Memories of Freedom

Memories of Freedom

An Indigenous Defense of Animals and the Earth

Rod Coronado

— 2025 —
Creative Fire Press

CREATIVE FIRE PRESS

Edited by David Skrbina

Creative Fire Press is a US non-profit educational publisher.

Library of Congress Cataloging-in-Publication Data

Coronado, Rodney (1966 -)
Memories of Freedom: An Indigenous Defense of Animals and the Earth

p. cm.
Includes bibliographical references

ISBN 978-1963-1432-01
(pbk.: alk. paper)

    1.   Activism, environmental

    2.   Animal Rights movement

    3.   Civil Disobedience

Printing number: 9 8 7 6 5 4 3 2 1

Printed in the United States of America on acid-free paper.

DEDICATION

This book is dedicated to everyone who has ever shed a tear for animals and our Mother Earth, and thought, "What can I do?"

DISCLAIMER

This book is a personal narrative recounting the author's past experiences, including illegal actions taken in the name of animal and environmental protection. The author accepted full responsibility for those actions, served multiple sentences, successfully completed probation, and has lived a law-abiding life for over two decades.

The unlawful events described in this work occurred many years ago and fall well outside the applicable statutes of limitations. They are presented solely for autobiographical, historical, and educational purposes. Nothing in this book is intended to admit, confess, or re-affirm any past criminal liability, nor does it constitute an admission of any conduct not already publicly documented, prosecuted, and resolved.

This book does not promote, encourage, or incite illegal activity. The author has chosen, for more than two decades, to pursue lawful, peaceful forms of civic engagement through legislative, educational, and community-based efforts, and offers this book as a reflection on that personal journey.

This publication constitutes protected speech under the First Amendment to the United States Constitution. It is not intended to serve as a manual, endorsement, or instruction for unlawful conduct. Any attempt to mischaracterize this book as advocacy for illegality is both inaccurate and contrary to the author's intent.

This disclaimer was prepared in consultation with legal counsel and approved by Steven Christianson, Attorney at Law.

CONTENTS

Memories of Freedom

FOREWORD

ON THE NEED FOR CIVIL DISOBEDIENCE FOR NATURE

The life story contained herein is one of the most compelling and courageous of our day. I can scarcely name a man—whom I know or have even heard of—with more fortitude, courage, and moral principle than Rod Coronado. He has an astonishing sense of purpose and mission, and a remarkable willingness to risk his own wellbeing and to sacrifice his own material interests for the sake of others—for animals, for nature, and for the planet as a whole.

It is easy to overlook how rare this is. The mass of people today are utterly indifferent to the suffering of the non-human world; a minority are aware and concerned, but do little about it; a few take personal action or make lifestyle changes; some even make careers of it; but virtually none put their lives or personal interests on the line in such a direct and immediate way as Rod has done. His is a life apart. The rest of us can only stare in amazement, that such a man is still possible in the present day.

In what follows, Rod offers his life story and his worldview in his own words, unfiltered by the media machine that so loves to distort and censor the truth. This alone is a rare event. Few serious activists in the environmental or animal rights movements have taken the time to put down in words their personal stories. In itself, this requires a kind of openness, vulnerability, and exposing of one's deepest thoughts and concerns in a manner that is hard to find anywhere.

But this is no mere autobiography; it is a lesson for humanity. Rod is, in many ways, a role model for those of us concerned about rampant social injustice, about the suffering of animals, and about the on-going—and accelerating—destruction of the natural world. He has chosen one path, and has thereby effected a remarkable imprint on society. He has shown us what one person can do. One person can bring a renegade nation's whaling fleet to its knees; one person can free thousands of imprisoned animals—animals whose lives were destined for misery, torture, and death; one person can inflict massive costs upon industry or academia when they pursue oppressive, cruel, pointless, money-grubbing, pathological gains at the expense of animals or nature; one person—of ordinary and humble origins, not unlike millions of other young men and women today—can change the world.

Of course, there was a price to be paid. This is unsurprising; all truly great social reformers and activists in history have had to pay a personal price—often with their lives. Fortunately in this case, it did not come to that. But still, Rod has had to undergo substantial and, for most of us, inconceivable hardship: a total of some six years in prison, long-term monitoring by the FBI, loss of friends and colleagues, a disrupted family life, foregoing of any real career or financial security, years spent under cover and on the run. But like all such men of courage and conviction, he has weathered the storm and survived countless assaults by the enforcers of the system. He did his time, and came out strong. Today, at the age of 59, he stands tall, unbroken by the adversity of the past. A family man, a father, a land steward, an honest worker—and still a warrior for environmental justice. No longer a front-line militant, but still an active and effective voice for nature. We have much to respect and much to learn from his story.

Rod's life-path, of course, was fraught with controversy. Confronted with modern society's unspeakable cruelty toward whales, seals, mink, lab animals, coyotes, wolves, and indeed to all of nature, he acted in the most direct and physical manner possible. "Direct action" means, if nothing else, direct and tangible interference with the machinery of destruction. It means to physically disrupt and block the means by which the damage occurs, through personal and individual action. Doing so demands, as I stated, profound courage and a deep-seated strength of moral vision. It demands a truly higher calling. In a sense, Rod acted on the Biblical dictate: "to destroy the destroyers of the earth" (Rev 11:18).

But this path is dangerous, illegal, and potentially fatal to oneself and others. Fortunately, and through careful planning and foresight, no one ever suffered any injury, let alone death, from Rod's actions—or indeed from *any* action by *any* animal rights or environmental activist, ever. Direct action is targeted at the material means, the physical infrastructure and financial methods, by which harm comes to animals and nature. Activists will destroy equipment, laboratories, whaling ships, fur farms, animal prisons—but never will they harm individual people. They will inflict massive financial loss, they will disrupt illegal or unethical activities, they will stop cruel hunting practices—all without physically hurting anyone. Sentient nature, they argue, is more valuable and more precious than any machinery of death and destruction. Animal wellbeing and the defense of nature is of greater value than profits or power.

But still, says the critic, such action is *illegal*. And if it's illegal, they imply, it's wrong. The law is the law, they say. We may not like it, we may be disgusted or appalled by it, but it's still the law. Laws are made by people to govern society in a rational manner. Laws may be inconvenient or bothersome, but they are necessary. And if we don't like them, there are means by which we can change them—at least, in a nominal democracy. If the environmental or animal activists don't like our present laws, say the critics, then they should work at a social and political level to change the laws. In other words, change the laws *legally*. Criminal action, they say, changes no laws; it is reckless, unilateral action by groups of self-appointed vigilantes. Any modern society must be a society of law-abiders. The alternative is social chaos or anarchy—or so they say.

This view is understandable but highly flawed, on multiple grounds. Here I will sketch something of a rational, philosophical defense of the very idea of direct action, of civil disobedience, and of nominally illegal action in the face of grave injustices against the non-human world. This will be an ethical argument, which is the only kind of argument that can be mounted against such injustice.

Abuse of Nature

Consider, first of all, why abuse of nature exists at all. (In what follows, I will focus on the living organisms in nature, i.e. animals and plants; abuse against such things as whole ecosystems or non-living nature requires a separate treatment.) Plants and animals are living, sentient beings. They perceive the world, they communicate, they feel, they possess a kind of intelligence, they have urgings and strivings. They want to live, grow, and reproduce. To harm or kill such living beings is therefore intrinsically wrong. They have value in their own right. Plants and animals can prosper and flourish, or they can wither and suffer. Hence, like all living things, they deserve, at least, moral consideration; and an argument can be made for something even stronger, namely, rights. In any event, they are the proper subjects of ethical treatment.

Therefore, a case must be made that any human-caused suffering is "worth it"—that is, that it brings greater good than harm. Does the benefit gained by someone outweigh, in any sense, the pain and damage that is caused to others? This is the calculation that we must make.

So: What is our justification? Why do we harm living creatures? Primarily for three reasons: (1) food, (2) fun, and (3) profit. Let me take a brief look at each of these.

First, let's examine the question of food. Begin with the obvious fact that literally everything we eat is, or was, alive.[1] We eat animals, animal products, and plants to survive. To live, we must take life.[2] But to live a maximally ethical life, the best possible life, we ought to cause minimum harm.

One obvious problem here is meat-eating, especially of industrially-produced animals. There is a triple ethical problem, in fact. First, the animals themselves—primarily cows, pigs, and chickens—are of course living, sentient beings who are being slaughtered for their meat. Every day, something like 190 million land animals are killed for food, across the Earth; this includes about 1 million cattle, killed each day. Second, we have the environmental cost, which is huge. Food animals now account for about 20%, by weight, of all animal life on the planet. They consume water and energy, and produce immense amounts of waste products (solid and gaseous), contributing substantially to the environmental crisis. Third, human health suffers; meat-eating is associated with various cancers, heart disease, obesity, osteoporosis, dementia, and shorter lifespans. In 2015, the World Health Organization classified processed meats as carcinogenic. Suffice to say that meat-eating imposes multiple problems on multiple levels.

Then there is killing or enslavement for fun: that is, for a hobby, for entertainment, or for luxury goods. Sport hunting and fishing are obvious examples, as is killing animals for fur (domestic or wild). But it also includes such things as circuses, zoos, rodeos, and other animal exhibits. It should be obvious that killing or enslaving living beings for the sake of fun or luxury is utterly indefensible from an ethical standpoint. The value to a person cannot possibly offset the pain and suffering of another sentient being, unless that other creature is reduced in status to a mere physical resource, devoid of all true value.

Both of these questions—food and fun—are bound up with the question of *money*. Animal agriculture pays; the hunting industry pays; the luxury clothing business pays; animal research facilities pay. As for plants, mass extraction of trees is also big business, as is ordinary industrial agriculture. There is big money to be made in the exploitation of living things, and this money flows back to governments in the form of political donations and lobby funding that serve to sustain the various industries. Laws

---

[1] With the sole exception of salt—the only mineral that we directly consume. And this naturally excludes such things as water and air.
[2] But even here there are exceptions. A fruitarian, for example, who eats only fruit and nuts, does not kill the tree or plant. Broccoli and cauliflower are technically the flowers of their plants, and harvesting them does not kill the plant. And such things as grains and seeds are often edible only after the parent plant has already perished.

are written and enacted under pressure from the very people who profit from those laws. It is a grotesquely self-serving and anti-democratic practice, one that perpetuates massive suffering of non-human life, promotes ill health among people, and contributes strongly to the destruction of the global ecosystem. And yet it is all "legal." What is a concerned person to make of this situation?

Some Ethical Lawbreakers in History

Throughout history, there have been notable individuals who found themselves on the wrong side of the law. They developed a strong sense of moral indignation at some particular legal affront to their ethical sensibilities, and they *acted*. For them, 'legal' was not identical with 'moral' or 'just.' For them, there was a higher standard to meet than the general obligation to follow the rules: it was to act consistently with their highest moral principles—principles that were widely considered to be rational, reasonable, and right. It is worthwhile taking a quick look at their lives and their examples.

Probably the first notable law-breaker in Western history was Socrates. Living around the year 400 BC, he was, in many ways, the founder not only of philosophy as we know it, but also of many of the basic precepts of Western civilization. Through his teaching of Plato (and indirectly, of Aristotle), Socrates today exerts an almost unprecedented influence on the modern world. When confronted with injustice, he was absolutely resolute; he would expose the ignorance or hypocrisy of even the highest men in the land, and would tenaciously defend the highest moral standards, even at steep personal cost. In the end, it cost him his life.

Socrates' unyielding exposure of official corruption earned him many powerful enemies, who eventually levied bogus charges against him; they even threatened to impose a death penalty. Forced to defend himself at trial, Socrates spoke most eloquently and movingly; for him, acting morally and justly was by far the most important thing, outweighing even the gravest of consequences:

> You are sadly mistaken, sir, if you suppose that a man with even a grain of self-respect should calculate the risks of living or dying, rather than simply consider, whenever he does something, whether his actions are just or unjust—the deeds of a good man or a bad one. ... [A]cting unjustly in obedience to one's rulers, whether god or human being, is something I

> *know* to be evil and shameful. Hence I shall never fear or
> flee…from things I know to be evils. (*Apology* 28c-29c)

The law 'required' Socrates to be pious and not cause trouble. It demanded that he conform and submit to the ongoing injustices of the powers-that-be. But he could never do that; his path was right and just, and it was the law that was wrong. In the end, and thanks to a corrupted jury, he was found guilty, imprisoned, and sentenced to death. But to the very end, he was unbroken; he had acted justly and thus accepted his fate.

As a second example, consider the many stories of Jesus, as related in the Bible. On the traditional view, he was indeed a 'law-breaker.' He violated local Jewish law by flouting Old Testament dictates such as not working on the Sabbath, and he violently "overturned the tables of the money-changers" in the Jewish Temple (Matt 21:12). Later, he was brought before the Roman governor Pontius Pilate and charged with "perverting the nation," failing to pay taxes, and "saying that he himself is Christ a king" (Luke 23:2). And in Acts, the apostles seem to be speaking for all Christians when they cry, "We must obey God rather than men!" (5:29). As with Socrates, Jesus and his Christians were willing to usurp the law in the name of a higher moral power.

American history itself contains a number of moral law-breakers, from the very beginning. The Boston Tea Party of 1773 was a blatantly illegal act. The American Revolution of 1775 was a dramatic violation of English law, among the gravest crimes imaginable. All the Founding Fathers were, formally, law-breakers of the highest order. But they did so in the name of justice and true moral principles. A century later, Susan B. Anthony was arrested in 1872 for insisting that women had the moral right to vote.

And there were some notable international examples. Gandhi was arrested and briefly detained in 1919 for encouraging mass non-cooperation with the ruling British colonialists. He was arrested again in 1922, found guilty of sedition, and sentenced to six years (though released after two). Yet another arrest came in 1930 during the notorious Salt March. There, British soldiers mercilessly beat nonviolent protestors, and in the end, between 60,000 and 90,000 were detained or imprisoned.

A somewhat similar situation occurred with Nelson Mandela, who was arrested several times in his fight against South African apartheid. He was imprisoned twice for short periods in 1952, and then again in 1957 on a charge of treason; after a three-year trial, he was exonerated. In 1961, Mandela and others formed a resistance group, "Spear of the Nation," that operated very much like latter-day animal rights activists. They conducted night-time attacks on military facilities, power plants, phone lines, and transportation infrastructure, all carefully planned to avoid any human injury. He was arrested again in 1962 and charged with sabotage and sedition; ultimately he and two others were found guilty and sentenced to life in prison. Thus began a grueling 27-year imprisonment. He would walk free only in 1990, going on to become South Africa's first black president in 1994.

And then we have Martin Luther King, another civil rights advocate who was first arrested in 1955 during the Montgomery bus boycott. Further arrests came in 1961 during the Albany desegregationist movement and in 1963 as part of the Birmingham campaign. It was during this imprisonment that he wrote his famous "Letter from a Birmingham jail" which included this memorable line—as relevant for the environmental movement as for civil rights: "We know through painful experience that freedom is never voluntarily given by the oppressor; it must be demanded by the oppressed"; or in the case of nature, "on behalf of the oppressed." In the end, King would suffer nearly 30 individual arrests prior to his assassination in 1968.

All these people were, in their day, called the worst of names: radicals, rebels, outlaws, thugs, terrorists. Today they are heroes. They acted not in their own self-interest but rather for the benefit of others—others whom they never knew, and others yet to come. They acted on behalf of the innocent, the vulnerable, and the unrepresented. That's why they are our greatest moral icons.

But perhaps the most relevant dissident and law-breaker, for the purposes at hand, was Henry David Thoreau. It is worth spending some time to reconsider his story.

Disobedience for Nature

Born in 1817 and dying tragically young (of tuberculosis) in 1862, Thoreau was a major figure in American literature, but he was also a naturalist, philosopher, and political activist. A friend and colleague of Ralph Waldo Emerson, Thoreau subscribed to the romanticism and so-called transcendentalism of the time. Like Emerson, he revered nature, but he also valued human autonomy and independence, and came to oppose the various burdens of government, particularly of a federal government engaged in such ethically atrocious actions as institutional slavery and an illegal war against Mexico.

From 1848 onward, Thoreau gave several local speeches on political topics. One particularly fruitful speech, "The Rights and Duties of the Individual in Relation to Government," was delivered in February of that year. It dealt with the moral right—and indeed, the moral *duty*—of citizens to resist unjust actions by their political institutions. By that time, the Mexican-American War was in its final phases, though at the cost of some 7,000 lives in total; and the matter of slavery was heating up, amidst a growing abolitionist movement. Thoreau viewed both issues as moral outrages, and he was appalled that his government—and his tax money—were supporting both. His speech would later be published in 1849 under the title "Resistance to Civil Government," though it would ultimately become known simply as "On Civil Disobedience." To date it is one of his most famous writings, and a landmark in American political philosophy. It was this essay that explicitly influenced both Gandhi and King.

At that time, political essays on behalf of animals or nature were unknown, and thus it is entirely to be expected that Thoreau addressed only human rights. And yet, he was a profound lover of nature. He cherished his time alone in the wilderness, and seemed entirely satisfied and content among the trees and meadows of eastern Massachusetts. But it was more than a beautiful landscape. Nature, for Thoreau, was alive and enspirited; he seemed to hold it in a kind of mystic reverence. In his journal of 31 December 1851, he wrote: "The earth I tread on is not a dead inert mass. It is a body—has a spirit—is organic... Even the solid globe is permeated by the living law. It is the most living of creatures." We can therefore well imagine that, given a more modern milieu, that he would have written on the need to defend nature *directly*, through non-violent civil disobedience, just as he did in the political sphere.

Thoreau was outraged at slavery and war; and indeed, in the present day, *modern society systematically enslaves animals and is at war with nature*. Many of the ideas and principles are thus identical; his ideas are as relevant as ever, in a new context. Let's recall a few of his more famous passages (with due apologies for the gendered language that was standard at that time):

> I ask for, not at once no government, but *at once* a better government. Let every man make known what kind of government would command his respect, and that will be one step toward obtaining it.

We all are inclined to follow the law, but what do we do when the law permits moral outrages?

> Must the citizen ever for a moment, or in the least degree, resign his conscience to the legislator? Why has every man a conscience, then? ... It is not desirable to cultivate a respect for *the law*, so much as for *the right*. The only obligation which I have a right to assume is to do at any time what I think right.

This resonates in our day, when the federal government seems to embody the height of corruption. How should someone respond to such a system?

> I answer, that we cannot without disgrace be associated with it. ... [Everyone] recognizes the right of revolution; that is, the right to refuse allegiance to, and to resist, the government, when its tyranny is great and unendurable. ... All machines have their friction; and possibly this does enough good to counterbalance the evil. At any rate, it is a great evil to make a stir about it. But when the friction comes to have its [*own*] machine, and oppression and robbery are organized, I say, let us not have such a machine any longer.

Great injustice, when made 'legal,' demands that we act; we must break the law:

> Unjust laws exist. Shall we be content to obey them, *or* shall we endeavor to amend them, and obey them until we have succeeded, *or* shall we transgress them at once? Men generally, under such a system as this, think that they ought to wait until they have persuaded the majority to alter them. They think that, if they should resist, the remedy would be worse than the evil.
>
> But it is the fault of the system itself that the remedy *is* worse than the evil. *It* makes it worse. Why is it not more apt to anticipate and provide for reform? Why does it not cherish its wise minority? Why does it cry and resist before it is hurt? Why does it not encourage its citizens to be on the alert to point out its faults, and *do* better than it would have them? Why does it always crucify Christ, and excommunicate

Copernicus and Martin Luther, and pronounce Washington and Franklin rebels? ...

If injustice is inherent to the mechanism of government, it will eventually cause the machine to falter; let it takes its course. But...

> if it is of such a nature that it requires you to be the agent of injustice to another, then, I say, *break the law. Let your life be a counter-friction to stop the machine.* What I have to do is to see, at any rate, that I do not lend myself to the wrong which I condemn.

Yes, the system can punish the law-breakers. It can put them in jail, lock them away. But it cannot thereby turn a wrong into a right: "Under a government which imprisons any unjustly, the true place for a just man is also a prison." In a nation that deliberately and systematically enslaves animals and indeed all nature,

> —where the State places those who are not *with* her, but *against* her—[a prison] is the only house in a slave State in which a free person can abide with honor. If any think that their influence would be lost there, and their voices no longer afflict the ear of the State, that they would not be as an enemy within its walls, they do not know by how much truth is stronger than error, nor how much more eloquently and effectively he can combat injustice who has experienced a little in his own person. Cast your whole vote, not a strip of paper merely, but your whole influence.

In other words, make *your life* your vote; don't just check a box once every four years. And fear not if you are a small minority:

> A minority is powerless while it conforms to the majority; it is not even a minority then; but it is *irresistible* when it clogs by its whole weight.

Thoreau realized that the power of the system was in its money, that the government, and therefore civil society, could only function with the financial support of its citizens. Therefore, one potent means of resistance was to refuse to pay one's taxes. If thousands of people refused to pay, on ethical grounds,

> that would not be [as] violent and bloody a measure, as it would be to *pay* them, and enable the State to continue to commit violence and shed innocent blood. This is, in fact, the definition of a peaceable revolution, if any such is possible. ... When the subject has refused allegiance...then the revolution is accomplished. But even suppose blood should flow. Is there not a sort of blood shed when the conscience is wounded? Through this wound [our] immortality flows out, and [we] bleed to an everlasting death. I see this blood flowing now.

Thoreau acted on his convictions; he refused to pay his taxes, and thus became a conscientious law-breaker:

> I have paid no poll-tax for six years. I was put into a jail once on this account, for one night; and, as I stood considering the walls of solid stone, two or three feet thick, the door of wood and iron, a foot thick, and the iron grating which strained the light, I could not help being struck with the foolishness of that institution which treated me as if I were mere flesh and blood and bones, to be locked up. ... I saw that, if there was a wall of stone between me and my townspeople, there was a still more difficult one to climb or break through, before they could get to be as free as I was. I did not for a moment feel confined, and the walls seemed a great waste of stone and mortar. I felt as if I alone of all my townspeople had paid my tax.
>
> [My jailers] plainly did not know how to treat me...; for they thought that my chief desire was to stand on the *other* side of that stone wall. I could not but smile to see how industriously they locked the door on my *meditations*, which followed them out again without let or hindrance, and *they* were really all that was dangerous. As they could not reach *me*, they had resolved to punish *my body*; just as boys, if they cannot come at some person against whom they have a spite, will abuse his dog. I saw that the State was half-witted...and that it did not know its friends from its foes, and I lost all my remaining respect for it, and pitied it. ...

To live a truly moral and noble life demands persistence and fortitude:

> *I was not born to be forced.* I will breathe after my own fash-
> ion. Let us see who is the strongest. ...
>   When I meet a government which says to me, "Your
> money or your life," why should I be in haste to give it my
> money? It may be in a great strait, and not know what to do:
> I cannot help that. I am not responsible for the successful
> working of the machinery of society. I am not the son of the
> engineer. I perceive that, when an acorn and a chestnut fall
> side by side, the one does not remain inert to make way for
> the other, but both obey their own laws, and spring and grow
> and flourish as best they can, till one, perchance, overshad-
> ows and destroys the other. If a plant cannot live according
> to its nature, it dies; and so a man.

Idealistic, we say. Fine words and fine principles, but unrealistic. "Why
should I suffer for animals, or for nature?" Why, indeed. When animals
suffer, or the Earth suffers, it may well be necessary for some humans to
suffer, for the sake of change—or else we will all suffer the consequences
of no change. Nature obeys a higher law. If we continue to violate her and
her creatures, we will certainly pay a price in the end.

A Life of Resistance

When looking at the broad sweep of Rod's life, it is hard not to see him as
the very man Thoreau called for: *the one honest person*, one of great moral
conviction, who would act in defense of nature. As Rod and others spent
their time in prison—not for harming people but simply for destroying
property and the means of exploitation—we are tempted to say, as Thoreau
did, that, in an unjust society, the only place for a just person is a prison.

"Be a counter-friction to stop the machine"—perhaps the greatest
slogan of civil disobedience ever written. Would that we all could act on
that imperative.

One man did. We now turn to his life, and his story. May we all find a
lesson in it.

— David Skrbina, PhD

Memories of
Freedom

CHAPTER 1
EARLY DAYS: 1966 TO 1985

Like many people, my family came to this country a long time ago. They did so to make a better life for themselves and their children. My family has always lived on this North American continent, but not in the country now called America. One of my great-grandmothers stowed away on a ship headed from Sonora, Mexico to San Francisco, California in the 1880s, while my other great-grandmother walked to Arizona from her homeland in the Rio Yaqui Valley of Sonora where our ancestors lay dead and buried. Their many sacrifices made my life possible.

Long before my grandmothers were born, the Yaqui inhabitants of what is now called Sonora, Mexico were fighting and dying to maintain their autonomy. We were here long before there ever was a United States of America or a Mexico. We were the ones who drew a line in the sand when the first Spanish Conquistadors arrived in our homelands in 1531; we told them that all the land around where they stood was our sacred homeland, Jiakim. Later, I would learn a lot more about this struggle from one of the last traditional leaders of the Yaqui Nation, a man whom I was fortunate to know before he passed on to his next adventure in the Spirit World.

My identity as an indigenous person was not something I knew much about—at least, until I lived and learned about my people while on the run from the FBI in the 1990s. My mother was the one who always told me we were Yaqui, but I didn't know what that meant. I remember getting a set of Time/Life Books ("with the look and feel of hand-tooled leather" as the television ads proclaimed), that included a volume titled "The Indians." I read every word, but most of them were not written by the subjects of the book, and they didn't move me as much as the pictures. I remember staring into the eyes of the portraits of those indigenous relatives who were staring back at me from a hundred years ago, with some sort of unknown connection that I felt deep inside of my young self. I felt like I had been abandoned in the future when what I wanted most was to be in their world.

Then one day when I was 14, my mother gave me the book *Bury My Heart at Wounded Knee*, by Dee Brown. She told me, "This is the story of our people." For those readers unfamiliar, this book became the first of my generation to teach of the genocide inflicted against this country's original inhabitants. Each chapter recounts episode after episode of American history, and American violence, when soldiers and settlers repeatedly betrayed the trust of indigenous nations and slaughtered them.

As I grew into my teenage years and started attending Live Oak High School in Morgan Hill, California, I was learning about the same time period covered in Brown's book, but without the perspective of the conquered peoples who were constantly betrayed and lied to by the US government. Even though I was only a teenager, after I read about the many nations of indigenous peoples that were targeted for genocide, with survivors corralled into a disease-ridden reservation system by our young government, I rejected my identity as a United States citizen.

My awakening to the violent history and truth behind our government's existence came not long after I had a similar awakening about our society's treatment of animals. Both of these shifts in my consciousness were only possible because my mother and father supported my compassion and empathy for animals and my desire for justice. Because of their inherent feeling for equality, and not because they saw themselves as activists, my parents never tried to dissuade me from "doing the right thing"— even when it wasn't popular to resist injustice.

Some Family History

My father Ray was born in Tucson, Arizona in 1939, the son of a pastor of a Spanish Apostolic church. They moved to California a few years after World War II. My grandfather—as I learned after his death—was a conscientious objector during the war, refusing on religious grounds to carry a gun. He was thus assigned to be an army chaplain's assistant, where he served proudly. When I was a child, I used to envision my veteran grandfather in the cockpit of a WWII fighter jet, engaging in dogfights with Germans or Japanese—both of whom were the enemy races, as my culture taught me. This was the image of a "WWII veteran" that television told me made them heroes in this proud nation, and so, naturally, I believed that my grandfather proved himself during his service by killing the enemy. In reality, what really made him a hero was his refusal to compromise his principles about war and violence. My grandfather is a WWII veteran and an American hero, but not for the reasons I was ever taught.

One day, not long before he died, we sat together under a cottonwood tree near his home in Fresno and talked about our spiritual paths and where they had led us. It would be the last time I would ever see him, at least on this plane, as I was then a fugitive; but my desire to know my family's history had led me back to my grandparents before they passed, and for that I am grateful and will always keep their memory alive with loving action.

Both of my parents struggled in their youth to rise above systemic oppression that would have preferred they both remain as farmworkers in the field, or on the assembly line of a cannery where they first met in Central California. Instead, my dad took my mom and left the conservative religious upbringing of his own childhood and moved to the San Francisco Bay Area in the early 1960s to start a family and, later, our own business in the growing Silicon Valley.

Some of their brothers and sisters followed them to the Bay Area, which was still mostly native wetlands, as I recall from my childhood. We would drive from San Jose to San Francisco for special occasions and I would always look out the window at the many birds that could be seen flying in the wetland estuary that reaches far into the San Francisco Bay between the two cities. My father's and mother's hard work and dedication to their family led them to open their own welding and steel fabrication business in 1977, which my brother and I worked at as children.

Hammer Elementary School

My dad taught us things that I was personally afraid to teach my own children later in life—like welding, and shooting firearms. I remember welding a stick figure person out of nuts and bolts, painting it black with spray paint, and wrapping it with a paper napkin and masking tape to give to my first-grade teacher, Mrs. Cannon. I also remember her squeezing me real hard in appreciation of the gift. That my father wasn't afraid to empower me with skills like welding, driving, and shooting demonstrated his belief that there was no reason we couldn't be successful like other people around us.

One of the other memorable things that happened a year later at the same school—Hammer Elementary in San Jose—was my having another indigenous person as a teacher and mentor: Mr. Lloyd Hill. There was never anything spoken about us both being indigenous, but Mr. Hill was the only teacher I ever remember coming over to our home for dinner. I remember bringing out my microscope after dinner to show him something or other, and I recall his genuine fascination at what I was showing him. He was probably the first indigenous person I ever met outside of my own mixed-blood family.

Possibly one of the reasons I remember my second-grade teacher so well is because of an incident that happened the following year in third grade. We must have had a substitute teacher who was unfamiliar with our classroom dynamics and discipline because what I remember is crystal clear: I was being told not to talk, for reasons I cannot remember, and when I refused to be silent, I was made to sit in the front of the room, facing the rest of the class. When I still refused to stop talking, the substitute teacher instructed two of the bullies in our class to cover my mouth with masking tape. I remember physically struggling against the larger two boys who eventually succeeded in taping my mouth shut. I was then returned to the front of the class while the teacher sent one of the bullies to ask Mr. Hill, my second-grade teacher and mentor, to come to the class to see me, to complete the humiliation.

I will never forget that day, not only because of what happened to me, but because of the intentional effort made by a white teacher and other white students to humiliate not only me, but Mr. Hill as well. As I sat in the chair with my mouth covered in masking tape, I could see the open door of our classroom. I remember Mr. Hill walking slowly by the door and when he looked in at me, his face was as I had never seen it before. His head was bowed and there was pure sadness in his face as he witnessed what was being done to me. That was the last time I ever saw him.

The years passed; we moved further away from San Jose and into a brand-new tract home my parents bought in south San Jose for only $44,000. My dad and I began raising parakeets, first as a hobby, then later as a small business. We would take our young parakeets to local pet stores to sell and travel to bird shows. I remember learning how to drive in the empty fields that still existed near downtown San Jose where my dad's shop was located. It was a Chevy step-side truck with "three-on-the-tree" manual shifting. This was about the same time that I began to become aware of how most animals were being treated by humans in the adult world around me.

The local newspaper ran a story one weekend about the use of animals in medical research. I saved the story and asked my dad about it. He told me those kinds of experiments were necessary to ensure the safety of the kinds of products that people used—including people like us. The idea that somehow I was responsible for those animals suffering was my first awareness to the institutionalized abuse of animals for food, clothing, and medicine. I was beginning to learn that my growth and evolution must include the acceptance of this kind of suffering if I was to become happy and successful in life. It was just a fact of life that animals were treated the way they are.

A Shocking Revelation

One evening in 1977 when my parents and I were watching television, I tuned into Public Broadcasting and saw what would alter my life forever. It was a documentary filmed by what looked like a bunch of hippies in Canada. They were out on the sea ice off Canada's eastern coast, a place totally foreign to me; but what drew my attention were the harp seals and their pups that these activists were trying to save. As my family watched, I quickly learned that it was the seal pups themselves, not the adults, that the hunters were after. Harp seal pups are totally defenseless, still being unable to swim. I watched as Canadian hunters would grab a seal pup by the tail, spin it around on the ice and then crush its skull with a few blows from long clubs.

I remember bursting into tears, and my mother quickly changing the channel. But I immediately protested and told her I needed to see what was happening. Through my tear-covered eyes, I sobbed as I watched seal pup after seal pup clubbed to death, the white ice of their ocean nursery covered in rivulets of blood. It still makes me cry just thinking about that day, over 40 years ago.

I was sobbing and crying as my parents sat with me, silently watching as the ruthless slaughter took place on our television. Who knows what might have happened, had there not been the one other human being I saw in that film that was doing what I felt was the only thing to do. As we watched, one activist threw himself over the bodies of the seal pups in a desperate attempt to save their lives. Others were standing in the way of the sealers ship as it burst through the ice of the seals' nursery.

Finally, one of the two men standing in front of the icebreaker handcuffed himself to a winch line being used to haul aboard bloody seal pup pelts. The sealers didn't stop, they didn't even hesitate. Instead they continued hauling aboard the pelts, dragging the activist through the icy waters before also hauling him aboard. I later learned that he was arrested for interfering with the seal hunt. The Canadian man's name was Paul Watson, and seeing his action that day convinced me of what I must do with my own life. I told my mom then and there that I wanted to go to Canada and join these people putting their lives on the line for animals. I remember my mom saying, "I just might go with you."

The Canadian seal hunt was, and still is, the largest slaughter of marine mammals in the world. Forty years ago, amidst all that seal pup head-bashing with clubs, when I saw Paul Watson and Robert Hunter going beyond just witnessing and documenting the slaughter, but literally standing in the path of the sealer's icebreaker, resolute human beings taking a stand, Indian-style, to stop this unnatural intrusion into the harp seal's nursery, trying to stop the slaughter that in moments would follow—I knew that was where I belonged. (Years later, I would get the opportunity to sail with both Paul and Bob Hunter on the Sea Shepherd ship, *Divine Wind*, into the North Pacific in 1987.)

Watson and Hunter's actions that day would be one of the only things that kept me as a young child from losing all faith in civilization and humanity, after witnessing the slaughter of harp seals. These courageous human warriors gave me the strength and determination to soon find and join their struggle to save our seas and planet.

I was only 12 years old. No child should ever be told to accept our society's appalling treatment of animals. No conscientious human being should ever teach a child that cruelty is an accepted fact of life. My parents understood that my empathy and compassion were going to make it difficult to grow up in today's world, so they supported my interests. When I didn't want to play football anymore, but instead wanted to go to the public library where I could look up old newspaper articles about Greenpeace and other activist groups, my mom would drop me off there after school.

Back in that day, they still had the old Dewey Decimal System in libraries. I would look up benign subjects like "Animals" and then dig through whatever folders were in the file cabinets on the subject. And that is where I found flyers from organizations like the Animal Welfare Institute and the Fund for Animals. Those pamphlets were where I saw my first images of wild animals caught in steel foothold traps, that are still in use today. But those images and the idea that there were others organizing against such activities, was my source of great hope. I am almost ashamed to admit it, but when I found an old newsletter from Paul Watson's Sea Shepherd Conservation Society announcing the purchase of a new ship to replace the first Sea Shepherd, which was sunk in Portugal in 1980, I stole it. I quickly sent off my membership dues. That was in the spring of 1981.

That same summer, when I was 14, anti-nuclear activists were in the news for blockading the entrances to Lawrence Livermore National Laboratories in the east Bay area where nuclear weapons were being developed. I would lay out the newspaper to read it on our carpeted floor after my father had finished reading, and in the stories about the protests, there were pictures of young people linked arm in arm, sitting in the road to the laboratory. The police were handcuffing and dragging the protestors away, but I saw in their faces a level of commitment that moved me, something I could relate to.

When I picked up the phone and my parents heard me calling Greyhound to inquire about bus tickets to Livermore, my mother interrupted me, saying that she would drive me to the protest herself. When we arrived the next day, the majority of the protestors had disbanded and we only saw a few activists driving around in a stereotypical hippy Volkswagen van. It didn't matter to me though; I was finally able to start doing something about all the things in the world that were breaking my heart as I was learning about them.

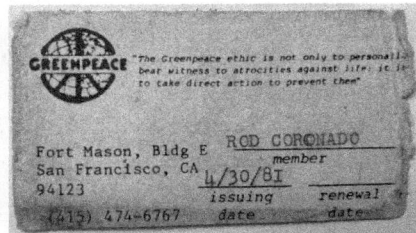

Sea Shepherd

ROD CORONADO

Member Since

January 1982

Marine Mammal Protection And Conservation

GREENPEACE "The Greenpeace ethic is not only to personally bear witness to atrocities against life; it is to take direct action to prevent them"

Fort Mason, Bldg E
San Francisco, CA
94123
(415) 474-6767

ROD CORONADO
member

4/30/81
issuing
date

renewal
date

After that day, I began mowing lawns to raise money to send to groups like Sea Shepherd and Greenpeace, and I began to clip every news article I saw about Paul Watson or any other activist group willing to confront cruelty and abuse wherever it was happening. I joined Sea Shepherd and Greenpeace, and I still have my membership cards from 1982. I began collecting signatures for petitions against the Canadian seal hunt and commercial whaling; whenever my family had over visitors, I would pull out my petitions and ask them to sign. I had joined the California-based Animal Protection Institute, which was very mainstream, but at the time produced a nice monthly magazine. I eagerly awaited each issue in the mail, reading them cover to cover the day they arrived. Each article exposed me to a different animal abuse issue, often occurring right there in my home state of California.

As one might imagine, my discovery of animals being used in cosmetics and medical research experiments was particularly disturbing to my young psyche, especially because of my love for the same species being used in such experiments, like cats, dogs, and rabbits. With the Canadian harp seal hunt, I had been exposed to not just the hunt, but to a corresponding direct-action campaign by real people to stop it. Regarding animal research, I had yet to be exposed to any other form of opposition other than writing letters, raising awareness, boycotts, and maybe protests. That would soon change, based on the actions of other compassionate people living in California in the early 1980s.

Paul soon announced that he was taking the new Sea Shepherd II to Soviet Siberia in the Bering Sea to expose the killing of endangered gray whales for use as feed (!) for foxes, on fur farms. I followed each newswire service story as the ship sailed from the Atlantic to the North Pacific, finally arriving on the scene in August 1981. When Paul landed a crew onto Russian soil and documented the fur farms, he was chased out of the area by a Soviet Destroyer. With each news report, I felt more and more connected to these earth warriors and animal defenders. Paul and his crew weren't a bunch of scientists; they were young committed people who couldn't stand by while crimes against the earth and animals were being committed. (Paul was about 30 years old at that time.) I understood that feeling and was envious of the crew, but proud to show my friends and family the articles from our local newspaper, which also lent them a good degree of legitimacy. I was a part of this struggle, but not quite ready for the battlefield.

My Teenage Years

As I became a teenager and my interests began to include the normal interests of a normal teenager, friends of mine would come over to play and hang out. They knew my interests in animals and didn't make fun of me because of it, maybe because most of them were Mexican and could relate to having sympathy for the oppressed. Whatever the reasons, I had support—not only from my family, but friends as well. I remember having the newspaper article from that first-ever story I read about animal experimentation pinned to my wall. A young friend, Steve, was in my room looking at the walls and taking it all in when he saw the headline on the news clipping; it read, "Who Will Save the Animals?" Steve saw it and then said, "Rodney will save the animals."

After my discovery of animal activism in the form of Sea Shepherd, Greenpeace, Fund for Animals, and other animal welfare groups, I became more aware of current issues beyond Canada's harp seal hunt and commercial whaling. The fur trade, for example, with its use of foothold traps and snares, had been killing furbearers on this continent for centuries, and the bloody business was alive and well.

My awakening as a young activist paralleled my parent's business success in San Jose, as my father's steel business rode the wave of the growth explosion taking place in Silicon Valley. My parents are hard-working people who sacrificed a lot to bring their young family to San Jose. I was happy to see our family prospering, but one evening, as my parents were getting ready to go out for a night on the town, my mom walked down the stairs wearing a brand-new red fox fur coat. When I saw her, I was silent but started to cry. That was the first and last time my mother ever wore that or any other fur coat.

At about this same time, our family moved to a much more rural part of Santa Clara County, to escape the growth taking over San Jose. We had almost two acres just north of Morgan Hill, California. There, I became aware of the round-up and often slaughter of wild horses and burros in the American West, as it was an issue I had read about during my library research. When the Bureau of Land Management (BLM) introduced its adoption program for captured animals, I convinced my parents to adopt two burros that had been removed from the Grand Canyon.

At the time, no one questioned the BLM's assertion that wild horses and burros were degrading the native desert ecosystem, having been introduced over the last century by various sources. Later I would learn that wild horses and burros comprise only about 2% of grazing animals on the western landscape, while commercial livestock comprise almost 60% on the same sensitive western ecosystems. But there was no money to be made from wild horses.

Nonetheless, the BLM's adoption program was meant as an alternative to sharpshooters killing the animals, so I happily took possession of these two burros; they lived with us for years yet never became tame or overly friendly.

By the time I entered high school, I was pretty resistant to the overall image of the American way of life. My family shared in the success, but still I knew that behind the veneer of happiness were animals being exploited to provide us luxuries. Vegetarianism was never really mentioned,

as most of my awareness came from fairly mainstream organizations focused on ending animal cruelty, not ending institutionalized animal abuse.

By far my greatest interest was in the type of direct action carried out
by Paul Watson and his young organization, Sea Shepherd Conservation
Society, on behalf of the whales and seals of the world. After my discovery
of Greenpeace, I read everything I could about the young Canadian organization; and I also learned that Paul Watson had been voted out of the group
because he had violated the non-violent principles of Greenpeace when he
took a sealers club out of his hands and threw it in the water. I could empathize with Paul because simply "bearing witness to atrocities against
life"—which is the motto printed on my 1977 Greenpeace membership
card—is simply not enough.

When Paul took his new ship, Sea Shepherd, back to the Canadian
seal hunt in 1979, his crew entered the seal nurseries with harmless dyes
that, after being applied to a seal pup's fur, rendered it commercially invaluable. Crew members hiked across the floating ice around nearby sealing
ships, painting every pup they found with the dye. These were the kinds of
actions that made sense to me.

After Paul rammed the Sea Shepherd into the world's most notorious
pirate whaling ship, the Sierra, in July 1979, I knew I had to join his crew,
even though at the time I was only 13. The next time Paul would travel to
the ice floes with the Sea Shepherd would be four years later, in 1983. I
was still in high school, so I had to settle for raising $150 to sponsor a half-
ton of diesel fuel for the ship's journey back to Canada. This time, the Sea
Shepherd would be seized on the ice and, after the crew was arrested,
parked in Halifax, Nova Scotia, where it would sit for over two years.

A Fateful Trip

I went about my life in California, struggling to finish high school, which I
hated. My friends and I went on camping trips for the weekend or I went to
an outdoor archery range, but for the most part, I was ready to begin my
life away from home. After moving to a more rural area and getting into
archery, I eventually tried my hand at bowhunting. I loved reading *Outdoor
Life*, a hunting and fishing magazine, because it was the only publication I
could find that addressed wildlife conservation. It painted hunters as conservationists, which made sense to me as someone who loved wildlife and
being outdoors.

I began hunting deer in the mountains not far from my home. One hot
afternoon, I stalked 15 yards from a resting blacktail buck and slowly

moved into a shooting position. When the wind shifted, the buck caught my scent and jumped up; as soon as he did, I fired my arrow towards his heart. The buck ran away, but in the dwindling light, I saw him limping. I decided to let the buck bed down where it would hopefully die, and I returned the next morning to track him. As soon as I reached the original spot where he was bedded, I found my arrow, which had only penetrated about two inches before hitting his shoulder blade, bending the aluminum arrow. I couldn't find any blood trail because the wound wasn't fatal. I hadn't achieved a killing shot, but just wounded him. I felt awful.

Later that same year, I was again hunting by myself outside of Yreka, California, when I got another chance to take a shot. Walking to my hunting blind, I heard the sound of deer running towards me, having been flushed by another hunter. I quickly sat on a stump immediately off the deer trail and remained motionless as the group of five deer, including a buck, walked just a few feet away from me. When the buck passed and was far enough away for me to take a shot, I released my arrow. This time, my arrow was low and hit the ground before bouncing up and striking the buck in the hindquarter. The loss of momentum took away the arrow's killing force and it now lay anchored just beneath the animal's skin. Another non-fatal wounding shot.

That was it. I quit hunting at that very moment. I had wanted to hunt because I believed it would bring me closer to nature and the wildlife I loved, but all I was doing was invading their homes and hurting them. I spent the rest of the week "hunting," but without my bow. With no intent to kill my prey, I instead simply watched. I happened upon a coyote that was asleep on a log, and I sat down and watched until the animal woke up, stretched, and ambled away. The next morning, I saw a black bear grazing on berries just ten yards away without ever noticing my presence. Coyotes could be hunted year-round without a permit and I had a bear tag, but I learned to get far more enjoyment from connecting with these wild animals without intending to kill them.

In 1984, my parents decided to take a vacation to Vancouver, British Columbia, during the summer of my senior year—which I was happy to join them on, knowing that Vancouver was also the home of Sea Shepherd's main office. As a member of the group, I had read that Paul was out of the country, so I didn't expect to meet him, but I still was excited to be where there was so much Greenpeace history.

When we had checked into our hotel room, I took my binoculars and searched the city skyline for where the map told me the Sea Shepherd office was, not sure what I was expecting to see. All I knew was that I was getting closer to my goal of joining Paul Watson on the Sea Shepherd. I picked up a local newspaper in our hotel's lobby and read an article about the proposed expansion of Vancouver's Aquarium to accommodate more captive cetaceans, in particular beluga whales, that would be captured from the wild. There was going to be a public hearing on the aquarium expansion, so I asked my parents if they would drop me off at the meeting place.

How strange it must have seemed to my parents, having been raised to believe that the best thing they could do for their children would be to give me the privilege and luxury that they never had. My dad wanted nothing more than for me to go to college. He realized that I had no interest in following in his footsteps by taking over the family business, a role that my older brother was more suited for, not me. Still, my parents begrudgingly supported my every desired turn towards a much less traditional life, even while growing up in one of the most prosperous areas of the country.

The night of the aquarium expansion meeting, my parents dropped me off in front of the public building where people were filing in and taking their seats. When the meeting began, Vancouver Aquarium officials explained their reasoning behind the proposed expansion, after which they took questions and comments from the audience. Part of me wanted to speak up, but I was nowhere near ready to stand up in front of a crowd of strangers and tell any authority figures what I believed, however strongly I might feel about the issue. Instead, I sat rapt with attention, listening to my first public meeting about wildlife issues, happy to be in a place where others like me also supported fewer whales in captivity.

As the meeting began to drag on, a citizen's name was called, indicating their time to testify; *it was Paul Watson*. My heart felt like it was pounding against the inside of my chest as I watched my childhood hero walk towards the microphone to deliver his condemnation of the aquarium's plans for more captive whales. When Paul finished talking, most of the crowd broke out in applause.

As others continued testifying, my heart continued to pound as I thought about what I should do. Here I was, less than a month after graduating from high school, with the goal of nothing greater than to join the organization led by the man that was seated just across the room. When the meeting ended, I made my way through the crowd towards Paul, and when I reached him, I introduced myself and shook his hand. I'm sure I must have been talking a mile a minute.

The first thing I remember Paul saying was that he remembered receiving the many letters I had personally sent him with my childhood donations. I had told Paul the truth, that I wanted to join his crew as soon as possible and do whatever I could to help save the whales and seals that he had already dedicated his life to. Paul told me about a project he was involved in: painting life-sized murals of whales in their natural environment, to help raise awareness. If I wanted, I could join that crew the very next day. Paul told me I could meet him at Sea Shepherd's office the next day. I knew exactly where to go.

When my parents showed up to pick me up from the meeting, I was elated and through the roof with excitement. I told my mom and dad that I had met Paul Watson and was going to leave the next day with him on his latest adventure. My parents were aghast. What they had hoped would be one last vacation together with their youngest son, instead became the trip where they would instead see me off on my first real adult adventure. My mom was the one who told me that, before I could go, she wanted to meet the man whose path I'd been following since I was 12. The next morning, I was standing outside the Sea Shepherd office while my mother spoke to Paul. I would be spending the remainder of my summer vacation with him as a volunteer.

When Paul took me to my parents on the eve of our trip home, I promised him that I would return. As soon as I got back, I packed my small car and drove north to Seattle to rejoin Paul on the latest mural project. I would spend the next five weeks mixing and hauling paint, and tabling for Sea Shepherd on the University of Washington campus. Later I was invited to fly to Hawaii to work on the next mural project, which lasted four months. I was the engineer for the project, which was a 20-story high mural of breaching humpback whales that could be seen everywhere on the Waikiki skyline. I was 18 years old.

Rod, age 18

Painting the Waikiki mural (1984)

I had been working with Paul for almost six months when he told me the Canadian government would be releasing the Sea Shepherd back into his custody. The next project would be the repair and refit of the ship so that it could embark on a campaign to interfere with the slaughter of pilot whales in the North Atlantic. I flew home for a short visit before buying a plane ticket to Portland, Maine. From there I would take a bus to Halifax, where the ship had sat, neglected, for over two years.

But I was exactly where I wanted to be: mentoring with an individual whose life was dedicated to the unapologetic preservation of the natural world. I never wanted to be a lobbyist or stand on some streetcorner holding a sign; I wanted to be directly involved with impeding the destruction of the Earth's remaining great whales, and in that task, there could be no greater teacher than Paul Watson.

CHAPTER 2
RAID ON REYKJAVIK

A short two years later, I was 20 years old, crouching in the engine room of a commercial whaling ship, in Reykjavik Harbor, Iceland, with my own Robert Hunter, a Cornishman named David Howitt. We didn't have permission to be onboard. We were acting on a bold promise to take direct action against any commercial whaling operation violating the International Whaling Commission's 1986 ban on killing whales for profit. I was there with the mission of sinking half the nation's commercial whaling fleet.

But before I can tell the story of the sinking of the Icelandic whaling fleet, I have to tell you about my evolution aboard the Sea Shepherd, as a warrior disciple of one of the greatest war captains of my generation. For over 40 years, Paul Watson remains nothing less than one of the bravest human beings I have ever met while fighting for animals and our planet. If we were living in the 19th century, his victories would be lined up next to other great earth-warriors like Crazy Horse and Geronimo (no disrespect to lesser-known warrior women, such as the Apache, Lozen, or my own Yaqui nation's Chepa Moreno—women warriors who fought alongside their more well-known indigenous rebels.)

My rites of passage came on the bridge and fore deck of the Sea Shepherd. Where I stood for hours gripping the wheel of the ship, as it rode the swells of the North Atlantic, listening to Paul, Robert Hunter, Al Johnson, Ben White, and other great warriors of the 1960s and 1970s regale of stories chasing pirate whalers into Russian waters or swamping sealers on the ice floes who were slashing the throats of harp seal pups in front of our crew. I heard stories of power. Not force, as is best represented with large standing armies, but *power*, like a thunderstorm. Power like that tapped into by Geronimo, who, when escaping pursuing military forces literally numbering in the thousands, would escape amongst the open plains of our homeland now known as the state of Arizona.

I learned that despite what Mao might have said, power does not come out of the barrel of a gun. Power is that beautiful moment when you realize that our greatest weapon is our heart—that the Earth spirits are there, not awaiting the calls of our reptilian brain, but because they want to hear the voices of our hearts. We come into this struggle, not because of our anger or rage, but because we love so much, that we can feel the suffering of others and see it as interconnected to our own desire to live free.

Paul Watson was my first war captain. I came to him with purpose and desire, and he taught me about the tactics and strategy of the guerrilla fighter in the late 20th century. You see, Paul isn't a politician. He doesn't reward race and privilege, like some non-profit groups that better resemble financial institutions than guerrilla insurgencies, Paul allowed me the opportunity to realize a dream I had, of making my life about protecting and defending the natural world I loved. He showed me the path, and once I had demonstrated my ability to walk it, he taught me that our struggle was always going to be underfunded and unsupported, that we might be criminalized, or beaten or killed, but that in choosing to be warriors, we were accepting those consequences that were a big part of our job's description. Many years later, I would learn that these principles were very similar to those of indigenous warrior societies, both my own and others.

Paul taught me that we were not the first, nor would we be the last, in a long line of warriors who had fought the onslaught of colonization and imperialism, and its impact on the natural world. Paul taught me something that would be echoed by indigenous elders I would later meet: that was that it's not only blood that makes an Indian, it's the courage to *live that way*, even when it is deadly dangerous to do so. To be Indian isn't something to be determined by the invading forces' offices of colonization who issue enrollment numbers; it's something we are because we choose to be ourselves, with our own beliefs, which centuries have proven to us, and which are the most sustainable way to live in harmony with others and our environment.

As an indigenous kid growing up in California in the 1970s, I was as far away from my native roots as an ant is to the sun. Paul was one of the only human beings I ever saw putting his life on the line and standing in the way of the world's whalers, sealers, and killers. I was a kid coming to terms with the brutal reality of how the human world treats animals and the Earth—generally like shit. And while the rest of the world was lining up for chicken McNuggets, it was Paul who stood up for the natural world. And he wasn't just standing in the way of the sealers' icebreaker. I next heard of Paul when I was 13, because he had rammed his ship into the world's most notorious pirate whaling ship, the Sierra. Such willingness to do what needed to be done made Paul someone I could respect and look towards for guidance in this life.

Growing up in the 1980s, I was already an ethnic and social outcast, not wanting anything to do with the world I was growing up in, let alone the careers. My heroes, and who I wanted to be like, weren't other non-

white people who were successfully assimilating into the dominant con-
sumer-based society; they were other human beings like Watson and
Hunter, fighting against the violent destruction of the natural world, trying
to protect life instead of profiting from it.

Joining the Sea Shepherd

So when I finally finished high school, I didn't sign up for the military, I
joined Neptune's navy and walked up the gangplank onto the Sea Shepherd in Halifax, Nova Scotia for the very first time. That was May 5, 1985.

The ship was a wreck. Paul had used the Sea Shepherd to blockade
the Canadian sealing fleet at St. John's Harbor in Newfoundland during the
1983 seal hunt. He would later take the ship onto the ice floes where seals
had given birth to their pups, to interfere with the sealers until the Coast
Guard arrested the ship and crew. I was one of the first to join the crew
since the ship was released back into Paul's custody. The ship had not been
properly laid up for the two years, and it would be months before we ever
got the main engines running again.

The summer of 1985 was filled with days waking up at 7 a.m. and
working until 7 p.m. on the ship's engines. An old British engineer by the
name of Jeremy Coon had joined the crew as Chief Engineer and was the
first experienced ship's engineer that I became close friends with. Having
spent my youth working on my father's construction company, I was ready
to apply my knowledge to the ship; I only needed guidance. Jeremy barked
orders to me and John, a local youth I had also befriended. John and I
would end each work day with a night of drinking in the local Halifax bars,
which were booming with the 80's music scene, which I also loved. We
would stumble back to the ship each night, sometimes unable to remember
how we got across the gangplank.

I made other friends, in the form of two French-Canadian sailors, Eric
and Jean-Pierre, who had jumped ship from a private yacht named the
Calita, where they had been stranded in harbor for months without any
money for food, let alone supplies for the yacht. Not long after, two other
British crewmembers from the boat also joined our crew: brothers Steve
and Nick Taylor. Both were experienced sailors and I quickly became
friends with Nick, who was the more gruff, reckless, and funny of the two
brothers. Steve would leave the ship not long after, but for Nick, the Sea
Shepherd II was the last ship he would ever sail on.

I had no complaints and couldn't have been happier on that underfunded derelict and neglected ship. That vessel was one of the few whose

sole purpose was the defense of the seas and the creatures living within. The fact that it had a big white stripe painted on the bow—an indication that she had been seized by the Canadian government—was just more reason for me to be proud as a crew member. Every morning, I would walk past the twisted steel support struts holding up the rear deck, a wound inflicted when a Canadian Coast Guard cutter, the John A. McDonald, rammed alongside the Sea Shepherd as her crew harassed sealers on the ice floes in spring of 1983. I remember being told by a ship supplier in Halifax, that he wished that ship was on the bottom of the harbor.

Another sad historic milestone for the environmental movement would take place in July 1985 when Greenpeace's flagship, the Rainbow Warrior, was blown up in harbor in New Zealand, killing one crew member. It was the first time that I would hear of deadly force being used against nonviolent protesters whose aim was peace; but it would certainly not be the last. Later it would be learned that the ship had been targeted by French agents after years of Greenpeace campaigns exposing the country's role in aboveground nuclear tests since the 1970s. It was a clear-cut case of government sanctioned terrorism, yet no government, even Britian (which the ship was registered under), would condemn France's attack. I had heard Paul Watson called a 'terrorist' numerous times for sinking illegal whaling ships like the Sierra without injury, yet here was a European superpower targeting an aboveground environmental organization with deadly violence, and yet nowhere was there any such condemnation.

Taking to the Seas

Finally, after months of greasy work, in July 1985, the Sea Shepherd again departed Halifax, Nova Scotia. She was headed across the Atlantic, to the Danish Faroe Islands, to interfere with the annual slaughter of thousands of migrating pilot whales. I'll never forget that amazing sensation when a ship you've lived on for months in port finally sets sail and suddenly you are bouncing across the waves with the constant hum of the ship's propeller turning as your soundtrack. When the ship swung out towards the open sea, I felt like a dream had finally come true for that young teenager from San Jose.

More crew had joined before we set sail, including Mark Heitchue, a young environmentalist from Richmond, Virginia, who was brought on by Ben White, veteran from the Soviet Siberia and seal hunt campaigns. Mark and I shared an engine room watch and became fast friends, spending nights on the aft deck listening to U2 and other popular 80's bands, with the stars as our only light. When our main engine oil line cracked, we were forced to make harbor in St. Pierre Miquelon in Newfoundland. The enclave was administered by France, though surrounded by Canada on all sides but the sea. Paul was certain that if we made port in Newfoundland, that the ship would again be seized by the seal-hunt-supporting government. Mark and I explored the island before finding the only bar in town, which better resembled a church. The stay was brief, but long enough for us to lose two crew members, Steve Taylor and Isabell, a Canadian.

Rod's Birthday with Paul Watson (July, 1985)

On those grey days crossing the North Atlantic, especially as we cruised along the coast of eastern Canada, I read Farley Mowat's *Sea of Slaughter*, which chronicles the European exploitation of wildlife on the eastern seaboard since the arrival of 15th century European explorers. What Dee Brown's *Bury My Heart at Wounded Knee* taught me about U.S. policy towards indigenous Americans, Mowat's book taught me about the long dark legacy of wildlife eradication by European explorers and settlers.

As we crossed the silent grey ocean, I imagined what it must have been like when whales were so plentiful on these very seas that they posed a navigational hazard to the earliest white mariners that came to these lands seeking fish, then fur. Most people also don't know that before the first colonists arrived, herds of eastern bison roamed the eastern seaboard. There were also brown, black, and white bears, the latter becoming known to us in modern times as "polar" bears, but their natural range dipped south into what is today's state of Maine. Woodland caribou were another species that was literally wiped out in "New England." On land and sea, one species after another was reduced to its oil and fur. For whales, the end began with the invention of the steam engine and explosive harpoon in the early 20th century. The targets were no longer just the slower whales, like right whales, who were so named because they were they "right" whales to kill because they swam slow and floated after being killed. As has often been the case with other indigenous wildlife, industrial growth and human expansion reduced the great whales that literally covered the world's oceans to a sliver of their original numbers in less than one century. Whales, wolves, bison, and bears—species that had coexisted with humans for thousands of years without ever the threat of extinction, were lost within many people's living memory.

I was exactly where I wanted to be: on the one ship that was plying the ocean, hunting the last remaining ships plying the ocean hunting the Earth's last whales. Since 1983, when the International Whaling Commission finally listened to the world's scientists and voted to end the commercial slaughter of great whales, I had been waiting to join Paul Watson and the Sea Shepherd. I knew only in the company of such a warrior would I ever get the opportunity to also sink a whaling ship. Paul showed the world that it could be done, and I sure as hell wasn't going to miss my opportunity to fulfill my dream by, instead, going to college to become a veterinarian or game warden (two professions where society says it's ok to protect animals.)

An Introduction to Iceland

On that first ocean crossing to the Faroe Islands, we pulled into Reykjavik harbor to refuel. The Icelandic police placed us under 24-hour surveillance, which was to be expected, with Paul's reputation for ramming and blowing up whaling ships. The police also had patrol vehicles next to the four ships owned by Hvalur Limited, Iceland's only whaling company, surviving solely on its illegal sale of whale meat to Japan. The company also had divers checking the whaling ships' hulls daily for explosives mines like those used by saboteurs to sink both the pirate whaling ship the Sierra and Greenpeace's Rainbow Warrior—which I thought was pretty bad-ass.

Here I was, a 20-year-old kid, in Iceland, on the Sea Shepherd, with the enemy's ships *right there*. This was before Iceland had been the first nation to violate the IWC's ban on commercial whaling, and when the story of the sale of whale meat to Japan had hit the news, in the fall of 1986. I wanted to get a closer look at the whaling ships, so I walked across the harbor to the long dock where the four ships were berthed alongside each other, and of course, the police and whaling ship crews were very interested in what I was doing. Still, I walked past the ships, taking pictures from the end of the dock, while two of the whaling ship crew posed for pictures in front of me and took pictures of their own. No words were exchanged. I went back to the ship, and later would wonder about something I had seen. Paul had already made the threat to take action against any whaler violating the IWC moratorium, so even then, on my maiden voyage, I was already thinking of a way to attack Iceland's whaling fleet.

A few days later, we departed Reykjavik's harbor without incident, and after an uneventful stop in the Faroe Islands, I returned home to California to work and save for the Sea Shepherd campaign to the Faroes the following year.

Forming a Plan

In June 1986, I rejoined the Sea Shepherd, which was berthed in Plymouth, England. I already had the plan to sabotage the Icelandic whaling fleet in my mind. It was a safe assumption that Iceland would not abide by the IWC ban on commercial whaling, so I already was coming up with a strategy. But what my plan needed, more than anything, was an accomplice. I knew I was in the right place to find one, not only because the ship was a magnet for young British animal activists, but the Plymouth community boasted a healthy population of anarchists and fox hunt saboteurs as well.

When I returned to the ship, I split my work between the engine room and the deck, not wanting to be relegated to being below deck in any confrontation, even though my skill set was better used in the engine room. But it wasn't necessary, because there were other skilled crew members from the local community who were joining us for the first time as well. Every day that I spent working on the ship while it was in harbor, gave me the chance to get to know these European counterparts, who were equally committed as I. A lot of our differences came in the fact that they were far more politicized than American youth like myself. Many of our volunteers were in their early 20s, but had already adopted strong political positions that they mirrored in how they behaved, what they consumed, and how they fought for justice.

Rod, Alice Clark, and Roland (1985)

Finally, the day came when we would leave Plymouth. I said good-bye to the young anarchist hunt-saboteur friends I had made, who had turned me onto punk rock and vegetarianism. We first set sail for Malmo, Sweden, where the annual meeting of the International Whaling Commission (IWC) was being held. There, they would decide what to do with member nations like Iceland who had no intention of observing the moratorium on commercial whaling that the IWC had passed in 1983, and that was meant to go into effect in 1986.

While the IWC meeting in Sweden was happening, Iceland's whaling ships set out to kill a total of 140 fin and sei whales in defiance of the moratorium, and then sold most of the meat to Japan. This would be the first blatant violation of the whaling moratorium that activists like Watson, myself, and an entire generation of enlightened citizens had fought for. That's all I needed to know in order to solidify my scheme to sink a whaler. The four Icelandic whaling ships I had already laid eyes on the previous summer were now pirate whalers, and thus they were fair game to any would-be saboteurs ready to defend the long-fought moratorium—namely, me and whoever else I could convince to carry out such an attack on a naval fleet in a foreign country. No problem!

Sea Shepherd (1986)

A hardworking Cornishman, and one of the hunt saboteurs from Plymouth, named David Howitt had joined our crew before we set sail for Sweden. David and I became friends when we would leave the ship after a long day of doing repairs. We would either go to the King's Head Pub, where the local hunt saboteurs met to organize the following day's hunt sabotage, or we would go to one of the local hunt saboteurs' homes where we would listen to records by the band Conflict, among others. It all sounded like screaming to me, but when I read the lyrics on the sleeves of the record, I began to see that this was the music that had inspired a generation of young people in Britain just like me.

The Conflict song, "This is the A.L.F.," was a how-to on getting involved in your own direct actions to save animals lives, whether it be slashing tires or burning buildings. These things were not even on my radar back in California, although I had clipped a small newspaper article once about people operating under the same name as the A.L.F., breaking into a research laboratory in my home state of California and rescuing the animals used in experiments there. I thought that was amazing. When I read that article, I wrote a letter to Alex Pacheco with People for the Ethical Treatment of Animals (PETA), who had publicized the raid and told him I wanted to join the ALF.

I never heard back from Pacheco (although I would years later, after I built more of a reputation…) nor had I learned anything more about the ALF until I met my young friends in England. The British animal rights movement was light-years ahead of any in the US, so the kindred spirits I couldn't find in my own life in California were much easier to find in the UK, once I had joined the crew of the Sea Shepherd, which attracted many young energetic animal defenders.

From left: **Veronica Behn, Peter Winch, Rod Coronado, Nick Taylor, Paul Watson, Jeremy Coon, Gabriella, Jim Frankham, David Howitt**

David Howitt was the only one of these new friends who would be coming back to the Faroe Islands with us. So when it became known that Iceland would continue to engage in illicit commercial whaling activities throughout the summer of 1986, I knew who I would ask to help me sink the whaling ships responsible for those illegal whale deaths.

Finally, one night after a long work day while in harbor in Sweden, I invited David to the rope locker of the ship for a smoke, where we could talk in private. As we both crouched amongst the piles of ropes, I recounted what I had seen the summer before in Reykjavik. David sat, rapt in attention as I described how I thought we might sabotage a whaling ship as an act of defiance to the violation of the moratorium. With a light laugh, David acknowledged that he took my offer seriously and began asking questions. By the end of the night, we had our plan. I told David I would approach Paul with the idea after the campaign to the Faroe Islands. Meanwhile we would both focus on the confrontation we expected to find upon our return to the Faroes.

The IWC's moratorium on commercial whaling would have no effect on the wholesale slaughter of smaller whales, which continues even to this day. In 1985, the Sea Shepherd sailed to the Faroes, but it wasn't until the following summer of 1986 that our opposition to the local practice of driving pilot whales ashore to be butchered was taken seriously. In 1985, we were allowed to go ashore, but the following year, the Faroese government banned Sea Shepherd from entering Faroese waters, despite the then-Prime Minister's open invitation to anyone opposed to the pilot whale drives.

Conflict in the Faroes

We were not content to respect our exclusion, so when we arrived outside Torshavn Harbor, rather than waste time in a stalemate, it was decided that a boatload of crew would go ashore and test the waters, so to speak. As soon as they set foot on dry land, the five crew members were arrested and detained

Within minutes of the arrest, it was decided that the ship's bosun, Nick Taylor, and I would take one of our ship's inflatables to the harbor in Torshavn and attempt to retrieve the inflatable left behind by the arrested crew members. As Nick and I approached the harbor, we could see a crowd gathering near the captured inflatable, with police present.

Nick and I made a plan to motor up to the captured boat, cut its mooring line and speed away. But as soon as we were close to the dock, a Faroese police officer jumped into our inflatable and wrestled control of the boat away from us. We were dragged ashore, as members of the angry mob screamed, "Kill them!" We were thrown into a police vehicle and driven less than a mile to the police station, where we were booked and jailed. I was told I was being charged with *attempted murder* of a police officer because of the knife I was holding at the time of arrest—the one that I had planned to use to cut loose our other inflatable.

The next seven days would be my first ever spent in prison for defending wildlife, but most certainly not the last. The five crew members that had been arrested and jailed had boosted the prison population of the Faroe Islands by 80%—the prison population being just seven inmates before our arrival. After the first couple days in captivity, Faroese officials offered to release us, but only if we accepted paid flights out of the country. The other crew quickly accepted, but Nick and I chose to remain, unless we were allowed to return to the Sea Shepherd.

After the first couple days, Nick and I began planning an escape from the jokingly minimum-security facility—not as a bold political statement, but because we were bored with the mandated labor of twisting fishing hooks onto nylon line while watching Danish overdubbed episodes of the TV cop show CHiPs. Our plan was to scale the chain-link fence during recreation time outside, and then run to the harbor, where we would then steal a boat to reach our ship at sea. The plan gave us something to talk about for a few days.

But before we could follow through on our plan to escape, after seven days in captivity, Nick and I were transported to Torshavn Harbor where, without any explanation, we were loaded aboard the nation's sole navy gunship, the Olivur Hagli. We anxiously sat under guard below decks where we could not see what was happening or where we were going. Instead, we listened to the RPMs of the main engine as it accelerated, then decreased speed repeatedly. We would later be told that the Olivur Hagli was attempting to overtake the Sea Shepherd as it openly violated the ban on entering Faroese waters. The two vessels played this cat-and-mouse game for a while, until the Faroese captain informed Captain Paul Watson that they were attempting to return his two remaining crew members.

At the nation's three-mile limit, the prisoner exchange was made, and we were transported aboard a military inflatable, across rolling waters, to climb up the Sea Shepherd's rope ladder and back into the arms of our friends. Back onboard the Sea Shepherd, it was decided that we should first return to nearby Scotland to refuel and better prepare the ship for what would surely be a confrontation when we returned to the Faroe Islands.

We sailed south to Lerwick, Scotland, where we spent three days outfitting the ship with fuel and supplies, as well as wrapping the entire railing around the ship with three strands of barbed wire to prevent "unauthorized boardings." I spent my 20th birthday in Lerwick, drinking beer and rum, and listening to The Smith's latest album "The Queen is Dead" on the monkey deck of the ship, with my deckhand friend, Pete Winch. We had lost more crew, after they realized we were going back to the Faroes, and they lacked the stomach for the confrontation with the navy that we most certainly expected. Left with just 16 crew members, we departed Lerwick one July morning, each of us taking shifts of six hours on, six hours off, to accommodate the loss of crew.

As soon as we re-entered Faroese territorial waters, the Olivur Hagli began pursuing us, attempting to board our ship. From their own small inflatables, the Faroese navy launched a tear gas assault on our ship. I was assigned to the foredeck with a fire hose, spraying cops in the face to try to throw off their aim as they fired gas projectiles at my friends on the deck and bridge. David Howitt was in the engine room, in over a hundred-degree temperatures and lingering tear gas, keeping the ship going. If the police got on board, we all knew we were in for a deserved beating after fighting them off with our hoses and with their own tear gas canisters, which we lobbed back at them—with an occasional steel wrench thrown in for good measure.

POLITIGARÐURIN
KRIMINALPOLITIDEILDIN
J. Bronckagøta 17 – 3800 Tórshavn
Tlf. (042) 11448
Stempel

Date
Fredag, den 230686
File No. 56K1-84130-00010-86   Alien No.

EXPULSION ORDER

An order was granted today for the expulsion of

Name
Rodney Adam Coronado

Date of birth   Place of birth   Nationality
030766   California, U.S.A.   amerikansk

The order was granted in pursuance of section of the Act on the Entry of aliens into Denmark   (see overleaf)

The expelled alien was ordered to leave Denmark within............... days after having served his sentence.
straks

At the same time the expelled alien was debarred from entering Denmark again/before
1. juli 1987
Date

The expelled alien was notified that

violation of the debarment shall be punishable by fine, mitigated or ordinary imprisonment for up to six (6) months;

as a member of the crew or as a passenger onboard an aircraft or a vessel he or she shall not be allowed to leave the aircraft/vessel upon arrival at a Danish airport/seaport;

entry into Finland, Iceland, Norway, and Sweden may take place only if a visa has been issued for the country concerned.

The Order may be appealed to the Ministry of Justice. If the appeal is filed with the Ministry of Justice within three (3) days from today's date or a request for an appeal is submitted to the Police, the expelled alien shall be allowed to remain in Denmark pending the decision of the Ministry of Justice.
Denne afgørelse er truffet af justitsministeriet og kan ikke påklages.
A copy in..........
of this Expulsion Order has been given to the expelled alien.

The expelled alien declares that he/she

☐ waives   ☐ wishes to file   ☐ wishes to consider

an appeal to the Ministry of Justice

According to article 14 of the Aliens Act, expences caused by deportation of an alien are to be paid of his/her own means.
I consent, that my resources, apart from the amount mentioned below for smaller necessities during the journey are being used to pay the fare at my expulsion from this country. This also applies to wages and a special allowance being paid on my release, which I am possibly entitled to from the criminal welfare. I have been informed that deportations normally are affected to the home country. However, if it is possible, I would like to be sent to one of the following countries.

Travelling money: kr. _____   Countries: _____

Expelled from Denmark (23 June 1986)

With the BBC film crew we had aboard, we were able to turn our confrontation into the climax of a documentary on the slaughter of pilot whales. We escaped to fight another day and began sailing back to England. Only David and I had another idea in mind for the whalers of the North Atlantic. After the battle with the Faroese police, I approached Paul with the idea. I told him that after our 1985 refueling stop the previous summer in Reykjavik, I had begun to think about the security on the whaling ships when they weren't on high alert, as they were when we visited. I told him I thought it was worth investigating, and if the opportunity presented itself, a person or persons, might be able to sneak onboard one of the whaling ships, enter the engine room, and open a seawater intake pipe, sinking one of the whaling ships in harbor.

To Paul's credit, even though I was a 20-year-old idealistic kid without much life experience, he accepted the notion that David and I could carry out such a plan in a foreign country. After all, David had proved himself in the fight with the Faroese, as had I. Paul would later say to media who were shocked at the young ages of the Sea Shepherd saboteurs, that in many cultures, including our own, this was the age young people took the path in defense of their land and freedom. The difference was, the young people in this ecological crisis were beginning to fight for the Earth instead of for a government.

When I finished proposing my plan, Paul kept his gaze focused on the ocean in front of us and asked me what we needed from him to support the plan. No laugh, no machine-gun questioning on how we might fail, just a belief in what I had to say. I would later learn that this was the most empowering thing a mentor can do for a younger student: simply help strengthen their belief in themselves.

David and I spent the summer of 1986 working to raise the money for our mission to infiltrate Iceland with the sole purpose of causing maximum economic damage to their whaling industry. I waited tables in a nightclub in London's Chelsea district during the nights, and I refinished antiques on Kings Road during the day. David went to southern England where he picked hops. Every few weeks, we would meet to discuss our plans and go over intelligence we had gathered on Iceland. When our work was complete, we would make a batch of paint-filled light bulbs and ride out on our bikes to smash the paint bombs on London fur shops. We had originally planned on early October for the attempted raid, when the fleet was being laid up for repairs and winter, but our plan had to be delayed by a couple weeks, due to the Superpower summit being held in Reykjavik between the US and Russia.

The Plan in Motion

Finally, the day arrived when we rode the London Underground subway to Heathrow Airport to catch our IcelandAir flight to Reykjavik. As we rode to the airport, I removed a patch from my jacket that read "Save the Whales, Save the Earth" with a picture of a fin whale. All we carried with us was our cameras, clothes and rain gear, underwater flashlights, knives, and a couple of maps. All the tools necessary for any action would be acquired in Iceland.

When we arrived in October, only the hardcore travelers were still around. We got beds in the local youth hostel, and one of our first tasks was to buy a pair of bolt cutters and a large adjustable wrench from a local hardware store. We wanted as much time as possible between the purchase of our tools and the action, in case anyone might remember the purchase.

On one of the first nights in the capital city of Reykjavik, we snuck out of the hostel late at night and crept into a scrapyard from where we could view the four 175-foot Icelandic ships that comprised the nation's entire whaling fleet. Hvalur ("whaleship") 5, 6, 7, and 8 bobbed in the harbor, tied alongside each other like four Riders of the Apocalypse waiting to unleash their evil on the natural world. The ships' superstructures were painted white with the bridge windows and portholes dark and imposing, resembling the empty eye-sockets of a skull.

Needless to say, we were a little intimidated. The reality of what was so simple to discuss in England was now staring us in the face in the freezing fall weather of a Reykjavik night, four very real ships floating in the safety of Iceland's major seaport...more than a little daunting, to say the least. But we knew it wouldn't be easy, so David and I began a series of late-night observations of the harbor, beginning that first night in Reykjavik.

Within two weeks of conducting night time surveillance, a clear and definite routine began to emerge of the day-to-day security of the Icelandic whaling fleet. It was abundantly clear that security was minimal when the ships weren't actively whaling. We knew any attack would have to take place late at night, so we began watching from the scrapyard nightly until we could predict the coming and going of the night watchman. Every Friday evening, a night watchman would relieve the day watch, carrying with him two bottles of Brenivin, a strong Icelandic vodka. No activity could be seen on three of the ships—the watchman staying on the fourth ship, the one furthest from the dock. A weekend night emerged as the best night for action.

In Reykjavik we saw photos from the whaling station, which was 45 miles from town—a separate facility from where the ships were. Tours were offered for the station, so David and I hitchhiked to the desolate station and were dropped off near the entrance. As we approached, not a soul was visible. The whaling season was over, and with it the demand for tours. David and I began to walk throughout the premises in broad daylight, gazing through windows at offices, machinery, and workshops, and it quickly became evident to both of us that we might be able to strike the whaling station as well as the ships. We knew we would have only one shot at the Icelandic whaling industry, and any risk to ourselves did not matter. Already we felt the chances were good that we would not get off the island, once our sabotage was discovered.

Iceland in (now) November 1986 was not a country that expected or even remembered the threats of a militant anti-whaling organization. Only one watchman was aboard all four ships. It was the off-season and the crews were ashore, with work on the ships restricted to daylight hours.

The week of our planned attack, the whaling ships were taken into drydock. One by one, they were pulled out of the water for repairs and cleaning, which is a major operation. David and I had planned on attempting to sink all three ships minus the one that housed the watchman. Now we were forced to sacrifice our third target. Our money was running low, and the fear of being discovered still haunted us. Maybe we were already under surveillance ourselves, and the police were waiting for us to act before they could legitimately arrest us?

Already David and I had read up on the Icelandic penal system and learned that the longest sentence given to any crime was eleven years. We also learned that Icelandic prisoners were employed making cement sidewalk blocks. From that day on, the jokes never stopped of how good we might become at building Icelandic sidewalks.

David and I had befriended two Swedish women who were also staying at the youth hostel while working at a local meatpacking plant. It was the same company that packaged the nation's whale meat, so we listened closely as the women described the company's labor shortage. The women said the company would often hire foreign travelers and pay them under the table without paperwork. It was a perfect opportunity to investigate whether the "Whale Meat Mountain" of surplus whale meat from the illegal 1986 season's kill was being stored at the facility. I took a job stuffing mass-produced wieners into vacuum packaging. During breaks and on my way to work, I surveyed other buildings within the large facility but found nothing related to whale meat, only the remains of domestically-raised farm animals raised for slaughter.

I was enjoying being a part of the Nordic working class and making friends with other Swedish workers when I was called into the boss's office. Apparently, my employment had been noticed, probably because I was the only non-white employee at the factory. I was told that I was prohibited from working, but that my boss would try to get an exemption. We walked to an immigration office together in downtown Reykjavik where my boss pled my case, but the ruling was firm: I absolutely was not allowed to work in Iceland without a work permit. What's more, I worried that this issue might draw attention to the expulsion order I had received in the Faroe Islands which also prohibited me from entering Denmark and Iceland. My boss was very apologetic and even offered to lend me cash until I was later paid. I thanked him for going to bat for me but said my goodbyes and returned to the hostel to deliver the news to David. I knew this event warranted us taking swift and immediate action before I might be discovered in Iceland.

Time to Act

Finally surrendering our fate to the whale spirits, we decided to act. We choose the night of November 8 for our task of vengeance. We said good-bye to our European friends and told them David and I were going to rent a car for our last day to do a little sightseeing.

On the morning of November 7, David and I checked into a different hostel, one where we had the privacy of our own room. We then drove to the airport on the morning of the 8th to pre-check our luggage for the 6 a.m. flight out of the country the following morning. It was to Luxemburg, but we did not care where it went, as long as it was not Scandinavia. Next, we drove to Iceland's only vegetarian restaurant for what might be our last supper. We had been saving our money for this last luxury but found the restaurant closed. Not to be disappointed, we bought food from a super-market and drove to a clearing above the whaling station to eat our meal and await the early winter darkness.

While eating, we listened to the car radio, and after our meal, we discovered we had drained the battery dead. Here our mission might have ended, had not a vanload of Icelandic youths, probably employed by the whaling station, come to our rescue. They towed our car until we could jump-start it, and then we waved goodbye and drove to our prearranged hiding place for the car, as night was fast approaching.

A rainstorm began to fall, adding a brilliant cover as David and I pulled on our dark raingear, gloves, and ski masks, and strapped on fanny-packs filled with flashlights and tools. I then placed the car keys on the top of the rear tire, and we began the long walk to the whaling station in complete darkness, bending into the wind and increasing rain. We couldn't even look in front of us, the rain was so torrential. All I could see was the dark ground at my feet as we walked on the road to the whaling station. At this point, we didn't care if we were out in the open. It was November in Iceland in a desolate region with no street lights or traffic. David and I had learned while hitchhiking in Iceland that if the first car that passes you doesn't stop, the second one will—except it might be four hours later. Once darkness had fallen, we saw no other vehicles on the road that night.

As we approached the whaling station, we were suddenly surprised by the sight and sound of a front-end excavator that was digging a trench at the station. This was the only visible activity at the station, so we dropped to our bellies on the ground and spent the next hour lying still in the freezing rain until the workman and his machine eventually headed off to the local town. As the lights of the machine disappeared, we stood up and shook the aches from our bones and leapt forward into action. Before we could start, we wanted to make sure there was no one else on the premises, so we carried out a brief search of the darkened complex. There were only a few small lights illuminating the station, but every building appeared to be empty. This was the time we had been waiting for. Not only would we attempt to board and sink one of the whaling ships in Reykjavik Harbor, but we now knew we could carry out a destructive raid on the nation's only whale processing plant as well.

Our first task was the sabotage of the six huge diesel generators that provided power for the station. David and I were both experienced diesel engineers, and we knew what was good for an engine, as well as what was bad. Before long, we were stripping off our outer clothing and sweating profusely in our handiwork as we removed valve covers and bent the metal rods with sledgehammers we found at the site.

Next, David and I moved on to the many centrifuges that processed whale blubber into a high-grade lubricating oil. Smashing the delicate equipment with our hammers, we next located what I could not find at the meatpacking plant I had worked: the Whalemeat Mountain. David had attempted to move the many crates of whale meat outside with a forklift, which were housed in huge refrigeration units beneath the station, but his forklift ran out of propane gas. We were forced to wedge open the refrigeration units and then sabotage the refrigeration units themselves, so that hopefully the meat would thaw and spoil. Unfortunately, it was November and the temperatures already cold for that time of year.

Once we had shut down the power for the refrigeration system, we next found a computer control room that kept the entire station's machinery fully automated and running smoothly. While I began more carefully cutting wires, David simply began smashing the computer panels with a pair of bolt-cutters until sparks flew and LEDs flashed and the beautiful music of machines dying all around us could be heard in the darkness. We had already been onsite for over an hour and there was no time to waste.

We moved next to the ship's store, where the spare parts for the four whaling ships were kept. Taking what we, as engineers, thought were the most expensive replacement parts, David and I carried the machinery to the edge of the docks where we unceremoniously tossed them all into the dark waters.

On one of those trips to the slipway, where hundreds of great whales had been hauled ashore to be slaughtered, I carried an armload of brand new, razor-sharp flensing knives used to strip away the blubber of a whale. I threw each one down the slipway, the blades making sparks as they hit the concrete before disappearing into the water.

Finally, after about three hours of tedious sabotage, we reached the main offices where record books detailing the illegal catches were kept in a filing cabinet. We confiscated all record books and poured cyanic acid we found in a warehouse throughout the building's database. Windows were smashed, and anything that looked expensive met the business end of our wrenches and bolt-cutters.

Days later, when I was back stateside, I watched the World News and would hear the station's foreman recount with shock how it appeared that the whole whaling station had been the target of an air raid. The total damages would easily be over a million dollars alone at the station.

We realized we could have spent all night sabotaging the station, but in the forefront of our minds, we knew the ships were waiting, so David and I looked at our watches and realized it was time to signal our retreat and return, sweaty and tired, to our awaiting rental car. Once there, I experienced a frantic moment as I reached for the keys I had left on the tire and did not find them there. With relief, I discovered that the high winds had been so strong as to blow them some feet away, where I found them with my flashlight after a brief desperate search. Now covered in grease and drenched in sweat, we began the pitch-black drive back to Reykjavik. We were already dead tired and the weather had made the roads treacherous, and often on the gravel road, our car would start to slide when it hit ice. Each time we worried we might run off the road and be stuck on the shoulder as the nation woke to our attack. I am convinced that many of my premature gray hairs were earned that night.

A Watery Grave

An hour after leaving Hvalfjordur, we reached Reykjavik Harbor, where three deadly ghost ships lay bobbing in the water, the fourth in dry dock. Resting, David and I ate some quick energy food and stashed our confiscated record books from the whaling station in the backseat. Taking a deep breath, we then opened our car doors and stepped back into the pounding rainstorm that made our ski masks and rain gear not just a disguise but a necessity. With hands in our pockets like two cold fishermen, we began walking down the dead-end dock towards Hvalur 5, 6, and 7.

The tides in the harbor were such that we were level with the ships' decks; so, to board, all we had to do was hop a few feet from the dock to the steel-plated decks. Moving quickly to Hvalur 5, David pulled out our bolt cutters and cut the hasp on the lock that shut the engine room hatch. Moving into the fully-lit engine rooms, David searched the ship for any sleeping watchman while I moved into the engine room and began lifting deck plates, looking for the saltwater cooling valve that regulated the sea-water that cooled the ship's engines at sea. By the time I found it, David had returned to announce that the ship was indeed empty. What I had found was the weed box that serves as a filter for saltwater pumped from the sea below the ship's waterline. By removing the cover, we would easily allow the entire engine room to be flooded in seawater.

Two down...

We began to wrestle off the sixteen or more nuts that held the valve cover in place, and when most were removed, water began to shoot out from the bolt holes. I tasted it, and it was salty. When the cover was fully removed, the ocean water would flood first the engine room and then the rest of the ship's compartments, dragging it to a watery grave in Reykjavik's deep harbor. Leaving the cover partially removed, we moved to Hvalur 6, where we repeated the process, quickly locating then removing that ship's salt-water weed box.

Finally, when we had all the nuts and bolts removed, we took a pry bar to the valve on the second ship, and with a little persuasion, the valve quickly popped free, releasing a flood of seawater that drenched both David and me. We fled the engine room and quickly returned to Hvalur 5, where we removed the last of that ship's cover bolts, and again the ocean began to rush in, looking like a fire hydrant left wide open.

The Getaway...

Now it was time to execute our escape. The whaling station had been demolished, and two 175-foot whaling ships were sinking fast. The time was just before 5 a.m., and the airport was almost an hour away. As David and I began walking away from the two sinking ships, we tossed our remaining tools into the icy waters and pulled our ski masks off just as we reached the car. Hopping into the driver's seat, I started the car and pulled onto the road.

Less than two minutes later, we were pulled over by a Reykjavik police car. My first thought was, "No, they can't be that good; they can't have been watching us this whole time..." Still, there we were, with two ships quickly sinking and minutes ticking away before our flight to freedom would lift off, possibly leaving us for the next eleven years to fine-tune our masonry skills at the local prison. And now an Icelandic police officer was walking to my window while David and I sat soaked in water, with engine grease all over our clothes.

The officer greeted me and then asked me to get into his car. Looking at David as he sat with eyes forward, I got out of our car and walked towards the back seat of the police cruiser. Once seated in their car, the officers ignored me and spoke to each other in Icelandic before finally turning around and asking me in plain English, "Have you been drinking any alcohol tonight?"

Almost laughing, I said, "No, I don't even drink!" which was a lie, and he then asked if he could smell my breath. It was tempting to utter a joke, but hot coffee on an IcelandAir jet was calling. So I breathed on him, and he wished me a safe trip to the airport, knowing that was where we were probably headed because of the early morning departure.

That police officer is probably still cursing himself to this day, after having had the nation's only saboteur since the Second World War in his police car, before then letting him go. Returning to the car, David told me he had almost bolted but thought it best that he wait for another moment for some signal from me.

Pulling into the airport, we grabbed our daypacks and quickly changed our clothes, dumping the grease-covered ones in the airport garbage can. We next went through Icelandic Customs without any incident, checked in, and grabbed our boarding passes. The polite ticket agent told us the flight was delayed due to the harsh weather. The words were what we least wanted to hear, and David and I spent the next 30 minutes staring at the clock, imagining the chaos erupting at Reykjavik harbor just about now. Finally, our flight was called, and we quickly boarded, still not feeling safe until hours later when we landed in Luxembourg.

As we landed, David and I gazed out the window, half expecting to see Interpol agents waiting for our arrival. They were not. We collected our luggage and walked out of the airport after making an anonymous call to the Sea Shepherd offices in the UK, saying only, "We got the station, and two are on the bottom..."

We then hitchhiked to Belgium, where we caught a ferry to England and then a bus to London. Getting off the bus now 36 hours after our action, I walked to a news agent and picked up a copy of the morning paper. A story on the front page said only, "SABOTEURS SINK WHALERS, photo page six..."

Flipping to the page, I saw one of the most beautiful sights in the world. There were Hvalur 5 and 6 resting gently on the bottom of Reykjavik harbor, only their skeletal superstructure peeking above the waves. Paul Watson was quoted as accepting responsibility for the attack, which he said was an enforcement action of the IWC's moratorium on commercial whaling that Iceland had violated. David and I embraced in the streets, laughing with the elation that only a realized dream can bring.

We were too young to realize the depths of what we had just done. Ours was the latest action in a long-running battle against commercial whaling, an industry responsible for wiping out and depleting all members of the Earth's great whales. If commercial whaling couldn't be stopped, what hope would there be for redwoods and rainforests also being destroyed for economic growth? Let alone animals dying in traps for the fur trade or in factory farms to feed the Earth's growing human population.

David and I had done what a responsible or ethical government should have done: shut down an illegal operation in violation of international laws and treaties. But governments do not exist to protect biological diversity from commercial exploitation by capitalists; no, their purpose is quite the opposite, to protect those responsible for destroying our planet.

Two whaling ships lying in Reykjavik Harbor in Iceland yesterday after being sunk by an environmentalist group.

Militants Sink 2 of Iceland's Whaling Vessels

By United Press International

REYKJAVIK, Iceland, Nov. 9 — Militant environmentalists boarded two of Iceland's four whaling ships early today and opened key sea valves, sinking the ships in Reykjavik harbor, a leader of an antiwhaling group said.

No crew members were aboard the vessels at the time.

Today, as the scuttled vessels' prows poked out of the harbor's 35-degree waters, police divers confirmed that valves had been opened on the 434-ton Hvalur 6 and the 427-ton Hvalur 7.

Paul Watson, president of the Sea Shepherd Conservation Society of Vancouver, claimed responsibility for the sinkings. He said a team from his group had sneaked into the engine rooms of the vessels and opened the valves, sending sea water pouring into the holds.

He said the team had taken care to make sure no one was aboard.

Mr. Watson is a former member of the Greenpeace environmentalist group who broke away amid bitter disagreements in the 1970's to form the Sea Shepherd group. The two groups maintain no contact with each other.

The two sunken vessels are owned by Iceland's only whaling company, Hvalur of Hvalfjordur, based 15 miles north of Reykjavik, the capital. The company said it would be able to refloat the ships, though much of their equipment would be ruined by the water.

Two other Hvalur-owned whaling vessels remained afloat in the harbor. Mr. Watson, in an interview from Vancouver, British Colombia, said the group did not try to sink them because "there were watchmen aboard."

"Our organization has the full right to sink the whalers because Iceland is violating the moratorium," he said, referring to the moratorium on whaling that the International Whaling Commission has decreed.

"I instructed our people they were not to use explosives to insure that no one could be hurt," Mr. Watson said. "We could have sunk the other two, but

Continued on Page A9, Column 1

New York Times, 10 Nov 1986; p. 1

I'd come a long way from being the 12-year-old kid who wanted to grow jojoba beans to help save the whales. I had found my war captain, and in following his lead, I was able to strike a legitimate target that he helped identify in the ongoing war to save the whales. Paul had been the only human on Earth to up the ante by targeting pirate whalers for sabotage and sinkings, and now with the Iceland action, we drew the focus of the world's media to the controversy surrounding attempts by commercial whalers to legitimize themselves in a changing world.

And we'd done it with nothing more than our own determination, wits, and some bolt-cutters.

The world's law enforcement community would still not wake to the threat of "eco-terror" for a few more years, but soon it would be identified as a major threat to economic interests involved in the destruction of wild-life and the environment. Make no mistake though, there were plenty of critics of our illegal actions—the loudest of course being Greenpeace, already the most vocal critic of Paul Watson's Sea Shepherd tactics and strategies. We were accused of "putting a gun to the head of Iceland" by the Canadian Director of Greenpeace. Yet, for years, Greenpeace's navy of multiple ships peacefully sat in harbor while Iceland's illegal whalers plied the seas, killing the Earth's last fin whales. By targeting the illegal whaling ships of Hvalur Limited, we wanted the world to know a new generation of eco-warrior was entering the battlefield.

The two Hvalur ships today—rusting away on the coast of Iceland

Rod and Paul Watson (3 December 1986)

CHAPTER 3

JOINING THE ALF

After the whirlwind of media surrounding the Iceland campaign, I decided to move to southern California, where I could connect with the many Earth First! activists from the then-multiple chapters that existed in California, as well as the veteran animal rights activists in the southern portion of the state. In January 1987, I was invited to a conference in Sacramento on "Civil Disobedience & Direct Action in the Animal Rights Movement" by Cres Vellucci, another pioneer in the US animal rights movement. Over the phone, Cres told me, "There's some people I really want to introduce you to …" This did not surprise me, as California in the 1980s was becoming a hotbed for radical environmental action, and the animal rights movement wasn't going to be left behind.

By this time, I was no longer naïve about the Animal Liberation Front. When I first read about the ALF's April 1986 raid on the University of California at Riverside that rescued hundreds of animals, I wanted to join those who participated, and thought I could simply find them. But I quickly learned about the risks involved and the level of secrecy that was required in order for such raids to be effective. After my time with my anarchist hunt saboteur friends in the UK, I knew the safer path was for me to build my own cell of the ALF.

After 1986, with the public knowledge that I had committed the raid against Iceland, most activists in both the environmental and animal rights movements knew what I was capable of, and some even felt obliged to tell me about illegal actions they had taken against developers, trappers, and an assortment of animal abusers. So when I returned to California after the Iceland raid, and began meeting the movers and shakers in the animal rights movement, it wasn't difficult to find someone who had participated in the ALF raid on UC Riverside.

After a series of payphone calls late one night in early April 1987, I drove from my home in Palm Springs to an AM/PM gas station, where I met one of the participants in the UC Riverside raid. I wasn't looking to join their group, I simply wanted to know how they had carried out such a successful raid against a well-financed educational institution with regular security so that I could begin searching for my own animal research targets. We drove together to a rabbit-breeding operation on the outskirts of

San Bernardino. My contact told me this was a breeder who had been supplying animals for research to laboratories in the UC system for some years now. We parked my van behind a small orchard that abutted the rear of the rabbit breeders and crouch-walked to the dimly outlined barns a couple hundred feet away. Inside the barns were dozens of white rabbits of varying size and age.

I'll never forget one thing my contact told me: "No matter how tight their security might seem, there is always a loose link." I remembered the lone security guard on the whaling ships in Iceland, who carried a plastic bag with two vodka bottles onboard at the beginning of his watch every Friday.

This was to be my first animal rescue and I needed help to pull it off. Friends I had met at the conference in Sacramento drove down to help; when they came, they brought along newspapers filled with stories about a recent arson at an animal diagnostic laboratory under construction at the University of California at Davis. This one action in April 1987 would bring national media attention to the issue of animal research, but it also was the beginning of the FBI's investigations into the ALF. It would lead to subsequent grand juries that dragged dozens of activists behind closed doors to testify about associates in the animal rights movement.

On the day of the action, I went to a Sea Shepherd crew member's home in Topanga Canyon, having been told earlier that he would lend me a vehicle for the raid that we expected would result in the rescue of dozens of rabbits. When I got to the house, my fellow crew member casually informed me that he was going to come along, as was our common friend and Captain, Paul Watson. The three of us drove back to my place in Palm Springs—and my friends were astonished when I walked in and told them that the Captain of Sea Shepherd would be driving our getaway van! All of us were in our twenties, and we really looked up to the movement's heroes like Paul. And though Paul and I had become personal friends, to the others he was still something of a legend. And this legend was not only giving us the thumbs up, he was coming along to help us steal a bunch of bunnies destined for painful experiments at UC laboratories like the one still smoldering in Davis.

So on this warm April night in the California desert, as we drove towards the Bloomington rabbit breeders, my friends and I celebrated the birth of a new cell of the Animal Liberation Front. Our feelings were only galvanized as we drove out of Palm Springs, where privileged youth our own age were out in the streets, drunkenly celebrating Spring Break. My older friend looked at them and exclaimed to Paul, "Look at those young people. Look at what they are choosing to do right now; and then look at these guys [us]! Look at what a beautiful thing they are going out to risk their lives for…"

The raid went off without a hitch. We rescued 113 white rabbits, most of them young bunnies, and about a dozen large breeding males and females. We drove the animals north and arrived late at night to my family's rural home, where we placed the rabbits in a barn. From here, they would be housed in different locations. But before we could do that, some broke out of the barn and had to be re-rescued by my parents, who offered up a weak cover story to the neighbors to explain the many white bunnies seen running around on Easter weekend.

We were just getting started. In early May 1987, Paul Watson was scheduled to speak at the Whole Earth Festival on the UC Davis campus, where another Earth First! chapter had sprouted. My colleague from Iceland, David Howitt, was in the country, so he joined me, as did many other local Earth First! activists in descending upon Davis, where the police were still very much interested in who burned the unfinished diagnostic lab a couple of weeks earlier.

It was here that I was able to meet many of the people who would, at different times over the years, aid me when I needed another body on an ALF raid. It was a good time for me. I was looking for others who were ready to take the kind of action we had taken in Iceland, while at the same time participating in above-ground protests that Earth First! and local animal rights groups like In Defense of Animals were organizing. These were the people who had begun fighting for animals and the Earth in my own home state while I was off sailing with Sea Shepherd; many became life-long friends.

Saving Wild Horses from the BLM

While at the Whole Earth Festival, Paul relayed a message that a long-time figure in the animal rights movement, Cleveland Amory, wanted to talk to me privately. Then age 70, Cleveland was something of an 'elder statesman' of the movement; he also became my unofficial mentor and adoptive godfather.

When I left Davis, I went to San Francisco, where I met with Virginia Handley of the Fund for Animals. Cleveland had instructed her to get in touch with me about the federal roundup of wild horses from public lands across the West. Cleveland's Fund for Animals had become famous for their campaign to rescue burros and wild horses that were being scapegoated by the livestock industry, which saw the horses as grazing competitors, even though they constituted a fraction of the number of cows allowed to graze on the same lands. (More than 600 million acres in the US, mostly in the west, are turned over to ranchers to graze their beef cattle, causing immense ecological damage.)

In California, the Bureau of Land Management (BLM) had designated 21 wild horse and burro "herd management areas" on the more than two million acres of public lands populated by wild horses in the state. The BLM says the combined "appropriate management level" for all such areas in all of California is just 2,200 animals. But the state had, at one time, around 30,000 wild horses. This means that, since 1971, the BLM rounded up over 27,000 wild horses and burros from public rangelands where they cause a fraction of the environmental impact that hundreds of thousands of cattle have on that same land.

In old-school fashion, Virginia coordinated a call between Cleveland and I, both on pay phones. I was told that the Fund was taking legal action to block the latest roundup of horses, which were being warehoused in corrals outside of Litchfield, California. Cleveland wanted me to give him an update on the horses' living conditions. I agreed to do the job, driving to the northeastern high desert of California with three new friends from the Whole Earth Festival in Davis.

From an overlook, the four of us nestled into a pile of lava rock and gazed over the corrals of the Bureau of Land Management facility where over 200 wild horses were awaiting transfer to "adoption centers"—in reality, little more than prisons for animals born in the wild. In one smaller corral, we could see horses standing still with just their tails swishing. These were the trained saddle horses used by BLM riders. But in the larger corrals, horses were running back and forth with their tails and manes flying; these were the wild ones. I had read the story of wild horses in America in Fund for Animal literature, but seeing these clearly wild animals being taken from their home, simply to make room for beef cattle, was heartbreaking.

After talking with my friends, I went back to a pay phone and again spoke with Cleveland. I told him that the corrals were located in a remote desert area with little highway traffic, and that if released from their corrals, we believed the horses could escape. He told me the Fund was tied up in the legal case, but he supported my decision to attempt a rescue mission. I remember him telling me to be careful and steer clear of the horses when we were in the corrals. Once we had cut the fences, he told me, "Run like hell!" That was the last time I ever spoke to my adopted godfather. Cleveland died in 1998.

Planning the Raid

We drove back to the San Francisco Bay area, where most of us lived, and prepared for the raid. Our plan was simple. We would enter the BLM complex of corrals and cut through dozens of six-foot-high fence posts, each six inches in diameter, that made up the corrals where the wild horses were kept. We reviewed topographical maps of the area to determine the direction that the released horses would need to take, in order to reach open range. Just to the northeast lay the 750,000-acre Twin Peaks wild horse herd area, where they could disappear amongst the jigsaw maze of desert mountains.

In the direction we expected the horses to follow, we would also cut hundreds of feet of barbed wire fence that stood between the horses and their freedom. Where we anticipated wild horses might cross the deserted Interstate 395, we would also cut fencing and erect two highway construction signs with flashing lights (that we stole from an urban construction zone in the Bay Area.) On the yellow diamond signs, we painted a black silhouette of a horse running, along with the words, "HORSE XING."

I will never forget the night we were preparing for the raid in my family's old horse barn in Morgan Hill—the same barn that served as a rescued rabbit refuge the month before. My father walked in on us as we were painting the horse crossing signs, but before we could say anything, he started chuckling and shaking his head as he turned around and walked out of the barn.

The next day, in clown-car fashion, five of us piled into an old van we had borrowed, loaded down with the crossing signs, bow saws, and camp gear. After getting my dad's help to start the delicate vehicle, we headed east into the Sierra Nevada mountains, which we would cross, then head north to the BLM Wild Horse corrals outside of Susanville, California. After picking up crew in the mountains that night, we started back towards the interstate, when suddenly…the van's brakes stopped working. Before I could tell anyone what was happening, the lights also went out. I immediately swerved the van into the road bank to the left, to avoid going off the mountain to the right. We narrowly missed boulders and gently came to rest on the shoulder of the road. Our flashlights came on and we could see that everyone was ok—even the vegan lasagna we had been given, which was resting flat on the chest of one of our crew.

Luckily, we hadn't driven far and we were able to discover the minor cause of the electrical and brake failures; we patched in a fix until we could reach a proper auto parts store in the morning.

We stopped at the airport in Reno, Nevada where we picked up a friend from Los Angeles who would also rent another car for the action. Together we drove back to Litchfield and made camp in the desolate BLM lands that make up most of northeastern California. The four of us who had participated in the earlier recon would lead separate teams of fence cutters, each team with a pair of bolt cutters and three-foot bow saw. It was Memorial Day weekend, and any human activity at the corrals was minimal. So when the sun set, we hoisted our packs onto our backs, bid farewell to our drivers (who would pick us up at a pre-arranged time on the shoulder of I-395), and in the fading light, began cutting barbed wire fences.

With one team remaining on barbed-wire fence-cutting, the rest of our crew approached the corrals that were just visible in the moonlight. Cutting the fence would be heavy work. First, we'd have to cut through the large posts, then cut the 4-inch square wire attached to the posts, then drag aside the fence with the posts still attached. We focused on the northernmost corrals where we had seen the young stallions earlier, but also separate corrals with mares and foals.

Time was on our side, and we spent the better part of three hours cutting and dragging fence. Each corral was 4 to 5 acres in area, so the horses, easily spooked, ran to the farthest side of the corral while we worked. When we had finished, we gathered together, formed lines, and started driving the horses out of the corrals. We walked about 20 feet apart from one another, but it didn't take much to get the horses moving.

While visibility was limited, we could literally feel the ground shaking as dozens of horses raced past us towards freedom. I was still dragging portions of fence when I heard the hoofbeats; I stopped my work just in time to see a group of young stallions running across the moonlit desert, their manes flowing. They were free once again.

Because of the holiday weekend and the remote location of the action, the media didn't pick up our press release from the action, but we knew law enforcement would be made fully aware.

Back on the Sea Shepherd

After the wild horse liberation, my attention shifted back to Sea Shepherd duties, as the organization was acquiring a new ship in the Pacific since the Sea Shepherd remained in the UK. But the BLM raid had galvanized some of the new recruits. There was no formal organization to our new group; we deferred to whoever put in the most work doing recon and knew the most about our targets. If I was seen as a leader, it was mostly because I was the person who made contacts and could secure funding because I was becoming a public figure in the movement.

Two weeks after the wild horse action, the ALF returned to UC Davis. These would be individuals who had become empowered to take action following the destruction of the animal diagnostic lab only two months earlier and then had joined us on the wild horse action. They understood that by taking direct action to rescue animals, they *were* the ALF.

On June 12 two of the ALF wild horse warriors from Litchfield, cut through a fence at the Raptor Center on the UC Davis campus and gained entry into an office, where they took keys to the turkey vulture cages. At the time, the center was experimenting on the vultures, feeding them the commercial poison #1080 to study its effects on California condors—of which, ironically, the last wild bird had been captured two months earlier. The raiders then released five of the turkey vultures being used for experiments.

Meanwhile, David Howitt and I arrived in Seattle to begin work on the newly-acquired ship that we would use to sail into the North Pacific Ocean. We would be hunting the Japanese drift-net fishery, which consisted of hundreds of ships that used miles-long nets to catch anything that swam across them. In their quest for edible fish, the drift nets also caught all kinds of unintended creatures, including dolphins and sea turtles, many of which died in the process. We spent the first weeks of June working on an old tuna fishing boat, before an agreement was made to trade the ship for a Japanese-built tuna fishing vessel. The trade was between Sea Shepherd and the Parkwest Children's Fund, a faith-based group that provides relief to people throughout the world with a fleet of ships.

In mid-June we set sail for the North Pacific, spending the next four weeks searching for the drift-net fleet—to no avail. It had been only a year since I left the Sea Shepherd II in England to carry out the Iceland campaign and now, with a crew of friends that included other new ALF members, being at sea again with such strongly committed warriors was amazing. We sailed north along the Queen Charlotte Islands as we built confidence with the new ship.

On my birthday, I was standing watch on the bridge when we began seeing a disturbance in the green ocean waters. Very quickly, the surface of the water was broken by the white and black tail fluke of what became a humpback whale. As we slowed our engines, the magnificent giant began spy-hopping, which led to full-on breaching his entire body out of the water, to then hit the surface with a huge splash. It was one of the best birthdays ever, especially to be sharing it with Paul, David, and many others of the great crew on that voyage. Seeing whales alive and joyously jumping out of the ocean was also the best reward for our actions the previous fall in Iceland. I've always believed that, as defenders of the wild, it would be a denial of a great source of strength to not draw from the power of the very animals we fight for—just as so many indigenous warrior-nations have done before us.

When we pulled into Dutch Harbor, Alaska to refuel, we were followed by a Japanese government surveillance vessel that had been sent to relay our location to the fleet; no wonder we found nothing. With limited funds, it was decided to end the campaign and sail into Vancouver, British Columbia. As much as I wanted to continue on the path of direct action with the ALF strategy, I still loved going to sea with a trusted crew of like-minded people—especially when those people were friends I had made in past campaigns.

Strategic Arson as a New Tactic

In August 1987, I flew home to California where I reconvened with some friends who had participated in earlier ALF actions that year. As much as we wanted to carry out live animal liberations, we knew that these kinds of raids required far more resources and put us at greater risk than raids intending to cause merely financial damage. Liberated animals are too easily replaced, and housing them requires exposing them, and ourselves, to the risk of recapture. Therefore, it was decided that we should use arson as a means of property destruction, as had been modeled in the UK, from where many of us aspiring radical animal liberationists took our lead. Only, we wouldn't use the ALF name to claim responsibility, but the then-more-radical British splinter group, the Animal Rights Militia, to claim responsibility.

My girlfriend Sophia and I had recently watched a documentary called "The Animals Film" (1981), which was the first video many activists had seen, depicting animal experimentation and other forms of animal abuse, including the confinement of veal calves in small crates that prevent movement. After I watched the film, I felt justified in targeting those industries for economic sabotage. I had already made the decision to follow my own path and my own law, so that same night we found a veal distributor in San Jose, and drove out to investigate. We brought along the only resources I had available on hand: a gallon of white gas for my camping stove and a lighter.

After walking past the location and determining that no one was on site, I slipped into the loading dock and found my way into the building. All lights were off and the place was mostly concrete and steel—hardly a good target for an arson attack, but we were determined. We found a store-room full of pallets with cardboard boxes. After piling boxes together, we lit the pile and fled. The next day, local media covered the story and we knew we were on a path of no return.

Target: Fur Shops

We decided to return to the ship in Vancouver, so my girlfriend and I drove back; I decided to stay with the other two remaining crew, David Howitt from my Iceland adventures, and Linda May, a veteran of the Divine Wind driftnet campaign. There wasn't a lot happening on the ship at the time, so the three of us would often wander into Vancouver, where I noticed quite a few retail fur dealers. Back in London, while David and I were work-ing to save up money for the Iceland campaign, we would sometimes ride our bikes past fur shops and pummel them with light bulbs filled with red paint. I invited David to join me on another such mission in Vancouver.

Before diving into my own personal campaign against the centuries-old fur trade, I'd like to provide a bit of indigenous history. By the late 16th century, after wiping out their own furbearing animals, the European fur trade had turned its attention to North America; thus began centuries of violence against the indigenous inhabitants and native furbearing popula-tions of the "New World." The first wave of European fur traders brought diseases that literally wiped out entire villages in what is today called New England. A smallpox epidemic introduced by a Dutch fur trader in 1633 left a community of 1,000 with only 50 survivors. Before the epidemic ended, a number of tribes had lost their individual identities in the land we now call Massachusetts. Entire indigenous nations were wiped out or forced to assimilate into other tribes and colonial life, all because of the economic demands of the fur trade.

Sadly, remnant indigenous survivors were quick to join the fur trade—not because they wanted to, but because it was the only way to sur-vive. Without the stability of pre-contact communal life, many indigenous people became trappers to obtain the guns, powder, and metal tools they needed for survival and subsequent warfare, as tribes fought for the control of lands to exploit for fur. In 1620, Samuel de Champlain listed, "bufles (buffalo) moose and elk" as important resources in New France. By the time of the first European settlement, many species were already near ex-tinct because of the fur trade. Other non-furbearer native species like bison, caribou, and elk would soon be decimated in the early colonial period.

For almost the entire 17th century, the French, English, and Dutch colonists fought with indigenous nations for control of the new fur trade, from New England to the Ohio Valley. It was even called the Beaver Wars, though most of us know it as "The French & Indian War." I am opposed to the commercial fur trade—not only because of the commodification of nature, but also because, as an indigenous person, trapping and the fur trade still represent to me an institution of colonization and extermination, one that continues to this day, with our government's support. To me, the fur trade, trappers, and the state wildlife agencies promoting trapping are all part of the same colonial oppressive mindset that began plaguing these lands hundreds of years ago. Such an industry is comparable to those that rely on child labor, illegal prostitution, and the illegal (and legal) drug trade to remain profitable.

Back in Vancouver, we started out small, hitting one or two shops a night; but after a week or so, we decided to hit more shops in one night. Unbeknownst to us, the Vancouver Police had been alerted to the fact that people were vandalizing fur stores in the downtown area, and they were on high alert. David and I had a strategy: one of us would walk up to the plate glass window and smash it with a brick or rock aimed at the corner of the glass. We learned the hard way, that if you throw a brick against an eight-foot square pane of glass, often the brick will simply bounce off the glass!

Sometimes we encountered homeless people or wandering drunks, and we tried to wait until they were out of view. Other times, I decided that I was far enough away to escape a detailed description, and so, with a hoodie over my head, I'd smash the glass anyhow before tossing in a few red-paint-filled light bulbs.

One week, while our Captain, Paul Watson, was out of the country, we made the poor decision to use the Sea Shepherd van to go on a smash attack. Linda May would be our driver, while David and I did the smashing. As soon as we hit the first fur shop with bricks and red paint, triggering the alarm, the police were dispatched to area fur shops to see if we would again return to vandalize the same premises. Stupidly, we did. After targeting one of the shops we had done earlier, David and I walked around the corner to our awaiting van and began to drive away. No sooner did we pull away, when out of nowhere, police cruisers surrounded us with their lights on (but sirens off). We were caught red-handed—literally, having red paint from our light bulb bombs on our hands and clothes. David's sweater, which was covered in red paint, was taken as evidence, and the three of us were hauled away to jail.

I felt awful. I couldn't have cared less that we got caught; what really humiliated me was that we were caught while I was left in charge of Sea Shepherd's ship and van, which now sat in a police impound yard. This was only my second time in jail, but I must say, it would be one of the coziest stays I ever had in police custody. The remand facility in Vancouver provided separate rooms with FM radios, and in our common area we had a sofa, TV, and kitchen with fridge stocked with juice. I chose to fast the entire time I was there, just five days.

City fur merchants claim to be targets of animal rights activists

By GORDON HAMILTON

Vancouver fur merchants say animal rights activists are waging a campaign against them after three businesses were struck by paint-bombs over the weekend.

Three people were apprehended in a vehicle registered to the U.S.-based Sea Shepherd Society after display windows were broken and red paint sprayed over merchandise at Grandview Furs, 976 Denman, early Monday. Damage is estimated at $5,000.

In separate incidents, Pappas Fur Designers Ltd., 449 Hamilton, and Avenue Furs, 4307 Main, were struck early Sunday morning. Half a dozen Vancouver fur merchants have repeatedly been targeted in recent months.

"This is not a light-weight thing at all," Constantine Pappas, of Pappas Furs, said after his store was sprayed with paint and peppered with metal nuts, apparently fired by a slingshot, early Sunday.

Charged with mischief are David Owen Howitt, 23, of England, and Rodney Adam Coronado, 21, and Linda Sue May, 21, both of California. They are to appear in provincial court today.

Sea Shepherd Society spokesman Scott Trimingham said the three are volunteer workers for the organization.

In a telephone interview from Los Angeles, he said the society did not authorize the action or the use of its vehicle.

"If we have an action we know about it. This caught everybody by surprise. This is the first time this

> I feel sick about this. You work six days a week and then all this happens.
>
> — Miriam Saariden

kind of thing has happened," he said, when asked about the link to the society through the vehicle registration.

Police raided the Sea Shepherd ship Divine Wind early Monday morning, Trimingham said.

The initials ALF — believed to stand for Animal Liberation Front — were sprayed on two of the stores sabotaged over the weekend but police spokesman Larry Yip said all three incidents are not necessarily related.

Trimingham said the society is not

affiliated with the Animal Liberation Front, which he termed a loose coalition. He said he does not know if any Sea Shepherd Society members also claim to belong to ALF.

Randy Claxton, Canadian Security Intelligence Service director-general for B.C., said Monday the intelligence agency is aware of the fur store attacks "but it's strictly a law-enforcement matter at this point."

Miriam Saariden, owner of Grandview Furs, said her store has been damaged several times in the past, the most recent being six weeks ago to the tune of $7,000. At that time, several other stores were also vandalized.

"I feel sick about this. You work six days a week and then all this happens," said Saariden, who claims she is closing her business because of the attacks.

Sept. 1987

After our arrests, the media reported that our attacks were only the latest that the same businesses had suffered. For years, they were the target of economic attacks by opponents of the fur trade. An International Commonwealth Conference taking place soon after our arrest had a planned fur show canceled, for fear it might draw protests during the Queen's visit. We were pleased.

When Paul returned from his travels, all he said to me, as I felt humbled and ashamed beside him, was, "The next time you do something like this, can you do it a little farther from the ship?"

Different friends pooled their money and got the three of us out on bail. PETA was also a sponsor. Another was a fellow ALF comrade, who ponied up $10,000 in cash to get me out of jail. Little did we know that years in prison would soon be in both of our futures.

David, Linda, and I went before the magistrate and requested permission to return with the ship to the US, which was granted. Only Linda would return to face the music. David would be arrested then released over a decade later.

This would be my first experience as a fugitive from justice. It was too tempting to simply say that I'd never go back to Canada again. I was only 21 and there was no way I was going to stop fighting to face a criminal trial or subsequent jail sentence. The true revolutionary should always strive to be free. And when you are captured, your priority should be to escape—to continue your struggle once again.

This was the feeling in the salt air as we pulled up our mooring lines on the Divine Wind and set sail south towards the California coast. On board were my fellow veteran crew members as well as another ALF friend from those first California raids. We were still just beginning, and together on that voyage hugging the Pacific Coast, we planned our next attacks. Much as we had in Vancouver, we targeted small fur and meat distributors in the San Francisco Bay Area where I still lived.

ACTIVISTS IN TROUBLE

In the midst of our society, there lies an industry with revenues in the billions of dollars. It achieves its wealth by the inhumane slaughter of millions of fur-bearing animals. It sells garments made with the hides of coyotes, bobcats, lynx, minks, foxes, and others whose role in the ecosystem, and whose inherent worthiness of life, are totally denied. The exploitation of fur-bearing animals has escalated to proportions that are not

Linda May and Rod Coronado—happy to be out on bail

tolerable to compassionate individuals. The fur industry has no place in a caring and respectful world.

On September 21, 1987, Rod Coronado, David Howitt and Linda May were arrested in Vancouver, Canada following two months of what the media called "a campaign against fur merchants." According to Canadian police, numerous area fur shops had been the targets of economic sabotage, their display windows smashed, red paint simulating blood sprayed on fur coats, and slogans painted on their doors and windows. Some stores report having been "hit" eleven times in the past two years.

As a result of these actions, at least two furriers have reported that they will be going out of business. Coronado, Howitt and May are charged with breaking and entering and destruction of property. PETA has paid $5,000 of their $30,000 bail.

PART OF A MOVEMENT

"We are no longer looked upon by the masses as a special interest group whose only concerns lie with the treatment of dogs and cats or baby seals, but a genuine movement of hundreds of thousands of individuals who believe that all life is

ACTIVISTS' DEFENSE FUN

In 1983 PETA establish the Activists' Defense Fund for legal fees associated with accuse animal rights activists Contributions may be earmarked for the Activists' Defense Fun

sacred and deserving of basic rights, which include freedom from pain and suffering.

"We can no longer tolerate the screams of our closest relatives, the primates, whose deaths are only calculated by redundant experiments, or the wolves, whose only value is assessed by the price of their pelts on the fur market. We must realize that we need to be relentless and utilize every form of tactic available to us if we truly believe that we can achieve world reform. The time has come for the total abolition of the fur trade. A campaign on behalf of fur-bearing animals is already under way, and it is our duty to see that no aspect of it is halted. Perhaps one day the real criminals — those who hunt and kill — will be behind bars, but until then we must continue to fight hard for the freedom of fur-bearing animals. It is perhaps our planet's most dedicated battle."   *Rod Coronado*

On Thanksgiving Day, with the Divine Wind floating at anchor off of the Santa Cruz Boardwalk, my girlfriend and I drove about an hour away and set fire to the Ferrera Meat Company's slaughterhouse. Two days later, unknown ALF allies, dueling banjo style, burned down a poultry warehouse also in San Jose. To say that law enforcement was taking notice would be an understatement. At least we did go a *little* further from the ship this time!

Still licking my wounds from having been caught in Canada, I turned my attention towards the Mojave Desert. This was the ancestral homelands of the desert bighorn sheep which was recovering from near extinction from market hunting in the early 20th century. The then-California Department of Fish & Game (it would soon change its name to Fish & Wildlife) had decided that recovery efforts were successful enough to allow limited "recreational hunting."

With my newfound Earth First! allies in California, we went to public hearings on the proposed hunt, of course to no avail. At the end of the day, the North American Bighorn Sheep Society would get their hunt and also be allowed to auction one permit to kill a sheep to the highest bidder—as a fundraiser for further bighorn "conservation efforts," of course. A trophy hunter paid $40,000 for his right to kill a bighorn in December 1987, the first year of a new bighorn hunting season in California.

We couldn't resist. I had freshly come from the animal liberationist training fields in England, where saboteurs had been shadowing fox hunters on horseback for decades. I even learned how to blow a hunting horn! Also, a British hunt saboteur had recently joined our above-ground animal rights group in Santa Cruz, so it was agreed that the Hunt Saboteurs of America would be founded by activists of many masks. We were members of the ALF. Some of us were also crewmembers of Sea Shepherd. Others were purely Earth First!ers but willing to help out on any animal liberation involving dogs (true story).

The 1980s were peaking; revolutionaries of many colors were joining forces to oppose animal experimentation, old-growth forest destruction, and this new thing called globalization. California was popping, with Earth First! chapters in over a dozen cities and animal rights groups in all of the larger metro areas. I did not feel alone. Crossovers between different friend groups were producing an amazing array of dedicated Earth warriors that I would draw from in coming years. Together we would become a force to be reckoned with and it would all be in the name of our animal relations. It was our time to rise.

We loaded our Subarus and Toyotas and headed south to the Old Dad Mountains in the first week of December 1987. We didn't know much about bighorn sheep hunting tactics, but we knew silence was necessary to approach within shooting range of these wary animals. Our tactics were simple: We would follow the hunters until they were poised to shoot, then blow compressed air horns in the hopes of scaring away any sheep within rifle range.

It wasn't difficult finding the hunter's basecamp; they were the only ones out in the middle of the desert mountains in December. We quickly learned to be stealthy and remain unseen until the last moment when we went to blow our air horns. Still, there weren't a lot of humans in the desert at that time of year, so the hunters were able to find us on occasion. In one instance, a hunter approached a hunt saboteur in a narrow canyon. From about 50 yards away, the hunter drew a pistol and fired two shots, one on each side of the saboteur. After he had reupholstered his weapon, the saboteur yelled, "Missed!"

In another encounter, a group of activists were rounded up and forced into a horse trailer. When one resisted, he was punched in the face by a hunter. The next morning, we approached the hunters' base camp on foot at dawn and noticeably caught them off guard (and hungover.) We told them that we were nonviolently resisting their hunt, but if they chose to be violent, then we too would escalate our tactics. They probably would have agreed to anything to get us out of their camp that morning.

The cat-and-mouse chase between hunters and hunt saboteurs would continue for a few years in the Mojave. It became an annual campaign where sometimes animal rights activists from LA would show up in the winter desert wearing t-shirts and converse shoes. When the majority of the campaign was spent trying to avoid capture by both the hunters and law enforcement, I decided to return to ALF actions. But there were many good adventures in the desert during those early hunts. Walking for miles without food and water, seeing bighorn sheep whose lives you might have saved…the pluses far outweighed the minuses.

Probably the funniest thing to come from our campaign was the "vegetarian special" that a Baker, California falafel shop had each week that we were in town for the bighorn sheep hunt. We ate there every day. The least funny thing to come from our campaign was the state legislature passing a hunter harassment law in direct response to our efforts to sabotage the sheep hunt. We must have been effective if the state felt it needed to pass a law specifically against us! It wouldn't be the first time.

Despite my arrest in Canada, I was still a member of the Board of Directors of Sea Shepherd, having been awarded the position for taking out the Icelandic pirate whalers. I was also still thinking about the two remaining Icelandic whaling ships that were left untouched by our November 1986 raid.

At our last board meeting in 1987, I proposed that David Howitt and I return to England, where the Sea Shepherd had been berthed since our 1986 Faroe Islands campaign. We would get the ship operational with the

intent of taking it on a one-way voyage back to Iceland, with the sole purpose of ramming the two remaining Icelandic whalers where they lay
berthed in Reykjavik Harbor. We would then scuttle the Sea Shepherd in
the harbor to complicate any resulting salvage operation. Our plan was to
then attempt escape on a rigid-hull inflatable boat that we would pilot 300
miles to the nearest Scottish land base on Flannan Island. We likely would
never have made it, but we had to try.

My efforts to convince the other Sea Shepherd Board members of another brazen and illegal campaign against Iceland was probably just my
own naïve hope that I could finish the job. But there would be many factors that would stand in my way. As the years went by, Iceland's whalers
would be in and out of the news, as the nation's sole remaining whaling
company fought for its own survival in a country where its practices were
coming under more and more domestic scrutiny and even opposition. Iceland might be in my future, but it was beginning to look further and further
away from the path I was currently taking on my warrior's journey.

Captured wild horses at the BLM's corrals in Litchfield, California

CHAPTER 4
ACCELERATING ATTACKS

In early 1988, David and I flew back to England for the first time since the Iceland ship sinkings. We made our way back to the Sea Shepherd II, which was now docked far up the River Severn, near the desolate town of Sharpness. It was a somber return for David and I. The last time we had been on the ship was to visit Nick Taylor—my friend, fellow crew member, and cellmate from the 1986 Faroe Island campaign. Nick was our trusted comrade who we had felt deserved to know that the truth about why David and I had abandoned the ship after the Faroes campaign the previous summer. Nick was one of the few people we confessed to about our then-planned raid against Icelandic whalers. It would be the last time we ever saw Nick.

That winter he would die from a drug overdose. Nick had admitted to battling drug addiction when we visited him and had explained how he had tossed some of the ship's medications overboard, because he knew his temptation to use the drugs wouldn't go away as long as the drugs were there. While I was back in England, I visited Nick's mother to give my condolences and then visited Nick's grave, where a small oak tree had been planted in his honor. Unfortunately, Nick was not to be my only personal loss; there would be other friends I had made aboard Sea Shepherd who would take their own lives, in their own long-battles with depression and substance abuse. I had grown up in a pretty safe middle-class neighborhood, but as I began traveling the world, and especially when I started spending more time with indigenous communities, I would continue bearing witness to the tragic loss of life of incredibly brave and beautiful people who fought beside me for the Earth and animals.

Back aboard the nearly-abandoned ship, the scene was very depressing. An elderly man had moved aboard as the chief engineer and he seemed content to call the ship his home for as long as possible; he had little interest in getting the engines up and running. And while we had the support of Sea Shepherd USA, we weren't getting much support from the UK office, which consisted of a married couple who only tolerated us because of our Iceland fame. It frustrated me that, less than a year after making Sea Shepherd so internationally recognized for our action in Iceland, we weren't being supported in our effort to finish the job by our then UK base.

The final conflict between us and the British crew was when a visiting friend from Plymouth, Dean, pulled out his hunting horn while aboard the ship, to call off a pack of hounds that could be heard chasing a fox near the docked ship. David and I had always participated in local fox hunt sabotage actions when we were in the UK, as they were organized every weekend during the hunting season. The UK Sea Shepherd officers told Paul that we were "organizing hunt sabs" from the ship. Finally, the husband flat out told me that our presence aboard the ship was costing Sea Shepherd money and we should go back to the US—this from someone who had never sailed a day in his life in defense of the oceans, nor even had the intention to do so.

Over the years, I would again and again be met with resistance from those I thought were my allies; but as I would learn, there's a lot of money being made in the name of animals and the Earth, and a lot of the organizations raking it in are more concerned with that money than the animals it was meant for. I thought Sea Shepherd led by Paul Watson would never be such an organization and it wasn't; but once the group gained worldwide attention with Paul's successful campaigns in Antarctica, and a board, not Paul, ran the group, they would oust him from the very organization he founded, much as had happened with Greenpeace in its early days.

Like Paul, after the Iceland campaign, I began experiencing what would become very common: being unwelcomed by those who believed the best path for animals and the planet is with fundraising and business incorporation, not commitment and sacrifice. The movement to protect not only the whales, but Earth and animals, was growing—but in the nonprofit sector, not in the trenches as many of us had hoped. More and more groups were entering the scene, promising to do more for imperiled wildlife—but not with direct action, but litigation and legal action. I had no problems with a diversity in strategy, but often it was these nonprofit groups that were the first to criticize direct action taken on behalf of the Earth and animals. What I learned was that, for many in the animal and environmental movement, the western model of imperialism—with its racism, classism, and privileged standard of living—was acceptable as long as the machine treated animals better. They had no problem with creating well-paying jobs for themselves, along with comfy retirement funds created from public donations on behalf of wildlife.

People for the Ethical Treatment of Animals (PETA) remains one of the few organizations that never condemned the ALF or direct action that saved animals lives. To this day, I have tremendous respect and appreciation for Ingrid Newkirk and Lisa Lange for the work they continue to do on behalf of animals.

After the bad feelings in the UK, I decided to come back to the western United States where I had left a small cadre of new friends and comrades ready to risk their freedom in the name of animals and the Earth. With renewed inspiration from my visits with UK hunt saboteurs and animal liberationists like Dean, we began planning more raids on animal breeders and factory farms.

While I was in England, a veteran Animal Liberation Front group struck the University of California at Irvine on January 29, 1988, rescuing 13 beagles used in air pollution experiments. My new group of ALF warriors were encouraged, but I would later find out a sad truth. Tensions developed within the group that carried out the raid, and the UC Irvine raid would be the last time that group ever acted together. I also would later learn that the dogs were not taken to safe homes to live out their lives, but were killed and their bodies burned in the desert by a disgruntled member who also was using some of the drugs stolen from the UC Irvine laboratories.

We were learning that good intentions were not good enough. Some animal liberationists believed it was better to kill an animal yourself humanely, than allow it to suffer in an animal research laboratory. For example, a committed animal rights activist in southern California told me that she worried about animals in nearby labs because of earthquakes. She said that if a big earthquake struck, she wanted to go to the labs and shoot the animals so they didn't suffer. We quickly learned that many activists supported humane euthanasia, and that some ALF cells in the US even believed in euthanizing animals rescued from farms and laboratories.

We didn't disagree that euthanasia was a preferred alternative when an animal was suffering, but we believed that every effort should be made to find a home for a healthy animal before you determine their fate. This would be one of the main reasons we shied away from live animal liberations in the 1990s, because finding homes for rescued animals was so dangerous and could lead to our capture, let alone the return of animals to a fate worse than death.

Animal Liberation in California

In the spring of 1988, we carried out multiple animal liberation actions in California, the first being a rabbit breeder in Hayward that supplied rabbits to nearby Stanford University research laboratories.

On the night before the raid, we drove our van to an apartment complex that bordered the rabbit breeding compound. The parking area was along a high wooden fence surrounding the rabbit barns. We loosened one of the vertical fence boards so that it could be swung aside to allow us into the compound. Not more than a few minutes had passed since we parked when we suddenly heard over our police scanner a report of a suspicious vehicle at our location. We drove away before any police arrived. Feeling lucky to have heard the call, we decided to postpone the raid for a day.

When we returned the following night, the weather had turned into a windstorm that provided excellent cover for our break-in. Three of us entered the barns and began loading rabbits into carriers. Because of the wind cover, I decided to enter an additional barn we hadn't previously checked out. Finding more rabbits, we began taking about ten from the barn when we noticed, on the inside of the door, that it was alarmed. We stared at the two connecting terminals that were separated and wondered whether the alarm had already been triggered. Our driver did not report anything to us over the radio, even though they were sitting listening to a police scanner that we knew worked. We decided to leave immediately with 73 rabbits in our van.

The media would later interview the rabbit breeder, Mike Westervelt, who said the animals were used for research in cancer, kidney diseases, AIDS, and birth defects and that the ALF is "just out there to...make it seem like we're killing the Easter bunny." Westervelt said his alarm had gone off at 10:55 p.m. on the night of the raid, but when he investigated, he found nothing out of the ordinary. "I carry a gun. They are so lucky, they should be playing the lottery." said Westervelt. It's my guess that the breeder blamed the wind for setting off his alarm and decided to turn it off, not knowing we were planning to break in less than an hour later. Of course, he wouldn't want to admit that he turned the alarm off for fear of voiding any insurance claim.

The day after the raid, I got a call from my sister telling me that my friend Victoria had passed away. Victoria was an elderly woman my sister and I had befriended because she was also a lover of nature and animals. She was dying of cancer when we met, but she would help fund our fledgling ALF cell, not knowing specifics of what plans were. She had died the night of the raid. I remember telling the other cell members that she must have been our guardian angel that night, which is why we didn't get caught when we triggered the alarm. Throughout the years, I would have many such guardian angels.

A Visit to Davis Poultry

A few days later, we visited Davis Poultry Farm in Gilroy, California, not far from my family's business and home. It's not uncommon to drive by the same buildings every day and not know what's going on inside them, but as I became an active animal liberationist, I learned how to look for factory and fur farms, research laboratories, and other nondescript buildings. The poultry farm had always been there as I was growing up, but it wasn't until that first hen rescue that I saw what it looked like inside.

The smell is the first thing you notice—a thick ammonia scent from the fecal matter collecting beneath the rows upon rows of chicken cages. There are thousands of hens in each typical egg barn. This one in Gilroy had three or four hens per cage, each of which was about the size of a milk crate. The hens live out their lives in such misery, never seeing the light of day or touching the earth beneath them. Chickens, like many animals, are meticulous groomers and in nature can take dust baths to rid themselves of mites and other irritations. On an egg farm, there is no such experience for a chicken.

The hens we rescued were again taken to my family's barn, where as soon as we removed them from their cardboard box carriers, they began to peck the earth with clipped beaks and take dust baths for the first time in their lives. They then surprised us all by bursting into the air with tattered wings to roost in the rafters of our barn. These hens were hundreds of generations removed from nature, but something deep inside them was stir yearning to be free. We gave these handful of birds the chance to be what nature intended them to be: not factory-raised egg machines, but living, loving, and feeling beings capable of simple pleasures like eating insects or roosting safely away from predators. In nature, the Dodo bird was hunted to extinction because of its inability to escape from human threats. With chickens, humans have created an equally docile animal to exploit by the billions, without ever worrying that they'll go extinct.

Maybe if we stopped forcefully breeding domestic animals for our exploitation, we could learn to appreciate them. Maybe if we returned to the way of our ancestors and treated the beings that sustain us with the respect they deserve, we could live in harmony, as caretakers not exploiters. All of us have been removed from nature, some to a greater degree than others. But one thing remains true throughout the animal world that I have witnessed, and that is the physical desire to be free from pain and suffering and live your life as nature, not humans, intended.

A few weeks after the raid on the egg farm, we organized a protest at the same location. Some of us were working with above-ground animal rights groups like, Progressive Animal Rights Alliance (PARA), a student group out of the University of California at Santa Cruz. At the protest, farm workers confronted protesters and wrote down our license plates. The police were out in numbers as well. Even though we had posted flyers for the protest in public places, including outside the farm, the workers and police still thought we were there to break in and rescue more hens. We left without any arrests or more hens.

We broke the first rule of guerrilla warfare. We were not maintaining a low profile; many of us were involved in above-ground organizing and protests against the same targets that we wanted to go after as the ALF. We knew that we didn't have long before criminal investigators would wise up and start looking at legal animal rights campaigning for clues to who was involved with the illegal side of things.

For the moment, we enjoyed a level of anonymity; but that would end once federal investigators began catching on to our tactics. It wasn't that every animal rights activist was prone to illegal activity, but our presence in mainstream above-ground organizing also allowed us to identify potential candidates for recruitment to the ALF.

For the April 24th, 1988 World Laboratory Animal Day, our animal rights group, PARA, organized a protest at the University of California at Santa Cruz. We would gather outside of classroom buildings, where we would also burn an effigy of a vivisector. This was a moral dilemma for some in our group, who felt it was making things too personal. But we also knew it would get a lot of attention, so we did it anyway.

The real action came when we led everyone in a march to a new animal facility that was under construction on campus. As we approached the busy work site, the workers stopped momentarily to listen to our chants, but didn't make a move—until five of us broke away from the group and ran towards the tall construction crane that stood over the site. Reaching the crane before the pursuing construction workers, the five of us quickly scaled the ladder as high as we could and unfurled a banner proclaiming, LIBERATE LAB ANIMALS NOW!

We thought that we would be immediately arrested, but the police were not ready to risk hurting anyone (thankfully), so they began negotiating with us to come down on our own. Everyone except our supporters had gone, and the police began setting up flood lights when it became apparent that we would spend the night on the crane. None of us had brought along food, and the police blocked any from reaching us.

Some of our friends tried to throw us apples and oranges, which the police stopped. These were the days before cell phones and texting, so we had no private way to communicate without the police listening in. But we knew others were trying to get us food. When night fell and the scene quieted, the police heard a disturbance and began investigating around the construction site. Suddenly they reached into the shadows and pulled out a young college student. On his back he had a pack loaded with food intended for us.

While the police were focused on our food resupply, one of our group silently climbed down the crane's ladder and made a run for it without the police noticing. After midnight, as we were trying to sleep, wrapped like a burrito in the banner we had decided to use as a blanket, some supporters on the ground started singing songs which drew the attention of the police.

Protesters and anti-vivisection banner atop the crane.

When the police approached the noisy supporters, our missing friend sprang into action and bolted back to the crane. The police only then knew that the loud singers were really just a distraction, and ran back towards the crane, reaching it just as our friend made it up the ladder and out of reach. We feasted on baked tofu, peanut butter sandwiches and other treats, but in my own head I knew this was the kind of friend I'd soon be asking to join my new ALF cell.

Our collective of radical activists from the San Francisco Bay Area, Sacramento, and Los Angeles areas were building a solid reputation for nonviolent civil disobedience, something that was a strong hallmark of the animal rights movement in California in the 1980s. Back then, it wasn't just young radicals like us who were willing to get arrested for animal rights, it was the leaders of mainstream groups like In Defense of Animals' Eliot Katz, who often was the first to be dragged away in cuffs. Women in the movement were the backbone, with leaders like Tanya Keogh, Betsy Swart and many, many more whose names and stories are books themselves. Working alongside such groups, we were able to carry out dramatic media stunts that got vivisection in the news while also forcing the University of California and other animal research facilities to redirect resources from research to public relations and security.

Another big target of Bay Area animal rights activists and groups was the proposed $21 million Northwest Animal Facility, where thousands of animals would be used in experiments that included biological warfare research. Nine of us met one morning in May in Sacramento, where we put on biohazard suits and gas masks and marched into a UC lobbyists office to protest the new animal lab. We barricaded ourselves in an office, but the puffy office furniture was easily pushed aside by the cops who arrested us.

Veal Cruelty

Back in the California radical underground, the target of our next ALF raid would be a veal farm, where male calves are taken from their mothers and raised in crates so small that they cannot turn around. Veal calves are intentionally kept anemic to keep their flesh tender for when they are slaughtered at just a month old. We knew legislation was pending in California that would ban such crates, and we hoped a raid on such a farm could draw attention to the issue.

In those pre-internet days, we often found our targets through the Yellow Pages of the public telephone book. We found a suspected veal farm outside of Santa Rosa, California and made plans to do a recon on the location on what turned out to be a foggy night. Two of us were dropped near the building we suspected had the calves, but the farmer's home was only a short distance away. We crept up to the windowless building and slid the large barn door open just enough to squeeze inside of the darkened barn.

Around us on each side were rows of calves, each chained by the neck and tethered to the ground in a crate that was almost as narrow as their thin emaciated bodies. As soon as we confirmed that there were calves in the barn, we exited and regrouped with our friends in the van and began making plans for the raid.

The hardest part would be finding homes for any veal calves we rescued. We had begun working with a spokesperson in southern California who had offered to deliver our press releases to the media and speak on the ALF's behalf, so we wouldn't have to risk arrest. One of the first tests of our trust was asking the same person to help us find homes for two veal calves. Within days, they told us that a farm along the coast would take the animals.

We were again using my own white Ford panel van that my father had bought at an auction for $500. The van had been used by a school district and looked as generic as possible, except for a few dents and the fact that it only had a driver's seat. The rest of the van was open space. Often, the navigator, or the person in the passenger seat position, would sit on an upended five-gallon bucket. For the veal raid, we covered the floor of the van in plastic and topped it with loose straw.

We drove north to Santa Rosa and found the veal farm as quiet as it was before. I had offered to be the driver, in order to give other cell members the opportunity to be a part of the rescue. We dropped off two members with radios and bolt cutters, and parked in a distant area to await word over the radio. The operation went over smoothly; about 40 minutes after being dropped off, we pulled up to the same spot and saw two dark-masked human figures with two very white-faced calves tottering on skinny legs.

We loaded everyone up in the van and slowly made our escape south. The calves were licking and suckling our hands and fingers and as I drove south across the Golden Gate Bridge. I remember looking behind me as the floodlights of the bridge illuminated the interior of the van and seeing three humans intertwined with two calves, all asleep in one huge puppy pile. We drove through the night and arrived at a beautiful farm at around 8 a.m. We backed the van up to an empty corral and watched as the calves stepped out freely onto the earth. After taking a few wobbly steps to gain their ground, they began to run in circles while kicking out their hind legs. With that image in our groggy heads, we loaded ourselves back into the van for the journey home.

Meeting a Legend: Dave Foreman

That summer of 1988, we loaded up our old Ford van with friends from Santa Cruz and drove to eastern Washington state for the annual Earth First! Rendezvous, which was held that year in the Okanagan Valley. Paul Watson even drove out from Seattle, and it became a kind of Sea Shepherd reunion as well. I had never been to any large national gatherings, and these were the early days, when "Rednecks for Wilderness" was a real thing—well before the days of political correctness within the movement. Earth First! was a *de facto* direct-action community in defense of Mother Earth, and I instantly felt welcomed. Mainstream animal and environmental groups, by contrast, would be very careful with their association with Sea Shepherd, let alone the ALF.

But this Earth First! movement welcomed David Howitt and I like hometown heroes at the gathering's big rally held on July Fourth. In front of hundreds of attendees from across wild America, the main EF! founder, Dave Foreman, called David and I up on stage. Once there, Dave introduced us to the movement and commented on what our actions in Iceland said about the youthful EF! element, such as our local chapter in Santa Cruz. He even led the crowd in singing "Happy Birthday" to me.

David Howitt, Rod, and Dave Foreman

The presence of radical animal liberationists within the Earth First! community would be the beginning of a new generation of Earth First!ers; it would give birth to many new things, such as the ALF's equivalent, the Earth Liberation Front (ELF), and other direct action groups like the Biotic Baking Brigade, which became known for smashing pies in the faces of corporate Earth-destroyers. Sure, there were clashes within the movement, such as when big game hunters within EF! opposed our sabotaging of the bighorn sheep hunt in southern California, but for the most part, our animal liberationist ideals aligned with EF!'s biocentrism and deep ecology. In those early days, we were all about making public the connections between animal and environmental abuse.

That summer, after the Earth First! gathering carried out a large protest and occupation of a US Forest Service office in eastern Washington State, some friends and I headed up to the northern part of the state. We wanted to attempt an arson of a livestock corral used in the annual Omak "Suicide" Stampede, a brutal horse race that is controversial because of the numerous injuries to horses during the race. Without much experience, I created a delayed starter device that failed to ignite—leaving only more evidence for any criminal investigators. Fortunately, I never heard of any fallout from this failed arson attempt.

Loma Linda's Frankenstein Laboratory

There would never be a shortage of horrible factory farms for us to raid, but we really wanted to carry out larger and more effective raids that would have a deeper impact on their targets. We gathered confidence and strength, knowing that we were capable of more. I began investigating Loma Linda University; I learned that the famous heart-transplant researcher Leonard Bailey, best known for his "Baby Fae" transplant of a monkey's heart into a human infant, had a research facility there, where he carried out transplant research.

Situated just south of Interstate 10, Loma Linda University's medical campus sprawls across a huge area bordered by residential and farming areas. The main campus was not our target. Security patrols on animal facilities within the hospital were way too frequent and infiltration difficult. We had identified a field research office used by Bailey directly between a railroad track on one side and a farm field on the other. Joining me on these recons would be an activist I had met in Santa Cruz. Together we would be dropped off in a small park, where the railroad tracks crossed the road. From there we would walk into the darkened areas along "Farm Way" where the lab was located.

In the 1980s, Bailey pioneered human-to-human heart transplants, but what he is most remembered for is his 1984 transplant of a baboon's heart into a human infant known as Baby Fae. The monkey's blood type did not match the child's and organ rejection occurred three weeks after the surgery, killing the child. While some ape-to-human transplants had been attempted with chimpanzees, they met with failure. Bailey pioneered lamb to young goat heart transplants, and a dean of medicine at Loma Linda once praised Bailey, saying, "He had worked for years on doing cross-species transplants in animals. We had a whole lab of animals that had someone else's heart."

We found the isolated laboratory to be without an electronic security system. We found an unlocked window and were able to make an unforced entry on multiple nights. Often, we reviewed and removed physical files in the lab's office and took them to an all-night copy shop, where we copied them before returning them to the lab the same night. On one of the bulletin boards in the lab, we found a joke photo of an anesthetized monkey lying on his side, dressed in a white lab coat, with a button that read, "Just Say No to Drugs."

Outside the laboratory were pens filled with young goats which were to be used in organ transplant research. But it wasn't just goats Bailey was experimenting on; he also used dogs in his research, though none were currently at the facility. For the raid, I called in all members of the cell I had been building across California. We were expecting to be rescuing numerous goats and needed all hands on deck.

On the night of the raid, August 15, 1988, five of us, clad all in black, walked through the dark of the railroad tracks leading to Bailey's lab and jumped over the low fence behind the facility. Although the lab was usually surrounded in silence, on this night a farmer was cutting hay in the field directly across from the laboratory. Myself and another cell member were planning on entering the building as we always had.

But this night, as I crept by a row of chain link kennels that had always been empty, I saw dark motion coming from one of the kennels. As I approached the dark figure, I saw a large dog. Startled, I accidentally kicked a metal bucket that rattled across the concrete kennel floor. Suddenly, a spotlight from the tractor turned on, as the hay-cutting farmer searched for the source of the noise. Luckily for us, dozens of baby research goats could be seen standing in the pens next to the lab, which he must have believed was the cause of the disturbance.

After a few moments, the light faded, and the tractor continued on its loops of the hayfield. Meanwhile, we entered the building and started emptying physical files into duffel bags which we handed to others to return to an awaiting vehicle. Another member poured red paint over the files that were not taken, and spray-painted "ALF" in three-foot letters and the words, "MURDERERS" and "ANIMAL TORTURE IS NOT SCIENCE."

All during this time, our van stood on call to receive young goats. Only, there was now a change of plans. Once we took the records and photographs that we wanted from the lab, our focus shifted to the animals. Upon investigation of all the kennels on the premises, we found two kennels, each with a large Labrador Retriever inside; both black dogs could be seen wagging their entire rumps and seemed happy to see us. In another kennel, we found five puppies that records would later reveal were delivered by a random source animal supplier from Sierra Vista, Arizona the day before, to be used in future transplant experiments.

The tractor finished cutting hay, and we were then again alone under the waning moonlight, with only the dogs to gather and load. The puppies would fit into a single large portable kennel, but the adult dogs would leave with us on leashes. The pups were the first to go, disappearing into the darkness towards our awaiting van. We were to follow behind with the two dogs.

I entered the first kennel and approached the black dog, which now cowered in the rear of the chain link kennel. I spoke gently to the dog while offering my hand, but the animal remained docile. I petted her and lifted her large body up into my arms and carried her to my comrade across the fence, who was waiting with a leash. When he set the dog down on the ground, she bolted away with the leash trailing behind her. We were in an unmowed field of grass, and in the moonlight, the dog's black shape could easily be seen playfully circling the two of us trying to recapture her. Just as we would approach close enough to grab the end of her leash, she would drop her forepaws forward with her rump in the air like a puppy, before running another circle around us, as if it was a game we had played every night of her life.

After what seemed like hours, but were only minutes, we caught the dog's leash, and with the other dog in tow, led them both to a new life and freedom. We took all the dogs to a safe house in Los Angeles and sorted through the pilfered documents, forwarding the most important to our media spokesperson. I chose to stay with the dogs that would be driven to Tucson, Arizona where they would eventually be homed.

I would later hear a crazy story from a new recruit that we had brought along as a driver on the Loma Linda raid. He was tasked with delivering the records stolen from the lab that we felt were important (and there were many) to our media spokesperson, who was to copy them and then destroy the originals. Our new friend was at the spokesperson's home copying documents, one page at a time, when a local reporter called for comment on the police raid on her home. Immediately, they realized the police were on their way and started cramming papers back into the duffel bag. The new member said that he could hear the sirens getting closer as he climbed over the back wall of the house in the quiet neighborhood in San Bernardino. He made a clean getaway. We all agreed he would make a great addition to our cell.

But I still had to get the dogs to Arizona. It was a hot day, easily in the 90s, as we barreled east on Interstate 10 in my un-air-conditioned van with seven dogs inside. We bought a kiddie pool which we poured water and ice into, while the puppies sat in the water. The big dogs lay on their sides fast asleep. We drove through the night, but now it was the next morning and the temperatures were quickly rising as we entered Arizona.

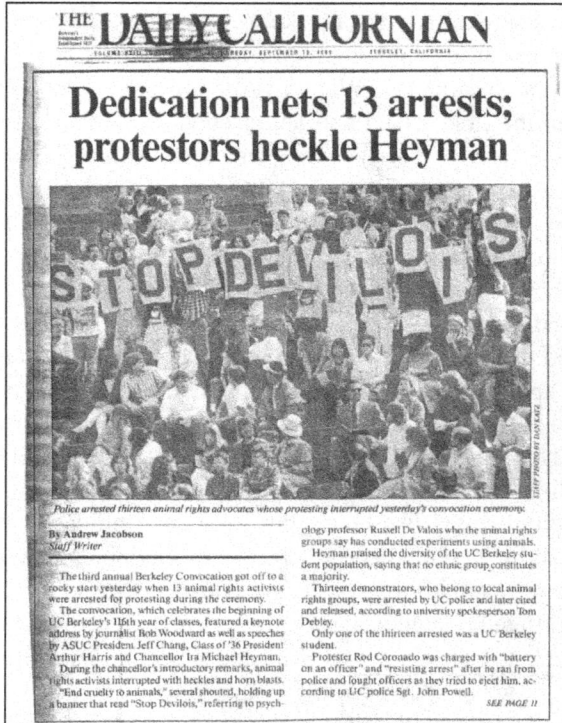

THE DAILY CALIFORNIAN

Dedication nets 13 arrests; protestors heckle Heyman

Police arrested thirteen animal rights advocates whose protesting interrupted yesterday's convocation ceremony.

By Andrew Jacobson
Staff Writer

The third annual Berkeley Convocation got off to a rocky start yesterday when 13 animal rights activists were arrested for protesting during the ceremony.

The convocation, which celebrates the beginning of UC Berkeley's 116th year of classes, featured a keynote address by journalist Bob Woodward as well as speeches by ASUC President Jeff Chang, Class of '36 President Arthur Harris and Chancellor Ira Michael Heyman.

During the chancellor's introductory remarks, animal rights activists interrupted with heckles and horn blasts. "End cruelty to animals," several shouted, holding up a banner that read "Stop Devilois," referring to psych-

ology professor Russell De Valois who the animal rights groups say has conducted experiments using animals.

Heyman praised the diversity of the UC Berkeley student population, saying that no ethnic group constitutes a majority.

Thirteen demonstrators, who belong to local animal rights groups, were arrested by UC police and later cited and released, according to university spokesperson Tom Debley.

Only one of the thirteen arrested was a UC Berkeley student.

Protester Rod Coronado was charged with "battery on an officer" and "resisting arrest" after he ran from police and fought officers as they tried to eject him, according to UC police Sgt. John Powell.

SEE PAGE 11

"Protester Coronado charged with battery on an officer and resisting arrest"

Finally, relief came when we saw water sprinklers running at an empty school. It being a weekend, we couldn't resist stopping to give the dogs some rest in the shade of the olive trees that surrounded the grassy school field. If you happened to pass us on that hot day, you would have seen two humans, two dogs, and five puppies frolicking in the spray of the sprinklers like one big happy human/dog family. We knew the pups had not experienced anything traumatic yet, but the adult dogs had never known human love. When offered a tennis ball, they ignored it. If a water hose was being held by a human, they would cower in fear.

Despite their obvious upbringing in a laboratory setting, these two retrievers still exhibited joy and love, even if at an inappropriate time during their rescue. Once we removed them from the concrete kennel, they immediately took to sleeping with me and my girlfriend as we hopped across California and Arizona. But as we got closer to the animals, we knew it would just make it harder when that happy day came when they would go to a forever home. I stood on the porch of my friend's house in Tucson on the day that both adult dogs were loaded into a Volkswagen bus for the drive to their new home. I cried as I watched the two black silhouettes disappear down the road, but I was happy. We had given seven dogs a new beginning without the threat of torture, and that made everything worth it.

I returned to the Bay Area. In September, I was part of a protest at the University of California at Berkeley against Russell De Valois, a notorious primate researcher whose experiments involved poisoning monkeys with illicit drugs. We disrupted a convocation ceremony and were dragged to jail, but released the same day. As usual after a civil disobedience arrest, I was feeling frustrated with the ineffectiveness of such tactics and was ready to get back to ALF work. Still, it was nice to know that for every such protest that ended in our arrests, there would be legal defense and bail provided by groups like In Defense of Animals. In retrospect, the leaders of these groups must have suspected that many of us were also in the ALF, but they were smart enough to never ask.

Dunda the Elephant

We identified our next target in southern California. We were recruited to take action against the San Diego zookeepers responsible for a horrific beating of an African elephant named Dunda. In May 1988, it became public that over a four-day period, zookeepers took turns beating Dunda with axe handles while the animal was tied down, spread-eagle, in chains. The abusers complained that their arms were sore after what they described as "home run swings" were inflicted on Dunda for hours at a time over four days. She had earlier been transferred to the San Diego Wild Animal Park as part of a breeding program, and handlers admitted that the transfer was handled poorly.

After the truth began to surface, the details of the beating received national media attention, but no criminal charges were being considered for those responsible. One of those who carried out the beating said they were hitting Dunda in the face with axe handles and, "they would hit her in any spot that they could get to," because she lashed out at them. After one beating session, the zookeeper said his hands were so sore he couldn't hold a pen.

Elephant Was Beaten 4 Days, Wild Animal Park Worker Says

By JANE FRITSCH, *Times Staff Writer*

An elephant handler at the San Diego Wild Animal Park said he saw colleagues carry ax handles to the barn where they were disciplining an African elephant called Dunda last February and said ax handles are commonly used at the park when elephants misbehave.

The handler, Steve Schwenn, said in an interview Friday that the beatings occurred in the early morning hours before the park opened to visitors and that the beatings were administered over a four-day period, not one or two days as zoo officials have said. Handlers sometimes emerged from the African elephant barn after the sessions complaining that their arms ached from the strain of beating the elephant, Schwenn said. He said he was not involved in the beatings, but spoke to other keepers who were.

Several Investigations

The discipline used to control Dunda in the days after she was transferred from the San Diego Zoo to the Wild Animal Park in February has become the subject of several investigations.

Officials of the San Diego Zoological Society, which operates both the zoo and the park, have said they believe no abuse occurred and that the controversy is a result of a factional dispute between keepers at the park and at the zoo.

However, Schwenn said Friday that he and some other elephant handlers at the Wild Animal Park agree with keepers at the zoo who have complained that Dunda's transfer was poorly planned and that she was beaten severely and unnecessarily.

The Humane Society of the United States said Tuesday that the Dunda incident was an isolated case of animal abuse.

The San Diego Humane Society, an unrelated group, has completed an investigation, but has not yet issued its report. The U.S. Department of Agriculture also began an investigation Tuesday, but no conclusion about the incident has been reached, according to Dr. Frank Enders, the veterinarian in charge of the department's San Diego area.

Schwenn said Friday that he has been troubled by the incident for several months and decided to come forward in an attempt to encourage others to say what they know.

"I think it's everybody's responsibility, whether they were involved or not, to come forward," Schwenn said. "I'm making a statement because I think it's our responsibility as elephant keepers and handlers. There's no sense lying about it. If we want the public to know the truth, we should tell the truth."

Schwenn said he believes the elephants at the park generally receive good care under the direction of Alan Roocroft, the supervisor in charge of elephants. "I don't have any dislikes for Alan or anybody there," he said.

"I think people should know that elephants are dangerous. . . . But I think you only resort to beating an elephant when there is no other means to handle the situation. There were other means to resort to first."

Schwenn said he was working at the Wild Animal Park on Feb. 16, the day that Dunda arrived, and that she appeared to be calm as she worked off the effects of a tranquilizer that had been administered for her trip from the zoo.

"When I observed her that evening, there was no damage to her at all. They even said she walked in like a baby," Schwenn said.

Schwenn said he didn't see Dunda again until more than a week after the barn and allowed to mingle with the rest of the African herd.

"The day they brought her out, she was putting her trunk on her head and feeling the sore spots. She kept putting mud on her head," he said. "You could see the swollen-ness. You could see by her actions that she was in some kind of pain. She was going by the water a lot and putting water and mud on her

Ax handle used to beat elephants at Wild Animal Park

head to relieve some of the pain."

The beating sessions began several days after Dunda arrived at the park and lasted for four days, Schwenn said.

Please see ELEPHANT, Page

When Dunda finally was allowed out of a barn and given access to other elephants, witnesses said her head was covered in visible sores and she wrapped her trunk around her head, and also placed mud and water over the wounds to relieve the pain.

As the Animal Liberation Front, we had never engaged in straight-up intimidation tactics directed at individuals, nor had we ever targeted the homes of those responsible for animal abuse. But this incident warranted an exception. Especially when the names, addresses, and license plate numbers of those responsible for Dunda's beating were revealed by a sympathizer who worked for the California Highway Patrol.

Another interesting development emerged at the same time. Probably the most vocal opponent of animals in entertainment in the 1980s was none other than the man who made his name in entertainment, famed game-show host (and enrolled member of the Rosebud Lakota Nation) Bob Barker. Through an intermediary, we told Mr. Barker of our planned revenge and asked if he would be our media spokesperson for the action. He instantly agreed.

On October 14, 1988, the night of the raid, we drove to the airport with a friend who rented us a car. We didn't want to be driving anything that might look suspicious, so we chose a late-model sedan that blended in. The good thing about rental cars was that they were usually almost new, and often more reliable than our personal vehicles. We all remembered the antique van used in the wild horse liberation. Also, rental cars are never expected to be driven by their owners—a good excuse, in case we ever got pulled over by a cop.

In the airport rental car parking lot, we transferred our three backpacks loaded with our ski masks, gloves, radios, red spray-paint, smaller cans of regular red paint, glass-etching fluid, and cash (should we become separated). We would be in quiet neighborhoods where the sound of breaking glass would surely draw attention, so we decided to use methods that were silent but effective. Glass-etching fluid purchased from hobby stores and applied to a sponge could be used to write messages on glass that could not be removed. We would also use leather awls, which are sharpened metal spikes, to puncture the sidewalls of tires.

The three of us drove in the rental car from Los Angeles International Airport to the Normal Heights neighborhood of San Diego, where Louis Bisconti, one of Dunda's abusers, lived. It was Friday night after midnight, but not yet bar closing time (when more police patrols would be expected). My accomplice and I hopped out of the car at a stop sign, one block away from our target. We walked up the sidewalk to the correct address, and, checking the cars, confirmed the license plate numbers we'd been given. We worked quickly. While one spray-painted "DUNDA'S REVENGE" and "NO EXCUSE FOR ANIMAL ABUSE" on Bisconti's sidewalk, the other poured red paint and paint stripper over his vehicles, punctured the tires, and applied etching fluid to the vehicles. As a parting message, we took a sponge soaked with glass-etching fluid and wrote the letters "ALF " on Bisconti's front house window.

As quietly as we had arrived, we departed to our planned pick-up location two blocks away. We left the neighborhood with no other cars on the streets and got on I-15 for the 30-minute drive north to Escondido, not far from the San Diego Wild Animal Park where Dunda slept. It was just after 2 a.m. now. We drove to the Escondido home of Alan Roocroft —the supervisor in charge of the elephants at the zoo and the man who signed off on the four days of beating with axe handles. We covered his two vehicles just like those in San Diego and left our ALF spray-painted calling card on his fence.

Finally, we drove to trainer Pat Humphrey's Escondido apartment and repeated the process on his two parked vehicles without any incident. We then hopped back on the Interstate for the drive back to the LA airport. After returning the vehicle, we used an airport payphone to call Nancy Burnet, Director of the Coalition to Protect Animals in Entertainment, and read her our press release demanding the firing of those responsible for

Dunda's beating. We also said we had taken our actions because no charges had been filed against those responsible for Dunda's beating, nor had the zoo changed its policy on the beating of elephants.

The next day, the executive director of the Zoological Society of San Diego was quick to issue a press statement, declaring, "We are outraged that the victims and their families have been terrorized in such a manner. Personally attacking our employees is purely reprehensible." Bob Barker took up the torch for Dunda, responding that the ALF had damaged only cars and property, but what the zoo's trainers did was the real violence that needed to be condemned. Barker also said, "They (ALF) decided for the first time to enter into battle to protect animals in entertainment. The red paint they used on the cars and homes represented the blood Dunda spilled." In a *Los Angeles Times* interview, he said, "I do not believe that type of discipline (the beating) is acceptable to the American public" and added that he had "absolutely no criticism" of the ALF's tactics. "They are certainly breaking the law for a good cause."

LA Times, **15 Oct 1988 (p. 1)**

It galvanized my belief in direct action as an effective tactic in defense of animals, to have someone I had seen on television since my childhood support the ALF and its tactics. Barker was quick to remind us all that property destruction could not compare to real physical violence when it came to taking a moral high ground. Many legitimate movements and causes have been forced to engage in physical violence to effect positive change; Gandhi realized this, as did Nelson Mandela.

In the year after our revenge attack, things had already begun to change within the zoo's elephant program. The popular elephant shows and rides were canceled, and following our raid, both trainers whose houses we targeted resigned from their position as elephant trainers, and were transferred to the construction and maintenance staff of the zoo. On the national front, the American Association of Zoological Parks and Aquariums drew up the nation's first guidelines for the handling of captive elephants in response to Dunda's beating.

Unfortunately, the elephant trainers who first spoke out about Dunda's treatment were the target of disciplinary actions and ended up needing legal representation. They were convinced it was retaliation for embarrassing the institution nationally. Dunda herself would continue to experience troubles assimilating with the other African elephants. Though her physical wounds had healed, she still found herself roughed up and pushed around by the elephant herd's matriarch. Eventually, she found a friend amongst the herd of eight elephants, and spent five more years in San Diego before being transferred to the Oakland Zoo, where she lived out her life as part of a complete family group.

At the Oakland Zoo, she would be honored and respected, something that was reflected when her name was officially changed to M'Dunda, the proper spelling of her name. In Oakland, she quickly built a reputation for her kind and gentle demeanor, and communicated with her herd mates by rumbling. She was often observed 'trunk twirling,' which is a sign of affection and intimacy for elephants. By 2019, M'Dunda had celebrated her 50th birthday with a huge public party; video of her eating her birthday treats was live-streamed on Facebook. Two months later, she was found dead, collapsed among her family members. A spokesperson said, "She was such a gentle being and closely bonded with her keepers. We'll miss her greatly." Rest in Peace, M'Dunda.

It was now November 1988. Our cell wanted to carry out an action against the fur industry, in solidarity with anti-fur activists around the country who traditionally protest on "Fur-Free Friday," the day after Thanksgiving, against the cruel practices of trapping and fur farming. We found an isolated fur retailer in Santa Rosa, named Del Conte Furrier, that was housed in a former residential home without any neighbors. At night, we watched the target for hours to ensure that there wasn't anyone living on the premises. On the night of November 24, we took one last look at the target to ensure it was empty before sliding underneath the building through a crawlspace. Once out of sight, we were able to pile combustible materials in a corner before setting a timed incendiary device.

Earlier we had found diagrams for building such devices using a wristwatch as a timer, but those devices proved too small and prone to failure. Instead, we devised a simple incendiary device that utilized a one-hour kitchen timer, 9-volt battery, and an automobile tail-light with the glass removed. We would create a basic electric circuit: when the one-hour timer expired, the needle would push together two bare wires, completing the circuit, and igniting the tail-light bulb which would be placed amongst flammable materials.

Using the new device against the furrier was also a test run for future actions where arson was a possibility. In the early morning hours, the timed device worked as intended, igniting a fire that caused extensive damage to the furrier—which would never reopen. As usual, no one was injured in the three-alarm fire. In our statement to the press, we stated that the fur industry was "a perverse business that needlessly murders millions of animals each year to provide humans with deplorable status symbols. The ALF will continue its war against this Nazism until the bloody fur trade is abolished from our society forever." With the success of our newly-developed incendiary devices, we were now able to include arson as a regular tactic when it could be carried out safely without harm to any humans or other animals.

In December 1988, three of us crane-occupiers from Santa Cruz were recruited by In Defense of Animals for a new campaign they were launching against the Yerkes Regional Primate Center in Atlanta, where hundreds of chimpanzees and other primates were being used in medical research experiments. We were to hang ourselves next to a large banner from a research building on the Emory University campus. We carried out the action, hung the banner, got media attention, and then were arrested. But what really stood out for me on the week that we spent in Atlanta planning the peaceful protest, was the lack of security at Emory University's animal facilities.

While scoping out locations for the banner-hang, we found a vivarium on the rooftop of one of the campus buildings where research animals were being held. I wanted to forget the banner and start doing recon for a proper raid on the university. But I was getting ahead of myself. I wasn't the only one with a radical lens in the growing anti-vivisection movement in America. Through Ben White, a veteran Sea Shepherd crewmember and Director, I had found a link to the already-existing ALF in my home country, and soon I would be meeting other ALF members, this time from the east coast.

CHAPTER 5

UNIVERSITY RAIDS, AND RETURN TO SEA SHEPHERD

Unbeknownst to our growing cell, in November 1988, San Jose Police arson investigators organized a meeting between federal, state, and local law enforcement to address our growing string of attacks—especially the unsolved three arsons against San Jose meat producers. In local media reports, investigators remained tight-lipped about their plans, saying, "We don't want these terrorist groups reading about what we're going to do in the newspaper." But what they *did* say was that representatives of the FBI, California Department of Justice, state fire marshal, San Jose and Santa Clara police, and San Jose fire departments were trading information, ideas, and names of possible suspects who might have set fires, stolen farm animals, and spray-painted graffiti throughout California, especially in Santa Clara County.

Ironically, two days before the law enforcement gathering in San Jose, we had conducted what we used to call "smash attacks," where we again targeted local animal industry targets like butcher shops and fast-food restaurants. We hit four targets within a two-mile area, slashing tires on delivery trucks, etching slogans with acid on windows that would be too loud to break, and also shooting projectiles from slingshots as we sat in the back of a moving pick-up truck. These were smaller actions that did not require weeks of planning; yet even these actions were gaining the attention of the FBI and other federal law enforcement agencies. Somewhere in Washington D.C., federal agencies more used to dealing with foreign terrorist threats were now becoming familiar with the growing threat of "animal rights extremism." This would soon take the label of being the most active domestic terrorist threat in the United States, despite our movement having never taken a life.

Back on the battlefield, we were feeling invincible. Another opportunity to test our latest fire-making abilities came in January 1989, when I arranged to meet up with a close ALF friend of mine outside of Sacramento, California. This wasn't far from UC Davis, where security was at an all-time high after the April 1987 Veterinary Diagnostic Laboratory fire; so instead, we decided that we would target two locations, The California

Cattlemen's Association offices in Sacramento and the Dixon Livestock Auction Yard less than 30 minutes away from Davis. We would set one of our timed incendiary devices at the auction yard, but we would be attacking the Cattleman's offices with good old-fashioned Molotov cocktails.

In our naïveté, we knew nothing about making Molotov cocktails. We had just seen them used in every 20th century armed revolution, and we wanted to give it a try. What we did know was that a mixture of gasoline and oil inside a bottle, with a rag as a wick, were the basic ingredients. On the night of our attack, we took an empty wine bottle and filled it with the mixture; we then took a rag, tied a knot in one end, and forced the knot past the neck of the bottle. We turned the bottle upside down until fuel could be seen on the rag sticking out of the bottle. Unlike our previous actions, we were acting with little to no reconnaissance. The office target was on a darkened city street, and the auction yard was totally deserted at night. Such an attack could only work against an industry not on guard.

Although we had targeted livestock operations in the San Francisco Bay area for animal liberations and two arson attacks, California's animal agriculture industry was simply too huge to be insulated against actions like ours. Nor did it yet realize what a threat our small group was becoming. Minimally-planned raids would only be something that we could do against an industry not on guard against our attacks. Of course, I have engaged in my share of spontaneous actions, but there is no greater insurance policy for not being caught than carrying out thorough surveillance on a target before a strike.

On the night of January 29, 1989, we drove towards our Cattleman's office target, parked a block away, and began walking towards the darkened offices—they were in a storefront in a row of brick offices, with a large plate glass window next to the entry door. When we reached the office, I looked both ways along the sidewalk and, not seeing any movement, pulled out a can of green spray paint and wrote in two-foot letters on the stucco building, "Earth First! Agri-Bus Kills!" Then I took a large rock and smashed it into the corner of the glass. The glass shattered and an alarm sounded immediately, but we both maintained our positions, while my partner lit his cocktail and hurled it inside. We both saw the bottle bounce off the carpeted floor and roll to a stop, with the rag fuse still smoldering. After running back to our vehicle, we both instantly knew that our choice of a wine bottle had been a fatal error. The glass was simply too thick to shatter on impact.

Not to be easily defeated, we drove to a liquor store and bought a 40-ounce bottle of beer that we dumped in the parking lot, refilling it instead with our fuel mix. Unfortunately, not more than 15 minutes after our first attempt, as we drove by our target in preparation for a second try, we could see a lone man standing outside the office, staring past the broken glass towards our fire bomb dud. We chose to keep driving out of Sacramento and on to Dixon for our next attack.

Dixon in 1989 was a ghost town. The auction yard was on the outskirts, with very little human activity anywhere to be seen. We parked our van near other empty vehicles in town and walked to the auction yard. It was dark, but the glow of the town's lights provided enough light for us to explore the large wooden structures that made up the auction. Only a few pens far from the main auction building housed any live sheep, and the rest of the main barn was empty. Inside the barn, we picked a spot underneath a stairway that opened up to another, higher level. There, we piled crates and boards haphazardly around the two jugs of gasoline and oil that we would leave next to our ticking incendiary device. Leaving as silently as we entered, I drove my friend back home to Sacramento.

After dropping him off, I got back on I-80 for my own drive home to the San Francisco Bay Area, only realizing then that I would be again driving past Dixon—although thankfully, on the Interstate. As I got near the town, I didn't need any signs to show me where the auction yard was: it could be seen easily from the Interstate, engulfed in flames, with flashing red lights and sirens from fire trucks blaring. I drove by slowly with both hands firmly on the wheel and my eyes on the speedometer; I didn't want to be pulled over for something as stupid as speeding, even though I wished I was driving 100 mph.

The next day, I drove to a phone booth far from my house and called the Associated Press to claim responsibility for the fire which caused $250,000 in damages without any related injuries.

We knew it wasn't an Earth First! tactic to burn buildings, but everyone in the movement knew Dave Foreman's controversial book, *Eco-Defense: A Field Guide to Monkeywrenching*. It detailed, among other things, how to burn billboards and heavy earth-destroying equipment. So we decided to throw our own wrench into the movement by claiming the Dixon fire as an Earth First! action. The media would interview Mike Roselle, one of the founders of Earth First!, and much to his credit, he told the reporter that anyone with an Earth First! T-shirt could consider themselves a member of the radical eco-movement; so the arson must be a legitimate attack. Another longtime Earth First! member and author of a book on livestock overgrazing would later write a letter to the *Earth First! Journal* detailing the connection between the Dixon Livestock Auction Yard and public lands overgrazing in California by commercial sheep herds.

Attention Moves to Tucson

A few weeks later, on February 21, 1989, some of my fellow crane occupiers from Santa Cruz carried out another crane occupation, this time at the University of California at Berkeley's partially-constructed Northwest Animal Facility. Meanwhile, after the Dixon arson, I spent most of my time out of state, carrying out reconnaissance at two targets: a dog lab at the University of Utah and multiple animal labs at the University of Arizona at Tucson. After housing the rescued Loma Linda dogs, our contact gave us a tour of university buildings that held animals for research at the Tucson college. This was clearly a campus without much security on their animal care facilities, and we wanted to take full advantage of that; we knew that, before long, this and other university animal research facilities would be locked down in response to recent ALF raids.

So, on one sunny day, I sat in a hot car as two women from our group walked into a university medical research facility, now that classes were out for the semester. After about 30 minutes, I started to grow concerned, when all of a sudden, I saw both of them emerge from the basement entrance of the building in broad daylight, each carrying a cardboard pet carrier. When they got in, they just said, "Drive. We'll tell ya later!" The two women later told me they had seen a note on a bulletin board offering up two former research cats for adoption. Neither cat had suffered noticeable trauma, so the researcher simply thought it'd be nice if they were adopted; otherwise they would be euthanized. Now they were the latest animals to be housed by our local rescuer contact.

On another occasion, as I explored the hallways of an empty research building, I encountered a female staff member in a white lab coat. I could tell she was more friendly than suspicious, so I told her that I was in the building wondering whether there were any seasonal jobs available caring for animals. She asked what kinds of animals I had worked with. Knowing there were rabbits in that particular lab building, I responded saying, "My father and I used to raise and sell rabbits..." Before I could continue, she was fumbling for her keys and asking me if I wanted to see her rabbits. I followed her down a hallway that led to a room with a locked door; when she opened it, every wall was lined with stainless steel rows of cages with adult rabbits in each one. After some brief small talk, I said goodbye, making mental note of the path leading to the rabbit room.

I spent a few weeks in Tucson carrying out surveillance. One night as I did my regular nightly rounds on campus, I noticed a dumpster outside of the microbiology building; it was filled with material obviously discarded from the laboratory building next to it. I came back a few hours later when there was no activity and climbed into it with a flashlight. Amongst discarded office chairs and broken file cabinets, I found garbage bags filled with office materials. Inside amongst the debris were receipts for animals purchased from breeders, old animal research protocols, and other clues as to what went on in the labs on campus. The biggest score was a roll of blueprints for the very microbiology building I was scouting, that told us where animals were housed when they were not being used in research experiments. There were many such buildings on campus, but the microbiology building easily housed thousands of frogs, mice, rats, guinea pigs, and rabbits.

Our local contact had also alerted us to another possible university target: an off-campus residential house nearby that served as the business office for all of the University of Arizona's animal care departments. The building was where all animal records were stored for the University, and our desire was to completely destroy it with fire, using one of our newly-tested incendiary devices. These were the days when much research data was still stored on site, as hard copies.

As our plans for the raid grew, we knew we'd need multiple people and vehicles, so I traveled back home to Santa Cruz, where I recruited two new members for the University of Arizona raid. Both were activists I had met at Earth First! actions and gatherings; both were committed vegans who did not hesitate to say yes when I approached them for help.

Much to our surprise, as we were preparing for the University of Arizona raid, news hit the local airwaves that four greyhound dogs slated for research had been rescued from the nearby Veterans Administration Hospital in South Tucson. We knew nothing about the action or who might have carried it out, but after running into another ALF cell in California, we knew we weren't the only ones committed enough to taking direct action on behalf of suffering animals. We were thankful to not see any changes in security at the university following the VA dog rescue, but we knew the longer we waited, the more likely the situation could change.

By now, it was nearing the end of March, when the semester would end and the campus would be empty for a couple short weeks. We decided to take action on a Sunday night when there were the fewest people on campus or inside buildings. For weeks now, we sat in our vehicles late at night watching the microbiology building from a distance, timing the length it took for the custodial staff and graduate students to make their rounds. We'd see an office light turn off, then moments later the corresponding person would exit the building.

As our veteran cell members started arriving from California, we quickly crowded the hotel room where all of our forced-entry equipment, disposable clothing, and radios were being wiped down and prepared for the raid. We pored over the blueprints I found in the dumpster, as well as the hand-drawn maps I made of other labs we intended to target. In addition to the microbiology lab and the off-campus office for University Animal Care, we would target a lab in the Shantz Building and another in the Life Sciences Department. It would be a brazen multi-building assault with different teams carrying out simultaneous raids.

We would have to use forced-entry tactics, as all of the buildings would be locked after 6 p.m. At the microbiology building, on the day of the raid, I went into an empty stairwell that led to an exit. The door could be opened from the inside when locked simply by pushing it. With my foot holding the door open, I took a screwdriver and removed the two screws that held the clasp that secured the closed (locked) door. I replaced the screws with much shorter ones that barely held the clasp in place. Later, a hard pull would be all that was needed to dislodge the clasp. This was one simple method that I used repeatedly over the years to get into buildings that only had daytime public access.

Back at the hotel room, we tuned into the local community radio station, KXCI, and checked the local TV stations. We were surprised to hear our friend Dana Lyons, a musician and fellow Earth First! activist, being interviewed about the University of Arizona's plan to build an observatory in one of the last remaining habitats of the Mount Graham red squirrel. He also described the area as a sacred place for the Apache people. I'd be returning in a few years to help defend the mountain, but that's another story.

Time to Act

Finally, it was time for our raid to begin. Our security lookouts were in place in university parking lots, watching for any unexpected entry into the Microbiology building. I then began the raid by walking up to the stairwell door I had rigged earlier and gave it a quick pull, dislodging the clasp from the door, which rattled to the floor. As I returned the original screws to the clasp—so that our point of entry would be hidden—three other ALF members entered behind me; we all pulled ski-masks and white lab coats out of our backpacks. Putting on a white lab coat to carry out a raid was something we had only ever seen the American ALF do in its video-recorded raids of laboratories. We liked the psychological value it had for the vivi-sectors to see us, not them, wearing one of the symbols of their authority as a "researcher."

We clambered up the stairwell with our hearts pumping and adrenalin rushing. There was always a chance that some unexpected grad student might push through a door at any moment, despite our months of painstak-ing reconnaissance. We had no contingency plans for encountering a hu-man, other than to try and escape. We were neither physically nor morally prepared to try to restrain anyone or deploy weapons.

At the top of the stairwell, we entered what university researchers called, "The Penthouse": a small animal research laboratory that sat atop the microbiology building. Each door into an animal room had reinforced glass, but no alarms. We pulled small steel mallets from our packs and smashed the glass closest to the door knob, then reached in and opened the door. The smell of cedar shavings used in the cages was the strongest smell; we could hear animals scurrying in the stainless-steel cages that lined each wall. With the lights now on, each team worked in a different room, loading first rabbits into bags that were being carried back to the ground floor. This was the same room I had entered earlier with the aid of the lab worker's key.

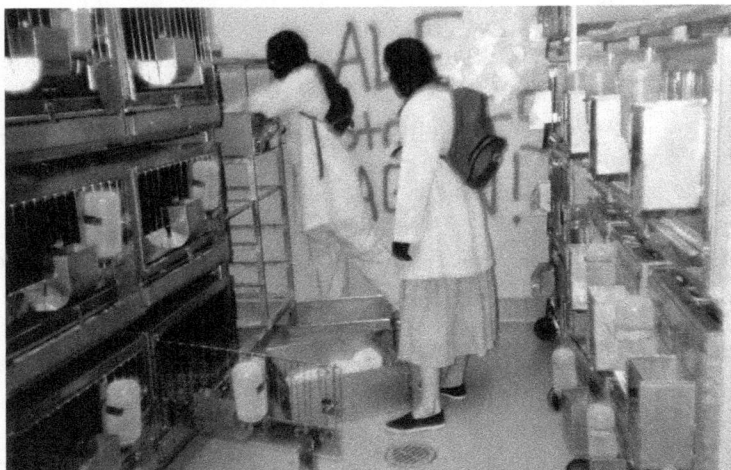

Two members at work in the "Penthouse"

There were five of us in the lab now; some were spray-painting red messages like "ALF Strikes Again" while others shuttled animals. When it came to the smaller animals like mice, rats, and guinea pigs, we left the animals in their cages and placed the entire cage onto a tall wheeled cart. With probably more than 500 animals in each cart, we wheeled the stacked cages into the elevator and pushed the ground floor button. We were on the fifth floor. The doors slid shut and we began our descent. Everyone's eyes were glued to the illuminated floor indicator light, waiting to see if anyone else was in the building at that exact moment and waiting for the elevator. It was the longest elevator ride of our lives, despite only being a few floors!

The doors remained closed until we reached the ground floor. Before descending, we had called over the radio for our pick-up, which would come in a bold maneuver where they backed up our white panel van right up to the doors of the microbiology building. It was a moment of complete vulnerability where, if a single person saw us, they would be able to quickly figure out exactly what we were doing and that it was probably illegal. Our tireless nights of recon paid off though, and no one saw the five masked figures in lab coats loading hundreds of animals into a van at 3 a.m., then calmly disappear into the desert night.

As soon as the van was loaded and gone, those of us remaining moved into the next phase of the raid. Two individuals would walk on foot to the north side of campus where the University Animal Care offices were located in the residential house, enter through the basement, and set a timed incendiary device amongst the desks and files. I stripped off my mask and coat and would carry out my next role without any disguise. All my faith was in my knowledge gained from my own countless nights watching the target buildings within the time frame of our now-occurring raid.

I was between two brick university buildings with a road separating them. Everything was awash in a glow of light from the university lights. My target was the Shantz Building; I had never been inside, but I knew animals were kept behind a locked basement-level door because of an extractor fan that blew air out of the room and onto the street. Whenever I walked by the fan, I caught a whiff of cedar shavings and urine. The fan was at head height, so I moved a recycling bin over and climbed on top to reach the sheet metal covering the fan. I cut through the material with tin snips, cutting a hole big enough for my body to slip through. Once the zagged circle of sheet metal had been removed, I still had to remove the actual fan with its motor and blade blocking the hole, but at least I could now see the rows of small cages inside the animal room.

With the electrical fan wires cut, I next cut two of the three thin metal supports holding the fan, and bent it out of my way. It's a good thing DNA forensics had yet to evolve to the level it is today, because as I pulled myself through the hole, the sharp edges snagged on my clothing and scraped against my body, leaving superficial cuts, but enough to bleed on the entry point. I lowered myself onto the floor and pulled an empty wheeled cart over to a wall of rat cages and started stacking them on top of each other. When I had two carts full, I radioed for my pick up.

The truck pulled up to the loading dock as if it was another authorized university vehicle, and as I wheeled out the carts to be loaded into the truck, another member entered the lab and spray-painted a message promising to return for the animals we were leaving behind. As I stood on the loading dock looking both ways up the well-lit road, I could hear air escaping out of the tires of university vehicles that were being vandalized by one of our members. When the truck was loaded, it returned in the direction it had come and began the long drive through the night to a rendezvous location, where supporters were waiting to receive the rescued animals.

But I had one more role to fulfill—to enter the Life Sciences Building and climb the stairway to the fifth floor, where another rooftop laboratory was located. Only this particular lab was empty and under construction. Because it was under construction, entry was quite easy. I began piling anything wooden I could find into a corner of the building near a window that I hoped would feed the fire in the mostly brick-and-steel building. I pulled a Tupperware container from my pack that had the delicate incendiary device circuit cradled in toilet paper. I made sure the two contact wires were just barely separated, so the one-hour timer needle could easily push them together in about 25 minutes. I connected the 9-volt battery terminal and set the device amongst my pile of combustibles and set a couple fuel bottles near enough that they would melt and discharge their fuel for the fire.

While I was setting the fire for the rooftop laboratory, another ALF member walked down the residential street housing the Animal Care offices. Without hesitation, they snuck beside the dark building and pried away a grate that led beneath the house. Crawling under, they placed an incendiary device amongst the wooden foundation and then fled.

None of the rescuers or the 1,231 animals rescued stayed that night in Arizona. We all headed in our different directions. It would be weeks before we began to comprehend the impact of the raid. We were working with a new sponsor now, one who recognized the validity of arson as a tactic. The University of Arizona raid was our opportunity to prove ourselves, not only to our sponsors, but to the entire vivisection industry, to which we now posed a serious threat. Our sponsors joked that the raid was more like one carried out by the P.L.O. (Palestine Liberation Organization) than by the ALF. But we were changing the ALF.

Immediately after the raid, as we headed in our different directions, a local supporter drove in the pre-dawn streets of Tucson, physically delivering our press release to numerous news agencies. They told me later that all they could hear the entire morning were sirens headed in the direction of the university.

In another funny twist, the morning after the raid, local Earth First! activists descended upon the University to protest the telescope construction that we had heard about on the radio the night before. The scruffy local protestors had no idea what had happened the night before and were shocked at the amount of armed law enforcement response to their meager protest. Later, university officials would say they mistakenly thought the two incidents were connected.

The University of Arizona's animal research department would be changed forever. Not only would security costs in the future take a larger chunk of the budget, but more oversight would come in the future use of animals in all university experiments. Vivisection would continue, but it would require more justification and come with far greater economic costs.

But ours was not an action to end the practice of vivisection, it was a raid to rescue its victims. We knew our actions alone would not result in any lab being permanently shut down, but we also knew that anyone getting into the field of vivisection would realize that they had to start looking over their shoulder more than before. The Animal Liberation Front was growing, and we had proven to industries engaged in animal abuse that we could carry out large-scale actions, with the rescue of 1,200 animals from the University of Arizona being the largest ever at the time. We hoped it would be a record soon broken.

The Final Voyage

I returned to the San Francisco Bay Area after the Arizona raid and began preparing for what would be my last voyage on the Sea Shepherd. While we were at sea in the Pacific on Paul Watson's newest ship, the Divine Wind, the older Sea Shepherd sat in the UK awaiting repairs. The ship had been moved to Ijmuiden, Netherlands where a crew was being assembled for an Atlantic crossing. I would join the ship in Europe and sail it across the ocean, then we would go through the Panama Canal and follow purse-seine tuna fisherman who were killing thousands of dolphins in their huge nets that were used to encircle the marine mammals because of the tuna that swam below them.

Beginning in the 1950s with the invention of synthetic netting and powerful fishing gear that could haul longer nets, the purse-seine fishing industry for yellowfin tuna quickly developed in the Eastern Tropic Pacific—a region that extends west from the coast of Mexico all the way south to Peru. It is the aquatic homeland of many important marine species, including the only penguin species in the Northern Hemisphere. In addition to sea turtles and giant manta rays, the eastern tropical Pacific is home to many species of dolphins such as the coastal spotted, eastern spinner, and the northeastern offshore spotted dolphins, all of which have a unique relationship with the other species with whom they share their ocean home.

Because large-bodied yellowfin tuna were always discovered swimming below equally large pods of dolphins, purse-seine fishermen began encircling the pods with large nets, capturing both dolphins and tuna. By the early 1960s, as many as half a million dolphins a year were being killed by purse-seine fisheries. By the time the United States passed the Marine Mammal Protection Act in 1972, spotted dolphins had been reduced to less than 20% of pre-fishery levels, with spinner dolphins at just 40%. Though efforts to reduce dolphin by-catch were greatly reduced in the 1970s, by the late 1980s, the kill had risen back up to tens of thousands of dolphins each year.

We would sail the Sea Shepherd into the Eastern Tropical Pacific Ocean for a confrontation with the purse-seiners from Mexico, Venezuela, and Costa Rica. I flew into Amsterdam in June 1989; Paul led me back to the ship where I would be later joined by old friends from previous voyages, as well as new British crew members. We only spent a few weeks in harbor before we set sail for Ireland.

One of the last tasks was to recruit a retired sea captain as an experienced seafarer for the voyage. Bill looked the part of a British sea captain, with his white hair and beard and always chipper demeanor. He shared stories of being torpedoed by Nazi U-boats during World War II, who targeted the merchant ships delivering aid during the war. One night while on watch, I saw Bill strolling down the deck toward me, ready to take over his shift. He was whistling as he walked across the gangplank and greeted me like it was the middle of the day, rather than a bleak 4am in the morning.

Bill told me the story of how he had been forced to retire because of his age, yet he still desired to be at sea. When the day came for us to set sail, Bill told me he had kissed his wife goodbye, and told how she was startled because he usually never kissed his wife goodbye. I was at the helm of the ship as our ship swung out towards the open sea, with the engines slowly churning, awaiting orders from Bill—when suddenly he began wheezing and then fell down on the floor of the bridge. Although we attempted resuscitation, the medical crew that responded said he had died immediately. While some of the crew were crying, I couldn't help but feel at peace, knowing Bill had died doing what he loved: captaining a ship at sea for another noble cause.

Unfortunately, before we could reach Ireland, we developed engine problems, requiring a stop in Falmouth, UK. While there, my girlfriend Sue and I rented a car and drove to London to visit my sister and pick up food donations we had solicited from various natural food distributors. We also visited the famous Brown Dog statue in Battersea Park, which was dedicated to an animal subjected to repeated medical experiments at University College London in 1903. The statue erected by British anti-vivisectionists led to fights in the streets between medical students and anti-vivisection, suffrage, and labor activists, which led to its removal in 1909. Only in 1985 was the statue rededicated as the UK anti-vivisection became the impetus for the global animal liberation movement which I was now a part of.

Brown Dog statue

In celebration of the UK movement's achievements, I also paid a visit to my old friends in Plymouth, where I saw the fire-damaged Dingles department store that was targeted by animal rights activists in December

1988; they set timed incendiary devices in the store so a fire would start late at night when the building was empty. Five other stores owned by the House of Fraser were also the targets of arson attacks because of the company's policies on selling fur.

Back aboard the ship, we readied ourselves for the crossing and for weeks at sea before ever reaching the dolphin-killing grounds. When the tugboats came alongside, we pulled up our lines and said goodbye to Britain, beginning what would be a 27-day crossing of the Atlantic. The watches were monotonous, with sea conditions amazingly calm. It was like crossing a huge pond, not the ocean. The boredom would only be broken when someone saw a whale, or when a breakdown allowed the crew to swim in the dead-calm ocean. After carrying out the raids on the west coast, I was frustrated with the day-to-day routines of ship life versus being engaged in hands-on action that required recon and preparation, which I preferred. When we finally reached Key West, Florida, I was ready for a break. The only time we got away from the ship was when we were on ship errands to get engine room parts; but that was enough.

Rod at Key West

We met up with Ben White, my other mentor and friend from my earlier Sea Shepherd campaigns. Ben was also active in the east coast Animal Liberation Front, which only made him more of a hero to me. Ben would be the campaign director for the tuna/dolphin campaign, but for now he would stay ashore and join the ship later when we reached the Pacific. We set sail for Panama with great enthusiasm for what lay ahead in the Eastern Tropical Pacific. The Panama Canal was incredible, but what I most remember was looking out into the dark forests on either side of the canal as we sailed through. From the darkness could be heard a symphony of animal sounds coming from the jungles. I could only imagine the many eyes watching as our ship sailed through the forests of Central America.

As we sailed north along the coast of Costa Rica, we received word from Ben that there were tuna ships in the harbor of Puntarenas preparing to go to sea; he would rejoin our boat the next day. We set our course for the harbor and sailed through the night at full speed. When we arrived, we dropped anchor and went ashore to get supplies, while Sue and I hung around the docks trying to pick up some intel on the tuna ships. Having been born in Peru, Sue was fluent in Spanish and she struck up a friendly conversation with a man on the dock who identified himself as the helicopter pilot for one of the tuna ships. Purse-seiners use helicopters to locate the flocks of seabirds congregating above large schools of tuna. They then launch speedboats to help corral the dolphins swimming above the tuna as the ship sets its net in a wide circle, eventually drawing it to a close.

Crossing the Panama Canal

The pilot told us they were to set sail later that night. We took the information back to the ship, where we discussed a plan of action. Paul and I wanted to put a dolphin-killing ship out of commission. While crossing the Atlantic, we spoke of ramming a purse seine ship at its stern, with the hope that we could disable its ability to lay a net. But with Ben White not yet

aboard, I didn't realize that he was opposed to such action, instead preferring to work with the Costa Rican government on a less-confrontational
solution to the country's role in dolphin-killing. Ben believed we might be
able to negotiate to save many more dolphins than we could by ramming a
ship, and his argument made some sense. But what Paul and I believed was
that, as the Sea Shepherd, our job wasn't to negotiate, but to decommission
vessels engaged in the decimation of the world's last marine mammals. By
contrast, Ben and many of the crew wanted a peaceful, non-confrontational
solution.

It became clear to the rest of the crew that I wanted Paul to use the
Sea Shepherd to ram a tuna ship. After Ben rejoined the boat, he held crew
meetings and included them in the decision-making process about the
campaign. I wasn't opposed to such consensus, but most of the crew had
never been involved in an environmental, animal or other political struggle, and to them, negotiating with a government sounded far more reasonable than ramming a ship. I became irate and began comparing Ben's and
the crew's ideas to those of the less-radical Greenpeace organization—the
very group that had kicked out Paul for being too radical in his desire to
save the lives of the world's last marine mammals.

When night fell, Sue and I found our pilot friend on the dock by his
ship where we were invited to share a smoke. We sat cross-legged at the
end of the dock on a hot tropical night, as Sue and the pilot spoke about
being at sea and about the dolphins. The pilot confessed that his ship had
so far this season been responsible for just over 50 dolphin deaths which,
for him, was an unfortunate consequence of an otherwise lucrative occupation. He also said they would be heading out to sea later that night.

Sue and I raced back to the Sea Shepherd in our inflatable and told
Paul and Ben it was now or never, if we wanted to stop this dolphin-killing
boat from returning to sea. Ben wanted to have another meeting with the
crew, while Paul and I were ready to make the decision and take action.
Yet, Ben was the campaign organizer who had raised the funds for fuel and
who was undoubtedly committed to the best outcome for dolphins, so it
was decided that we would follow his course of action—but only for now.
Within minutes, a plan was concocted where five of the women crew
would take one of our inflatable boats and chain themselves to the anchor
chain of the tuna ship, thus preventing its departure.

But I was disgusted! Here we were, the most radical marine mammal
protection group on the planet, and yet we had chosen to chain ourselves to
something rather than send it to the bottom of the ocean. This was a
Greenpeace tactic, and not why I chose to sail with Paul.

After the women were found connected to the ship's anchor chain, crew members attempted to dissuade our crew from the protest with "seal bombs," which are essentially large firecrackers used to deter seals from eating the fisherman's haul. This was rural Costa Rica, not California, and I thought that our actions here were more likely to cause injury than the more "radical" action of targeting a large piece of steel with another large piece of steel.

With Sue translating, a deal was eventually made with the captain of the tuna ship. We would retrieve our protesting crew, and in return he would allow us to look at his catch books which confirmed the number of dolphins we already knew the ship had killed that season.

When the confrontation was over, the crew held *another* meeting, and there they asked Ben to kick Sue and I off the ship! When Paul heard about the vote, he said that he would sooner kick off every other member of the crew before dumping the only man responsible for sinking two whaling ships [in Iceland]. Paul and I weren't always on the same page with tactics, but I've always known that his allegiance, like mine, lay with the people most willing to take action for animals, not those who only talk about it.

With our crew back onboard and the tuna ship on its way to sea, Ben left the ship once more, and we set sail ourselves for the Eastern Tropical Pacific tuna fishing grounds. Paul and I were resolute that we would ram the first dolphin-killing tuna ship we encountered.

Encountering a Tuna Ship

After only a day at sea, and with information gleaned from the tuna captain's catch records, our radar picked up a stationary object about 12 miles away. It was night, and we were confident it was a tuna boat, so we stopped our own engines and drifted within radar range of the vessel. As dawn approached, we started our engines and edged closer to the other ship. Once it was within view, it was easy to see that it was a purse-seiner, resting between sets. I wanted to ram the vessel without warning. Paul felt that our action must be filmed, otherwise it might be covered up by the ship's company or simply ignored by the media. At the time, I couldn't have cared less about documentation. I wanted to send a message to the dolphin-killing industry that if you engaged in the slaughter of marine mammals, your vessel will become a legitimate target.

We began circling the ship with our own vessel, drawing the full attention of that ship's captain and crew. When we rounded the stern of the tuna ship, placing us within range of ramming the net-launching boat dangling from the stern, a crew member climbed onto the gear for a better look at us—but also placing himself squarely in danger, should we ram. Paul swung the wheel to starboard, but before we could take further action, the tuna ship fired up its engines with plumes of black smoke shooting into the air and began sailing away from us at full speed.

As the tuna ship disappeared over the horizon, many of us were on the bridge, silently watching as the tuna ship out-ran our slower ship. One of the crew, who was a former Greenpeace captain said, "I wish we had a faster ship." Paul replied, "I wish we had a helicopter." I said, "I wish we had a rocket launcher."

Heading Back to California—For One More Attempt

Not too long after discovering that the tuna ships we wanted to pursue were much faster than the old Sea Shepherd, it was decided to sail north to Mexico; at that point, Sue and I decided to jump ship and return home to California rather than wait for the ship to arrive much later. The encounter with the tuna ship in Costa Rica had shown me that the tactics I was committed to were not always in line with Paul Watson's Sea Shepherd. At the time, I didn't care about media attention; all I wanted to do was cause financial losses for the industries engaged in animal abuse. But Paul knew that direct action on the seas could only be successful if we were able to document those actions we were willing to take to protect the seas. I begrudgingly agreed, which was why I left the ship in 1989 to return to the kind of direct actions we had begun on the West coast.

When I returned to California, I recruited one of my friends who had carried out the UC Davis raid on the raptor center in 1987; we wanted to conduct our own attack on the American tuna industry that was also responsible for dolphin deaths. I knew my time was best spent with the Animal Liberation Front, not Sea Shepherd, but I still wanted to make a mark on the industry I had just spent my entire summer trying to stop.

We rented a car and drove down to San Diego, which was the home port of the US tuna fleet. Once there, we scouted out multiple targets, including a tuna ship that was tied alongside a dock. The other targets would be the offices of a tuna company and the headquarters of the Inter-Tropic Tuna Commission, which was responsible for ensuring that US tuna fishermen reduced their incidental by-catch of dolphins. While there had been protests targeting the US dolphin kill, no one had ever targeted the industry for direct action; security at the locations was scant, although we didn't spend much time investigating.

We drove to an industrial supply shop and purchased 50 feet of steel cable that we would attempt to wrap around the underwater propeller of the tuna boat. If we could get a couple wraps around the propeller shaft, when the ship started up its engines, the cable would become entangled, requiring expensive repairs or even drydocking. At the offices we were targeting, we would set incendiary devices or use Molotov cocktails. We spent the day preparing the incendiary devices and gathering equipment we would need to dive on the ship. My friend would be the diver, as she was far more confident in the water than I was.

When late night finally arrived, we drove to the docks and parked amidst restaurant-goers, skulking through the shadows to the side of the darkened tuna ship. While I remained on dock on watch, my comrade climbed down a ladder on the dock to the ink-black water. There she disappeared under the ship—only to pop out a moment later. explaining the difficulties involved with the task. Without a weight belt, it was nearly impossible for her to stay underneath the ship long enough to wrap the cable. After many frustrated attempts, we were forced to abandon the idea in order to focus on the remaining targets that night.

Tired and wet, we drove to the long dock that housed the Inter-Tropic offices, parked our rental car, and grabbed a small duffel bag with the incendiary devices. At the end of the dock, the office building was unlit and empty. I had earlier discovered an unlocked bathroom window, into which we now both climbed. Once inside the offices, I began searching for a good location to place the incendiary devices—when suddenly an alarm went off.

We both darted for the open bathroom window, making it out with just with enough time to crawl underneath the dock, as red-and-blue flashing lights approached. We could hear police voices, and their flashlight beams danced over the building that we had just vacated. A few moments later, a police patrol boat came alongside the offices and used its spotlight to search under the very dock where we were hiding. We were crouched as far underneath the building as possible, but my friend's foot was still sticking out a bit. Thankfully the light beam just crossed our hiding place without discovering the both of us hidden there with our duffel bag filled with fire-making tools.

After what seemed like hours, the police retreated. We waited another hour, just to be sure, before climbing out from under the dock. The parking lot was totally empty except for our rental car, which had three Molotov cocktails in the trunk. Close call! We couldn't believe our luck as we drove away. We had paid the price for not carrying out better recon and knowing all the complications that came from our desperate attempt to inflict damage on the tuna industry. A bit wiser, we abandoned any idea for an attempted attack after our near capture, and quietly returned to northern California.

Once I returned home, I quickly discovered that the above-ground activist community was being targeted by the FBI in its search for the underground ALF members responsible for our many attacks in recent years. My residence in Santa Cruz was a magnet for radical activists, and thus it also became a magnet for law enforcement hunting the ALF. If I was to keep on the direct-action path that I believed was most effective, I would need to change my routines, separating myself from most of the friends who were then engaged in legal forms of protest in California and the rest of the country.

Getting arrested protesting a new animal testing facility at UC Berkeley

CHAPTER 6

MONKEYS, POWERLINES, FUR FARMS...

As much as I loved being at sea with old friends and alongside my mentor Paul Watson, after returning from the Sea Shepherd tuna/dolphin campaign, I decided to focus on animal liberation activities on land. I knew I could apply our direct-action strategy against other vivisection and fur industry targets and that was my priority now, rather than being at sea, which was my childhood dream. That was a dream that had already come true, yet it had led me down roads leading to many an animals' nightmare. I didn't want to be beholden to any one organization any longer, and so together with Jonathan Paul, my friend from Santa Cruz, we started Global Investigations, as a private investigation company with a focus on exposing animal abuse. Our hoped-for clients would be the many national organizations who were familiar with our reputation for effective direct-action campaigns.

Jonathan and I started Global Investigations after being hired by various groups to carry out civil disobedience actions. Our thinking was that with GI, we could turn our activism into a paying job without swearing allegiance to one organization, as many of our friends had done to make a career out of their activism. It wouldn't take long for us to get our first job.

Before Jonathan and I could get to work officially, I was called out to Maryland to meet with a prospective client. I trusted the messenger, so I accepted the invitation and found myself sitting in a Bennigan's chain restaurant late one night, awaiting my patron. This person told me a long story I had already heard, but not with the ending involving me. I was being asked to ascertain the possibility of liberating the last remaining Silver Spring monkeys, which had been at the center of the longest-running animal rights case in history.

These monkeys were 17 wild-born macaques held since 1981 at a government-funded research lab called the Institute for Behavioral Research, located in Silver Spring, Maryland.[1] Brought about as the result of undercover work in 1981 by Alex Pacheco, one of the founders of PETA (People for the Ethical Treatment of Animals), the Silver Spring monkeys

---

[1] *Editor*: These monkeys should not be confused with the feral monkeys, also macaques, currently living in Silver Springs State Park, Florida.

were the subject of invasive and traumatizing experiments that Pacheco exposed, resulting in the first-ever legal rescue of laboratory animals in US history. But their freedom was short-lived. The experimenter fought in court, ultimately winning the animals return, but the legal battles continued as the remaining monkeys were slowly killed off in continued experiments.

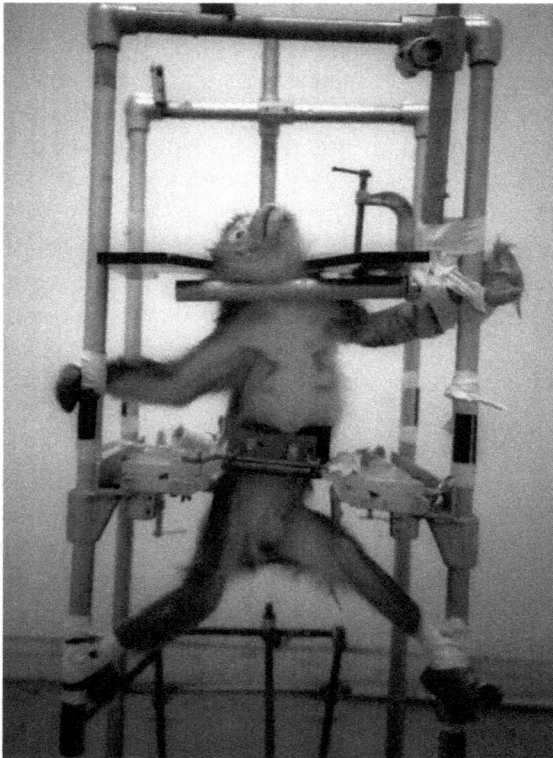

One of Pacheco's photographs

Now the courts had ruled in favor of the vivisector one last deadly time, with the remaining four monkeys being cleared for one last round of painful experiments, for no more reason than to deny the budding animal rights movement a victory.

The remaining monkeys were being held at the Tulane University Primate Research Center deep in the swamps of Louisiana, just north of New Orleans, along the banks of Lake Pontchartrain. I was told that every resource I required for the liberation would be made available and cost was not a limitation. I was given a Pennsylvania driver's license with a false identity, matching credit cards, and an envelope loaded with cash.

I flew from Maryland to Mississippi, where I rented a car and drove to New Orleans, to meet with another individual who had been hired for the same purpose. Together we were to infiltrate the grounds of the primate center and locate the four remaining Silver Spring monkeys. I bought maps of the area and noticed that the Abita River led right to the edge of the primate center. We found a camouflage duck hunting boat for sale on the side of the road, paid the asking price with cash, and drove the boat to our hotel parking lot.

There would be three of us involved in the initial reconnaissance: a driver and the two of us going into the facility via boat. The first night, we launched our boat at sunset at a busy boat launch without any undue attention. We were just two more guys going out in a boat. We motored to a beach near a highway rest area and waited until nightfall. At about 9 p.m., we got back in the boat; I put on a pair of infrared goggles that would help me navigate the windy river without light. As we sped across the open water in total pitch blackness, I hoped we wouldn't strike any floating logs or alligators that might pitch us into the ink black swampy waters. As we neared the primate center, we began to see lights coming from the floodlights that stood over the entire facility. We cut our motor and paddled the last few hundred yards. As we approached, we began to see the tops of their cages and could hear the primates chattering.

Mooring our boat just 70 feet from the fence line, we crouched and spent just over an hour, simply watching for any human activity. I had learned when doing recon on a new target that it was a good idea to first watch the target from a safe distance to ascertain if there were any regularly-scheduled security patrols. If any such patrol operated on the hour, we would notice from our secure position.

Without any signs of security, the two of us crouch-crawled to the six-foot chain link fence that simply ended near the forested swamp.

Before we could simply walk onto the grounds, we inspected the opening left where the fence ended. We could see a stationary infrared security device that shot an invisible beam to another stationary device about a hundred feet away. We pulled back into the woods to discuss our next move. I told my partner that I felt confident that as long as we didn't break the infrared beam, we could avoid triggering the alarm. I volunteered to crawl on my belly close to the stationary security device in an attempt to slip in. I made it past the beam without incident and signaled to my partner that I was going to approach the main monkey housing area, which was a square structure with an open courtyard in the middle.

The main building sat on footings that created a three-foot crawl space underneath the entire building. I removed a ventilation grate and crawled under the building, pulling the grate back into position once I was in. I crawled towards the courtyard and peeked through another grate to see the tops of rows of cages through the high glass of each room lining the courtyard. I decided to just sit and wait another hour to see if there were any patrols. After about 30 minutes, an alarm sounded. I knew I hadn't triggered it, so I stayed put and remained on high alert. After the alarm had stopped only a minute or two later, I saw a security guard with a flashlight enter the courtyard and take a quick walk around the buildings before disappearing from where he had come.

I crawled out and back underneath the security beam and found my partner waiting where I had left him. I asked him what he thought the alarm was. He told me that after I had left, he had decided to "test" the alarm by breaking the beam to see what would happen. I was furious! But I didn't say anything there in the field. I just suggested that we return to our pick-up spot by the rest area.

When we got back to the hotel, I lit into the skilled partner I knew only by reputation. I told him it put me at great risk to trigger an alarm without my knowledge. I was done working with such an inexperienced fellow. I told my handlers that I could do this job, but not with someone who put me at risk without communicating what he was doing. The next day, he was gone.

I flew home under my false name and got in touch with my ALF cell members. I told them I was working with another group on an action out of state and needed trustworthy help. A quiet young member volunteered, and a few days later we were driving back to Louisiana in a rental car. I felt relieved knowing I was choosing from a pool of warriors who had already proven themselves in previous actions. They knew my security protocols and routine, as well as being fully committed to risking their own freedom for that of others.

I was now being trusted by people I had incredible respect for, to find the Silver Spring monkeys and rescue them. It sounded like an impossible task. The remaining monkeys were not in good health. Some had spinal fusion from spending their entire lives in cramped cages. We would have to anesthetize them all before carefully transporting them via boat to freedom. But before we got that far, it was my job to simply locate the four monkeys amongst the hundreds of others being held for experimentation.

It was sometime around the beginning of January 1990 that we rented a hotel room by the week and began to spend every night surveilling the primate center. The boat was risking too much attention on our nightly patrols, so we opted to walk along unlit residential roads that ran near the remote research center. Each day, at around 5 p.m., we would drive north, crossing the 24-mile-long Lake Pontchartrain Causeway to Covington, the closest town to the primate center. Once there, we would wait until dark and then get dropped off half a mile from the facility, walking on roads until we reached the facility's remote maintenance yard on the edge of their property.

During daytime, we had lots of time to kill. We found the best vegan restaurant in New Orleans and rewarded ourselves weekly with their amazing meat substitutes they made from pecans. At least we were already friends and knew each other well enough to get along when we weren't working. Even better, we had become so familiar with the security routine at the primate center, that we knew when we could easily approach the fence line and scurry under the infrared beam. I knew exactly when the security guard would be walking the courtyard of the primate building and could safely climb out from under the building and walk the courtyard with a flashlight as soon as he left, knowing it would be at least another hour before he returned.

Inside, I saw hundreds of monkeys crouched in cages as I poked my flashlight into their darkened rooms behind the glass of the inner courtyard. Some had labels on their cages that indicated they were "infected." The monkeys had no stimulation devices or physical companionship to help them endure their painful ordeals, for which the only release would be death. My heart began to break each time I entered that courtyard. Each night, I searched row upon row of cages, looking for the faces of four monkeys I had only ever seen in photographs.

After midnight, we exited the facility and rendezvoused with our driver to begin the drive back to our hotel room. I remember laying in the backseat as we bumped along the causeway's dead-straight line back to New Orleans, listening to Sinead O'Connor's "I Do Not Want What I Haven't Got" and thinking about those monkey's sad faces. Their eyes would glare into my flashlight beam, trying to see the creature behind it. To them, I was just another one of their captors or torturers. They had no reason yet to believe otherwise.

Failure

Finally the time came when I had to report to my patron that I could not
locate the Silver Spring monkeys. We peered over a map of the facility I
had drawn from my memories of the many visits there. I pointed to all of
the buildings I had inspected; the only remaining building was situated
directly next to the security headquarters. My patron asked about that one.
I told them I knew nothing about it because it was too close to security and
too exposed for me to carry out surveillance. My patron asked me to attempt the surveillance anyway, but I refused, saying it was not safe and put
me at too much risk of exposure.

  I did not have the history with these individual animals that my patron had. And time had run out on the legal battle to regain the monkey's
freedom. A court had just made a crucial ruling allowing the remaining
Silver Spring monkeys to be returned to the original owner and experimenter, who was determined to use them in one last invasive experiment. I
suggested we rescue other healthier monkeys being used in research and
then plant incendiary devices in the empty administrative offices, which I
could access from the building's crawlspace. I wanted to do something,
anything, to this hell hole for monkeys. It wasn't just the remaining Silver
Spring monkeys I was concerned about; my history was now with those I
had seen for myself suffering at the hand of man. I couldn't just walk
away… But in the end, that's exactly what I did. I never heard from my
patron again.

  Weeks passed before I read the news accounts of the final experiments conducted on the remaining monkeys. Within a year, they would be
euthanized. My feelings were being hardened—not to the suffering of animals, but to the industries that were killing them. Rescuing prisoners of
the war on nature would remain a noble goal, but what I wanted to do now
was put those industries completely out of business. Reform was not possible. I wanted maximum destruction, not minimal damages.

Next Mission: The Power Grid

I returned home to my budding ALF cell in California, where raids were
being planned on local targets. But I was learning that in order to truly impact the industries abusing animals, we had to find bigger targets and
weaker links. The animal agriculture industry was too massive of a target
for our one cell's direct action. We could burn down hundreds of slaugh-

terhouses and it would do little to satiate the world's craving for meat. Eventually, we would be caught and our minimal impact removed.

On the environmental front, 1990 was the 20th anniversary of Earth Day; but instead of demonstrations, rallies, teach-ins or speeches that were the usual Earth Day tradition, the event had become an opportunity for corporate despoilers themselves to get involved in the planned festivities as a means to promote a "greener" image. It was the beginning of an era and "greenwashing" was just beginning its cycle. Pesticide-maker and GMO-king Monsanto donated $15,000 to Earth Day events in St. Louis, Missouri, which led to fractures in the local environmental community. In other states, corporate executives themselves got involved, as was the case in Alaska with a former oil company worker organizing the state's events; while in Portland, Oregon, resource extraction industries were paid sponsors, and criticism of timber practices was forbidden at official Earth Day events.

I lived in Santa Cruz at the time, in a house full of other activists. One day, we started joking about sabotaging a planned electric guitar Earth Day event coming up. Our conversations began after receiving a flyer from Darryl Cherney, a longtime Earth First! organizer and a personal friend whom I had joined on more than a few redwood protest lines. Darryl had circulated a flyer depicting the earth breaking free from its corporate sponsorship, but it also featured an illustrated image from the cover of the book *Eco-defense: A Field Guide to Monkeywrenching* by Dave Foreman. The graphic was accompanied by the phrase, "Go out and do something for the Earth...at night." That was all we needed to put our next plan into action.

We researched the power grid, locating where the transmission lines emanated from the coal-burning power plant operated by Pacific Gas & Electric (PG&E) that ran from the Moss Landing station to Santa Cruz and other cities. We knew any power outage would quickly be re-routed and restored. And we knew we were putting some people with health conditions at risk. Yet, power outages in the region were not uncommon, and rarely resulted in serious injuries or death. Our action would be a planned inconvenience.

On the first night (yes, there were more than one) we ventured out to target two small powerlines and to investigate just how to topple a 100-foot steel tower carrying high voltage power lines. The smaller lines would help ensure that power wasn't easily redirected. At a remote power transfer station, we found no signs of human presence and made quick work of cutting most of the way through two wooden power poles. We didn't want the lines to fall immediately, but we knew it would only take a strong wind to knock these smaller poles down.

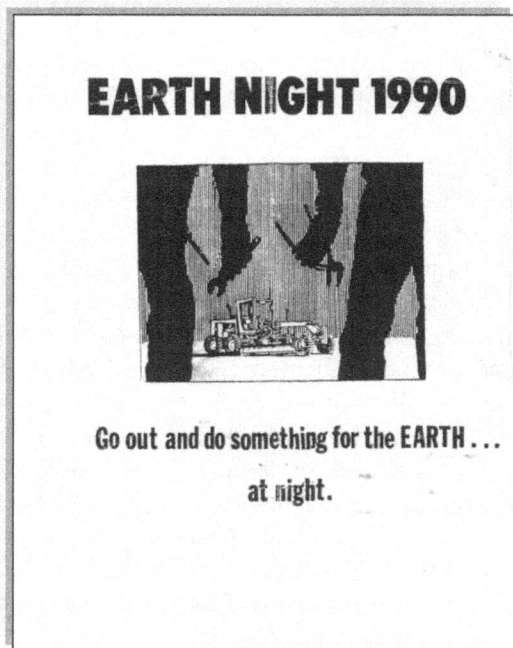

Darryl Cherney's flyer

We knew dropping a much larger transmission line involved removing large bolts connecting the towers to their base, but with tension from the lines, there would be some geometry involved and none of us were good at math. We knew we had to concentrate on removing the bolts from three of the four legs that we wanted disconnected. The fourth leg would bend under the pressure from tension on the line. As a target, we chose a pylon on a "soft" corner, where tension would pull the tower inwards and away from us.

We brought socket wrenches, open-ended wrenches, and cheater pipes to attach to the end of the socket wrench to give us more leverage. We didn't need the leverage on many of the bolts, but as the tension grew on the few remaining bolts holding the tower to its base, those bolts seized up and could not be easily removed. We were forced to retreat, leaving the tower with more than half of the bolts removed. We would return the next night, hoping no one bothered to investigate in the meantime.

The powerline ran across farm fields with only a few lights from small farm buildings illuminating the fields. The following night, we struggled to cross the freshly-plowed fields and found the targeted transmission tower still intact—and no FBI agents hiding in the bushes. This time we brought with us a hacksaw, sledgehammer, and chisel to separate the tower legs from their base. As we cut through each remaining bolt, the tension in the powerline, and our own bodies, grew. We knew this tower would fall. With only a few bolts holding all the pressure, I began cutting each bolt with the hacksaw.

Once I'd cut the head off of the final bolt, I jammed a chisel between the gap of the tower leg and base and took a swing with a small sledge. The leg shot out into space with spring force action, allowing the hundred-foot tower to begin its collapse over our heads onto earth. As the tower began to fall, the lines snapped with loud pops that sounded like gunshots, and a brief flash illuminated the entire area. For a split second, I could see my friends frozen in shock and surprise. We ran away from the lines, stumbling over the plowed rows that felt much deeper and higher than they were before. As we ran, we watched as power grid after power grid lost power, turning the world around us pitch black.

The drive home was surreal; every light was out. Back home, we drafted a press release by hand, claiming action under the name "Earth Night Action Group," in homage to Darryl's flyers. The official investigation would last for years, with some accusing the FBI of staging the sabotage to discredit environmentalists. In carrying out the action, we also were giving a revolutionary salute to other struggles that engaged in powerline sabotage. The "Bolt Weevils" are one such American group that come to mind: Midwestern farmers who grew frustrated with their treatment by a big power company and the lines crossing their farms. The farmers loosened the bolts, allowing the wind to later bring the powerlines down. We also were saluting those indigenous struggles in South America, like Peru's "Tupac Amaru," who fought for the rights of the poor and indigenous populace. They also often targeted the rural country's power grid.

The next day was another on our revolutionary agenda, with a planned protest at the Pacific Stock Exchange that turned into a near riot. Still exhausted from the past two nights of powerline sabotage, some friends and I got at the head of the march and led a small crowd in smashing bank windows and tossing smoke grenades into the streets. We were met of course by an unofficial group we would refer to as the "peace nazis" because they always appeared when radical activists began destroying corporate property, screaming at us to stop. These people still believed compassionate capitalism was possible and that change would only come from peaceful protests. I always reminded anyone who said this of the treatment of other peaceful protestors—including Brian Wilson, an anti-war activist who, while blocking train tracks to a weapons facility, had both legs severed when the government train refused to heed protestors' attempts to stop. I will never forget the horrible slogan I heard from military supporters following that violent crime against a peaceful protestor; they wrote, "You provide the legs and we'll provide the arms!" As emboldened as we were becoming, we still knew that with our increasingly brazen actions we were awakening the monster of American Repression. It wouldn't be long before we felt the heat at home.

San Jose Mercury News **(24 April 1990)**

A Near-Fatal Car Bomb

On May 24, 1990, Jonathan Paul and I were practicing music in our Scotts Valley home; we had faint hopes of becoming a band, but never got beyond our infrequent practice sessions. During this particular session, there was a knock on our door, and when the friend who answered the door returned, he said, "Rod, there's a deputy sheriff at our door who wants to talk to you..." I said, "Tell him to fuck off!" and laughed; but he didn't. When I walked out of the room, I could see the police officer peering into our windows. I opened the door, but before I could speak, he asked if Judi Bari and Darryl Cherney were expected at our house later that day. In fact, they were—for another benefit concert, which we were always hosting for one campaign or another. But this was something strange.

I always practiced serious security culture, never wanting to divulge any information to a cop without a warrant, but I could tell that something was amiss. The officer then told me that Judi and Darryl had been involved in "a serious accident" and it wasn't yet known whether they had survived. I was in shock. The officer kept returning to questions around the intent of their visit, which I found bizarre, considering the intensity of news he had just delivered. I regained my composure, stopped asking, or answering, questions. Convinced that he wasn't getting any more information, the officer left.

Not 15 minutes later, we received a phone call from a friend telling us what really happened. Darryl and Judi were the victims of a *car bomb* that had been placed under the driver's seat of Judi's Subaru. The bomb ignited as they were leaving Berkeley after a show there and heading to their next gig in Santa Cruz, where we would host them. Whereas the sheriff's deputy left me not knowing whether either victim survived, our friends informed us that Darryl escaped with minor injuries while Judi's injuries were serious and would eventually haunt her for the rest of her life. Judi died seven years later, in 1997, from cancer.

Incredibly, the FBI immediately assumed that Darryl and Judi were *not* victims of a car bombing, but of transporting *their own bomb* which had prematurely exploded—and that is the story that was fed to the news and that went out on the wire to media outlets everywhere. The media reported that the bombers themselves were the victims. Within days, the narrative would be corrected, but it would be years before the FBI was held accountable for their actions—with a successful lawsuit that left Judi's surviving children with a cash settlement. For the time being, Darryl was accused of being an orchestrator of much more violent actions than we could ever carry out, and we knew this was the beginning of an era where the FBI would continue to target those it believed were involved with the ALF and its illegal activities.

The FBI pointed to the flyer Darryl had created, promoting sabotage in the name of the Earth, but in reality, Darryl was part of what some of us activists referred to as "Ecotopia Earth First!" because of their steadfast adherence to nonviolent and pacifistic principles. Few Earth First!ers in northern California at the time promoted illegal eco-defense in the early 1990s, opting instead for a campaign of nonviolent civil disobedience that targeted corporations—such as the corporate owners of the infamous Maxxam Corporation which had purchased Scotia Lumber, one of the last commercial old-growth redwood forest logging operations in the United States. Darryl and Judi were simply the latest in a long line of peaceful leaders of a nonviolent protest movement to become the target of physical violence in America in the 20th century.

2 Earth First! Members Hurt By Bomb in Car

Radicals reportedly suspected in Oakland blast

By Michael Taylor and Elliot Diringer
Chronicle Staff Writers

Two leaders of the militant environmental group Earth First! were injured yesterday when a pipe bomb ripped through their car as they drove through Oakland.

An Earth First! organizer, Karen Pickett, said police told her that the two will be booked on charges of transporting and possessing explosives. Police declined to comment.

Judi Bari, 40, and Darryl Cherney, 33, both of Mendocino County, were taken to Highland Hospital in Oakland. Bari, who was driving her white, four-door Subaru station wagon, was listed in serious condition with a broken pelvis and internal injuries. Cherney was in good condition with facial cuts.

Oakland police, who were investigating the bombing with the FBI and the federal Bureau of Alcohol, Tobacco and Firearms, acknowledged that Bari and Cherney were "being detained," she at the hospital and he at police headquarters.

Police and FBI agents searched the Oakland house where Bari spent the previous night and detained a member of the household for eight hours yesterday, said the household member. He declined to give his name but said he belongs

Page A16 Col. 1

Investigators discussed damage to the Subaru station wagon in which the blast occurred

San Francisco Chronicle (25 May 1990)

To this day, no one knows who really planted the bomb in Judi and Darryl's car. But as the media and FBI pointed their fingers at members of my own community of activists, I was starting to feel like we were giving our enemies an easy target as we paraded around at night carrying out illegal actions, while in daylight we were the public face of the very same movement to protect animals and the earth. It started to feel like we were doing *too* much, and maybe being *too* visible.

Not long after the car-bombing, I heard news that was simply impossible to believe. In February, South Africa had released Nelson Mandela, the radical leader of the anti-apartheid movement after 33 years in prison. Now Mandela was on a tour that was bringing him to the San Francisco Bay Area where he would deliver a speech at the Oakland Coliseum. Tickets were no longer available, but that didn't stop my friend Gently and I from going. We stood in the parking lot, looking sad, as we asked hundreds of smiling attendees if they had any extra tickets. Finally, Gently, being a longtime follower of the Grateful Dead, started yelling, "I NEED A MIRACLE!" The expression was a common one to other concert-going "Deadheads"; and it meant that you needed a ticket. I thought it was hilarious that my white dreadlocked friend was shouting the wish to a predominantly black audience, when suddenly a family approached Gently. I was no longer skeptical!

With two tickets in hand, we entered the coliseum and were greeted with the sound of Malcolm X's speeches as they were broadcast over the stadium PA system. This was the same stadium I had been in numerous times as a child to watch an Oakland Raiders football game; but now I was here listening to historic calls for justice from a hero long stolen from this world. The stadium was filled with explosive joy. It was like we were all coming to a surprise birthday party. Finally, the recorded speeches stopped and members of the band, The Special AKA's, came on stage and began singing their celebrated anthem, "Free Nelson Mandela"—only when it came to the title of the song, the band had changed the words to "Nelson Mandela is Free." As they sang these words, a tall elderly black man walked onto the stage with his fist held in the air, and the entire stadium erupted in cries and applause. Gently and I stood with our fists in the air surrounded by thousands of others with tears pouring down our faces. Here was the man who had fought for his people and nation with every means available until it led him to prison. Now the system of Apartheid he had fought was collapsing and he had risen from its rubble.

When Mandela began speaking, I couldn't believe what I was hearing. After thanking all of us in the world who had supported his struggle, he began talking about apartheid in America. He told us he had spoken to indigenous leaders and learned of the US Indian Reservation system and how it was modeled on the South African government's oppression of its indigenous population. He told those of us gathered that day, that we needed to attack the apartheid that was happening right in our own country. Nelson's visit was life-changing for me and came at time when I knew I had to follow my own path and not that of any larger movement. Hearing his words only confirmed what I was already feeling.

The Utah Dog Kennel

In the months that followed the car-bombing, I spent much of my time flying around the country carrying out reconnaissance on possible targets. There were dogs at the University of Utah we were hoping to rescue, more at the University of California at Davis that we felt confident we could grab, while at the University of Connecticut we investigated a lead there, and there was a fox fur farm in Pennsylvania; all these were brought to our attention by the above-ground animal rights movement or through our own leads.

I spent a month in Salt Lake City following a lead we received via the ALF support group. A letter came in from someone on the janitorial staff at the University of Utah's dog lab, telling us about abuse they had witnessed. I drove out to Utah and lived out of our group's van in the national forest that surrounded Salt Lake City. I rode my bike onto campus and found an overlook that gave me a view of the dog kennel we hoped to break into.

Each night as I sat against a large rock staring at the kennel, I'd listen to the dogs barking and would be instantly be reminded of Richard Adams' novel, *Plague Dogs*, about two canines that escape from a top-secret government laboratory. I read the book during the day and did recon at night. In the story, there are two dogs, Rowlf and Snitter. The latter dog was a pet before ending up in a research lab, so there are many contradictions Snitter must work out about humans. He shares memories of home life with a bewildered Rowlf, who, as a purpose-bred dog, never knew love. All he knows of humans are those who place him in a tank to swim until he drowns, only to be revived and forced to repeat the experiment another day.

I knew that each of the many dogs I could hear barking from the University of Utah's kennels was either a Snitter or a Rowlf. I knew that each one was capable of love, loyalty, and friendship if only given the chance. I knew that each animal that suffers at the hands of humans in a laboratory is equally capable and desiring of love, loyalty, and friendship—maybe not with humans, but certainly with their own kind. I saw farm and lab animals become loving companions to humans who showed them love. I knew that all those dogs or any animals in such dire straits needed was help from a few humans ready to empathize with their suffering.

After weeks of planning, our West coast cell of the ALF gathered in Salt Lake City for the raid on the dog kennel. On the night of the raid, a partner and I were in a university parking lot, parking the van that we would use for the action, when we were immediately stopped and questioned by a university police officer. Despite our alibi that we were visiting a friend in the hospital, the officer asked to see our ID, which we provided. We were released without any further incident, but we both knew that if we carried out a raid on the same campus that night, any suspicious activity encountered by any campus police would be later scrutinized.

When we broke the bad news to others back in the hotel room, everyone wanted to call off the action—everyone except my partner and I. My friend showed total resilience and indifference. He said the cops could prove we were in the parking lot, but that's it. His priority was doing everything he could to rescue those dogs barking in the kennel. But we were overruled, and so everyone got back on an airplane to California—except me. I drove the 800 miles back to California, feeling deflated. I shared the feelings of my friend; I didn't want to give up all the work we had done and turn my back on those dogs. But I was part of a larger group that believed in consensus, so I begrudgingly agreed to head back home to California.

As I approached Elko, Nevada, I drove past a few acres of netted pens in the desert and saw a sign identifying the location as a Chukar game bird breeding farm. Chukar are a popular species amongst bird hunters, and this farm bred and sold the birds to private game farms and some state wildlife agencies. I stopped for the day, waited for nightfall, and walked across the outskirts of town to the farm. It was clearly empty of humans, so I approached the pens where hundreds of birds were kept.

As I crept close to one pen, suddenly the birds flushed and flew straight up into the netting before landing back on the ground. The noise startled me, but with no one around, I knew I had little to worry about. After surveying the pens, I crawled into an office window and ransacked the files and equipment. I placed all the paperwork that looked important in the center of the office, including a cash box that had about fifty bucks in it. I wanted them to know their money was tainted. I poured oil, paint, and anything I could find over the pile, and then grabbed a utility knife from a work table and returned to the pens outside.

I began cutting the nylon netting on each cage, removing large panels and dragging them aside. As I did this, hundreds of the chukars erupted skyward—only now they weren't hitting the net, they were flying free. After I had cut large holes in every pen, I began the long walk back towards the glowing lights of Elko, as chukars could be seen walking and flying in every direction. Looking back, I would say my actions were reckless, in that I eschewed any safety protocols to satisfy my frustration and sadness about not rescuing the Utah dogs. But I also knew that I was passing through a state where no one knew me, nor had I been seen anywhere around the last-minute target.

There might not have been much strategic value in the ALF releasing a few hundred birds from a game farm in Nevada, but what I realized was that the further we went from California or areas with a history of animal rights activism, the more likely we were going to find suitable, unguarded targets.

Target: Mink

It was late spring 1990 when I flew to meet Priscilla Feral with the group Friends of Animals. We had spoken on the phone and I had been referred to her by Betsy Swart. Friends of Animals was involved in a campaign against the commercial fur trade which, for animal welfare and rights groups, meant a focus on fighting the cruelty inherent with trapping. For decades, the public had been shown photos of animals languishing in traps or the severed paw of an animal in a trap, the captured prey having twisted or chewed off their own foot to escape the steel jaws of a still commonly-used foothold trap.

The year 1990 was also when the European Union banned the importation of fur from countries that did not use humane trapping systems. The international fur trade, led by the Canadians, was quick at work developing "best management practices" for trapping that would establish standards for "humane" traps.

But it wasn't trapping that Feral was concerned about, but rather fur farming. Since the early 20th century, animals such as fox, chinchilla, and mink have been bred domestically on farms for their fur. Within the United States, there were just over 650 fur farms, according to the US Department of Agriculture.

Most of the fur farms in the United States were raising mink, utilizing the easily available animal by-products from farm animal agriculture as a food source. Because of the huge amount of production of cows, pigs, and chickens in this country, fur farmers are able to rely on a cheap, yet protein-rich diet for the small carnivores they were raising for their fur.

Now the fur industry was claiming that animals raised on fur farms were the "most humane" source of fur. Within the global anti-trapping movement, there was concern that if public consumers were convinced of this, the struggling fur trade might find new life in fur farming. Graphic video was making its way around the world of foxes being anally electrocuted in Asia, but no video existed of conditions on US fur farms. Friends of Animals wanted to hire our new company, Global Investigations, to find out what fur farms in this country looked like.

This would be our first real job. Little did I know it would also be our only paid job.

We would begin in Oregon and Washington state, where most of the West Coast fur farms were located. Utah and Michigan were other big states for fur farming. Jonathan and I drove north from California and stayed with friends of his in Seattle. We drove outside of Everett, Washington, where the rolling green fields gave way to forested hills. The fur farm we were looking for was a mink farm; and when we saw it, we knew exactly what it was. Much like factory farms raising chickens, mink are often raised in long windowless barns in rows of cages that are often less than a foot wide.

We parked our truck about a quarter mile from the farm and walked along the pitch-black road until we could see the farm; it lay across from the most amazingly beautiful field of wildflowers—a stark contrast to what we would see inside the barns. It was dark, but we could hear the scratching of literally thousands of small animals and smell the ammonia of their waste which was piled up underneath their wire-suspended cages. Occasionally and without warning, a mink would make a harsh shriek as we neared the cages. I could see the small mink turning around in circles repetitively, and I would soon learn that this was a behavior normally seen in zoo animals. Known as "stereotypical behaviors" with captive animals, these can include pacing, rocking, swimming in circles, excessive sleeping, self-mutilation, excessive grooming, and mouthing cage bars. This sad evidence of captivity is seen in many species, including primates, birds, and carnivores.

The self-mutilation was evident in mink that had first clipped the fur off their tails; others would eventually clip much of their body fur. Some fur farmers called this "lion syndrome" because it left the mink looking like a lion's mane, because the only fur it couldn't clip was around its head. These were behaviors so evident in mink, not only because of their intense confinement, but also because they are an extremely territorial species who, in the wild, do not tolerate trespass from other mink, except perhaps when looking for a breeding partner. Mink have yet to be domesticated. They are still in their genetically wild state, having only been mutated for the sake of fur color. Otherwise, most mink on North American fur farms are 99% genetically wild.

We took our photos, walked the rows of cages, and noticed all the paper cards affixed to each cage. These cards held the vital information on breeding that allowed the fur farmer to differentiate between breeder mink and mink that would be killed at seven months of age during their first winter.

We drove back to Seattle, where we searched maps for another mink farm in Sweet Home, Oregon. This farm was also situated in a forested area, so we could park our truck over a hill and hike into the farm like we had in Washington state.

Once it got dark and all the lights in the nearby home were out, we drove to our hidden parking space and trekked overland to the farm. As soon as we got within sight of it, a dog started barking and then a light turned on in the house. We saw a human figure step outside the door and speak to the dog before returning indoors. Once the coast was clear, we approached the familiar mink barns and were exposed to the usual conditions within this intensive confinement system.

The rows of wire cages were connected together and each cage was divided by a simple sheet of thick plastic. Each mink could hear the one next to them; often you could see mink frantically scratching at the plastic in an attempt to reach their neighboring mink, which they would probably kill. On this farm we also documented mink that were beginning to self-cannibalize, beginning with their own tails. It was heartbreaking and tragic to be discovering another form of commercial animal exploitation, only this time the victims were undomesticated native wildlife in the beginning processes of domestication that would only lead to the constant death and suffering of countless generations of mink and other furbearers to come.

When I returned to California, I was a changed person. The fur industry had always been a personal target, because of my early belief in it being not only an institution of animal abuse, but also a weapon of early colonization. Now the fur industry was in the process of establishing itself as another farm animal industry. I started researching fur farming, gathering addresses for more farms that we would visit over the summer of 1990. At the same time, we contemplated our next move with our ALF cell, which had drawn the attention of the FBI and several federal grand juries that were investigating our crimes across California and the West.

Earlier that year, our small group had attempted a break-in at Simonsen Laboratories outside of Gilroy, California, not far from my home. After weeks of recon, we were in the middle of attempted entry when I inadvertently stepped on a window sill as I lowered myself from the ceiling, which I had accessed via the roof. With alarms blaring, we fled on foot as a security vehicle could be seen speeding to the scene. I was heartbroken that my simple mistake had cost the many lives we had hoped to rescue instead.

Back home, my brother who worked for my family's construction company told me about a building under construction not far from our home in Morgan Hill, California. Since the project was seeking building contractors to complete the job, blueprints were available for job estimates, which my brother shared with me. The building was to be a satellite extension for Simonsen Laboratories, a large animal breeding facility that we had targeted earlier without success.

By the end of June 1990, the building was completed, and the first animals were being brought into the facility for breeding purposes.

On the night of July 1st, we again loaded up our trusty white van and I was driven only a couple miles from where I was then living with my parents; the driver dropped me off in the empty but lit parking lot of an industrial complex. These were still the days before such parking lots were under camera surveillance. I walked up to the façade of the building and, using a large steel pipe that was connected to the side of the building, climbed up to the first story roof. Once atop, I located the exhaust vent over an animal room and began removing the small self-tapping screws that held the rotating vent in place. With the vent removed, I could then access the fan within, which I also removed with a few screws and by cutting the electrical wire that powered the fan.

As soon as the fan was removed, I could smell the now-familiar scent of cedar shavings and animal urine. I was now in the crawl space between the roof and the ceilings of each room in the building. I took out a utility knife razor and cut through the sheetrock of the ceiling, pulling away pieces until the hole was large enough for my body to fit through. I then climbed back outside and onto the roof and called for backup. The van pulled into the parking lot and two individuals came towards me, each carrying a stack of plastic animal carriers. From atop the roof, I threw down a line and pulled up the empty cages, then another ALF member climbed up to the roof to help receive the guinea pigs.

The rest of the raid went off without a hitch, but the rescue would be fraught with complications. We had made out-of-state arrangements for the guinea pigs to be handed over in a hotel parking lot in Denver. So another member and I began the long drive immediately after the raid, east over the mountains towards Colorado. We spent a night in a hotel room where we changed the animals' bedding and fed and watered them. We stood in our hotel room filled with cardboard boxes, with the separated guinea pigs whistling and chirping as we kept an eye out for any signs of danger.

Once we arrived in Denver, we realized, with alarm, that our contact might not be coming. We couldn't call and ask questions over the phone, so after waiting an entire day, we came up with other plans. I reached my contacts in Tucson, Arizona who had helped us house the Loma Linda dogs, and they thankfully said to come on over. We then made the long, 900-mile drive to Tucson without losing a single animal. We had to fill my friend's spare bedroom with their fresh cages. It was decided that we'd split the animals into two groups: one would be housed in Arizona, while the other would be taken to Southern California and housed there.

I rented a car and drove 50 of the guinea pigs to another friend's home in Glendale, Arizona, where I next placed "free to good home" ads in a couple local newspapers. I also paid for an anonymous phone service to field the calls. Within days, I was taking interested calls and visiting the prospective adopters to see if they were suitable. I wanted to ensure that the animals would not be bred or used for commercial purposes. Most of the guinea pigs went to homes already living with the species, but perhaps my favorite homing was to a small school, where one classroom adopted two of the animals. After explaining their care to the teacher, I was quickly ignored as the children surrounded the new guinea pig enclosures. I left with the feeling that our mission had been accomplished: of giving these 100 individuals a better life than they would have had in any research laboratory.

The responsibility to find safe homes for rescued animals is the most important task for an animal liberator. Anyone might be able to smash a window or start a fire, but providing humane care for a sentient being is no small duty when you've assigned yourself the label of rescuer. To be an ethical member of the ALF, one must put their own interests behind those you've chosen to represent. The safety and security of the rescued is the reason behind every mission.

Sadly, as we increased our capabilities at carrying out animal liberations, the effort necessary to house rescued animals grew beyond our ability

—especially with law enforcement breathing down our neck after each raid. I will never condemn the rescue of an animal if they are provided a better life. There is no greater demonstration of our human compassion than taking such an action. But housing just 100 guinea pigs stretched our small group to its limit and put us all at risk. I spent over a month in Los Angeles overseeing the placement of just 50 animals.

Yet we wanted to strike at the finances of animal exploitation in such a way that our raids made a difference beyond the lives of the animals we were rescuing. But how were we to do this to an industry as strong and established as the medical research industry? We knew arson was the tool that caused the most economic damage, but unless we were targeting a much smaller industry, our attacks would just be absorbed by the nation's vivisectors and the university's that support them. They would become "the cost of doing business," and little would change.

After the fiasco housing the guinea pigs, I was leery about continuing to work with some activists whose principles I was beginning to question. Some in the ALF and the radical animal liberation community were most concerned with the media attention our actions received and less about the welfare of the animals we were rescuing. I felt like that was a major disconnect that I could not enable or support, so I began to make inroads into recruiting new members for the ALF who were not known to law enforcement or even the activist community.

In late summer 1990, I began meeting a group of friends living in southern Oregon who were part of the early struggles to protect old growth forests in the region in the 1980s. They were living in Ashland and working in a supportive vegetarian restaurant that fed activist travelers along the I-5 corridor. We had seen each other repeatedly at Earth First! gatherings and protests, and by now, these folks were becoming friends.

In August 1990, I obtained a short list of fur farms in Montana from Cres Velucci, my old ally and friend in Sacramento who had helped bring my early ALF cell together. After our exploratory mission in Washington, we decided to head to fur farms with other animals, such as fox, bobcats, and even Canada lynx. With names and addresses in hand, I recruited an ALF friend from Santa Cruz to be my partner on what would be our first official undercover investigation of fur farms. For this action, we'd be posing as prospective young fur farmers looking for good breeding stock to start our own farm. I'd even rented a post box and paid for a telephone service so that I could hand out an address and phone number if necessary; remember, these were the days before burner cell phones and Google numbers.

Randall and I drove to up to Washington state in late August to leave our own vehicle, which was traceable back to many a recent protest and hunt sabotage. Not that we expected any delving into our back story, but my ALF experience had hard-wired me for such security protocols on any action, and this was no different. In exchange, I borrowed a van from a Sea Shepherd supporter.

What was different now was the fact that we wanted video documentation of conditions on fur farms, and not to actually rescue any of the probably thousands of mink, fox, bobcat, or lynx. This made sense to us because we believed in the power of the truth as seen through the lens of our cameras. The embattled fur industry was desperate to survive in the midst of the European Union's partial ban on the importation of furs from animals caught in inhumane traps, and was laying great hope in the green-wash sell of fur farms as humane alternatives to the use of foothold and body-gripping traps most commonly used by trappers.

Friends of Animals hired us to gather evidence of the actual conditions in some of America's 600 fur farms and the techniques used to kill fur farm animals. Video of anal electrocution of foxes in Korea became public and the outrage against fur farms was growing. What the anti-fur movement needed was compelling evidence that conditions seen on fur farms in other countries was similar to those in the US.

We set our sights for Polson, Montana, where I had an address for a bobcat farmer. It was good to be on the road again with another new mission to focus on, one that didn't have the level of high security that West coast animal research laboratories were calling "the new normal." Still, this wouldn't be an easy sell; we would still be complete strangers to any fur farmers we met. For this work, I would need to create an alias for any in-person meetings we had with fur farmers. I chose the name "Jim Perez" as my cover for the entirety of the investigation.

I decided to stop at a Montana Fish, Wildlife & Parks office in the area to see if I might get any information from the staff about where I might find breeder mink. It was a good time to ask, as the agent on duty casually said I should get in touch with Bruce Campbell, who had a small fur farm not far away. They didn't have Bruce's number, but they knew he also owned a beauty salon in a local shopping mall and that was where we would eventually meet him later the same day.

Bruce was a former biologist for Montana Fish, Wildlife & Parks who retired from the department but still operated the salon and a small fur farm with a couple hundred mink, four bobcats, and two Canada lynx on his property. It wasn't hard to strike up a friendship with the man, as he shared many of my same loves of wildlife and the outdoors. This would be the first fur farmer that I actually met, rather than avoiding a meeting by sneaking onto their property without their knowledge to film their animals. We could film at night and possibly some at daytime when no farmers were around, but what we really needed was video footage of the killing methods used on mink farms.

Target: Fraser Fur

Bruce would help us by providing a few names of farms we did not have, including the Fraser Fur Farm outside of Ronan, Montana. It wasn't out of the ordinary for someone to get in touch with Bruce about his fur farm experience, but his was a small operation compared with most mink farms, which can house thousands of animals. Still, our friendship with Bruce allowed us the opportunity to make plans to return to his farm in November during "pelting" season, which is exactly what we did.

Before we left Montana, we wanted to visit Fraser Fur Farm. After having called the owners and mentioning that Bruce was a friend of ours, we were invited to come and take a look at some mink that were available for us to purchase. Bruce Campbell had acquired his breeder mink from Fraser, so we told the fur farmers we were very interested in buying mink and maybe even a cat or two. Stu Fraser was the elder who had started the fur farm with live lynx he had trapped in the nearby Mission Mountains. Before this investigation, I had no idea native endangered wildlife like Canada lynx could be raised in captivity, let alone to be killed for their fur. At the time of our investigation, it could be safely said that there were possibly more Canada lynx on Montana fur farms than there were in the wilds of the state where they belonged.

Fraser Fur Farm was on Terrace Lake Road, east of Ronan, down a dirt road with the majestic Mission Mountains in the distance. We drove up and parked amongst the mink barns and met Stu, who gave us a tour of his operation and led us through his mink barns. We saw his son feeding the animals from a motorized cart loaded with wet food that was slopped on top of each mink cage, each barely ten inches wide and separated by plastic dividers. As is common, the incessant sound of scratching and scent of musk could be heard and smelled. Mink are solitary animals that travel miles each night, coming together only to breed. They are their own worst predator and will easily attack larger animals with their sharp teeth and strong jaws. Being forced to live next to hundreds of others of their kind causes them to not just scratch at their walls in a futile attempt to escape, but also to self-mutilate.

We kept our visit short but again mentioned a desire to learn about the pelting process. We told the Frasers we didn't want to go through all the trouble of raising mink only to not know how to properly process them at the end of the season. This usually begins at the end of November, when the fur hits its peak condition as winter approaches.

Randall and I then decided to spend the night in the nearby Mission Mountain Wilderness Area and take an unofficial look at Fraser Fur Farm. We parked in the forest and hiked along North Crow Creek to where we could begin to make out the telltale long metal barns with exposed sides. There was human activity in the area, so we quickly abandoned any idea of infiltrating the farm to get video footage. Stu's sone could be seen driving a tractor with a visible sidearm on his waist.

Beyond the trees where we hid, it was easy to see a row of bobcats and lynx, most repeating the same stereotypic circular motion of pacing their cages that we discovered was common on fur farms. This was one of the latest constructs against nature created by humans in the last century especially, as wild animals became the subject of a captivity industry that was feeding zoos, private game farms, and other nefarious collections.

Seeing these animals—which were nothing less than a few generations out of the wild—it was unmistakable that their suffering was beyond the physical, though that evidence was abundant on fur farms as well. What was perhaps more disheartening was knowing that these bobcats and lynx could see the mountains which were their native habitat, just beyond the wire of their cages. Their feet would never feel the earth or a cold mountain stream. Their legs would never propel them into the air to catch a grouse or snowshoe hare. These were the latest victims of a centuries-old fur industry, desperate to continue its murderous rampage against the fur-bearing animal races of our continent. If there were not enough lynx in the wild to feed the fur trade's lust, then that industry would take lynx, bobcat, fox, and mink and raise them in cages just like chickens.

It was less than a year since I was setting incendiary devices and crawling through laboratory windows at various animal research facilities, but this fur farm investigation was a very different kind of action. We were exposed. We knew that, should we be successful, afterwards it would become known to every fur farmer in the country who we were. Any thought of anonymity would be forever lost and the fur farm industry would certainly increase their security, as their existence became known to the rest of the world.

Also, I wasn't emotionally ready for how affected I was by the conditions on America's fur farms. I had seen farm animals in the worst of inhumane conditions, but there was something different about seeing what were once fierce and wild animals subjected to the same spirt-crushing conditions. Every fur farm we visited in 1990 was located in a beautiful mountain area, where not too distant relatives of the imprisoned animals still roamed free. I remember seeing the trap injuries on a lynx's paw during the tour of Fraser Fur Farm. Though the injury was from long ago, this was an animal who had known the liberty of freedom in the wilderness. Her children would from now on forever be taken and killed before they would ever know their rightful place in the natural world.

I was still committed to the mission of obtaining video evidence of killing practices on US fur farms, but I couldn't help but think of how it might be possible to release hundreds of these animals from captivity. I had already seen feral mink that had escaped from their cages living near fur farms. I often would see them as I snuck up to a farm from nearby woods. For the moment, we took our videos and mailed them to Friends of Animals, asking that they not be released until we had returned to our fur farm contacts in the fall for the killing season. Back home in Santa Cruz, we began to feel the heat of surveillance, as federal grand juries were convened to investigate the ALF's crimes, including our Earth Night Action Group's toppling of powerlines in Watsonville, California. The animal rights community in Sacramento and Davis was getting the most attention as arson investigators continued to chase down leads in the still-unsolved Veterinary Diagnostic Laboratory fire in April 1987, when our group was just beginning. While others in my local activist community remained in the San Francisco Bay area, I was ready to begin living the lifestyle that matched our guerilla activities. I was spending more time in southern Oregon with friends unknown to law enforcement and without activist histories. It was time for me to leave the city and return to the wilderness.

Our contacts at Friends of Animals were very pleased with our progress. They supported our request to not release any video footage from the farms we had filmed in our first visit to Montana until we completed our investigation. While I was getting more immersed in the investigation, my activist friends around me were continuing the local struggle against vivisection at universities and organizing sabotages of California big game hunts for elk and bear, as well as the annual pilgrimage to the Mojave every November for the desert bighorn sheep hunt. Randall was one of those participating in other environmental campaigns that winter, so I was forced to find another partner for my return to Montana. When I received word from

Bruce Campbell that he was planning on pelting out his mink the following weekend in November, I was forced to find someone quickly.

Suddenly I remembered a friend I had made in southern Oregon—a woman named Maureen who had told me in confidence one night how much she supported the ALF and would love to participate in a raid if she could ever be of service. My father had helped me purchase a Subaru wagon—not the best vehicle for an undercover operation, but one that would serve the purpose of traveling across Montana in winter time. I drove north on I-5 from the Bay Area and pulled into Ashland around 9 p.m., heading straight to the vegetarian restaurant I knew Maureen worked at occasionally. She wasn't there, but the cook told me she was moving into a new house with friends right around the corner. I found her scrubbing the bath tub. After a brief hello, I explained that I was on an undercover investigation of fur farms in Montana and needed a cameraperson to help film the killing of mink. She didn't hesitate and responded affirmatively—as if I had just asked her to go to a friend's party. We would leave early the next morning.

On the long drive, I was able to describe the situation with Bruce Campbell and Stu Fraser, as well as prepare Maureen for visiting fox farms we had yet to see in Montana. Maureen was a committed vegan, but she understood why we were doing things differently than an ALF-type action. Whereas an ALF raid might want maximum destruction and economic loss, this was a raid to gather evidence to reveal to TV-addicted America, depicting how mink are being killed by fur farmers today. We knew some used gas, but we also knew there were more primitive methods. Maureen and I would visit a fox farm where the farmer described killing his foxes by crushing their chests between two boards, standing on the top board. This kill technique is called "chest compressions" by trappers and fur farmers, and is one of the cruel methods of dispatch that does not damage the fur, like a gunshot might.

We headed for Butte, Montana, where I knew of a fox farm. I had never made contact with the owner because of the remoteness of the farm, which made it safer to approach on foot from the surrounding forest. Randall and I had located this fox farm from the list given to us by Cres Velucci on our earlier summer trip. Because we were able to climb the fence and easily film the animals, we decided to come back in the kill season and see if it was possible to hide in a tree or something, to film the killing. These were the days before remote trail cameras and other similar devices, so we needed to be physically within view, and theoretically it was possible on this farm, which was surrounded by tall trees that could be easily climbed.

After spending a night in a windswept hotel, I walked across the street to a pay phone and called my old friend Betsy Swart, who was now working for Friends of Animals. I told her we had arrived in Montana and were heading onto our first farm to see if the killing had begun. She told me that video evidence of anal electrocution being used in America could have much greater dire consequences for the fur industry than it had from the Korean evidence of anal electrocution. I agreed, but told her that so far, we had seen no evidence to support it being used in Montana. Stu Fraser said he shot his cats and gassed his mink, and the one fox farmer crushed their chests, but on this particular farm, I wasn't sure how the farmer killed the captive foxes.

Snow was on the ground as Maureen and I parked our Subaru on a dirt US Forest Service road not far from the farm, which was surrounded by national forest land; this made our approach easy and legal. The farm was not within sight of the farmhouse, so we waited until midday when we knew the farmer wouldn't be feeding. As we approached from the tree line, it was easy to see that no one was at the farm, except for the foxes. With Maureen standing watch, I jumped the fence and headed towards the rows of wooden cages which were half-plywood nest boxes two feet square, each connected to a wire cage the same size. From the nest boxes, foxes stared at me as I crouched amongst their cages. I walked towards the small barn within the compound. Outside of it, I found an All-Terrain vehicle parked with a hose tapped to its exhaust pipe leading to a plywood box. This was the fur farmer's *homemade gas chamber*, using hot carbon monoxide to kill the foxes now staring out at me from their cages. To them, I was just another human like the one imprisoning them, possibly there to continue the killing. How could I prove to these animals that it was more important to film their suffering than to set them free? That was a human argument, not one for the animal world.

After retreating to Maureen's location, we discussed whether we should try to locate a tree to film the gassing of the foxes, which, with the location near the barn, made it almost impossible to see without being noticed. We decided to return to our hotel and call Betsy to see how she wanted us to proceed. On the drive down the forest road, our car started sliding on a curve and went off the road, enough to get stuck. I grabbed my mountain bike that I luckily had inside the car and told Maureen I would ride back to our motel and call a tow truck—which I did.

Biking my way back to the car, a highway patrol officer's cruiser passed by me and pulled over to a stop. The officer rolled down his window and asked if I was the owner of the Subaru that had went off the road nearby. I answered Yes, and he offered me a ride back to the scene. I didn't want the ride, but knew if I refused, I'd raise suspicion. So I took the front wheel off my bike and piled it into the cop's car and climbed in to the front seat. We made small talk as we drove back to the car, where Maureen was still waiting. The officer told me it was state law to report all accidents, and since I had called the tow company, he heard the dispatch and came to investigate. We arrived back before the tow truck got there, and the officer asked for my driver's license. I gave him my false Pennsylvania driver's license attached to a real person's identity, but with my picture on the forgery. The tow truck driver soon arrived, and as the officer sat in his car, I dealt with my car.

After I paid the tow truck driver and he left, I returned to the patrol vehicle which still had my bike in the back seat. The officer said he was waiting for a call back on my ID. (Gulp!) I then heard the dispatcher say over the radio that there was no record of that license in the state of Pennsylvania's system. The officer looked at both sides of the license and told the dispatcher, "Well, I have it right here in my hands, so it must be somewhere in the system..." In what seemed like hours, but was probably only moments, the officer shook his head and handed me back my fake license and said I could get my bike out of his car. As I hurriedly put my bike's front wheel on, the officer creeped forward and said, "Next time, over a cup of coffee!" I smiled and waved as he drove away, trying my best not to drive away immediately, knowing he'd be in front of us the whole way back to our hotel, should he discover my ID as a fake and return to look for us. We left after his car was out of sight, gathering our belongings from the hotel and hitting the highway headed north to Bruce Campbell's farm.

Along the way, I stopped to call Bruce Campbell, who told me he would start pelting his mink in a few more days. Knowing we had time, I then called Stu Fraser to ask if I could stop by and check out his pelting operation, which was much larger than Bruce's farm, with a couple hundred mink. Stu told me it was fine to stop by, knowing we were on our way to Bruce's.

We stopped at a nearby department store and bought a purse for Maureen to use for hiding our camera. We were no longer using the older bulkier VHS camera recorders, like we did for the University of Arizona and other earlier raids; now we were using a much smaller camcorder that used videotapes smaller than the size of an audio cassette tape—for those who remember such things. In one end of the purse, we cut a small circle the same size as our camera's lens. Maureen would do the filming while I did the talking.

We pulled our Subaru up to a large barn without windows and walked quickly through the rain, inside the barn, where we found not just Stu, but about four other men who were each facing a workbench with a dead mink hanging from its feet in a steel Y-shaped device. Each end of the "Y" was sharpened to a spike so that the skinner could hang the mink from the rear tendons on each leg. Once they had skinned around the anus and rear legs, they could pull the hide off the animal as if they were peeling a banana. The smell of musk from the mink excreted in fear was everywhere, but I'd bet the fur farmers hardly noticed it anymore. Stu showed me a gallon zip-lock bag hanging on a nail that was being filled with mink penises. He explained they were a special order for a man wanting to use them as toothpicks.

On the Fraser Fur Farm, a motorized cart with a carbon dioxide gas chamber was used as a killing method. The cart could be slowly rolled between the rows of mink cages as fur farmers filled the box with mink. Stu led us outside to where we could see his son operating the mobile gas chamber. Maureen was already filming as I asked questions about the technique. As the fur farmer moved the cart, another man reached inside each narrow wire cage with a gloved hand and pulled out the mink, who were biting and screeching in futile resistance. In an arc, the man would swing the mink into the gas chamber which had a one-way door. I could only imagine how horrible it must be for the mink to be flung into the darkened chamber filled with dead and dying others. For most of these mink who were raised and killed at less than a year old, this would be the only time they would have ever touched another mink since they were taken from their mother's nest box.

Maureen and I kept our cool, managing to talk for what seemed like hours. When we finally left and headed towards a motel, we felt gutted. We were in utter shock at the brutality we had witnessed, a bitter end for a horribly short life of cramped torture. Even worse: When we reviewed our videotape, we couldn't see much, as Maureen was unable to see what she was filming when she held the purse against her side. There was a lot of the roof of the barns, and the sound of the gas chambers engines drowned out much of the mink's screaming. We were deflated, knowing we couldn't possibly go back and try to film again. That would certainly raise their suspicions. We would have to hope for better luck on other farms we would visit later that fall, especially Bruce's.

Return to Bruce Campbell's Farm

We arrived in Lakeside, Montana, with a heavy snow falling. Maureen and I checked into a nearby hotel and called Bruce. He wanted to take us out to dinner, but knowing it would be impossible to hide the fact that we were vegans at a Montana restaurant, we instead offered to cook for him at his place. Anticipating such a meal plan, we hit a co-op in Bozeman and bought a ground beef substitute. We then bought two jars of spaghetti sauce at a regular supermarket, one that was vegan and the other with ground beef. At our hotel, we dumped out the real beef sauce and refilled the washed jar with the original label with the vegan sauce and fake meat. At Bruce's house that night, we cooked him a nice spaghetti dinner with garlic bread that he had no clue was a ruse. The meal disguise allowed us the opportunity to break bread with someone we thought we never would: a fur farmer. But Bruce and I easily struck up a friendship, with him being a lifelong outdoorsman and hunter and my own early adulthood years spent exploring the mountainous west; this allowed us to talk easily about things we both enjoyed.

In the morning, we arrived early at Bruce's and were met at the door with his wide smile as he rubbed his gloved hands, saying, "Let's go get some mink!" At the entrance to his own skinning shed was a pyramid-shaped pile of long black mink bodies. Inside the shed, he grabbed two five-gallon buckets as he told me stories about having been bitten by mink. His operation was small and did not require the mechanized process we witnessed at the Fraser Fur Farm. Instead, Bruce would use his gloved hands to manually break the minks' necks. He would later say that some-times after the mink had bitten him, it felt good to hear that neck pop.

We were far more comfortable explaining to Bruce that we wanted to film his pelting operation so we could learn more carefully his techniques. He had no hesitation with us filming, and so, with Maureen holding the camera easily in plain sight, the three of us walked towards the mink barns. I stood by to help, but all I was doing was making sure I wasn't blocking Maureen's camera angle as Bruce focused on his task. Flinging a wire cage door open, Bruce shot his gloved hands into the cage, pulling out a squirm-ing and screeching mink. The mink would always immediately bite hard onto one hand, allowing Bruce to use his other hand to take control of the animal's twisting body. With the animal against his legs, he would then bend the head back until the snapping vertebrae could be heard, silencing the mink's struggle.

I carried the plastic buckets that began to get heavy as they were filled with the beautiful bodies of the now-dead animals, their fur looking like one big blanket in the bucket, except with small feet and faces still attached. Once, a mink broke free of his grasp and hit the ground running directly towards me. I quickly stopped his escape with my own gloved hand, holding his body pinned against the ground until Bruce re-took control. He was grateful not to lose the $40 he was expecting to get from each pelt. But inside, I knew I had betrayed an animal simply to build confidence with a fur farmer, which meant betraying my instinctual desire to do more. When the buckets were full, we returned to the pelting barn where Bruce went to work skinning the animals, as we watched and filmed. The skinned carcasses were heaped into a pile with bared teeth and black, dead eyes. I asked Bruce what he did with the carcasses; "dump them in the local landfill," he said.

When the skinning was done, we returned to our hotel and immediately connected our camera to the TV and replayed the videotape. This time the image was crystal clear; but it seemed far worse when being viewed privately and not while undercover. Maureen and I burst into tears and had to turn the camera off. Accomplishing our goal had come with a horrible price for our spirit. We both knew we had carried out an undercover job that would eventually spare thousands of animals from the cruelty we had just witnessed; but for those animals whose lives were ended before our own eyes? I felt like I had betrayed them, just as I had for the mink whose escape I stopped.

But we regained our composure, and I made a call to Betsy Swart with Friends of Animals and let her know we got the footage they desired and would express-mail it right away. We had succeeded, but it felt like an empty victory.

Then the hotel phone lit up. It was Bruce. I listened as he told his story of wanting to get out of the fur business and admiring our desire to getting started in it. He wanted to offer us some of his breeder mink at a very good price. I let him finish talking before explaining that I would need to discuss this with Maureen and other partners. Maureen and I quickly came up with a counter-offer: we would ask Bruce to sell us everything and everyone still alive on his fur farm. I called him back and said that we wanted to buy not only his breeder mink, but those he was still planning to pelt out later that week. We also wanted to buy his two lynxes from Fraser Fur Farm and four bobcats, complete with cages, feed, and equipment. The next day over coffee, Bruce detailed his offer; it would be $14,000 for everything but the barns themselves.

Later that night, after making dozens of calls in my activist network, I heard back from a small animal rights group interested in providing funding. I am ashamed to have forgotten their name now, but they would probably have preferred it that way, given what was to become of my work on fur farms. While Friends of Animals was content with the neck-breaking video, the idea that we could rescue, rehabilitate, and then release 60 mink, four bobcats, and two Canada lynx would turn this nightmare into a dream.

We left Montana, heading west to gather our funds and prepare for the legal liberation. I stopped in Pullman, Washington, to pay a visit to Rik Scarce, a professor and author who had recently spent time with me while researching Earth First! and Sea Shepherd, for his 1990 book, *Eco-Warriors: Understanding the Radical Environmental Movement.*[2] From Rik's place, I called Linda May, a wildlife rehabilitator living in Washington state with none other than David Howitt; both had been with me on the Divine Wind in 1987, and it was there that I became friends with Linda. I called her for advice, and after a bit of discussion, she offered up her land outside of Port Angeles on the Olympic Peninsula. There, we could gradually rehabilitate the animals and release them back into the wild.

We had asked Friends of Animals for help with funding and housing the 66 furbearers, but they could only offer permanent, caged homes. Maureen and I promised each other that any rescue must include the eventual release of all healthy animals. That was our price for what we had chosen to witness. For thousands of mink I saw on fur farms that year, death would be their only escape, but for these 66, we could provide the life that nature, not man, had intended. I accepted Linda's generous offer, and we went to work planning the liberation.

In late December 1990, Jonathan Paul, Kris Maenz (an Earth First!er from Montana), and I drove a Ryder rental truck back to Lakeside, with Jonathan following in his own truck. We all camped out on Bruce's floor and shared another vegan meal with him before waking the next day, amidst deep snow, to disassemble his farm. The rows of mink cages would be stacked on either side of the rental truck, with the six cat cages in the area over the cab. All the feed and equipment would go into Jonathan's truck.

The mink were easy to load; we simply cut the wires suspending the rows of cages in the air, and then secured them inside the truck. The bobcats were moved using livetraps, but the lynx had to be sedated with ketamine, administered via blowgun—which Bruce also sold to us. Ketamine, Bruce explained, wouldn't make the animals unconscious, it simply immobilized them. They were still fully aware of their surroundings. Once darted, the two cats drooped over, allowing Bruce to move them with a large net into our travel cages. Although these two lynxes had spent their short lives in cages, they were still genetically wild animals—and they looked the part, as they growled whenever we approached.

---

[2] Revised in an updated 2006 edition.

When the last cats were loaded and we gave our money order for $14,000 to Bruce, we said our goodbyes and began the long drive west to Linda May's land on the Olympic Peninsula. I drove the Ryder truck until it began fish-tailing in the snow, when Kris, who was much more familiar with driving in the snow, took over; together, we all made the long drive through the night, stopping every few hours to check on the animals who remained remarkably calm, despite the growing smell of musk and urine.

When we arrived at Linda's, we backed the Ryder truck down her long driveway and unloaded the animals, placing their cages on the ground with tarps to protect them from the rain and snow. David and I immediately went to work building better, more spacious shelters. Maureen would join us in a few days, but until then, Linda, David, and I took turns feeding and caring for the animals. We built larger cages with frozen lumber and scavenged materials. Within a few days, we had created decent cages that were larger than those at any fur farm.

The Rehab Begins

Not a day passed that I was not stressed about the animals receiving the care they deserved. We couldn't vilify any fur farmer for their treatment now. It was our turn to show these animals, and the world, how we believed they deserved to live.

Included in the purchase of the fur farm was enough pelletized feed and frozen meat to feed the animals for a few weeks. As our rehabilitation project took shape, we were able to move from Linda's school bus home to a cabin on the Elwa River that we would also be tending. We slept at the cabin, and at dawn every day, we would wake up and prepare food for the cats and mink. The mink ate a pelletized food, which we would shift into a more raw-meat-based diet, but the bobcats and lynx ate mostly raw meat that was supplied by a feed company in Washington state. When our supply ran low, I drove to Edmunds, Washington to buy more raw meat from the Northwest Fur-Breeders Cooperative.

The Co-op was a conglomerate of fur farmers from Washington, Oregon, Idaho, and Utah that produced the needed feed and materials used by over two dozen fur farms across the West. With the legitimate inquiry that I wanted to buy feed for my fur farm, I was able to purchase the raw meat we needed. Meanwhile, my mind was already scoping out the Co-op as a possible future target of the ALF.

In the early days of the rehabilitation project, I was informed by my contacts in Friends of Animals that our neck-breaking video footage filmed in Montana would be used in an upcoming segment on fur farms on the national news show, *60 Minutes*. We were elated. It felt like a form of vindication to be able to share the trauma we experienced with the rest of the television-viewing world. I was glad our investigation had borne fruit, but I still felt unfulfilled with the accomplishment. Saving 66 animals was a blessing, but not enough for future generations of mink. With a solid crew of volunteers comprised mostly from my friends in southern Oregon, I felt it was safe for me to ask to leave the project for a few days to accomplish one more task in our undercover fur farm investigation.

Global Fur Auction

I contacted Friends of Animals and explained that while we had documented conditions on America's fur farms, including obtaining the neck-breaking footage, the last link in my mind was to follow the path of the animal's pelts as they entered the international fur market via auction. Fur auction houses have been a plague on this continent for almost 400 years. The first auction house was established in the late 1600s in what is now Quebec by the Hudson Bay Fur Company. In my conversations with fur farmers, I learned that most of their pelts entered the fur market through the Seattle Fur Exchange, an international auction house in Tukwila, Washington that is now called the American Legend Auction. The auction house is owned by a cooperative of fur farmers from the United States and was founded by the mink farmers in the midwestern states of mostly Wisconsin and Michigan. At the time, it annually traded in over $100 million of fur from 20 countries, though American Legend claimed that its mink were the finest in the world. The fur producer Nordfur said of American Legend's mink, "Since mink fur is indigenous to North America and has been raised there for more than a period of 100 years, the development in the art of mink production has given ALC the right to name its fur the finest in the industry."

My plan was simple: I wanted to use my contacts in the mink farm industry to gain entrance to the annual auction occurring in February. I wanted to show the path of a typical young mink on an American fur farm, that is slaughtered in their first year of life at seven months old. I needed to see where these animals' miserable lives ended and who would be the buyer of their fur. I was given a budget of $250 by FoA and began making calls. I spoke to fur farmer Stu Fraser in Montana who gave me the name of their broker at the auction house and also permission to mention their name. When I called to speak to the broker, explaining that I had recently purchased breeding stock for a new fur farm, I was warmly welcomed and invited to the auction. I called Sea Shepherd's former chief engineer Carroll Vogel and asked if I could crash at his place in Seattle, to which he readily agreed.

I tried to dress the part, but I was still very self-conscious as I parked far from the auction house. I entered the antechamber of the auction house where a few people were milling about and quickly went to an auction representative and asked for Brian, the broker I had spoken with. When he emerged from another room, he was all smiles and offered to give me a quick tour. He led me into a warehouse filled with wheeled carts like those used for clothing, only these were loaded with bundles of furs from different animals. Brian explained that I was a little early and that usually the fur farmers arrived the next day. Today was primarily the international buyers inspecting the furs that would be auctioned over the next couple of days. But since I was here, I was welcome to have a look around.

He soon left me in the massive warehouse alone, so I looked around me and started wandering through the aisles of literally hundreds of thousands of furs, each from an animal no different than the 66 "furbearers" now in our care. I made eye contact with some buyers wearing white lab coats and they asked if this was my first auction—as if it wasn't obvious. They were very friendly and demonstrated how to run my hands over the fur to inspect the guard hairs and determine fur quality. After they left, I began pulling different bundles of furs and carried them to one of the many well-lit inspection tables made available to the buyers to inspect. I was in.

The next day, I was joined by many other fur farmers who had traveled to the auction to see their pelts sold and visit with industry friends. We all sat in a room separate from the auction area where the lot numbers for pelts were listed on a lit board with the sale price. Almost all the buyers were from Korea and other Asian countries, with a few European buyers as well. After the sale, I headed to the hotel where most fur farmers were staying and hung out at the bar, where I easily struck up conversations with "other" fur farmers. I remember asking one for advice for a new fur farmer, and he said, "Sell your farm."

The next morning, I woke up at Carroll's house and had coffee with him before we both left to work. Carroll was reading a newspaper article as he said, "Wow, Rod, you work quick!" The article he was reading was about the recent decision by the Hudson Bay Fur Company to end its centuries-old practice of selling fur coats through its Canadian storefront businesses. Although the company's other retailers would continue their sales, this action by the oldest fur buyer in North America was another indicator of the fur industry's dire straits created by the anti-fur movement.

The last day of the auction was mostly a members-only meeting that, as a visitor, I was not allowed to participate in. After mingling with other fur farmers, the meeting was announced and everyone began filing into a private room for a closed-door meeting. As I became the last one in the room, Brian came over to me and invited me into the meeting. Even now, I was still carrying my mini analog tape recorder that I'd use to record conversations. I went into the bathroom, turned on the recorder, and then joined the line of fur farmers entering the private meeting room.

While auction business was initially discussed, it was clear that the focus of the meeting was a discussion of strategy to deal with the continuing crisis created by anti-fur activists. The fur farm industry was where the fur trade was attempting to make its last stand. Declining fur prices were already ruining wild fur prices, and the hope was that fur farmers would dominate the remaining market. In order to do this, the industry had to convince the public that fur farming was the humane alternative to trapping. An industry group had been created—The Fur Farm Animal Welfare Coalition—and media strategies were being developed to counter the claims that fur farming was just another cruel form of intensive confinement of animals.

Another high priority for discussion was continuing support for research intended to benefit the mink farm industry. A few cents was levied from every pelt sold at the Seattle Fur Exchange and put into the Mink Farmers Research Foundation, which had been created in 1954 to address the diseases encountered on fur farms (but not in the wild). This research project would be instrumental in helping fur farmers survive depressed prices by helping lower the costs for raising mink to pelting age.

After the meeting, I was introduced to Harold DeHart, the founder of the Fur Farm Animal Welfare Coalition as a budding new fur farmer not afraid to get into the dying business. Harold wrapped his arm around my shoulder and pulled me close, saying, "We gotta stop these people before things get as bad as they are in England. Right now, people are burning down stores selling fur and releasing farm animals. We can't let that kind of thing happen here." My presence was being noticed—but not as easily accepted as I first expected. As I was being introduced to other members of the Coalition group, I noticed one member staring at me with great suspicion, even as others attempted to recruit me to do public relations work. I was getting in deep quick. I decided to get out as soon as possible. It was the last day of the auction and everyone else was saying their goodbyes, so, not long after the suspicious stares, I exited and headed back to the sanctuary.

On the drive home, I stopped again at the Fur Breeders Cooperative in Edmunds, Washington to buy more wet raw food for the cats. As I walked through the office and large warehouse to pick up my order, I started thinking about how to break into the building after hours. I had seen a conveyer belt that led into the building through a small side entrance that delivered fresh fish byproducts to a large meat grinder. I made a mental note and continued home to my human and animal friends.

On the drive home, I couldn't stop thinking about the Mink Farmers Research Foundation. Here was a fur industry group that funded vivisection not to save human lives, but to keep costs on fur farms as low as possible at the expense of the animals' welfare. On top of that, it was the last hope of a dying industry that was plagued with ever-decreasing market prices for their final product, fur. In my ALF activism I was questioning the strategic effectiveness of random attacks on targets, rather than a concentrated campaign against one weak animal abuse industry. The fur farm industry might have been the target I was looking for.

By this time, my exposure to the trauma animals were experiencing on fur farms had changed my life. My first awareness of animal abuse had taken place when I was just 12 years old, as I witnessed the harp seal slaughter broadcast on PBS. This time, I was witnessing the violence in person. Becoming aware of such a level of socially-accepted abuse and trauma is not something you can easily accept and then continue to go about your life ignoring it. For me, there was an obligation in being a human—a member of the very species inflicting the violence. That made me responsible in part for the actions of my own species. I had learned if you ever want to really help animals, that's what you need to do: raise awareness to the abuse and hold the human abusers accountable and responsible.

So while I stood staring across this warehouse filled with the skins of hundreds of thousands of abused animals, all I really wanted to do was find a way to burn the whole thing to the ground. Centuries of fur animal abuse in North America had led to the budding development of fur farms, and if we didn't want to see mink becoming just another exploited species, the movement needed to act now.

When any of us ignores or turns a blind eye to systemic abuse in our society, it grows stronger and more ingrained in our culture. But when more people become aware, and choose to do something about it, that's when change can happen. It happened when I first saw those seal pups being clubbed, and I now hoped it would happen when the nation saw the mink we filmed getting their necks broken. This rehabilitation project would be another form of direct action and a chance to prove to the world that mink, bobcat, lynx, and other "furbearers" were not just farm animals or commodities to be traded on the open market; they were free wild beings that played an integral part in their native ecosystems and had every right to live free rather than in 10-inch-wide cages by the hundreds of thousands.

An Improved Sanctuary

Back at the "sanctuary" in Washington State, as we began calling the collection of pens and cages on Linda's land, we needed to build larger enclosures for the cats. They had spent their entire lives in cages standing on wire; now it was time for them to feel the earth beneath their feet for the first time. Once again, we didn't have the money to build them the enclosures they deserved, but that wasn't going to keep us from doing it. David and I began visiting remote "Park and Ride" lots on the Olympic Peninsula that had chain-link fence separating the paved parking lot from the encroaching wilderness and forest. The fencing was a ridiculous waste, but I guessed was required for liability or some other reason. Nevertheless, without causing much notice, we visited a remote Park and Ride lot one night with David's old van, and spent three hours working by headlight disassembling and rolling up chain link fencing that we'd use to build cat pens. When we needed more hardware, we would find another state-owned area and appropriate it.

We built the pens outside of human view where the cats could begin to become less accustomed to humans. In order for their successful rehabilitation, they would need to begin to disassociate humans with being fed. Instead they would need to learn that approaching a human could lead to their death. We built visual barriers on the side of the pens where we approached, and fed them outside of their view. When we moved the bobcats and lynx into the new pens, their noses were glued to the ground, sniffing every new scent available to their deprived acute senses. Their bobbed tails twitched back and forth as they explored their new temporary home. Once prey became abundant in late spring, we hoped to return these felines to their natural homes.

I spoke to wildlife rehabilitators who told me bobcats loved old clearcuts and that the challenge wouldn't be whether they could survive, citing the example of feral domestic cats. Rather, the challenge would be to keep them from being attracted to human habitations that they might associate with food. To combat this domestic desire, we would introduce a natural diet including live animals, such as rabbits and quail, or roadkill that we happened across.

When the time came to introduce a more wild diet, I purchased quail and rabbits from domestic breeders. At first, the cats were unfamiliar with live prey. But once we stopped feeding them, they quickly showed interest in their live food. Purchasing and feeding live animals was a moral dilemma that I only accepted because it would be a short-term measure. These animals would not need to be fed live animals or any animals forever; this was a rescue *and* rehabilitation project. For me, animal liberation for fur farm prisoners meant helping them return to their native habitat with the greatest opportunity for survival. Animal liberation did not mean these "rescued" animals spending the rest of their lives in bigger cages. They all had their teeth and claws and inherent wildness still intact. A few generations of captivity would not erase that.

Our sanctuary was home to two lynx, four bobcats, and 60 mink. While the cats needed larger pens to build muscular strength and hunting abilities, the mink required pens that were just three feet by six feet, with logs and baths made from cutting the bottoms of five-gallon plastic buckets. It was not much of a challenge to reignite the minks' wildness; they were already fierce beings, quick to bite any finger that strayed close to their cages.

Before we could release any of the mink into the wild, we had to ensure they were not carrying any disease that could be transmittable to their wild cousins. In order to do this, we would need to take blood samples from every mink and send them to a testing facility that catered to fur farmers. Linda and I geared up for the project with heavy clothing and leather gloves. I was the most familiar with handling mink, having visited and seen many fur farmers moving animals from cages. With a row of glass vials by our side, I'd open the cage door and quickly dart my gloved hand into the cage in an attempt to pin the mink to the ground. Having done that, I would then let the mink latch onto my gloved hand and, with their mouth occupied, I'd pull the mink out of the cage, hold its hindquarters, while Linda clipped a toenail and drew a small amount of blood. On a couple occasions, the mink twisted out of my grasp and darted away towards the surrounding forest.

On almost every mink farm I've snuck into, I've seen feral mink living just outside of the farm's perimeter fencing—ones that escaped just like ours did. But we didn't want these mink living so close to civilization where they might kill someone's cat or get into a chicken coop and themselves then get killed. So when our mink escaped, we ran after them, cartoon-fashion, with big fishnets. Their freedom would come soon enough.

Only one mink died on our sanctuary. Without any previous indicators, the young animal became agitated and vocal, twisting their body in apparent pain before succumbing to death in less than two minutes thankfully. We took the young female's body to a vet who had necropsied mink in vet school and said he had seen the condition before and that it was common on mink farms. Intensive confinement was the cause of such neurological defects as farmers cross-bred animals for mutations in fur color. Sometimes this breeding caused genetic defects, such as blindness in lighter-colored or albino mink.

Remember, we are talking about a species that had only seen the inside of a cage for perhaps 75 years. Before the 1920s, mink were only found in the wild, which was the basis for the breeding stock of many American fur farms, especially in the West. By the 1990s, mink farming was seeing what would probably be its economic peak time, with American black mink like ours fetching nearly $40 at auction. Although fur farms in Asia were producing far more mink than America, mink raised in the United States on the scraps from factory farms were still producing the most valuable pelts on the international market.

And though genetic mutations were now common amongst farm-raised mink, we knew that once our mink bred with other wild mink, their recessive genetics would not last long in their wild offspring. Freedom for fur farm prisoners meant returning them home where the impact of fur industry's abuse could be erased through wild breeding. We weren't just advocating for the rescue of 60 mink; we were fighting for the total liberation of a species.

Mink on fur farms never experience open water except from a plastic or metal dish. When we placed six-inch tall plastic five-gallon buckets filled with water into their cages, they immediately would investigate and quickly climb in, often spinning in a tight circle until all the water had been jettisoned from their bath. When this happened, the mink would stop and raise their heads, wondering where this new discovery had gone. When we isolated the mink and introduced live mice into their cages, not one animal refused to immediately attack and kill the small animals. Then with their quarry extinguished, the mink might lounge about before casually eating their meal. There are stories of mink killing beyond their means, especially when they get into a chicken coop. They will not leave a single animal alive. In the wild, mink are also known to cache large amounts of food to minimize their time away hunting. I remember reading an account where a great blue heron was seeing flying with a mink latched onto its leg.

Time To Be Free

When April came to the Olympic Peninsula, and remote forest roads became accessible, we were able to reach the wilder forest regions. The blood tests had come back negative for disease, so we began plans for our first release at the end of the month. We wouldn't release males and females together, wanting them only to bred with other wild mink. We also only wanted to release mink where a water source was available, which, on the Olympic Peninsula, was nearly everywhere.

The last preparation for total freedom would be a blessing from a Blackfoot medicine woman I had met in Montana. She shared her homeland with the ancestors of our mink and understood the work we were doing. On a beautiful morning, she came to our sanctuary and burned sage and sweetgrass and said a prayer for the animals. When she finished, she presented me with her sage bundle and instructed me in the ceremony I should conduct before each release to ensure their long life and freedom. As the smoke drifted over the many animal cages, I couldn't help but cry. Seeing the friends who had made helping these animals their priority, given so much of their time and love to this project—all these things were powerful and made me feel that what we were doing was truly sacred work, not just for these animals but for ourselves as well.

When the day came to release our first mink, we loaded two animals into their nest boxes and packed them into my Subaru. We drove deep into the forests and found an isolated stream surrounded by a moss-covered forest. We carried the mink on our backs, with straps attached to the nest boxes so we could carry them like a backpack. We burrowed the nest box into the river bank and then opened the cage. The mink quickly exited with their noses to the ground and soon found the river's edge. Without hesitation, the lithe animals entered the water, one by one, and began swimming fully submerged with only their noses and faces visible above the surface of the water. When the mink came out of the water, their nose led them to a burrow in the ground, where they disappeared. Moments later, we saw their black head poke out from the hole, as if to let us know that our job was done.

Every mink release was similar and equally rewarding. We would find a remote water source with good habitat and signs of prey, and watch as the freed animal explored their new home. After watching literally thousands of mink suffering on fur farms and seeing hundreds of thousands of their furs up for auction, finally seeing this one small group of animals returning to a natural existence was beyond satisfying. We were literally watching as these animals rediscovered the life that was intended for them.

And even if they only survived a few days, their lives of freedom, were surely better than a cruel death at the hands of man. I was also conflicted with the realization that once these animals were free, they faced the same threats other wild animals faced every day, from both humans and nature. There was simply no way to ensure their safety outside of our sanctuary. But a life in a cage is hardly a life at all for a mink, and I soon came to accept that true animal liberation would mean only that these mink themselves had any control over their destiny and that this was how it should be.

As the last of the snow melted, we continued releasing mink across the Olympic Peninsula and also in the Cascade Mountains of Washington. Each release was therapeutic for those of us who had seen mink on fur farms. And as we were left with fewer and fewer animals, we were able to increase the size of the remaining mink cages, until only a few animals remained.

By the first week in May, we began focusing on the release of the lynx. We knew the bobcats could survive in the footprint of human intrusion into the forests, but lynx are solitary animals that require large tracts of wilderness to survive. We opened a map of Washington state and picked the most remote and roadless area of the state, just south of the North Cascade National Park. We then located the nearest unpaved roads to the area and made that our destination.

At night, we placed live-trap cages against the lynx pens and lured them in with rabbit carcasses. The cages were then covered with tarps to keep the lynx sheltered from our view, and each cage was on wooden poles that protruded from each end for us to carry the animals deep into their new wilderness homes. Once the animals were loaded, I lit sage and sweetgrass to give our vehicles one last blessing before we re-entered the world.

As it happened, we missed our main ferry off the Peninsula and were forced to take a different one that delivered us to the middle of downtown Seattle. No one on the ferry knew that our vehicles were holding the elusively shy wildcats. I was nervous as hell that we'd be pulled over or somehow the animals would be discovered and confiscated. I simply could not let that happen. Thankfully, the ferry ride was uneventful, and as the sun rose, we found ourselves slowly climbing into the Cascade Mountains, ever closer to the home these animals deserved.

The national forest roads had only recently become accessible, following the snowmelt, and at our trailhead there were no other vehicles. We immediately began a six-mile hike into the wilderness with the animals. Not far along the trail, the passage had been washed out by recent storms, making the area even more remote—at least, until the trail could be repaired. We joked about what we would say if we encountered another hiker. How else could we possibly explain what we were doing with two lynx in cages? The hike was physically grueling but worth every step.

Finally we came to an area of the trail clogged with fallen trees and we decided to release the animals then and there. Unlike the mink, this time we would release the male and female together. These were genetically pure lynx, unchanged from the few generations of misery they had spent in cages.

We placed the cages next to each other, as four of the five of us stood in the distance, watching from a hidden vantage point. I stood between the cages with my heart leaping into my throat; I said an awkward prayer and goodbye before grabbing each cage door with my hands. I slid the plywood doors upward and open, and retreated to the hidden vantage point. The lynx remained in their cages, crouched towards the back for about 15 minutes. Then slowly the female began inching out, followed soon after by the male lynx. The two animals did not run but instead slowly melted into the wilderness, their fur providing the perfect camouflage in their native home. We waited a bit before retrieving the cages, and never saw the animals again. It had been less than six months since these lynxes were wasting away on a fur farm, and now, with a little help, they were back where they belonged.

Back at the trailhead, we collapsed for the night, exhausted. We had retrieved the animals' cages and broken them down so that we could easily carry them out, and left them next to us as we slept. In the middle of the night, I was awoken by the sound of growling. I opened my eyes but kept my body completely still, as the growling moved around our camp. I could hear the sound of clawing and tearing against wire and then realized that the cages covered in our lynx's scent had attracted another wild lynx that was now investigating these trespassing lynx smells. When the wild lynx finally departed, I discovered that everyone of us had been awakened, only like myself we each were too afraid to turn on a flashlight or say anything. This night-visitor had the power to instill a primal fear that we loved experiencing. Creatures as wild and free as lynx should instill a level of respect and fear when encountered; that is what it means to be wild and free from human domination. That is what has driven men for centuries in their vain attempt to conquer the wild that is represented by every wild and free-living animal.

One More Step

When we arrived back at the sanctuary, spring was quickly giving way to summer and the mink barn was empty. The only residents left were four bobcats that had been living isolated in the forest for over two months now. The first to be released would be the young females who were only slightly bigger than a large house cat. We didn't want to release the bobcats on the Olympic Peninsula because of the increased traffic in hikers with summer's approach, so we chose an area in the Cascade Mountains near Mt. St. Helens. The area was devastated by a volcano in 1981, but now, just ten years later, the forests were rebounding. There were also many old clearcuts in the area which we knew the bobcats would like.

We spent the night in a forest clearing and gave the young female bobcat one last free meal of a rabbit carcass. After this, she would have to fend for herself. In the morning, we cut away the tarp covering the bobcats' transport cage and let her get acclimatized to her new surroundings. I pulled open the door on her cage and walked away to watch from a distance. The cat slowly emerged from her cage and started walking away through the forest with her head turning in every direction, taking in all the new sights and smells of her new home. In less than a minute, she was gone, never to be seen again by us friends or any other fur farmer.

The remaining three bobcats would be next, with the last to be released being the oldest male. We had given this one bobcat the name Rufus, because he was the most accustomed to people and therefore the most likely to be drawn towards humans. For this reason, we knew we'd have to take Rufus deep into the wilderness where there was the least chance for a human conflict. We chose the Kalmiopsis Wilderness Area in southern Oregon because of our familiarity with that region. This would be the only release I did not take part in.

At the now-empty sanctuary, we loaded Rufus into a van with backpacks and gear for the humans that would be carrying him to his new home. By now we had a routine where the last thing to be done before our vehicles loaded with animals moved out, was to burn sage and sweetgrass to bless the animals on their journey towards a new life. As much as it was a relief to be so close to completing our project, I couldn't fend off a strong sense of helplessness as the last of these animals under our protection left that protection. We knew the bobcats would be vulnerable as they struggled to adapt to a new wild life, facing competition from other predators and threats by humans, but this was the life that was intended for them. As the van pulled out of Linda's dirt driveway, I cried as it disappeared, but was quickly comforted by Linda. She grabbed me by the shoulders, saying, "You've given these animals the freedom they deserve, and now it's up to them. We've prepared them the best we could. They've learned to hunt, they've learned a new life, and now they are back where they belong. That couldn't have been possible without all of our love and help. Now they are truly free."

Except for Linda, I was now left alone at the sanctuary. I walked amongst the empty rows of mink pens that were now silent. I had completed part of a promise I had made to the mink whose necks I had witnessed being broken. I had given their relatives the life they deserved. Now it was time for me to complete the other part of that promise, which was to attack the industry that had been created to destroy these indigenous relations of mine. No one else knew the vulnerabilities of the fur farm industry like I did. I knew the industry was in a struggle for its own life and I wanted to help push it over the edge. We were no longer assisting the wounded from the battle; it was now time to return to the war.

I said goodbye to Linda a few hours after Rufus left and, with my Subaru loaded, drove off the Peninsula and onto Interstate 5 south. My next stop was Corvallis, Oregon, home to the nation's oldest dedicated experimental fur farm on the Oregon State University campus.

Fraser Fur Farm

Bobcat at Fraser Fur Farm

Memories of Freedom

Jefferson Fur Farm

Seattle Fur Exchange

CHAPTER 7

GOING FOR THE THROAT:
OPERATION BITE BACK

Oregon State University's Experimental Fur Farm

In the dark new moon of May 1991, I found myself on the roof of a shed at Oregon State University's Experimental Fur Farm. I gazed over five rows of mink cages at the main laboratory that had provided aid to fur farmers since the 1920s when it was first created. I had driven all day, and when I arrived in Corvallis, I ate dinner and waited for it to get dark. We had discovered the location of an experimental poultry farm on the rural campus some months before, and I learned that the fur farm was nearby. Here was the nation's oldest fur farm research station, and it was now primarily focused on lowering fur farmer costs in an ever-declining market. I had also learned while I was at the Seattle Fur Exchange Auction that the Northwest Fur-Breeders Cooperative in Edmonds, Washington, donated feed for the station's 1,000 experimental mink population.

As I continued my surveillance, and after an hour passed without any sign of a security patrol, I climbed from my perch and walked towards a five-foot fence that surrounded the mink barns at the station. I walked the length of the fence until I came to an unlocked gate. As I opened it, I heard a rustling noise and noticed a loose mink that was just a few feet away from me, against the inside of the fence. I held the gate open and stood back, and after a few seconds the mink ran past me and, after crossing the threshold to freedom, bolted in a sprint in the direction of Oak Creek which ran behind the farm.

I had seen loose mink on a mink farm before, which is why they always used a guard fence to keep strays from truly escaping. I was sure the farmers had already written off the now-free mink and it would not trigger a security concern. This was still before any fur farms had ever been raided by the ALF outside of the UK and Europe, where they had already been targeted. Fur shops were often targets, trappers were always dealing with trap sabotage, but fur farmers were still off the animal abuse radar as far as the public was concerned in the US.

After watching the mink rustling away towards a new life, I started thinking about how to save future generations of mink from ever experiencing the misery of a fur farm. In all honesty, I had already begun thinking such things upon my return from the fur auction. Now I was again in a position to strike, only this time I knew all roads of ensuing investigations would invariably lead back to me. I was already known as an ALF member because of the Canada arrests in 1987; if I was to use the information I had gathered in my undercover investigation for Friends of Animals to carry out more ALF raids on vulnerable targets, I knew I would eventually be caught.

Then as now, I thought about all those mink, bobcats, lynx, and fox that I had seen on fur farms, especially those whose cruel deaths I had personally witnessed, and thought, "What's the worst that can happen to me?" No one was going to wring *my* neck; *I* wouldn't get the gas chambers; death was hardly certain, as it was for all animals on fur farms.

As I pondered this, the warm night air carried the sound of hundreds of paws scratching at wire with the occasional shriek from prisoners inside their cages. I had made a promise to the mink on Campbell's fur farm. I promised them that their deaths would not be in vain. I promised that I would do everything within my power to destroy the industry which had destroyed them. Now it was my time to keep that promise and I was ready to strike.

I began inspecting the perimeter of the laboratory and quickly found a small bathroom window. By standing on the fence, I could now see that the window was slightly open. I slid it completely open and hoisted my body into the bathroom, then slowly lowered my feet onto the seat of the toilet. The building was old. I saw no signs of electronic surveillance or alarms, so I decided to continue exploring without my own outside security watch.

It soon became abundantly clear that this was the building that housed the archives of research records from the last 70 years of fur farm research, as well as laboratory equipment for the research performed at this essential station. The offices of the head researcher, Ron Scott, also adjoined the lab. This was still the "analog" era and only a few computers were onsite. Most of the data was hardcopy. A fire here would do the trick. My only worry was whether any fire we started would endanger the imprisoned mink just outside.

The goal was simple: destroy as much irreplaceable research and equipment as possible without detection. When I left the laboratory, I continued searching the farm campus and located a wooden barn by the creek containing all the experimental feed and mixing equipment for the station; it also stood a safe distance, and downwind, from where any animals were caged. I decided this would be one of two targets of the first raid on a fur farm research station by what we would begin calling the Western Wildlife Unit of the Animal Liberation Front, or WWU-ALF.

Preliminary investigations had already proven that experimental feeds and mink diet were the backbone of all fur farm research currently in progress at OSU. This experimental feed being developed would ensure optimum pelt quality and yet remain economically feasible for farmers struggling with lower pelt prices at auction. We also knew that the already high cost of this feed was being covered by the Northwest Fur Breeders Cooperative, and without this donation, the research station would have to cut into its research budget to pay for the feed. Drawing back from the station that night, I felt elated, not sad, knowing that our next nighttime visit to this farm would hopefully be the last—and one that the mink researchers would never forget.

I drove back north to Portland to the home of a recent Earth First! friend I had met. Diana lived in the Burnside District; she had come up to the sanctuary and helped with a couple releases, and during that time, we got to talking about a lot of things; I knew I could trust her.

I didn't want to approach the usual suspects amongst my list of West Coast ALF and EF! contacts; the FBI was breathing down a lot of activist's necks as they searched for my friends and I who had begun torching farms and labs in California and Arizona. For this campaign, I needed warriors who were not on the FBI's radar, so I began approaching folks I had met after leaving the San Francisco Bay Area.

I told Diana about what I had discovered through my research, and then showed her a slide I took from the lab depicting a dead mink. We both talked about how the focus of fur farmers was often on controlling the breeding cycle through light and diet. Researchers were mimicking nature in an attempt to control when female mink breed, all without compromising fur quality. Diana was in. Together, she and I would traverse Oregon recruiting members for the WWU.

The following days were spent choosing the warriors, as well as a night for the raid that would offer adequate darkness and minimal activity, both on the premises and on the neighboring campus and houses. In late May 1991, I received word that state charges against three ALF activists accused of a raid on University of Oregon labs in 1986 were being dropped, so we decided, "What better way to celebrate this victory, than with another ALF raid in Oregon!"

Time To Act

When the sun set on June 10, 1991, five newly-recruited warrior friends and I gathered around a campfire on national forest lands just outside of

Corvallis, awaiting our time to act. We checked battery power on radios, reviewed hand-drawn and topographical maps, and covered up in bright college attire to hide the dark clothes we wore beneath the disguises. I felt a joy in the air that rarely inhabits our ranks as we readied ourselves for a night that we hoped would bring long-awaited justice to the nation's largest fur farm research station.

Packs were organized with the assorted equipment necessary for each individual member, and cash was also distributed to each warrior who would be on foot in case of separation, as well as maps with predetermined routes out of the area. We went over plans should we need to retreat and discussed each of our roles; only when everyone was crystal clear about their responsibilities did I feel that this new group of warriors was ready for the raid.

With the growing darkness as our greatest ally, we gathered for a last vocal moment and each of us expressed our reasons for being there that night. We spoke of what we hoped to achieve for our mink relations. These were all new friends who had proven themselves to me in many ways how much they were dedicated to the defense of animals and the Earth. I have been so blessed to find such beautiful human beings in my life, who have earned my love and respect as I witnessed their strength and commitment to animals and the Earth. At this moment, because of what I had learned about the vulnerabilities of the fur farm industry, I was grateful for such a group of warriors. As we piled into our separate vehicles, I was proud of this small handful of people who were about to risk all for our Mother Earth and her creatures.

Within the hour, we arrived in Corvallis and broke into separate groups. A driver would stay with a vehicle, ready to receive stolen records we intended to review before destroying. I dropped off two people to begin approaching the station from a nearby school yard. Once I parked my trusty Subaru, I hopped on my mountain bike and caught up with the rest of the crew.

When we found each other, one of the new recruits confessed that while he was walking across the darkened lawn of the school, a neighbor had turned a flashlight on his face, demanding to know what he was doing. He said he was heading home from a local bar, which apparently was convincing enough. Even so, I asked him whether he felt like his security had been compromised. At the time, he sported long hair and a beard, which he said he would rather cut and shave than call off the raid.

We decided to continue with the raid and descended into the nearby creek that led to the station. Without a spoken word, using only hand signals, we deployed ourselves to our various lookout positions, and hearing no radio warning, we began our night's work. Diana and I entered the laboratory the same way I had that first night. The bathroom window remained open and unlocked.

I moved into Ron Scott's office, where we used cut-up garbage bags to cover the window so we could work with some light without drawing the attention of the groundskeepers' house, which was about 75 yards from the lab. I filmed Diana stuffing records into duffel bags before putting the camera away and helping rifle through desks and filing cabinets, taking all the material we could from the on-going feed experiments. While we were in the offices and laboratory, my soon-to-be short-haired friend walked up and down each row of mink cages, removing every single breeding identification card from the cages to confuse the researchers, as there was no other way to identify the animals. Research photos, slides, and documents were loaded into backpacks along with the vivisectors' phone books, address books, and other material that would reveal supporters and financiers of the station's dirty work. After this, every single file, research paper, and archive in the station was spilled onto the floor and every available liquid poured onto them; eventually, a water line from the bathroom was broken that would soon flood the entire floor.

Once the records were either taken off site or moved into the barn for burning, I then focused on the most expensive laboratory equipment I could find. To avoid noise, I carried some computers and electronic scales into a walk-in refrigerator where I could smash them on the floor more quietly, while Diana smashed microscopes and test tube samples stored in the refrigerator. Veterinary medicines that might come in handy for rescues in the future were loaded into a fanny pack and sent out with the rest of the records. Lastly, the red spray-paint came out, and we left the WWU's calling card along with some suggested advice to mink vivisectionists—that, and the telltale 'ALF.' Exiting the research building the same way we entered, our forces began their withdrawal as I took on the role of demolitions; and with one watch-person, I stayed behind as everyone else headed to our pre-arranged rendezvous point over an hour away.

With a one-hour delay incendiary device tucked in a Tupperware container in my backpack, I entered the experimental feed barn, using the official "ALF key" (bolt-cutters) to cut the clasp on the padlock. The barn was full—not just of feed but also hundreds of mink nesting boxes in various stages of construction. But the most valuable piece of machinery was an industrial feed mixer that would surely be destroyed by the ensuing fire. Placing the device near the structural center of the building, I began piling wooden nestboxes around the device with other kindling. I called over the radio and got an all-clear, which meant I could now set the device. With the one-hour timer ticking, I pulled on my ski-mask and fled the crime scene. We hated leaving the mink behind. But we knew this was just the beginning. Back in the laboratory, Diana couldn't help but spray-paint on the wall of Ron Scott's office, "WE WILL BE BACK FOR THE KITS!"

Within minutes after I had set the incendiary device, all our drivers and lookouts had regrouped, carrying plastic trash bags containing all tools and evidence of our presence. In a few more minutes, with mountain bikes loaded and all confiscated research documents and photos in a safe car, we drove at the speed limit across county lines to the nearby interstate highway, where all clothes worn during the action were distributed in various dumpsters. Shoes worn during the action also were thrown away and all tools, although new, were deposited in the nearest river.

At about this same time, fire erupted in the experimental feed barn, demolishing the feed supply and all equipment in the barn, as well as the barn itself. Over 1,100 mink watched from their cages as the barn burned to the ground, and fur farm researchers groggily arrived to survey the smoldering damage. Within minutes, television cameras were on the scene, as federal and local authorities began wading through 70 years of fur farm research, all now down the drain.

After the raid, we rented a hotel room where we could go through the confiscated records to determine which were worth keeping, and which would be burned. We also needed to make VHS tape copies of our burglary of Ron Scott's office, which we would drop off at Portland TV stations along with our press release that ended with the statement, "…until the last fur farm is burned to the ground."

The attack left morale among the Northwest's fur farmers at an all-time low. Thanks to the global anti-fur movement, fur prices had already collapsed. Now fur farmers had to wrestle with the uncomfortable revelation that not only had virtually every research project at OSU's Fur Animal Research Station been destroyed, but also every name, phone number, and address of farms in the northwest was now in the hands of the WWU-ALF. Through media reports, we also received confirmation that we had seized genetic logbooks along with vital research records necessary for the continuation of research, crippling future experimental efforts with the remaining imprisoned 1,100 mink.

The blow was too much for the tight-budgeted research lab to endure. When 1991 ended and OSU's mink herd was killed, the Oregon State University animal research department decided to cut funds to the experimental fur farm. Within six months, the OSU Experimental Fur Animal

Research Station closed its doors forever. In our first strike against the fur farm industry—in what we were now calling "Operation Bite Back"—and less than six months since our fiery raid, the nation's largest fur farm research facility was effectively destroyed.

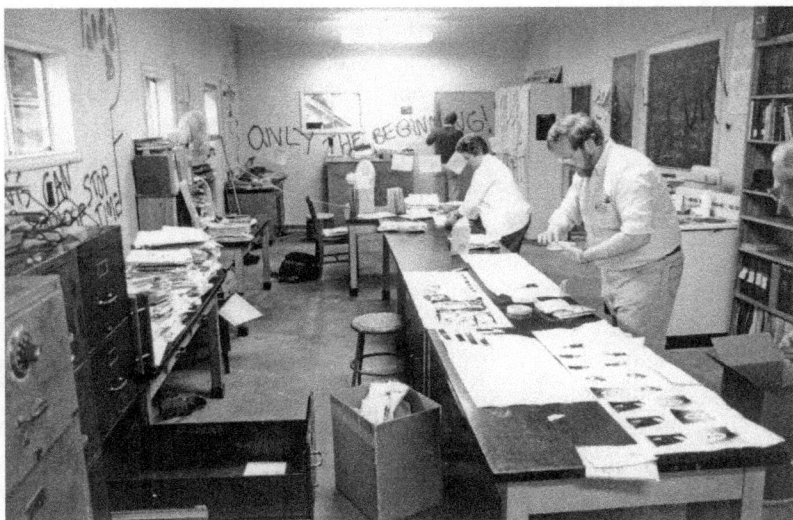

Cleaning up after the raid

Biting the Hand That Feeds You: Northwest Fur-Breeders Co-op

While the other members of our group returned to their hometowns and normal lives, Diana and I began the task of cataloging the data we had seized from the experimental fur farm. We had already identified the importance of the Mink Farmers Research Foundation from my infiltration of the Seattle Fur Exchange; now we were able to see what experiments were being conducted at which laboratories. It also became glaringly obvious from the lab records how important the Northwest Fur Breeders Cooperative was to fur farmers in Oregon, Washington, Idaho, and Utah. Not only was the co-op donating feed for OSU's experimental fur farm, they were also the main conduit for experimental feeds developed for western fur farms.

Although there were once 60 fur farms in Snohomish County, in 1991 only 20 remained—but still constituting the largest concentration of fur farms on the West Coast. The farms were "producing" between 125,000 and 150,000 mink pelts a year, which sold at an average price of around $30. Since 1947, the fur breeder's co-op supplied feed and other needed supplies to most fur farms this side of Montana. While fur farmers were once the primary customer for the inedible chicken and fish that the co-op processed into feed, the pet food industry was slowly becoming an equal consumer—so much so that the co-op had recently changed its name from the "Northwest Fur-Breeders Co-op," to the "Northwest Farm Food Co-op," which was much more sanitized.

Over beers at a Burnside pub in Portland, Diana and I discussed the possibility of an attack on the Co-op. I had been inside the offices a few times buying feed for our rehabilitation project and remembered how lax security appeared to be. Why wouldn't it be? Who would want to break into a fish and chicken feed manufacturer anyhow? Already the fur farm industry front group, Fur Farm Animal Welfare Coalition, was moving into a defensive strategy with its media response to the OSU raid; surely the Co-op would soon be on the defensive with more security, if it wasn't already. We finished our pints and rode our bikes back to Diana's place, where we quietly loaded gear into my Subaru for a drive the next day to Edmonds, Washington.

This was the waterfront home of the Northwest Fur-Breeders Cooperative. Located on the docks of Edmonds, the NW Co-op serves as a local feed manufacturer, processing tons of factory-farm chicken and fish by-products, and churning it into the food that keeps northwest fur farms operational and profitable. Operating as a hub, the Co-op weekly sends out diesel tractor-trailers to its member farms, distributing feed, nesting materials, and other equipment.

On the night of June 15, Diana and I stood above the docks of Edmonds, watching the co-op's 11:00 pm shift end its business for the night. A nearby restaurant was still open, but the rest of the dock was dark and empty, as I remembered it from earlier visits. We had been watching the building for over an hour without the notice of any dedicated security patrol. We parked nearby where Diana could watch from the Subaru while I entered the building. In my pack was a radio with an earphone extension so I could listen to any warning of a police response to my planned break-in. Diana also had the police scanner that we used in the OSU raid, and through earlier reconnaissance, we became familiar with the 'normal' radio traffic and knew the codes used by the police responding to calls.

I walked casually along the docks like I was a Co-op worker leaving the night shift, while stopping intermittently to survey the scene that lay before me. When I passed into the shadows behind the Co-op, I quickly darted behind two tractor-trailers parked against the building while the trailer's refrigeration units buzzed loudly over the surrounding sounds of the docks. The smell of fish entrails permeated the air as I donned a pair of disposable coveralls that I would use to crawl through the small feed conveyer belt entry into the building.

I had located the access window for feed products in my earlier visits and I now crawled into it, carefully lifting my pack with an incendiary device into the building. With continued radio silence signaling the all-clear, I began surveying the empty building to ensure that no late-night employees or watchmen remained before attempting to set the incendiary device. Upon confirmation of an empty building, I entered the warehouse portion of the building where feed, nesting, and pelting materials were stacked to the ceiling on wooden forklift pallets. Opening a ceiling vent to allow a little air circulation to fuel the fire, I set to work assembling the incendiary device around pallets of flammable shipping materials. When the device was set, I left the warehouse and entered the office where I had earlier bought feed for the bobcats and lynx in our rehabilitation project. I pulled out a can of red spray-paint and left the ALF calling card, accompanied with a mink paw encircled within the female symbol for the mink mothers at OSU, whose young the ALF were unable to rescue.

An unexpected police patrol circled the restaurant and Co-op parking lot, but never stopped. When I received the call that everything appeared normal, I exited quickly and quietly through the crawlspace I had entered. I walked back to the car, stripped off my coveralls, and climbed inside as Diana drove off towards Interstate 5 where we would make our escape south, back to Portland.

Within 90 minutes, and just after 2 am, a total of 70 firefighters from five districts responded to the four-alarm blaze that injured no one, but effectively destroyed 75% of the NW fur breeder's warehouse, causing an estimated $750,000 in damages. It would take four hours to extinguish the fire, which would flare up again the next day, causing additional damage. The operations manager for the Co-op reported that the fire destroyed 20,000 pounds of mink bedding, 10,000 pounds of ground corn cob used in pelt processing, and mink feed. We delivered a press release to the Associated Press which stated in part that we had started the fire "with the hopes of causing maximum economic damage to an industry that profits from the misery and exploitation of fur animals."

Following the OSU and then the Northwest fur-breeders raids just a few days later, the fur farm industry went ballistic. A $35,000 reward was offered for the capture and conviction of ALF warriors, and fur farmers announced in the media that they were now arming themselves against further attacks. Local police were confused, saying, "We've had no indication, prior to this, of any problems. There's been no picketing, no literature down here with fur breeders, so it's really unexpected." Both the FBI and Bureau of Alcohol, Tobacco and Firearms (ATF) were called in to investigate the arson, now that it was confirmed that our actions were part of a multi-state conspiracy to commit arson against fur industry targets.

Meanwhile, the fur farm industry had the rude awakening that their worst fears expressed in confidence to myself and "other" fur farmers at the Seattle Fur Exchange, were now coming true. The vice-president of the Northwest Fur-breeders Association was quoted saying that the OSU arson should have set off warning bells in the industry, "We should have gotten a security man here after the (OSU) raid. That was definitely an oversight on our part. Obviously, anyone with a (fur) farm in the area is going to be concerned, and we're going to have to start watching our backs." The second phase of Operation Bite Back was now complete. The American fur farm industry was now officially under attack, and they knew it.

The fur farm industry mouthpiece group, Fur Farm Animal Welfare Coalition, held a press conference in Seattle asking animal rights groups to denounce the ALF. Granted, none publicly did at this time, but neither did any come forward to support the ALF. The group also began warning other Washington state fur farmers to be on guard for further attacks; at the time, the state was the fifth largest fur-producing state in the nation.

And so the summer of 1991 began with my new cell of the ALF back in action. Training continued, and confiscated research papers and fur farm trade journals were reviewed to determine how best to break the next link in fur farm animal abuse. Diana and I began following up on leads of other potential targets with other new recruits, and searched veterinary medicine files for possible future actions.

WSU fears sabotage of research on furry animals

An otter basks in the sun at the WSU fur research facility, while Professor Fred Gilbert sits on the other side of the pool.

In July 1991, an article appeared in a Spokane, Washington newspaper, describing the impact that recent ALF raids had had on Washington State University's fur animal research program. As we had recently learned, WSU's lead vivisector John Gorham was working to remedy the 'confinement diseases' suffered by mink on the farms. Within days, we were on our way to WSU in Pullman, Washington, to ascertain whether a raid might be possible.

The Night of Stars Falling: Washington State University

After both the OSU and Fur-Breeders raid, Diana and I hit the road and headed east to visit friends in Montana who worked on the *Earth First! Journal*. I wanted to get out of Oregon, where federal authorities were sifting through the ashes and beginning subsequent investigations into the animal rights movement. I also wanted to make sure our actions were accurately represented in the radical environmental newspaper.

While in Montana, I also disappeared for a day and drove south into the Bitterroot Valley to spy on the Rocky Mountain Fur Company that I had visited the previous summer. The mink and fox farm was on my short list of potential next targets. Although friends had heard about both the ALF raids and our fur farm rehabilitation project, no one was connecting the dots or asking suspicious questions about my own involvement. Folks were enraptured with their own lives and political issues, and the hand of law enforcement investigating the ALF had yet to show itself in Montana.

At the Rocky Mountain Fur Company, I followed the river that ran behind the farm and, in the remaining daylight, came to the far edge of the farm's many rows of mink cages. Except for OSU's experimental fur farm, it had been over half a year since I'd been on a mink farm. The only mink I had seen since were the 59 we rehabilitated and released. I had grown intimately familiar with "our" mink and seen firsthand how well they transitioned to their intended wild life. Watching them swim, play, and hunt was hard evidence of their capacity to recover from the trauma of fur farm misery. Now, I was seeing again what had drove me to attack the mink industry. The ammonia smell of the animals' waste lingered over the incessant sound of mink scratching against the wire and plastic of their 10-inch-wide cages.

On the boundary of the fur farm, I came to a small mountain of skeletal remains of literally thousands of dead mink. This was the dumping grounds for the carcasses that were left to rot behind this concentration camp for animals. It was a brutal juxtaposition before my eyes. The beautiful Bitterroot River weaved past the farm with huge mountains on either side of the valley, filled with birdsong and natural life. This was the home world that these mink would never experience for themselves. Never would they swim in the rivers waters or feel the soft earth beneath their feet. As I retreated quietly from my lookout post, I vowed to return to attempt a raid that would target the pelt-processing building of the farm, which was far enough removed from the farm itself to be a target for destruction by fire.

After departing Montana, we headed back west as we busied ourselves researching all that we could about Gorham's research. We knew that this was also the time to begin reconnaissance missions on the Washington State University campus that spread out across the rolling hills of Pullman. Fortunately, I knew someone who lived in Pullman: Rik Scarce, an author who had interviewed me for the book, *Eco-Warriors: Understanding the Radical Environmental Movement*. Rik and I became friends, so it wasn't unusual to now call him up and let him know we'd be passing through town. Because we wanted to spend all our free time combing the campus looking for the experimental fur farm, we refused Rik's invitation to stay at his home and instead rented a motel in nearby Moscow, Idaho.

Like most of southeastern Washington, the Pullman area is a grass-covered plain devoid of trees, having been mostly deforested by the timber industry. We already knew that the location of the USDA's Experimental Fur Farm at WSU was hidden from the public, but how difficult could it be to find unmistakable mink barns?

Our first step was the tried-and-true tactic of riding mountain bikes like casual bicyclists on every road, trail, and path that crisscrossed the WSU campus. All the while, we checked outlying buildings and kept our noses to the wind for the easily recognizable scent of mink musk.

While searching for the fur farm, we discovered that WSU was a nerve center of animal research on native American wildlife. Grizzly and black bears, mule deer, elk, and bighorn sheep were just a few of the many animals we soon discovered wallowing in the misery of concrete pens and corrals on the sprawling rural campus. Serving as prostitutes to the livestock industry, WSU vivisectors were busying themselves in studying bacterial and competitive grazing threats that native wildlife posed to cattle and sheep on public lands. Never before had the ALF discovered vivisection on America's wildlife outside of OSU's mink farm, and now we strategized about the logistics of ways to transport these larger once-wild animals. Unfortunately, our limited resources and a shortage of warriors would prohibit us from spiriting away bears or deer, so our focus remained on the mink.

The newspaper article we had received also discussed a fur-bearer research facility on campus, where vivisector Fred Gilbert tested underwater traps on beavers. His lab also housed wolverine, fishers, badgers, and martens. We would attempt to locate Gilbert's laboratory and liberate the wildlife prisoners there, if at all possible. Gilbert's research was funded by the Canadian fur industry, as well as the Mink Farmers Research Foundation, and even the USDA. It was the result of the 1990 ban on the importation of furs into the European Union because of the cruelty associated with trapping methods. Out of the ban came the development of "Best Management Practices" for trapping, which became a system for testing every type of animal trap manufactured in the world, to determine if it was capable of "humanely" restraining or killing the targeted animal. Gilbert's experiments were focused on body-gripping traps intended to *kill* their victim's, unlike foothold traps which are intended to simply hold the animal until the trapper returns. Gilbert's experiments used drowning tanks where mink, otter, and beaver were monitored as they struggled in the steel jaws of body-gripping traps. His research determined that beavers took up to 13 minutes to die in the traps.

John Gorham's research targeted Aleutian disease, encephalopathy (known in cattle as Mad Cow disease), and other diseases that could economically wipe out a fur farmer, should their mink become affected. To conduct his research, Gorham would grind up infected mink brains and force-feed them to healthy mink until they contracted the chosen disease. Animals in his laboratory often died slow deaths as the paralysis of their disease slowly developed in their bodies, causing nervous disorders and hemorrhaging. To fur farmers across the world, Gorham was "one of the world's leading researchers in fur farm diseases," according to a 1991 article in *Fur Rancher Magazine*.

On a hot July afternoon, I stood with binoculars staring at a long building on Airport Way, the main road to the regional airport. The building was unmarked, yet cages could be clearly seen behind an eight-foot-high chain link fence. We would need to return at night to confirm our suspicions that we had found the hidden experimental fur farm.

In the early evening of a full moon before the lunar rising, Diana and I drove to a dead-end dirt road about a mile from the target and hiked to the suspected fur farm. We walked the perimeter, until we determined that no infrared or motion detector alarms surrounded the facility. Being a potentially federally-funded research station, we expected as much. There wasn't any electronic security, so we scaled the chain-link fence topped with barbed-wire to reach the suspected mink barns. Sure enough, through the night air we could hear the unmistakable sound of mink scratching at their cages.

I lifted the latch on the unlocked gate that led into the mink barn and began surveying the area; I soon located a control group mink who had not been infected with any disease, alongside those who had. Once familiarized with the layout of the facility, and having determined that no watchmen or watchdogs were around, we began to pull back to the chain-link fence. Hearing a car approaching from a distance, we quickly climbed the fence—when Diana got snagged by the barbed-wire on top of the fence. As the headlights of the oncoming car became visible, Diana wrestled with her pant leg, finally freeing herself. She jumped from the fence and sprinted across the road to cover, just as the car approached and passed by, as we lay hidden on the roadside. It was a university police car.

I climbed out from the roadside ditch in the pre-moon darkness and noticed that the headlight beams of the police car had made a 360-degree turn and then went out. We walked onto the shoulder of the road and instantly became suspicious. Pulling out a pair of binoculars, I looked into the distance down the darkened road; and straight ahead, I could make out the outline of a car parked on the shoulder with its lights off. Quickly, the two of us darted into the surrounding bare hillside, just as another police cruiser came speeding from the opposite direction on the same road. The first cruiser gunned its engine and turned on its headlights in an attempt to sandwich us in—the first car having certainly by now seen us crossing the road away from the farm. As we scrambled into the knee-high grass, the two police cars came together at the fur farm and shined spotlights into the facility, and then later, into the surrounding hillsides where we were hidden. This research facility was obviously expecting a visit from the ALF.

As we lay on our bellies in the sparse hills surrounding the farm, the moon began to rise clear and bright, illuminating the entire area with bright revealing light. One police cruiser was inching along with its lights off, just feet away from where we now were. The other patrol car parked on a ridge overlooking the entire fur farm compound. We remained motionless just as a group of coyotes began to howl, as the moon lifted herself into the sky. Something sounded out of place though, as most of the coyote cries were concentrated, and coming from the direction of another small building above the fur farm. Still other coyotes could be heard howling from the distant hills. It became plainly evident that coyotes were being held captive in one of the buildings we had yet to discover. With little to do but wait it out, we cursed our luck for being trapped under the moon's bright light, but were grateful to have the imprisoned coyotes revealed to us. Finally the police cruiser gave up the hunt and drove away, and we hiked the long way back to our hidden car.

The element of a surprise attack was gone. Not only did WSU's animal researchers have the raids at OSU and the NW Co-op as warnings, but now university police had spotted trespassers near the hidden fur farm. Within days, security was increased. And when Gilbert's lab was finally located, nestled in a grove of pine trees, we saw that an infrared perimeter security system was in place. The beaver sheds were clearly visible just beyond it. Despite the increased security, cautious reconnaissance continued.

The next day, with binoculars, we located the kennel on a hill containing the 12 coyotes we had heard the night before; all were the subjects of sarcocystis research. Sarcocystis is a disease that is not fatal to coyotes or sheep; the disease passes through a coyote's system in a few short weeks, while the parasites contain themselves within the sheep, destroying the economic value of their meat and wool. Coyotes commonly spread the parasite in their feces, where it's transmitted to sheep grazing on lands everywhere in coyote country. The coyotes for these experiments were conveniently provided by the USDA's Animal Damage Control Program— survivors of aerial gunning and gassed-out dens where their families had perished.

We called a strategy session to discuss the future of any actions at WSU's fur research stations. We had located our target, but in the process, we also identified other new potential targets. We decided that, in order for any attack to be successful, we would need more than just two people. Other warriors with various degrees of experience would be needed if we hoped to strike the fur farm, Fred Gilbert's lab, and now the coyote pen as well. By mid-August, only one additional ALF warrior confirmed their willingness to risk an attack on the already highly-guarded WSU research facility. We soon learned that Gorham had been chosen as the USDA's 'Researcher of the Year' for 1991, and would be out of town the week of August 21 to receive his award. That would be the time to act, both strategically and psychologically. The raid would be a four-pronged attack. We would first enter the Veterinary Building on WSU's downtown Pullman campus where Gorham's office was located, then strike the fur farm, Gilbert's lab, and finally release the coyotes from their hilltop kennel.

On a subsequent night recon of the coyote pens, I was shocked to discover that the building was almost without any security except for a small padlock on the kennel building, which I was able to easily get around without any signs of forced entry. When I entered the kennel, the coyotes were all very skittish and withdrew to the back of their cages. In the shadows, I could make out the frightened creatures with their tails tucked between their legs.

A Night for Action

As the sun set on August 12, 1991, in a motel room miles from Pullman, the three of us gathered around maps, while scanning local police frequencies to get familiar with the normal radio traffic in the quiet rural area. Earlier that day, I drove to nearby Lewiston, Idaho to rent a small truck to transport any rescued animals. In my pack that night were heavy gloves to handle the mink, forced-entry tools for the Veterinary Building, bottles of acid, bolt-cutters, and red spray paint for the coyote pens. The acid was an alternative to fire and would be poured over hardcopies of any research records we uncovered in Gorham's office.

We agreed on a means of communication for necessary radio transmissions, and pick-up points and times were finalized. We had already been driving through the area for weeks, pointing out spots near the road where warriors could be dropped off and animals picked up. This time, there was no full moon, but there would be the annual Perseid meteor shower, according to weather forecasters. When we settled on the final emergency contingency plan—should the police become alerted to our raid—we drove away into the night toward the distant glow of lights that was Washington State University.

Diana parked outside of the Veterinary Building as a security lookout, just as the last late-night student exited the bottom level of the building and drove away. Using the same technique as I had at the University of Arizona, I approached the door the student had just exited. Earlier that day, I had entered the building while it was unlocked and removed the door clasp, replacing it with two shorter screws that could be easily dislodged with a little force to detach the lock-plate that held the pin of the door lock in place. With a quick pull, I dislodged the clasp, collected it from the ground, and began climbing the stairwell to the third floor where Gorham's office was located.

I entered the fully lit hallway and walked to the door of Gorham's office. I slid a nearby file cabinet over as a step and climbed on top to reach above my head to remove a ceiling tile in the hallway just outside the office. In the ceiling crawlspace, only thin sheetrock separated the hallway from Gorham's office on the other side of the wall partition. Using a small keyhole saw, I cut a hole big enough to climb through and punched into the dark office of another one of "the world's leading fur farm researchers."

I lowered my pack first into the dark office, then climbed onto Gorham's desk. I took a quick survey of his files and began dumping research papers, computer discs, photo slides, and other important papers onto the floor. I grabbed address books and other fur-related intelligence. Everything else was smashed or tossed onto the floor. I saw a brand new computer that lay beside the desk, still in its box. Lifting the computer over my head, I smashed it to the ground, and proceeded to do the same to every piece of research and computer equipment in the room—the ALF version of therapy.

Looking out the window, I saw Diana in her lookout position, but without any communication over the radio coming from her, I knew we still had the "all clear." I pulled a can of red spray paint from my pack and began spraying the message, "John Gorham, this is what happens..." when the paint clogged and sputtered to a stop. Tossing the can onto the paper-covered floor, I then pulled from my pack a one-gallon container of muriatic acid and poured it over the complete mess until fumes forced me out of the office.

As I exited down the hallway, I passed a gurney with a Plexiglas box filled with white mice. It was labeled "irradiated 8/21/91." I scooped up the box and, holding it under my arm, fled the building, completing phase one of the WSU attack. Dropping off the mice with Diana, I then hopped on my mountain bike and began pedaling madly off campus towards the remote experimental mink farm on Airport Way.

Dumping my bike some distance from the mink barns, I quickly vaulted the chain-link fence and approached the building adjoining the mink barn. On the warm evening, I could see an open window, and as I approached, could soon hear the telltale sound of a man snoring. We knew security would be increased, but if the sleeping watchman was all that had changed, I felt confident in proceeding with the planned rescue of six mink. Earlier recon had revealed someone walking through the barn as late as 11 p.m., to check on the mink. Feeling confident that there would be no additional security patrols because of the presence of the sleeping watchman, I continued by taking an empty shipping cage for mink that had been recently sent to the facility. I cut the small lock on the mink barn with bolt cutters, and entered with my empty cage. I placed the cage against the nest-boxes containing live mink and, with my free gloved hand, used a piece of plastic to encourage the mink out of the box and into the cage.

Within just a few minutes, I had six inquisitive mink loaded and ready to go. When I left the mink barn, I replaced the cut lock with a similar duplicate; if the watchman decided to conduct a visual inspection later that night, he would see nothing out of place. I brought the mink to the side of the darkened road and called over the radio for pickup. After Diana had received the mink, I got back on my bike and began riding down the dirt road that led to Fred Gilbert's fur animal research facility.

I had earlier discovered infrared security measures in place, which meant I must enter over the electronic beam and not through it. Taking a ladder from a nearby barn, I leaned the ladder against the top of some chain link cages and climbed onto the roof of the facility and over the infrared beam without breaking it. I had one objective at Gilbert's laboratory: I wanted to locate and seize the videotapes that recorded his drowning experiments. The tapes had become the subject of a public records request by a news outlet investigating his controversial experiments on behalf of the fur industry, and I knew if we could release those tapes to the media, his research would only fall deeper into question. I came to a locked window that I knew had to be broken; but time was of the essence and I knew breaking into the building might trigger other unknown security measures. With great regret, I decided to come back to Gilbert's lab after I had released the coyotes—something that I knew I could do with minimal risk and something I would deeply regret not having done if I triggered an alarm at Gilbert's lab.

Coyotes Free Again

When I reached the hilltop coyote kennel, I took my bolt cutters and began clearing low fencing surrounding the kennel in order to provide a better escape route for the coyotes. I then walked up to the kennel and cut the lock on the chain-link gate, and entered. Moving down the row of cages, the coyotes became anxious and excited. One by one, I cut the locks on the cage doors and swung the doors opened. Each coyote leapt out of the kennel and quickly disappeared into the darkness. The only sound of their liberation was the sound of the grass as they ran through it towards freedom.

While most of the coyotes fled the kennel area immediately, others could be heard in the distance, howling from the dark shadows of the wild, just as we had heard them before. Meanwhile, one coyote hung back in the kennel and was attempting to sneak past me back towards the last cage in the kennel that I had somehow missed. Frustrated that the liberated animal was not fleeing, I reached out quickly in an attempt to grab the coyote by the scruff of his neck. When my gloved hands touched fur, the coyote turned his head and bit me on the arm. That's when I began understanding why this coyote would not leave. Huddled in fear in the furthest corner of the last cage, I could then make out another coyote which was listed as a young female. I took my bolt cutters and cut the last remaining lock, and threw her cage door open as the male stood only feet away from me, waiting.

The female ran towards him and when she reached him, they briefly touched noses before bolting off together into the darkness, as stars began shooting across the sky in a magical brilliance accompanied by the sound of coyotes howling. I began crying, just as I am now remembering the love between those two animals. The love those last two coyotes had for one another was so strong that the one male refused to leave this hell until his mate was also free.

I stood for a moment alone on that hilltop as shadowed figures ran through the tall grass and across the plains as the sky was exploding with falling stars. It was one of the most magical moments of my life; it revealed the deep love and devotion that could be shared not only between coyotes but now with us human allies willing to risk it all to give them the freedom they deserved. I took another can of spray paint and in two-foot-tall letters wrote across the back of the now-empty kennel: "AMERICAN WILDLIFE, LOVE IT OR LEAVE IT ALONE—FREEDOM FOR FUR ANIMALS NOW!!!"

Riding back down the dirt road, I felt like something had been unlocked or freed between the worlds of animals and humans. With our actions, we demonstrated to mink, bobcats, lynx, and coyotes that there were still some humans who recognized their kind as kindred spirits worthy of sacrifice and love. I had heard coyotes being called every bad name in the book: "vermin," "pests," "varmints," and even the label "furbearer" intimated that their value was only as a commercial product. Now I was feeling what I had only read about, or heard in old stories from times before, when the veil between the human and animal world was very thin. My allegiance to the human world had been abandoned. The world I was fighting for and craving was the one that existed on this continent for centuries before the colonizers arrived, when the people of this land recognized animals not as commodities to be exploited, but animal relations deserving of reverence and respect. Those last two coyotes showed me the world that is still waiting for our return—the world that can be ours again if we are brave enough to break free from the constraints of a brutally violent world to embrace again our place in the rhythms of life.

As the sun rose the following day, the evidence of the raid was quickly discovered by veterinary students who normally fed the coyotes. As the authorities were alerted, both vivisectors and WSU administrators were furious that the cagey ALF had pulled the wool over their eyes. And fur animal researchers' attempts to deny that research projects were funded by the fur industry were dispelled by ALF-released documents stating the contrary.

After all the rescued animals were released, we drove to Spokane where we delivered a press release to the offices of the Associated Press:

> As a result of continued exploitation of fur animals by WSU and USDA researchers, the ALF has been forced to respond in defense of wildlife and wilderness. We believe that coyotes, mink, beaver, otter, marten, and fisher have the right to live unmolested in their native habitat without the fear of exploitation by the fur and livestock industries. ALF shall challenge policies which allow grazing of livestock on lands traditionally used by native American wildlife. Until coyotes and other animals live free from the torturous hand of humankind, no industry or individual is safe from the rising tide of fur animal liberation. David Prieur, John Gorham, Fred Gilbert, David Shen, William Foreyt and Mark Robinson (all researchers funded by the fur industry) —beware. ALF is watching and there is no place to hide.

While the fur farm industry mourned the loss of the second-largest recipient of Mink Farmer Research Foundation funds, and although Gilbert's laboratory escaped the attack, his experiments did not. A Seattle television station filed a legal action against Gilbert and Washington State University for the release of his videotaped underwater trap experiments on beavers. Claiming that the videotapes were the property of the funder (the Fur Institute of Canada), Gilbert refused to release the tapes, while Washington residents were shocked that their university was being used to benefit the Canadian fur industry. Within a year, Fred Gilbert quit his post as the head of the Fur-Bearer Research Facility and retreated to a British Columbia university to continue his work, outside of the US. As for Gorham, his selection as Researcher of the Year was tarnished by the destruction of his ongoing research, which was rendered useless by stolen computer records and acid-damaged files, slides, and records. Gorham attempted to distance himself from fur farm research, only to later be featured on the cover of *Fur Rancher Magazine* in late 1991, as an honored guest on a tour of Russian fur farms overseas.

Meanwhile, somewhere on the Lochsa River on the Nez Perce Indian Reservation, in northwest Idaho, six mink swam for the first time in their lives in the world intended for them. I took the ten mice I had rescued and released them on the edge of a meadow where they could hopefully spend the rest of their lives in peace. As I sat watching these lab-bred mice, hundreds of generations away from having been wild, some were climbing tall stalks of grass to reach the seed pods at the end of each stalk, feeding on this new wild food. Even these mice knew what they were meant for in life and, surprisingly enough, it had nothing to do with us humans. Sure, they might be picked off by a hawk on their first day of freedom or eaten by a snake, but we were learning that that was what true animal liberation meant —freedom from the shackles of their human intended miserable destiny.

Two of the seven coyotes we rescued were later recaptured, but the other five were never seen by WSU researchers or police again. A WSU spokesperson stated, "They were not infected with anything that would cause a danger to the [wild] population." As summer turned to fall, we prayed that a new coyote family was beginning its preparations for the coming winter, their tattooed ears covered over by thickening fur. We hoped that they would soon forget their life in a cage and forever remember the Night of Stars Falling—and their human relations who came to free them.

Four Failures

The day after the raid on Washington State University, I picked up my friend Rik Scarce and his family from the Pullman Airport, in the far east of Washington state, and just down the road from the experimental fur farm. Rik was on vacation and knew nothing about the raid, nor had I shared with him any information about the fur farm research being conducted at WSU. Rik was a sociology professor and writer who had just published *Eco-Warriors*, about the ALF, complete with my interviews, and I knew he would immediately be a suspect. It felt a bit deceptive to not warn him of what might come, but I believed it was best if he honestly knew nothing of my involvement.

With my trusty Subaru again loaded with my bike and belongings, I departed Washington state—but not for my home in southern Oregon. Instead, I picked up a trusted friend in Missoula, Montana and drove south towards Utah. From the stolen documents from OSU's experimental fur farm, we had identified another vital feed supplier for America's western fur farmers. At the time, Utah led the country in the number of fur farms. I had seen mink pelts at the Seattle Fur Exchange Auction from Utah farms that boasted proudly of how their mink were the descendants of wild mink trapped in the 1920s. From those captive mink came the tens of thousands living (and dying) on Utah's fur farms today.

By September of 1991, US fur farm and federal law enforcement forces began to anticipate an all-out war by the ALF. Photographs of known activists were circulated among fur farmers, and extra caution was exercised when hiring farm help. The 1991 pelting season was drawing near, and with it the anxiety among fur farmers that they would be the next target of the ALF. Their fears were justified.

In the southern suburbs of Salt Lake City, in the small town of Sandy, stood the Fur Breeders Agricultural Co-operative. It was founded in 1939 by local mink farmers who wanted to consolidate the production of mink and fox feed in order to provide feed at a reduced cost to members. Without such a co-operative, mink farmers were often competing for feed sources. As the years passed, the Co-op started delivering feed to nearby farms with a fleet of tractor-trailers. Most deliveries followed the same routes to fur farms, which were within a 40-mile radius. The Sandy facility didn't only mix the raw feed ingredients and deliver feed, it also maintained a small mink research farm on the site.

I was of the mind that we needed to strike while the iron was hot. The longer we waited, the more likely that we would encounter stronger security, especially following three confirmed raids on fur farm targets in the last three months. My friend was justifiably wary when I suggested an attack on the Fur Breeders in Utah. I argued that I was relatively unknown in that state; once, Jonathan Paul and I drove to Coalville, Utah where many mink farms were visible from Interstate 80 as one drove east out of Salt Lake City. Jonathan and I had ridden our bikes to a huge mink farm on the south of town, stashed our bikes in daylight, and belly-crawled to a maze of fox pens located beyond the mink barns. We took pictures until the farmer came to feed the animals from a motorized cart and were forced to hide as he went about his feeding.

I had briefly spoken to a Utah fur farmer at the Seattle Fur Exchange, but that was the extent of my connection to Utah fur farms. Meanwhile, it was my friend from Missoula who wanted to tell me about a federal USDA research program that used coyotes and other wildlife in experiments to develop better lethal and nonlethal population control measures. The USDA's Predator Research Facility was located in Millville, Utah, not far from the Utah State University in Logan that worked in unison with the 140-acre research facility where over 100 coyotes were used in field experiments. As wildlife advocates, we had long known of the federal government's Animal Damage Control program, which later changed its name to the more innocuous sounding "Wildlife Services." In defense of crops, fish, and livestock, the USDA-administered agency hunted down and killed wildlife by the thousands, including on average about 80,000 coyotes a year using aerial gunning, traps, poisoning, and bounty programs.

We wouldn't be far from Logan when we travelled to Utah, so when we arrived in the state, we spent a late afternoon outside of Millville where we found a place to park our car in a nearby canyon that had US Forest Service land access. We hiked the open foothills that rose above the research facility, which was easy to see with its many chain-link-fence coyote pens, some pie-shaped, with observation towers where researchers watched the coyotes as they approached experimental baits and traps. From a distance of about a quarter mile, we sat under a hay barn and watched the facility with binoculars.

Everyone realized that fur farms were now on high alert, so we began to think about targeting other research entities, such as those involved in experiments on wildlife to develop poisons, traps, and lethal control weapons. Washington State University's USDA research on grizzly bears had piqued our curiosity about invasive wildlife research, and now we discovered a whole other chain of research facilities dedicated to addressing "wildlife conflicts." Now we stood looking at a federal laboratory developing predator control tools being used to kill hundreds of thousands of coyotes, mountain lions, badgers, wolves, and other native wildlife "in conflict with humans or their livestock." It was the same story as with us indigenous people—our own survival and desire to live free were the only crimes we ever committed that led to our systemic oppression and genocide. I saw the Predator Research Facility as the modern soldier's fort, only the animals of this land were the last to still be conquered and dominated.

We didn't want to strike this new division of native wildlife research without conducting much more reconnaissance and research, but we all agreed the proximity to publicly accessible lands and lack of security at the remote coyote research facility made it a good target to attack in the future. We hiked back to my Subaru and turned our attention back to a target much more likely to be on guard for an attack.

We rented a motel room in the seedy part of Salt Lake City and, on our first night, I got dropped off near the interstate exit closest to the Fur Breeders. Because of the feed deliveries, trucks were coming in and out of the facility and people could be seen milling about near their trucks. I circled the entire area and got on a dirt path that followed the slow-moving river behind the compound. Like many waterways near fur farms, I could see the occasional feral mink swimming in the moonlight. I passed the small mink farm and looked over the barns. If any fire was going to be a part of the plan, I needed to ensure that the mink were a safe distance away. But they would be endangered if we targeted the main feed building, so I was forced to target another building on the compound.

On the north end of the compound was a large warehouse that I decided to investigate. The building was without lights, but from the roof I could still hear the conversations of truck drivers not far away. I found a roof hatch that I could just lift high enough to unlock the clasp holding the small door closed. The building did not seem to have any apparent electronic security; instead it felt like the presence of employees around the clock was security enough. I climbed down a wooden ladder into a room filled with fur farm equipment and other unused materials. I checked adjoining rooms and found them all to be equally empty of life. I wanted to target the feed equipment needed for the actual operation of the Cooperative, but all of those buildings were either occupied or too close to the mink barns. I exited the building and returned the way I had come from behind the compound.

The next day, we practiced with a much cruder incendiary device than the one-hour timers we had been using since burning down Del Conte Furrier in Santa Rosa, California in 1988.[1] We would use a lit cigarette tucked into a book of matches; when the cigarette burned down to the matches, it would ignite the matchbook and any other fuel source I piled around it. This was August 28, 1991—just two weeks since we had raided WSU's fur farm and offices, and now we were ready to continue our attack on other integral links of the US fur farm industry.

It was just after midnight on a balmy night as I walked along the Jordan River behind the Fur Breeders compound. In my pack were my mask, gloves, a couple quarts of an oil-and-gas mixture, a pack of cigarettes, a lighter, and a can of red spray-paint. I would need little else on this raid. I quickly circled the property and climbed the fence close to the building we were targeting. I entered through the same roof hatch and quickly started piling flammable material against a wooden stairwell. Before I set our device, I checked the building one last time and peeked out a window to where I could see workers talking a couple hundred feet away. I went to a far wall and spray-painted the letters "ALF" along with a crude print of a mink paw. I returned to the pile by the stairway and set the matchbook device between the two plastic fuel containers. I lit the cigarette, took a

[1] See end of chapter 4.

drag to make sure it was well lit, and placed it between the row of matches in the book. I would have only about 15 minutes before the device ignited.

Within five minutes, I was back on the road leading to the interstate off-ramp where I would be picked up. It was pitch dark, and I could only be seen if I stood exposed on the shoulder. I waited in the shadows for what seemed like hours, but my getaway car did not show up. I pretended that I was hitchhiking, in case an approaching car was my ride, but in doing so I also made myself visible to every other vehicle. I knew that anyone in the area might become a witness, once the fire erupted and investigations ensued.

Without any way to communicate directly with my driver—this was before cell phones—I decided to find a payphone and call the motel where we were staying and leave a message describing my location. I then called a cab and took it to the local supermarket, where I was eventually met by my ride. By now it was almost dawn, and knowing nothing about the success or failure of our action, we decided to get out of Utah as fast as possible, before getting caught in any net of federal investigations that followed every new ALF raid.

No fire ignited. Only years later in court records would I learn the story of how the cigarette had failed to light the book of matches, and instead, how the butt that touched my mouth provided a DNA sample that gave federal investigators their first real clue in the investigation into Operation Bite Back.

I retreated to my mountain hideout in the Little Applegate River Valley of Oregon. I felt safe there—a place where only my local friends knew exactly where I lived. By now, hanging out with Diana in Portland was not wise. Federal investigators were visiting Earth First! houses and beginning to ask questions. I met with two friends who had helped carry out the OSU raid and gave them an update on the ensuing raids that were successful and the one that was not. They were willing to help with a more local action against a mink farm, so we decided to borrow a tactic from animal liberators in the UK and Greenpeace, which was to use a harmless dye to ruin the commercial value of light-colored mink. The tactic had first been pioneered by Paul Watson and his Sea Shepherd crew when they sprayed their dye on seal pups during the 1981 harp seal hunt. Soon after, animal liberators then used the tactic on British fur farms. We would spray the dye on the mink in the cages, which was quiet, yet economically effective.

I was opposed to the mass mink releases that had already occurred in Europe and the UK, knowing how ferocious mink can be to their own kind. Mass mink releases in a single location invariably result in fatal fights, not to mention the impact on local ecosystems, let alone nearby chicken coops! I wanted our actions to be in line with our argument that fur farming wasn't an animal welfare issue, it was a question about whether humans should domesticate a native species for commercial purposes, without consideration for the animal's importance to the greater ecosystem. Of course, we also believed in the rights of each of these individual fur farm prisoners to have an opportunity at freedom; but it was hard to justify when I knew it meant our actions would also result in the death of some of those prisoners.

We chose to target a mink farm in Sweet Home, Oregon that Jonathan and I had investigated the year before. We purchased henna from a health food store and filled garden sprayers with the dye. Each of the three of us carried a sprayer as we left our vehicle and began a half-mile hike over a small mountain to our target. The fur farm looked no different than when I had seen it before. We came out of the forest, and started to walk the circumference of the farm, staying well away from the farmer's house, which was located about 300 feet away.

As soon as we rounded the first mink barn, a dog began barking, and within seconds, lights came on in the house and someone ran out of with a flashlight beam directed towards the mink barns. Instinctively, we fled back the way we had come, ditching the sprayers when we reached the forest. We knew this farm was on guard for such an attack, and that meant the police were probably already on their way. A quick escape was what mattered most, even though it again meant leaving behind more evidence of another attempted raid. This was bad; investigators would have material evidence and yet we had no impact. In my mind, every raid was already bringing us—or at least me—one step closer to being identified or caught.

Not to be discouraged, the three of us regrouped the very next night, and came up with another plan for an attack on another mink farm. Earlier that year, as we searched for possible mink release sites on the Olympic Peninsula during our rehabilitation project, we discovered a mink farm on Steamboat Island near Olympia, Washington. It had a small processing building apart from the mink barns that I wanted to target for destruction, so we spent a couple hours watching for additional security measures before preparing for an attack the following night.

Leaving our vehicle about half a mile away near the main road, we walked to the farm and slowly crept up to the corner of the short guard fence that encircled the mink barns. I told my other two friends to keep watch from the location while I entered the farm. I climbed over the fence and started walking in a crouched position along the length of the first mink barn. Inside I heard the scratching of many mink, something that was becoming a familiar night sound for me.

When I reached the end of the mink barn, I stayed crouched and looked back in the direction I had come. I could just make out a figure with a flashlight turning and walking away from me. I assumed it was one of the friends I had just left, but when I crouch-walked back to them, both were still there and waiting for me. They said they hadn't moved since I left them. I then said quietly, "We're going to turn around and walk away as quietly as possible." I didn't want to tell them that I had just seen a night watchman—one who could have walked right up to me, on their fur farm with fire-making materials. We again ditched more evidence as we fast walked back to our car, but it wasn't apparent that our intrusion had been detected. No alarm had sounded, which was good because otherwise we could have been easily cut off on the small island.

Not long after, *Fur Rancher*, a fur farm publication, posted a reward poster for information on the culprits of recent ALF raids that included a composite sketch of one of the primary suspects—a dark-skinned individual that looked like me. The publication also advised farmers to arm themselves and be prepared for possible break-ins leading up to the ever-important pelting season near Thanksgiving. The industry's fears were now confirmed, at least with the attempted arson in Utah which left behind crucial evidence. With the two botched raids in the Northwest, I decided to head back to the only other fur-farm region that I was familiar with, Montana.

In December of 1990, I had visited Huggans Rocky Mountain Fur Company while on my last tour of the state's fur farms. I had visited the farm before, but I wanted to see the company when it was in the pelting process, so I got invited back on the same trip when we purchased our "own" fur farm. During my visit, I toured the main pelting building where mink and fox were skinned, their hides stretched and dried. The company processed not only their own pelts but those from many smaller farms in the area. The building stood apart from the rest of the mink barns and farm, so I wanted to see if it was possible to break in while it was loaded with the year's harvest of pelts and burn it to the ground.

The Bitterroot Valley has one road that leads south to the town of Hamilton; anywhere further south is treacherous or impassable in winter. We needed to be prepared for the possibility of escape, should we be forced to abandon our vehicle during any attempted action. One of my friends from the previous two attempts was still willing to join me on this winter raid, so together we purchased cold-weather gear, including snow camo, should we be forced to travel by foot. Our plan was to approach the farm on bicycles, then cross onto the property on foot and attempt to break into the pelt processing building. Once inside, I would set a one-hour timed incendiary device.

The night of the raid, December 12, 1991, we parked my Subaru on a Forest Service Road about a mile from the Huggans farm and rode our bikes down the dark and icy state highway that abutted it. The ice caused us to crash numerous times before we were forced to give up on the bikes and walk the last half-mile. When we reached the far perimeter of the farm, we crossed the barbed wire fence on the highway shoulder and started walking in the snow along the farthest mink barn. We realized that the snow left clear signs of our entry and path, for anyone who might be on security patrol. We sat for an hour to see if anyone was walking the farm on a regular schedule, and without any activity, we crept closer to the pelt-processing barn. I approached it and began inspecting the sheet-metal exterior. I found an extractor fan blowing air out of the building, and looked for the screws that held the sheet-metal panel underneath the fan. I removed about eight screws with a pair of vise-grips before being able to bend the panel far enough to enter the building. Inside, I could see hundreds of mink pelts stretched onto drying boards.

Just as I was about to enter the building, a dog walked from around the corner of the same building and froze, staring at me. It began to growl, and I knew if it started barking, someone would come to investigate; there would be no hiding that I was in the midst of breaking into their pelt barn, not to mention my path in the snow. With the dog still growling, I carefully retraced my footsteps in the snow back to where my friend was, and together we decided to retreat. We were simply too vulnerable to take any further risk, once the dog became aware of our presence.

Back at the Subaru, we hastily loaded our bikes and climbed back inside, with one small fuel can and one undetonated incendiary device. I drove back onto the main state highway that led north into Hamilton. But no sooner did I enter the town's limits than a police cruiser pulled behind me, following me the entire length of town, before finally circling back to his territory. As soon as the cruiser turned back, my friend and I started ditching evidence out the window: batteries, the timer, fuel cans, it all went out the window. Had we been pulled over, Operation Bite Back would have ended that night.

Back at our motel room, we counted our blessing and began the long drive back to Oregon.

The Malecky Ranch: A Success

Earlier in the year, while reading a copy of *Fur Rancher* magazine at the science library at WSU, I had seen an ad for a fur farm up for sale near Salem, Oregon, just down the road from OSU. I called the number listed and spoke to the owner, Hynek Malecky. He explained that he was interested in not just selling his mink operation, but in maintaining a partnership in a future joint venture. I told him I'd let him know if I was interested. Benefiting directly from OSU's research, Malecky had developed a state-of-the-art mink operation and was now, with the declining market in mink pelts, in need of additional financing to keep his fur business alive. No bank would dare loan money to a fur farmer, not only because of the instability of the fur market but also because of the recent ALF attacks in the Northwest. Malecky Mink Farm was just one of many farms teetering on the edge of bankruptcy. The Western Wildlife Unit of the ALF just needed to give it a little push.

Having returned to Oregon, I decided to head over to Malecky's farm in Yamhill, and after a cold and rainy night of reconnaissance, discovered almost no security there. What was a bit difficult was approaching the fur farm through the patchwork of private residences that surrounded it. But I navigated my way there, and after confirming that the mink barns were empty, I inspected the nearest barn and discovered it was the feed and pelting barn. That would be our target. I returned to my vehicle and drove south to the home of another friend I counted on to be my getaway driver. It would be a simple attack, with just me being dropped off for about 30 minutes at the most.

Less than two weeks since crashing our bikes on the icy highways of Montana, on December 21, here I was, jogging down a black-top road on my way to the next action. The light rain provided good cover and I had no problem re-entering the pelting barn. I located the structural center of the building and began gathering mink nesting boxes, pelt-stretching boards, and other available flammable materials, to build a pyramid of combustible items. I then placed the one-hour kitchen-timer delayed incendiary device beneath the whole wooden mess. Finally, I set flammable liquid in an open plastic container surrounding the device, twisted the kitchen dial on the timer, connected the nine-volt battery, and fled the building—mentally noting on my watch when the device was to meant to trigger.

Separate from the mink barns, this nerve center of the operation housed feed-mixing equipment, refrigeration units, drying drums for the mink pelts, skinning racks, and the assorted supplies necessary to keep a mink farm operational. Standing in the darkened processing building, I imagined the farm in full operation: the mobile gas chambers unloading still-quivering mink to the waiting skinners, and the smells of musk while the pelts are stripped from the minks' warm bodies like banana peels. I was more than glad that such a scene would never again occur at Malecky Mink Ranch.

By the time I rendezvoused with my pick-up driver, there was still half an hour left before ignition. Thirty-two minutes later, the device ignited. Before fire trucks could reach the scene, the heart of Malecky Mink Farm lay in ruins. One fur farm down, 600 to go. The action was clean and smooth.

By the time federal investigators arrived, the only evidence they found was a burned-down fur farm. Not even the telltale 'ALF' was spray-painted anywhere. We had decided that doing so would only leave evidence that might narrow the scope of suspects. Spray painting would only help law enforcement to conclude that the fire was arson, and not accidental or an insurance scam. This action—which took place after the pelting season—ensured that there was not only a minimal risk of harming animals on the farm (since most had already been killed), but also destroyed expensive pelts that were still in the processing building.

Having successfully carried out another attack on a fur farm, we turned our sights again to recipients of Mink Farmer Research Foundation funding. Idaho State University received a small grant to do fur animal research, but to our surprise, by far the lion's share of funding went to Michigan. I contacted a source for funding future actions, and once I had the funds, I could again recruit friends for another drive, only this time across the country to Michigan—a state where I had never been before.

CHAPTER 8
A TURNING POINT:
MICHIGAN STATE UNIVERSITY

In January of 1992, People for the Ethical Treatment of Animals (PETA) ran a series of radio announcements in western Michigan, drawing attention to Michigan State University's animal experiments by Richard Aulerich, whose primary laboratory animal "models" were mink. Unbeknownst to PETA, Aulerich was also the second-largest recipient of annual grants by the Mink Farmers Research Foundation, and had for the past 32 years provided vital research developments to the US mink industry. No discussion of mink farm disease research omitted Aulerich from the conversation. We kept on finding his research work cited in correspondence seized from OSU and WSU, and knew his work was an important link in the fur animal research chain. Through his service to the US government and the mink industry, Aulerich had been awarded federal grants to use his mink for toxic experiments involving the force-feeding of PCPs, dioxins, and other industrial pollutants. Published research records detailed how poisoned mink died violent deaths in Aulerich's laboratory, suffering severe internal hemorrhaging before vomiting blood and finally dying after being fed only feeds laced with contaminants, as part of the infamous Lethal Dose 50% (LD50) test.

Students at MSU would later tell us that a 39-mile stretch of the lower Fox River, which feeds Lake Michigan, used to be home to the largest concentration of paper mills in the world. Despite PCP productions having been banned almost 20 years ago, these pollutants remain in the mud and sediment along the river and lake, causing high levels of PCP in fish and other wildlife. Another area situated at the mouth of the Grand Calumet River at the southern end of Lake Michigan has the largest accumulation of industry-contaminated sediments in the Great Lakes. Students were frustrated that, despite all dioxin in the Great Lakes being traced to less than 200 factory stacks, and all PCP traceable to five industries, the only remedies were to entrust these corporations to voluntarily clean it up, or to conduct animal testing on the contaminants to determine their danger. A 1990 study showed 100% mortality among test animals exposed to sediment samples from the Grand Calumet.

Rather than study contamination in wild mink and otters in the Great Lakes region, Aulerich chose to cause further suffering by experimenting on mink and otters from his fur farm. We had also been given information by students about Aulerich making keychains for his students out of the severed paws of his vivisected mink.

To the American mink industry, Aulerich represented the last hope for the conquering of diseases commonly found on fur farms. OSU's Experimental Research Station was out of the game, and Gorham's research was in tatters. The Fur Animal Research Station at Michigan State University was on alert against attacks by the ALF, following the raids in Oregon and Washington. When PETA radio spots fingered Aulerich, MSU increased its already strengthened security. During the fur farmer and research hysteria, and because of our earlier actions, we decided to carry out one last experimental fur farm attack. This one would be on behalf of the Lake Michigan ecosystem, but it would also serve to stop mink suffering at the hands of Aulerich, and to draw attention to the real threat: industrial polluters.

Of course, it was a grand scheme in a dangerous time, but I knew if we were successful, we would have accomplished a major coup against the US fur farm industry by destroying much of their vital research and development in the face of collapsing fur markets.

My trail, however, would soon be compromised. On an earlier trip to Montana, I had forgotten a datebook in a shopping basket that had a fake ID hidden in the binding. When I was driving east to Michigan, I stopped at the store to retrieve it and was told it was turned over to the police station. I should have stopped then, but instead I went to the local police department in Missoula and was told I could pick up the book. When I was led into a room, I was surrounded by plain clothes cops asking me about the fake ID. No one said a thing about any ALF actions, but I knew my days aboveground were numbered. I was eventually given back my datebook, minus the fake ID, and allowed to leave the station. When I got back to my Subaru, my friend in the passenger seat began asking me what happened when I interrupted, "Is anyone following me? Let's get the hell out of here!"

The public story I told my friends in Montana was that I was driving east to get copies of fur farm footage I had shot for Friends of Animals while employed as a private investigator. Everyone knew we had completed our fur farm rehabilitation project, and I now wanted to make my own video documentary of the project using both fur farm footage and film of the mink, bobcat, and lynx whose releases we had mostly filmed. The real story, though, was that I wanted to get a look at the Michigan State University campus to determine whether a later raid was possible.

A Fateful Detour: Little Bighorn

On the drive out of Montana, I stopped at the infamous Little Bighorn Battlefield Monument. There, in 1876, Lakota, Cheyenne, and Arapahoe forces annihilated George Armstrong Custer and his 7th Cavalry after his trespass and violation of the Fort Laramie Treaty. I had been reading Peter Matthiessen's *In the Spirit of Crazy Horse* (1983), which chronicled the century and a half of abuse by the federal government of the Lakota and other plains indigenous peoples. At the Monument, there were acknowledgements of the loss of white lives, but not much mention of the indigenous perspective on the tragic battle, which cost nearly as many native lives as those of the invading soldiers. The lack of representation was offensive and a continued disrespect to the sacrifices made by indigenous people on this continent in their resistance to the genocidal American policies of the 19th and 20th centuries.

When I walked into the battlefield museum, again the story was presented from the invader's perspective; in one display case, there were sacred Sun Dance ceremonial objects and a Ghost Dance shirt. The Ghost Dance phenomena rose in the closing years of the 19th century when a holy man by the name of Wovoka received a vision that would give hope to many of the shattered tribes who had survived the brutal hand of Westward Expansion. Practitioners of the dance believed that if they performed ghost dance ceremonies, their lost relatives would return and the white man would be driven from the land. It was a ghost dance that led to the 7th Cavalry's later slaughter of ghost dancers and other men, women, and children at Wounded Knee in 1891.

In my anger, I spontaneously decided to see if I could break into one of the museum's display cases that held two pistols belonging to a fallen 7th Cavalryman. Perhaps I could use the pistols to "ransom" for the repatriation of the sacred objects on display. The case proved too difficult to break into without a tool to cut the small lock, so I instead turned my attention to a leatherbound journal attached to the wall in a small plexiglass case with four screws. When I grabbed the screw heads with my bare fingers, I found that they were loose enough to remove. I went back to my car and told the friends with me to wait and I'd be back in ten minutes. I also put on a small fanny pack after dumping the contents onto the driver's seat.

Walking back into the nearly empty museum, I could hear a film playing in a room that was staffed by the only museum member on that Tuesday morning in midwinter. I went back to the wing of the museum that held the journal. I removed the remaining screws, removed the case, lifted the journal from the wall, and put it in my fanny pack before replacing the empty case and screws. I walked back to the car and drove away.

The leather diary belonged to a Lt. McIntosh from Custer's 7th Cavalry. Notably, it had a bullet hole through it, fired by an indigenous warrior defending their family and homelands on that fateful day at the river called Greasy Grass, from a morning military ambush during a sacred Sun Dance ceremony. None of the story from the perspective of the Lakota, Cheyenne, and Arapahoe people was represented at the Battlefield Monument; that issue had been brewing long before I stole that journal. Not until years later, while I sat in prison, did I take the time to write about my motivations behind the theft, which I shared in a 'zine I made called "Strong Hearts."

It was Custer and his 7th Cavalry who, earlier, and in a blatant violation of the Fort Laramie Treaty signed by the same indigenous nations, led a mining expedition into the sacred Lakota holy lands, the place of origin, *Paha Sapa*—known today as the Black Hills of South Dakota. There he discovered gold. He then announced it to the media, which instituted a gold rush that flooded the region with trespassing miners. When the Lakota and other tribes expressed outrage at this violation of their treaty with the US government, they were offered pennies per acre for the heart of their Earth-mother. That money still sits in a bank; the Lakota still today refuse to accept money for their land. They want the return of the lands that were stolen from them.

When the Lakota attempted to evict the gold miners in the 1870s, the US military was sent in to "destroy the hostile Indians." "Hostiles" were any Indian who refused to live life in near starvation on the reservations where disease and social disorder was rampant. In 1876, US forces engaged with the so-called hostiles on the Rosebud River and got their asses kicked. General Crook—who, along with Custer, led the attack—later recounted the battle, crediting the Lakota and Cheyenne warriors with incredible acts of bravery, including that of a woman who charged into the midst of the battlefield to rescue her wounded brother.

Two weeks later, Custer discovered an immense encampment on the Little Bighorn. Not wanting to wait for reinforcements from Crook, Custer ordered a daylight charge on the camp of over 3,000. Lakota and Cheyenne warriors rallied to defend their people from the man they called "The Chief of Thieves." With shouts of "Brave hearts forward, coward hearts to the rear!", indigenous leaders Sitting Bull and Crazy Horse led their people to victory, completely destroying Custer and his 7th Cavalry of over 200 men. Many of the soldiers were mutilated by the indigenous women in retaliation for the mutilation of women and children by these very same men. Custer's body was left alone because no Lakota or Cheyenne wanted to dirty themselves by touching it. Yet, some women took leather awls and poked holes in Custer's ears, saying, "In your next life, with these added holes, maybe you will listen when we tell you Lakota lands are not for sale."

The victory at the Greasy Grass signaled the end of the "Sioux Wars," as the whites called them. Increased military repression led to the defeat of the Lakota Nation, and one by one, leaders such as Sitting Bull and Crazy Horse led their battered and broken yet proud people onto the reservations where many remain today. Within a few short years, hundreds more would be slaughtered after both Sitting Bull and Crazy Horse were assassinated on the reservation for trying to lead their people in a new way of life. As bands of Lakota survivors fled towards the camp of one of the last surviving great leaders, Red Cloud, in the midst of a brutal winter in 1891, soldiers corralled nearly 300 men, women, and children near the Wounded Knee River, where they were massacred.

By the late 1960s, things began to change, as the restless spirits of those whose blood was spilled by the US government began to fill the hearts of young indigenous men and women. An indigenous resurgence was born from the continuing abuses by the government, and consequently, the American Indian Movement (AIM) was born. AIM warriors converged on Lakota reservations on the invitation of the elders whose relations had fought and died at the Greasy Grass and other battlefields.

AIM fought tribal government corruption on the Pine Ridge Reservation that was covering up the transfer and sale of mining rights for tribal lands and targeting opponents with violence. AIM also began to rebuild the traditional community structures of their people, bringing back the old ways of the sweat lodge and sun dance ceremony to young people. AIM returned something to the reservation that the US government thought it had destroyed: the memory of who we are as indigenous people, people with our own proud heritage of resistance, and an identity with a culture that keeps our connection to Mother Earth alive.

It wasn't long before corrupt officials and the US government sent back in a modern-day Cavalry, launching a counterintelligence program that planted infiltrators, agent provocateurs, and smear campaigns against AIM's most vocal leaders. The FBI also supplied arms and ammunition to opponents of AIM, who threatened, intimidated, and murdered some of the

movement's finest young traditional leaders. By 1980, over 150 AIM activists had been murdered, with no investigation into their suspicious
deaths. Many went to prison, including Leonard Peltier, who was imprisoned for the killing of two FBI agents who, like Custer, had charged into a
peaceful Lakota encampment with guns ablaze. As a noble gesture on his
last day in office, President Joe Biden granted clemency to Peltier; he was
released on February 18, 2025, after spending nearly 50 years in prison for
his actions in defense of indigenous homelands and people.

In 1992, when I visited the Greasy Grass battlefield to pay my re-
spects to my fallen indigenous brothers and sisters who had given their
lives to defend Lakota sovereignty, I was outraged at the presentation of
Custer's defeat as a great tragedy committed by Lakota and Cheyenne
"hostiles." No mention of the violation of the Fort Laramie Treaty by US
forces or the justifiable response by indigenous people defending their
families and way of life from sanctioned butchers. I decided to counter this
disrespect of indigenous sovereignty and heritage with the theft of the cavalryman's journal, which I later learned was taken from a Lakota woman
by a soldier distributing food rations.

After the spontaneous action, we decided to visit friends in Boulder,
Colorado, even though it was out of the way. But we had a hidden agenda:
to also investigate the USDA's National Wildlife Research Center, which
was another federal laboratory developing predator-control poisons and
tools used to kill hundreds of thousands of coyotes, mountain lions, badgers, wolves, and other native wildlife "in conflict with humans or their
livestock." We borrowed a friend's car so we wouldn't be using my own
car, and drove to the Research Center, which was surrounded by a high
steel-post fence. Beyond the fence was the entire compound of many acres
with roads leading to separate buildings. We climbed the fence and moved
through the shadows towards a windowless building that looked like it
housed animals. The buildings were solid brick, but I was sure that, with
plenty of recon, I could find a way in.

Like the Predator Research Facility in Utah, we were already planning for our next campaign that would target federal predator-control research, perhaps after we had neutralized Mink Farmer Research Foundation targets. We approached a research building, and two of us climbed
into a dumpster next to the brick building. We began emptying plastic trash
bags collected from the researchers' offices, pulling out discarded documents that might indicate the focus of current research. We found documents that spoke of efforts to develop better sterilization methods to be
used for coyotes and we also found work schedules for field researchers,

including an upcoming itinerary for the testing of new poisons on badgers in Texas. The paperwork included descriptions of the staff and vehicles and even their hotels. But we felt powerless; we knew that we could easily thwart this sinister experiment by, say, attacking the researchers' vehicles while they slept in their hotels. But such an attack would only put the entire predator control research community on alert, making any future attacks on predator research facilities much harder.

My friend cried as we drove back to our other friend's house, and I openly shared with her my own frustration, but I really respected her determination to want to address this latest discovery of lethal wildlife research. Again, this wasn't animal research being done to save human lives; it was research into developing better methods of *eradicating native predators*. I promised her that I would turn my full attention to targeting the USDA's predator control research as soon as we were finished with targeting fur farm research. It made me feel less alone in my own feeling of desperate determination to prevent a further atrocity against wildlife. So many people loved wolves, coyotes, bears, and other animals, but who knew they were the subjects of invasive experiments to develop ever-more sinister ways to kill them? Despite the trend in the development of nonlethal methods, such as contraception, agents of Wildlife Services to this day still prefer lethal methods that result in over 60,000 coyotes being killed a year by the USDA agency.

The next morning, our attention was brought back to something else. Our host came into the kitchen where we were drinking coffee and showed us the daily Colorado newspaper. Inside was an article about the theft of the cavalryman's journal from the Little Bighorn Museum. Not treating the crime as seriously as our ALF actions, I had pulled out the journal and shown it to my friends when we first arrived in Boulder. We all were caught off-guard by the attention to the theft. We were used to the attention we were getting from our crimes against fur farmers, but now I was carrying out radical political actions that were drawing attention not only to continuing indigenous resistance, but to a subset of people willing to break the law and cheekily target historical artifacts of their oppressors.

My friends were not against the spontaneous action, nor were they opposed when I told them I wanted to issue a press release accepting responsibility for the theft on behalf of what I called the "Crazy Horse Retribution Society." I took the name from the radical off-shoot of the British Hunt Saboteurs Association, the "Hunt Retribution Squad," which targeted fox hunters' vehicles, sometimes burning them. So I drafted up a press release, which read as follows:

The Crazy Horse Retribution Society accepts responsibility for the theft of Lt. McIntosh's notebook from the battlefield monument. It was done to draw attention to the continued genocide inflicted on Native American peoples and lands by the US government. Custer's defeat at the Battle of Little Bighorn is described at the battlefield museum as a tragedy. The real tragedy is what leads native peoples to such drastic actions. Rape, mutilations, poverty, religious persecution, and cultural assassination carried out by the 7th Cavalry continues to this day by other US agents of repression on reservations across North America.

Misrepresentation of the struggle of Lakota, Cheyenne, and Arapahoe to maintain their ancient traditions by fighting imperialist assimilation has forced native people today to take action. The desecration of native religion by the profane display of sacred objects in museums and the destruction of sacred lands to mine uranium and coal for bombs and televisions is not conducive with the lessons given by the Great Spirit.

We demand equal representation at the battlefield in the form of displays and exhibits approved by the American Indian Movement. The explanation of the justified actions of Crazy Horse and Sitting Bull to defend their home and people at the Little Bighorn is necessary before the notebook can be returned. Until the US Government recognizes native sovereignty and suspends exploitive attitudes, teachings, and behavior against First Americans, we will rise up against the modern Custers of US society.

After surreptitiously dropping off the press release at an Associated Press office in Denver, I mailed the stolen journal to a safe address where I could collect it later. I didn't want to make any decision in haste as to what to do with the book, but I certainly did not want to be carrying it with me as I was planning other actions against alerted fur farm researchers in Michigan. (In the end, I would burn that journal as a hated symbol of the genocide of indigenous people.)

We said our goodbye to friends in Boulder and continued east on our winter adventure, camping along the way on frozen ground, until we reached Michigan.

On to Michigan

In the records from OSU, we knew the Michigan experimental fur farm was on "Farm Lane"—which was easy enough to find on a grey February day, as we drove around the sprawling rural campus in East Lansing looking for the tell-tale sign of long windowless barns. Like OSU, the mink farm was located next to an experimental poultry farm. The area was remote and the farm appeared empty, or at least without any obvious signs of increased security, like a barbed wire fence, lights, or onsite residence. It was enough for me to know that the location was remote and easily accessible to a state highway that ran past the mink barns. After the failed attempts and mishaps, I wanted better escape routes.

We next drove to the campus and to Anthony Hall, which is a huge stone building with hundreds of offices inside. I walked through the snow and past students, entered the building, and walked the main hallways until I found what I was looking for: Aulerich's office—which I intentionally walked right past. All I needed to do was get a good look at the door and surrounding walls to know whether I could get inside or not. At the bottom of the researcher's office door, there were wooden ventilation slats, about 10 inches high; I knew that I could easily cut through those with a small saw blade, assuming noise was not an issue.

When I got back to the car, I didn't say much, since we had a friend with us that we were dropping off on the east coast. But I knew that as soon as that task was done, I wanted to come right back. And as crazy at it seems, that's exactly what we did. After a nice Ethiopian dinner in Washington DC, and a couple night's sleep, my one friend and I drove straight back to East Lansing.

Along the way, I purchased the necessary equipment to build a one-hour time-delay incendiary device; I also bought several disposable break-in tools that I could leave at the scene. No longer did I want to be caught with equipment from an action once a crime had been committed. From now on, the only thing I wanted to carry away from a raid were any valuable research records or other damaging material.

For this particular raid, we conducted very little reconnaissance: just one night parked a few hours across from Aulerich's office and, on the same night, an approach to the fur farm to determine whether there were motion lights or other security measures. Confident that there were no heightened security measures in place, even after the PETA ads, we decided to again strike while the iron was hot.

The next night, we prepared ourselves in another motel room not too far from East Lansing. We were only two people: one driver and myself as the lone break-in operative. With the increased awareness nationwide, I felt safer acting alone, just as I had with the torching of the Malecky Mink Ranch. For this raid, I would be first dropped off on the state highway near the experimental fur farm, where I would break in, damage what I could without fire (because of the proximity to the mink barns), rescue two mink, and then return to the highway. There, I would be picked up and driven to Anthony Hall, where I would break into Aulerich's office, plant an incendiary device, and then escape.

A Night to Remember

As a light rain fell on the MSU mink barns on the night of February 28, 1992, I lay crouched low to the earth in a dark and heavy winter jacket, my heart pumping from both the cold and adrenalin. Cars rumbled by on the nearby highway as I cut through a chain-link fence and entered the perimeter of the Experimental Fur Farm. I stationed myself with a clear view of all incoming roads and the occupied quarters of the sleeping caretaker near the poultry farm.

When I felt confident that my trespass had not been detected, I made my way to the main barn and climbed onto the roof of the field laboratory. It was a corrugated sheet metal roof held down with small self-tapping screws. I went to work removing enough screws to remove one portion of sheet metal roofing, exposing the rafters of the building and ceiling loft; once inside, and after cutting a hole through the interior ceiling, I lowered myself onto the floor where I could then easily climb down to the main feed and research area.

Without any exposed windows to the outside, I switched on my red-tinted headlamp to preserve my night vision, and began to remove hinges on a door leading into the main office laboratory. There was no alarm visible on the door, so I quietly lifted it aside.

Upon entering, I began to carefully destroy all the research equipment in front of me. I quickly searched for files and research records, grabbed some mink breeding records, and then began pouring muriatic acid over feed-mixing machinery for the experimental mink farm, as well as over all the research equipment and documents that were left in the offices, and now piled on the floor.

I saw a freezer against the wall of the lab; when I opened the door, I saw about 30 round balls of aluminum foil the size of softballs. When I picked one up and peeled away the foil, I could make out the severed head of an otter. Much of Aulerich's research on PCP levels in the Great Lakes involved otters, and alongside the dark mink barns, I found one lonely otter remaining in a cage with little more than a small wooden nestbox for comfort. This was Alice, the sole remaining experimental otter prisoner who now watched as I entered and left the laboratory where so many of her kin had died. When I saw the beautiful animal, my heart broke because I was in no position to also rescue this new-found prisoner. We would take two mink because we felt confident they could survive with no rehabilitation, but the otter we simply were not logistically prepared to carry away safely that night. I took out my small video camera and filmed the freezer full of otter heads before turning to more demolition work.

After the laboratory feed-mixing room and research office were wrecked, spray-painted messages were left for Aulerich and other researchers, including "WE WILL BE BACK FOR THE OTTERS."

After I exited the lab through the hole in the sheet metal roof, I climbed down and entered the perimeter of the mink farm itself and began to remove every identification card from the mink and about 16 ferret cages. But before I removed the cards, I located two mink slated for future contamination, yet tonight, still healthy. I set up my video camera on another cage a few feet away and filmed myself as I loaded two mink into wooden nest-boxes separately for their journey to freedom. The nearby busy highway kept me from opening all the cages and releasing all the mink. As always, the hardest part was leaving behind the hundreds of other mink, as well as ferrets and otter, that we knew would soon be poisoned. I left the two mink in their nest boxes close to the highway where we could retrieve them later. It was now time to catch a ride back to campus.

Fire in Anthony Hall

The newly-formed Great Lakes Unit of the ALF had arrived and was now walking towards Anthony Hall on the MSU campus, looking like typical college students returning home from a late-night out. I had an earphone beneath my hooded sweatshirt that kept me in contact with my lookout parked in a nearby car, monitoring a police scanner. With radio silence indicating an all clear, I cut across the lawn in front of the building and dropped into a storm drain depression below a bottom story window. The latch on the window was ajar, as I had discovered on one last walk past the building earlier that night. Now, with a long thin strip of metal, I slid the latch completely open and swung the window open. I climbed into the building, landing on the desk of an MSU dairy researcher. Closing the window behind me, I kept watch for a few minutes to ensure that my entry had not been detected.

Once I passed through the office and was inside the building, I walked the lit hallway to a stairway and up one level to the office of Richard Aulerich. During my earlier daytime reconnaissance in the building, I studied the open office door and did not noticed any type of alarm system in place. I now approached the closed door and got down on my knees and with a large screwdriver, broke through three of the wooden vent slats on the door until I could reach up and open the door from the inside. I then ducked in and shut the door, not leaving any of the broken pieces of wood visible from the outside. Aulerich's office had a receptionist area, complete with a glass case filled with mink pelts for display—nothing like pride in one's work.

I opened all the file drawers in every office and dumped their contents onto the floor; I didn't care about what the research might reveal to the ALF, I just wanted it all destroyed. When I had dumped enough paper and other flammable material to start a fire in the stone building, I removed my pack and opened the plastic container that contained the one-hour time-delay incendiary device, cushioned with toilet paper for safe handling.

Suddenly, I saw flashing red and blue lights through the windows outside Aulerich's office. I was startled for a moment, but quickly regained my confidence, knowing that my lookout would have notified me if it was cause for alarm. In a few short minutes, the patrol car drove away, as did the motorist he had pulled over.

I continued in my task, and decided at the last minute to fill up my pack with a few computer discs, color slides, and selected research documents. I then set the incendiary device. After radioing my lookout, I returned to the basement-level office. Before I exited the window, I glanced around the research office through which I had entered; the nameplate outside the door had said "dairy research." I decided to slide all the computers and office equipment onto the floor before I rolled out of the window into the storm drain. After a quick clothing adjustment, I returned on the path I had come. My getaway driver pulled up to me a short distance away, and in minutes we were safely on our way back to scoop up the two mink from the shoulder of the darkened highway.

Back on the main campus, within the hour, a fire erupted in Anthony Hall. It totally destroyed 32 years of fur animal research by Aulerich, and over ten years of unpublished research by another vivisector. With this final attack, all major recipients of Mink Farmer Research Foundation

(MFRF) funding were effectively neutralized, leaving the US fur farm industry struggling more than ever to survive. Never before had the ALF successfully eliminated the research and development arm of an animal- and Earth-abuse industry as it did with the MFRF. But even as the ALF earned its title—as an effective threat to industry research—activists from across the nation began to feel the oncoming wave of federal police repression, as joint law-enforcement taskforces accelerated their hunt for the ALF renegades.

Meanwhile, only hours after the raid, on the shores of a remote lake, the two liberated mink from MSU's experimental fur farm were given their last meal by human hands—a road-killed rabbit and protein-rich cat food—before being released back into their native habitat, where they quickly disappeared into the lake's underbrush. It was what could be called a "hard" release, but we felt it was still better to put nature in charge, rather than let humans decide their fate.

Lansing State Journal, **29 Feb 1992 (p. 1)**

Richard Aulerich in his burned-out office

We returned to our motel room where I wrote a press release and placed it with some of the stolen research materials into a FedEx box that I would send to an address I was told could receive such information. I had used such intermediates in the past to deliver stolen documents— something that put parties on both sides at great risk. This time would not be an exception. I dropped off the package at a nearby FedEx location, before we left the area, heading south this time in a big loop that would end back at Oregon in early March 1992.

We had successfully carried out this last great attack, but it would be the last time I ever felt safe travelling under my own identity. The jig was up. The Feds were figuring out that "Jim Perez" was Rod Coronado was the ALF. It would only be a matter of time before they had enough pieces of the puzzle to prove it, or at least get an indictment.

CHAPTER 9

HUNTING THE ALF

After the MSU raid, we split up. I drove south and west before returning to my cabin home in southern Oregon. With Aulerich's research in ashes, we knew there was little left of the Mink Farmer's Research Foundation's funded research. There were still small funding recipients, but without another attempt on the Fur Breeders Co-op in Utah, it was hardly worth the risks that would certainly be involved in targeting researchers in Idaho or Wisconsin, where we hadn't even scratched the surface of the state with more fur farms than any other at that time. Still, I was not unhappy with what we had accomplished in the eight months since the last bobcat was released from our fur farm rehabilitation project.

In delivering the materials seized from the MSU raid to an intermediate, I had absolved myself of the risks involved with contacting the media, as I had before; but I also was involving People for the Ethical Treatment of Animals (PETA), the largest animal rights group in the nation, and one which had often spoken on the ALF's behalf following actions, predominantly on the East Coast.

Internally, we always referred to ourselves as the unofficial "West Coast ALF," knowing there was also a "East Coast ALF" whose actions were known, but not the identity of its members. My dear friend, Ben White from Sea Shepherd, was the only person I knew on the East Coast who had participated in the "True Friends" action that rescued two chimpanzees from the infamous SEMA Labs in Maryland in 1986, just a month after our raid on Iceland.

Now, with not just Ben's help but Paul Watson, Cleveland Amory, and other mentors, I had created an underground organization for animals capable of crippling a targeted American industry. Of course, the Department of Justice categorized the Animal Liberation Front as a terrorist organization; we became a legitimate threat to capitalist enterprises that exploited animals. It was a dangerous precedent and one that warranted a serious response from the FBI and the Bureau of Alcohol, Tobacco, and Firearms (ATF) investigators who were chasing us.

I spent the remainder of March 1992 enjoying the life I had created since leaving the San Francisco Bay Area. I was living in a simple one-room cabin with a wood stove and small propane oven. I carried water from the nearby creek and was ten miles from the nearest paved road, with coyotes as my closest neighbors. I felt very connected to the animals and places I was fighting to protect. Their plight was not some abstract concept or perceived injustice; it was the reality of a relationship with humans that began when the first colonizers arrived. Ever since, native wildlife has only known warfare from the hand of man. My deep look behind the locked doors of laboratories and fur farms had shown me the true level of suffering humans inflicted on animals, not the polished propaganda version that organizations like Fur Farmers of America were promoting as the narrative.

On April 1st, I received a call from a Sea Shepherd friend in Los Angeles that I had visited recently. He said he had something to fax to me: a copy of a search warrant that had been served at a PETA member's home in Maryland the month before. From the warrant, I learned that my package of stolen MSU materials had been intercepted because the account number I had used was invalid. At the time, I chose to use the number and drop the package into a drop-box rather than take it into a Fedex store in person.

The warrant stated that incendiary device materials found at OSU and MSU indicated that both devices had been built by the same person, but they couldn't yet prove who it was. The FBI also stated that I was responsible for the ALF attack on WSU and that federal grand juries were convened in Oregon, Washington, and Michigan to gather evidence in order to issue indictments against ALF members.

When Fedex opened the intercepted package and saw the suspicious materials, they contacted law enforcement. Inside the package was materials stolen from Aurelich's MSU office and the videotape I had made of the severed otter heads and the rescue of the two mink. The Feds used handwriting forensics to match my writing to that on the package label. Federal investigators had already concluded that I was involved in the WSU raid, and now they were certain I was responsible for the MSU raid as well. So they served the search warrant to a longtime PETA member whose address was the one I had been given to send our press release and any related materials. For the FBI, it was the jackpot they were looking for in their hunt for the ALF.

Inside the Maryland home, investigators found not only evidence related to my attacks on fur farms, but all of my handwritten maps and notes from my 1990 investigation into the possible liberation of the Silver Springs Monkeys from Tulane University in Louisiana. Unbeknownst to me, the address I had been given was also used as a safe house to store the equipment and intelligence from my earlier investigation. Burglary tools, radios, night-vision goggles, fake identification, and euthanasia drugs were carted away as evidence.

It took me a few minutes, but after processing the information in the search warrant, I knew I had to leave my cabin immediately. Although I had kept the location private, I had recently shared my location with an activist friend from Santa Cruz who wanted to visit—but I hadn't heard from him since. The lack of communication made me suspicious. My parents had already been harassed since the Fall 1991, being asked questions about my whereabouts and whether I was organizing illegal activities from their home. My mother would later tell me that, one time, the agents came with a long-haired, bearded young man who my mom said, "He looked just like one of your friends!" I was now highly suspicious that my cabin in Oregon had been compromised, so when I read the warrant, I knew it was time to go.

I had been in touch with Sea Shepherd friends in Los Angeles recently because they asked me to deliver a car from Eugene, Oregon that had been donated to the group. The new sportscar was owned by a wealthy hippy who followed the Grateful Dead. He now felt guilty about the purchase and decided to absolve himself by giving the car away. So I dropped the car off, spent a few days with old friends in the area, and then decided to move there for a while—or maybe even flee the country on the Sea Shepherd, which was set to sail to the North Pacific Ocean in more pursuit of Japanese drift-net fishing. David Howitt was on the Sea Shepherd's new former Coast Guard patrol boat, which was renamed the *Edward Abbey* and berthed in Marina del Ray, California.

So, back in Oregon, I loaded up my Subaru with a few belongings, mostly camping gear, and put the rest in a rented storage locker in Talent, Oregon.

One of the last things I did before leaving my beloved mountain home was to destroy the cavalryman's notebook that I had stolen two months earlier. Perhaps the "right" thing to do would have been to send it back, but it would still be some time before the National Park Service was ready to tell the story of indigenous peoples' resistance at the Greasy Grass, aka Little Bighorn. So, in a small act of personal defiance, I decided to burn the booklet in my wood stove before I vacated the cabin. I read through one last time the entries from the Lieutenant, about breaking up fights between the soldiers and his lists of supplies for the journal. The entries were daily until they abruptly ended on June 26, 1876—the day a bullet from an indigenous warrior pierced both the book and trespassing soldier. I tore off the cover and burned the pages one by one, before emptying the ashes from the stove behind my cabin.

I said goodbye to the coyotes who had been singing to me, who, every time I heard them at first, thought they sounded like crying women. For me, those cries represented the cries of their people, not just here on this mountain, but in the federal pens of the Predator Research Facility and other labs carrying out research on coyotes and other native wildlife. I was hearing the voices of my wild animal relations, and with that understanding, I knew I would have to again act in their defense.

A Brief Move to LA

I arrived in Los Angeles and stayed with David on the *Edward Abbey*. I helped prepare the newly-acquired vessel and even did some door-to-door canvassing for Sea Shepherd a couple times. The Feds' attention was not in southern California, but in the San Francisco Bay Area where my family lived, and the northwest, and now Michigan. I was able to associate with old friends and help out the ocean campaign coming that summer. It was during my time on the *Edward Abbey* that Los Angeles burst into flames during the riots that followed the acquittal of police officers who had beaten Rodney King. We rode our bikes down major streets as grocery stores were being looted and cops were taking defensive formations, circled up like a wagon train of cowboys being attacked by Indians. One group of officers stood with their legs firmly apart with shotgun shells dumped in a pile on the hood of their car for quick reloading. It was a real war zone.

Some businesses around us would burst into flames while others nearby remained untouched, possibly because of the "BLACK-OWNED" that had been spray-painted across some storefronts. At night we walked up to the top of the tallest parking garage we could find and watched as multiple fires burned across the city, and the sound of sirens and police helicopters was all you could hear. In many areas, police helicopters were kept away by gunfire from below. It was the first time I witnessed such a level of armed resistance to police brutality and our country's horrible history of violence against Americans of African descent.

Later, Paul Watson and I attended a concert by John Trudell at a small nightclub; John was a Lakota activist and poet who became the national spokesperson for the American Indian Movement. He was also one of the occupiers who lived on Alcatraz Island for over a year beginning in 1969, claiming the abandoned prison as Indian Land. Trudell's voice could be heard during the occupation from the pirate radio station the occupiers operated during the siege. Trudell was now addressing the recent riots in LA and giving his reflections as a longtime fighter against colonization.

After the concert, I met with Trudell and told him a little about the fur farm rehabilitation project, and shared with him some articles I had written about the ALF's campaign against fur farms. He was one of the few survivors of the FBI's campaign of violent repression that targeted AIM members and was a symbol of what a modern indigenous warrior looked like. Shaking hands with him was, for me, how shaking hands with the president of the United States must feel for other people. Crossing paths with this hero and icon of indigenous resistance was more than serendipity, it was perhaps an omen of what was to come.

Heading out to the Reservation

In May 1992, the world came closing in. David Howitt was called to testify to a federal grand jury investigating Operation Bite Back. Both he and Linda May would cooperate, telling authorities everything they knew about the rehab project and nothing else, neither of them having been involved in any of the actions I took after leaving the rehab project the previous June. By again tracking my phone records, the Feds were able to determine that I had called a storage rental facility, and when they ran my alias 'Jim Perez' past the managers, got a match. Armed with a search warrant, federal agents emptied my storage locker; it was filled with not just my personal belongings but copies of fur animal research papers and a manual typewriter that contained a ribbon that hid one of the messages I had last written:

> ... largest fur processor in Montana. After my investigation I discovered that all of the fur farmers in Montana used the same company to prepare pelts for auction. The Huggans Rocky Mountain Fur Company is a building I have been in before. It is all wood, with no alarms and no close proximity to animals. The targeted building contains all the drying racks and drums used in pelt processing. If we could cause substantial damage to that equipment, we would cause a serious disruption to the pelting season ...

Now federal investigators knew I was responsible for the attempted attack in Montana as well as the attempt in Louisiana.

And there was more. In my storage locker, the Feds also found the article I had saved from the Colorado newspaper about the theft of the cavalryman's notebook—a truly stupid move after having decided to burn the journal, which was the only other evidence of the theft in my possession. Now authorities had contacted the National Park Service and were able to match my fingerprints to those found on the notebook's plexiglass case in the museum. The federal charges against me were stacking up.

Again, I needed to leave my temporary sanctuary with friends and head somewhere with no direct history of my involvement. I met an author and Sea Shepherd supporter friend of mine in LA, Marc Gaede. Marc had written a book about a Lakota man who dedicated his life to helping indigenous people find sobriety through spirituality: *Sundance: The Robert Sundance Story* (1994). The man's family were Hunkpapa Lakota—Sitting Bull's people—and Marc said the elder of the family had actually told him if he ever needed a place to hide out, the Standing Rock Reservation would be a good place to do it. With a couple of phone calls, I confirmed with family members that I could stay on their 2,500 acres of land on which they raised horses. So I bought a plane ticket to Rapid City, South Dakota, and said goodbye to the West Coast. I boarded the plane with one backpack, about $3,000 in cash, and no plans on what to do next.

The evening air was warm as I left the Rapid City airport and headed into town to rent a motel room. I needed to find a way to the remote Standing Rock Reservation, and there was no easy way to get there. After a good night of peaceful sleep, feeling like I had truly escaped from the world where I was known, I grabbed breakfast then walked to a car dealership I had seen on my way into town. There, I found an older Subaru wagon on sale for only $1,800. I paid cash for the car and drove it off the lot. I grabbed my gear from the motel room and began the four-hour drive to Standing Rock. The Plains region was breathtaking. I had only ever traveled through on the Interstate, but traveling the Plains on small, lonely, two-lane roads takes you into another world.

Outside of the tiny reservation town of Wakpala, I pulled down the long dirt driveway to the McLaughlin residence. There I met my hosts, Pat and Victoria McLaughlin, two Lakota elders who welcomed me with just a little guarded suspicion. The public story I told them was that I was writing a book and looking for a place to write with solitude. I followed Pat as he drove his pickup truck about a mile from his own home to what looked like (and was) a dilapidated small home with a collapsed foundation. As we pulled up to the property, a red-tail hawk flew out of the basement. Pat told me he leased a grazing allotment to a white rancher I might see occasionally, but other than that, I probably wouldn't even see another Indian unless I left the family's land.

Pat looked like a cowboy, not a stereotypical Indian. He grew up during one of the most repressed times for Lakota people. He would tell me about bathing in the Missouri River every day before it was dammed, because his family did not have running water. When Bureau of Indian Affairs officials discovered his family's living conditions, they declared the home unsafe, kidnapped young Pat, and forced him into boarding school. And yes, 'kidnapped' was the term used by Indians who had members of their families stolen this way. Pat told me about how in boarding school he would be burned with steam by the janitor as punishment for speaking his native language of Lakota.

When he was a young man, like many Lakota people, Pat enlisted in the military for the fight overseas during World War II. He told me it was the first time he had left the reservation, and that within days of arriving in France, he was tossing hand grenades in street-to-street fights with invading Nazis. When he returned home to the reservation, he was still subjected to existing racism, not welcomed as a war hero. He turned towards his people and got involved with tribal politics, ascending to chairman of the tribe—an office he had recently left, but he remained on the tribal council.

At this time in my life, I didn't have elders. Sure, I had mentors like Paul Watson, Ingrid Newkirk, and Ben White, but I did not know what it meant to have *an elder*, someone like myself but with many more years of experience and wisdom as an indigenous person struggling to survive in the Invader's world. Pat was one of the first indigenous elders I was blessed to have in my life, for guidance and protection. He was my only visitor at my cabin, and we sat around my small campfire outside the house and drank coffee while he told me stories from his life and the land. He reminded me that this land was still Indian Land, and that there was a power and magic in it that still survived, to those willing to look and listen for it.

I spent my days walking the prairie, getting familiar with the sparse landscape which, it turned out, was not sparse at all. In each small crevice of the hills there was a sliver of trees, hiding habitat for a variety of species. It wasn't uncommon to find eagle feathers below the scraggily oak trees where the birds roosted, or in the prairie dog town's where an eagle had captured prey. I sat with binoculars and watched the prairie dogs from a hidden rise. If I heard the animal's warning whistles, I could then locate an approaching bobcat or other predator. Here was land where no white man was allowed to trap or hunt and where the animals existed as they had for generations before the white man.

One day, Pat's son, TJ, invited me to drive up to Grand Forks, North Dakota, to visit his ex-wife and child's mother, LaDonna Brave Bull and her partner Miles. Over coffee, we talked about experiences we had with racism in America. Only recently had I experienced racism in South Dakota, but these friends shared stories of horrible treatment by store and restaurant owners who regularly treated Indians with disrespect. It was the first time in my life I had ever heard other indigenous folks talk about such things.

I became quick friends with LaDonna and Miles and I agreed to join them when attending an upcoming Pow Wow at a state prison where their son was incarcerated. My new friends knew nothing about my real identity; they said all I needed to enter the prison was a driver's license, which I had in another name. When we arrived at the prison, all that could be seen were the high stone walls and guard towers atop of them. I wasn't concerned as I lined up, signed my name, and showed my ID to the guards ushering in visitors for the Pow Wow. Within moments, I was in the open prison yard. It was surreal to be visiting a prison, let alone one where dozens of indigenous people were visiting with relatives as drums beat across the yard. I was intrigued by the wooden-framed dome structure that I knew to be a sweat lodge, and how odd it seemed that something so ancient was allowed in a prison. In time, I would begin to learn the value of our traditions, especially for incarcerated indigenous people—which I knew, deep down, that I would soon experience personally.

An Assault by the Feds

Despite the relative sanctuary that I felt I was in, I still carried with me a certain level of fear and anticipation of arrest. Like the proverbial thread pulled from a sweater, once the Feds intercepted the FedEx package sent from Michigan, they began to uncover other key evidence that led first to the search warrants and then, in May, to a dramatic raid on my cabin in southern Oregon.

What unfolded on that bright and cool spring morning in the Little Applegate River Valley of Southern Oregon, was never officially acknowledged, probably because it failed. It would be years before I heard the story from one of the few eyewitnesses: my neighbor Chant Thomas, whose phone I had used on occasion. Chant was getting ready to leave for work around 7:30 a.m. when a well-dressed couple pulled up in a truck with a camper, asking if he could help them find Rodney Coronado's cabin. Being the veteran forest defender that he was, Chant was immediately suspicious of the two and told them he had never heard of me and that they must have the wrong address. He then drove away.

A few miles down the mountain, where the pavement ended, the Feds were waiting for the signal from the two agents in the camper. Another resident would recount that, as he drove the mountain, he was passed by several black vans with government plates. One van guarded the bottom of the dirt road while the others went to a public trailhead near my cabin ... to wait. From over the mountains came the *thump, thump, thump* of helicopter rotors as the aircraft flew towards a clearing near my cabin.

What happened next was almost comical, if it wasn't for the fact that, once again, the federal government could have injured or killed innocent people. The helicopter landed in the clearing of another neighbor's A-frame cabin and out charged armed agents. They ran towards the residence of my elderly neighbor and kicked in her door. She screamed for her life as the agents demanded to know where Rodney Coronado was; she pointed to my cabin hidden in the woods across the river. Realizing their mistake, the agents scurried across the wooden bridge that led to my recently-vacated cabin. Rushing to the far side of the river, the agents found the cabin, which was now empty except for a single hawk feather I left dangling in the doorway.

The raid impacted the local community; two locals were detained and questioned, and another, a Vietnam veteran, was so pissed off that he flew his own tiny helicopter to the scene and buzzed the government's chopper as it flew back empty-handed to Medford.

Following my trail, federal agents next tried to catch me in Santa Cruz, California. As the *Sea Shepherd II* and *Edward Abbey* were setting sail for the North Pacific in a rainstorm in late June, they were hailed by a Coast Guard vessel and told to be prepared to be boarded. It was a vicious rainstorm when ATF, FBI, and Customs agents boarded the Sea Shepherd and demanded to see everyone's passport. They searched the ship and asked if anyone had been transferred at sea. The ships would again be searched by the FBI on Canada's Vancouver Island. Paul Watson would later say they boarded the vessels "with a small army," including police dogs.

Many of my old Sea Shepherd friends were some of the first to be questioned by federal authorities hunting the ALF. Many had been visited by me during my fur farm investigation, and others, like David Howitt, were working on the ships when I was aboard them in spring 1992. Later, the office manager of Sea Shepherd's Marina Del Rey office was repeatedly harassed and subpoenaed because of her suspected connections with me.

She had bought my Subaru while I was still in LA, giving me some cash to live on in my early days on the run.

The Feds greatest weapon for both investigating the ALF and for intimidating its supporters were federal grand juries convened following the multi-state Operation Bite Back crimes. PETA employees suspected of handling press materials related to the MSU raid were subpoenaed, as were PETA's employee records and photos. Other activists from the US animal rights movement were soon subpoenaed. One of them was Jonathan Paul, my friend and Global Investigations partner, and also one of three men who were indicted in Oregon in 1990 on charges relating to a 1986 ALF raid on the University of Oregon. Paul was also a suspect in numerous ALF actions in California, as well as the toppling of power lines on Earth Day 1990.

Back on the reservation, I felt lonely and isolated from all my activist friends, but was very much aware of the danger I faced, even though I had yet to learn of the attempts to arrest me on the West Coast. I knew many of my friends would be at the annual Earth First! rendezvous in Southern Colorado. The gatherings were also an unofficial place that some of us gathered to talk about illegal activities to protect animals and the Earth. I knew I couldn't just drive up to the registration table and check in, so I looked at a national forest map and found a spot about ten miles from the gathering where I could drive and park, far from the event and from any suspicious criminal investigators.

I waited until morning to set out, carrying only a light pack with my sleeping bag, pad, and some food and water. I kept off trails and hiked over a ridge that led to the Animas River. When I thought I should be getting close, I started smelling wood smoke and heard voices and laughter still far away. It was dusk, so I waited until dark to approach the main trail leading to the event. It was dark by now, so I felt comfortable paying my $20 without drawing attention to myself. Luckily, the person checking in late-night arrivals did not ask for my name.

I walked the quarter-mile trail that led to the gathering in darkness, taking advantage of the fact that the crowd here discouraged the use of headlamps; it was called "Hippy mace" to shine your headlamp in an unsuspecting person's face. I made my way to the large central fire where a crowd had gathered, with most drinking. I kept to the shadows and surveyed the scene for danger, friends, or those I didn't want to see. When the crowd had filtered away to only a handful of people, I approached a trusted friend and tapped him on the elbow. He was shocked to see my face but quickly regained composure and walked with me to a place where we could talk in private.

My friend helped me find a place to camp far from others, yet close enough for chosen friends to visit. I even got to spend my birthday in a hot spring surrounded by people with whom I had spent the past five or six years fighting to defend the wild. Sometimes we called ourselves Sea Shepherd, sometimes the Animal Liberation Front or Earth First!, but we were all part of the same generation of Earth warriors, like Paul Watson and Cleveland Amory, or Crazy Horse and Sitting Bull. These were among the very few people willing to risk their own freedom for that of others.

One of the friends I met there was Jonathan Paul, who had recently had his charges dismissed for his alleged role in the 1986 ALF raid on University of Oregon labs in Eugene. Jonathan and I had worked together mostly on animal rights issues but he was now being targeted by the grand jury in Spokane, Washington investigating the WSU raid. Our older friend, Cres Velucci, was one of the animal rights movement's loudest critics of the grand juries hunting ALF, and always advised activists to "plead the Fifth" and invoke their constitutional right against self-incrimination.

Now with federal grand juries investigating the ALF in nine federal districts, Jonathan would be the first of many of my friends who refused to cooperate with federal investigators. Exerting pressure on him to testify at the Spokane grand jury, the US government hoped to gather information that would lead to the indictment of not just me, but other suspected ALF warriors. When Jonathan pled the Fifth Amendment and refused to testify, he was granted immunity from prosecution. When he still refused to testify, he was imprisoned on contempt-of-court charges, with the judge believing that imprisonment would coerce him to testify. He was wrong. Jonathan sat tight-lipped in jail for six months before his imprisonment was deemed to be punishment rather than coercion, and he was released.

Another friend called before the Spokane grand jury was Rik Scarce, author of the 1990 book *Eco-Warriors* that contained interviews with me and other ALF members. My phone records had again confirmed that he and I were friends and that I occasionally visited his Pullman, Washington home before the WSU raid. Rik's then-fiancé was also subpoenaed to the grand jury. Soon thereafter, Friends of Animals—who had financed my undercover investigation of US fur farming—began fully cooperating with the authorities.

For most of those called to testify, like my own family members, there was nothing to tell. I didn't mind if they answered questions about me because they didn't know anything about my involvement with the

ALF. Of course, it would be ideal in a movement for no one to cooperate with politically-motivated grand juries, but many of the people being intimidated and traumatized were innocents, like my mother or the parents of a friend I stayed with in Michigan before the MSU raid.

Meanwhile, in response to information seized in the Maryland house of the former PETA employee, another grand jury was convened in Louisiana in the summer of 1992 to investigate leads on the aborted plans to raid the Delta Regional Primate Facility at Tulane University. By the end of 1992, over 30 activists had been subpoenaed, many of them testifying about their knowledge of the ALF.

The year 1992 would be remembered as "the year of intimidation," in which dozens of grassroots activists and others saw firsthand the repression that the FBI and ATF was causing to those who supported ALF direct-actions. As with any movement worth their weight, despite this intimidation, many activists weathered the storm and refused to be intimidated by the government agents hunting the "terrorists" rescuing animals from laboratories and fur farms.

Most people would assume that, with nine federal grand juries and a multi-divisional task force of FBI, ATF, state, university, and county police forces investigating the ALF, that us warriors would be hunkered down somewhere, hiding from the law. I *was* hiding, but that didn't stop me from planning more actions. After leaving the Earth First! gathering, I drove back to South Dakota to await word from friends I had spoken with in Colorado. I was not content to simply hide out on the reservation; I still wanted to target the federal government's Predator Research Facility in Utah. But my pool of potential warriors was shrinking. Most of my friends were still living in areas with active grand jury investigations. It was time once again to recruit new warriors for a raid.

At the Earth First! gathering I had attended in Colorado, I made plans for a few friends to visit me in South Dakota at my reservation hideout. I had told them under no circumstances should they drive their own vehicles, for fear of any tracking devices that might have been attached to them. When I drove to the Sitting Bull Memorial where we were to meet, I was shocked to see Jonathan Paul in his own truck. But I was still happy to see the old friends he had with him. After explaining that he had had his truck scanned for any devices (something I was dubious of) we decided to leave his truck off the reservation on an old farm road.

We friends then went to work discussing the possibility of attacking the Predator Research Facility, but Jonathan was already on the FBI's radar so that path seemed like a dead end. It was decided that we should travel out of state to recruit any needed new warriors.

After our visit, when it was time for my friends to leave, we made our plan to retrieve Jonathan's truck. We treated the situation with extreme caution because I was extremely suspicious about Jonathan's truck having driven all the way from California to South Dakota, then stop and sit for a couple days, then start heading west again. If the FBI had placed a tracker on the car, this would be where they would set any trap. I was driving in a friend's car which we were certain was unknown to the feds. The plan was for us to all drive west, but in separate vehicles and not close together. It was late at night on the Plains when we pulled into a small town to fill up with gas at separate gas stations. I pulled in first, then saw Jonathan's truck across the street. With little other traffic on the road except for us, the next car that drove by aroused my suspicions. It was the only other car on the road at that hour and, after passing our gas stations, continued down the remote state highway. When we got back on the road and were leaving town, in the shadows of the shoulder of the road, with its lights off and backed into a field while facing the highway, was the same suspicious car.

We had radios with us that were on, so I told our friends that I suspected we had been compromised. We decided to meet briefly to discuss a plan of action on the dark shoulder of an intersection where we could also split up. As we hurriedly made a plan, in the distance we saw the lights of an approaching vehicle which suddenly turned and stopped. I was now certain we were being followed, and the presumed tracker on Jonathan's truck had indicated that we had stopped again. We were being followed, but not with a force large enough to attempt an arrest. The feds were probably simply trying to confirm my location, before planning any assault. We hugged each other and said quick goodbyes before I hopped into the Subaru owned by my friend from New Mexico, Jay, and we quickly drove off down the intersecting dirt road that crossed the highway with our lights off. Jonathan sped off on his same route west toward home, with his federal tail not far behind. When he returned home, they were waiting: he was met by federal agents and given the subpoena that would eventually lead to his imprisonment on contempt charges for not cooperating with the federal grand jury in Washington state investigating the WSU raid the previous summer.

Before my friends had arrived for their fateful visit, I felt extremely lonely and was very much expecting a possible raid by federal agents searching for me. I started losing sleep, and only felt safe when walking the immense prairie during the day, where I would sometimes nap, feeling safer sleeping during the day. On one of these days, I thought about my community of friends with Sea Shepherd and my new friends in Oregon, and how I could never be in their lives again as a fugitive from justice. My fear of being arrested or shot were amplified not only by my being a fugitive, but in the last year, the world had seen the FBI and ATF botched raids against Randy Weaver in Idaho and on the Branch Davidian homestead which left dozens of women and children dead. The Spirit hunters were very real in 1992 and the memory of their murderous reign against Black Panthers, American Indian Movement members, and other domestic insurgents was very much in the forefront of my mind.

One day as I walked the prairie, feeling afraid and overwhelmed, I started crying and surrendered to the emotions I was then feeling. As I cried, I looked up and saw a low-flying red-tail hawk circling over me, turning its head to observe what must have been a strange phenomena. It wasn't uncommon to see wildlife up close, on the huge expanse where no hunting was allowed, but as this hawk circled over me, I felt she could sense I was in some form of danger. I was still walking, but now I stopped because there was a coyote standing about 50 feet away from me, staring at me as he stood broadside. Like a wave, I felt all my fears lifted as the coyote stood staring at me. Without audibly hearing the words, in the fresh air created by the lifting of my sorrows, I could hear both the hawk and the coyote. They said, *"Now you know what it feels like to be hunted. Now you know what it feels like to be one of us... Do not be afraid. We are families and our homes have been attacked for hundreds of years, but we are still here. There is much power to help you, but not when you still believe in what you fear more than you believe in us."*

When I heard—or rather, when I felt that message coming from those animal messengers, I really started to cry; I knew I had just been rescued by the same beings I thought I had been rescuing all these years. All I know is that, from that moment forward, I was no longer afraid. And I knew it was now extremely important that we carry out what might be our last action against the Predator Research Facility. Coyotes were an indigenous nation of beings who knew only war since the Invaders arrived, yet they have been one of the only predators who have expanded their range in the face of such genocide. I was now seeing them as my ancestors saw them: not as 'others' but as my own living relatives. They had children just like us, they had families just like us, and humans have waged war on their communities for generations, but still they persisted. Still their survival was resistance.

With this vision fresh in my heart, after the close call in South Dakota, Jay and I drove west to Washington state to recruit warriors for the Utah raid. We visited old Earth First! friends I had made at the gathering in the Okanagon in 1988 and soon found a trusted friend who was willing to travel to Utah for the planned action. Next, we visited Port Angeles, where I attempted to contact David Howitt who was at anchor on his sailboat. He must have also been under surveillance because after we attempted to call him over the radio, two suspicious Coast Guard members appeared. When I then tried to hike onto Linda's property where we had carried out the rehabilitation project, I saw a mustached man sitting in a vehicle watching the road. It appeared that the feds had many people under surveillance in their hunt for the ALF.

Not to be discouraged, we got back in our car and drove to Colorado on our way to Utah for more surveillance. In Colorado, I learned of a friend from California who was passing through town. I made plans to meet him. Lief had helped me out with the guinea pig liberation near my hometown, so I knew I could trust him. After exchanging pleasantries, I asked if he might be interested in helping out with another action. He replied, "Sure! Whatever I can do to help, you know you can count on me!" I said, "Don't you want to hear about it before you decide?" To which he responded, "No…I trust you, whatever it is, I'm sure it's worth the risk." With Lief, we now had three warriors and were still hoping to recruit two more.

When we reached Utah, we visited another friend who I hadn't seen in a couple years. She was now working as a wildlife rehabilitator and was out of touch with old activist friends. Fortunately, she also readily agreed to participate in the raid once we had explained that the target was the same federal agency that had been killing tens of thousands of coyotes every year to protect the livestock industry.

Time for Recon

With a crew recruited, I could now turn my attention to the physical reconnaissance that was warranted for this next attack. Although the USDA's predator research had yet to be targeted by the underground, it had long been a target of the above-ground environmental and animal movements. We needed more people because we wanted to do as much as possible during our one-time strike that would surely lead to a change in security.

We wanted to hit Wildlife Services in two important, and somewhat adjacent, locations. Our targets were the offices of the USDA's lead coyote researcher, Fred Knowlton, on the Logan campus of the University of Utah and the connected USDA Predator Research Facility eight miles south outside of Millville. Those were the primary targets. The secondary would be the USDA National Wildlife Research Center's Pocatello Supply Depot, which manufactures the wildlife damage management products developed by researchers for the "Wildlife Services" program. This was the factory that was responsible for manufacturing and distributing such lethal products as the M-44 cyanide device which injects lethal poison into the mouth of its victims, mostly coyotes. Another weapon of mass destruction produced was the "Large Gas Cartridge" (EPA Reg. No. 56228-62) whose directions state, "Must be used in active coyote dens only." Other lethal tools, like a livestock protection collar with a reservoir of the lethal compound 1080 intended for coyotes, were currently being developed by the PRF in Millville. We wanted to hit both the research and manufacturing division of this vile agency responsible for the death of literally millions of native predators and other wildlife.

Pocatello Supply Depot

Registered Pesticides for Coyotes

Coyote. Photo: USFWS   Coyote. Photo: USFWS

Fumigants
     Registered Products –(GUP)
          Large Gas Cartridge 56228-62 USDA-APHIS: R, C, NC.

Use Directions: Must be used in active coyote dens only.

Use Restrictions: Must obtain Endangered Species Bulletin prior to use. Must contact USFWS regional office (406-449-5225) for information on endangered or threatened species in your area.

We drove the two hours from Logan, Utah, to Pocatello, Idaho, and camped in a canyon overlooking the small town. The Depot was on the edge of town near the railroad and far from any human habitation. We wanted to burn the building, which we knew contained dangerous chemicals. Any fire might pose additional risks to the public and firefighters. But we also knew if no homes or humans were threatened by the fire and it was deemed dangerous, it might simply be contained and allowed to burn.

I had been here once before, on that fateful failed attempt to burn down the Fur food co-op in Sandy, Utah. On that trip, we had scoped out the location, but hadn't gone further. Now I was climbing onto the roof to search for possible entry sites. I found one in the form of a roof hatch that opened onto the exterior of the building from inside the main building. Now on this scouting mission, I could lift the hatch just high enough to see a small clasp securing it. I could just reach the clasp with my fingers enough to dislodge it, and I was in. Inside were pallets stacked to the ceiling with various pesticide-labeled products, including some with strychnine; these were poisons meant to be fed to prairie dogs and other wildlife. The darkened warehouse might be alarmed for motion, so I took a small rubber ball that I got from a quarter vending machine and, from my elevated position, threw the ball towards the floor. No alarm sounded—either it failed, or there simply wasn't one. Whether the trick worked or not, I retreated from the building feeling like I could later return and plant an incendiary device. We would ask two of our team to carry out the Pocatello Supply depot raid.

When we returned to Utah, one of the first things we did was walk the campus of the University of Utah to locate Fred Knowlton's office. Once we had identified that it was a ground floor office, I turned my attention towards how we could get inside of it without having to walk any halls where someone might see us. The exterior window in Knowlton's office looked out into a U-shaped courtyard. The landscaping and shrubs below the window would offer some visual protection, but we also would be extremely close to the University Police station on campus just outside of the courtyard. We wouldn't need a police scanner to know if we'd been discovered; I could just look over my shoulder. At night and from behind the shrubs, I was able to discern that the trim around the glass window into Knowlton's office could be removed, and then the window. Whether it was alarmed or not, I would not know until I had removed the glass.

Once I was confident that I could gain entry, Jay and I focused on a few nights of all-night recon of the Predator Research Facility. The lab is located on the Wasatch Front, just south of Millville and at the foot of what is called the Millville Face of the Wasatch Mountains. On the opposite of the Wasatch Valley, to the west, lies the Great Salt Lake.

Every night as we conducted recon, we heard the main group of re-search coyotes in a kennel building yip and howl in response to wild coy-otes living in the first draws and canyons to their east. The wild coyotes could only be heard faintly, but the congregation at the research facility would sing together—dozens, if not more coyotes howling at one time. It was heartbreaking.

We saw a house on the property of the lab, with a single vehicle parked in front. We were pleased to note that whenever the coyotes howled, the watch-person in the house took no notice, with the lights still out in the house. Once I felt certain that there wasn't a nighttime security patrol, I decided to venture closer to the actual laboratory and again, search for an entry point. The lab was a sterile rectangular building with a sheet-metal exterior and almost no windows, except for one in a bathroom. In all my sneaking around as an ALF member, it's funny the number of times I've been able to gain safe entry into a target building through a bathroom window. They are usually cracked open just enough to clear the air inside.

Feeling confident that I could enter through the bathroom window, I then focused on the multiple chain-link-fenced pens that housed coyotes undergoing experiments. Some were being fed a diet laced with poisons, and others were the subject of various livestock-related experiments, all in search of better ways to kill coyotes. It was dark enough that I was walking upright next to a pen when I noticed a coyote following alongside me from inside the fence. When I realized this and stopped and turned around, the coyote quickly turned and darted away. Other coyotes in nearby pens could be seen watching me as I passed, probably wondering what this two-legged was doing out at night when all the others came around during the day.

In October, we again gathered around a small campfire in the national forest near the Idaho border. We were five warriors. We went over the plans again and again, and still came up short a person. We needed six: two for the supply depot in Idaho and four for the raid on the lab and cam-pus office. My old friend from the Okanagon, Stephen, offered to carry out the Pocatello raid alone without any additional security or a driver. It would be extremely risky, but better than taking no action at all. The rest of us would travel to Logan and then Millville. Before we separated, I gave Stephen some cash and went over everything I could remember from my recon. The last thing I gave him was a fully-assembled incendiary device with a one-hour timer.

The rest of us drove to a motel in Logan where we prepared for our part of the action. Jay and I had only known each other since we met at the Earth First! Rendezvous in Colorado earlier that year, but we both believed more in indigenous ways than in those of the Invader. She was the first ALF warrior I knew who brought ceremony into our actions. I welcomed the recognition that the animal liberation struggle that I was a part of was also part of a much larger struggle in North America against colonization by indigenous inhabitants as well. But what made things different now was that it wasn't just me recognizing that are struggles were connected; or that our power came from the Earth and those countless people who had lived and died on these lands fighting for a similar way of life. We spoke of this as we geared up for our action, that we were new warriors asking for strength and guidance from this sacred centuries-old resistance. Now we smudged ourselves as I had been instructed and prepared for battle.

Into Battle

The first leg of the action would be Jay and I entering the courtyard where Knowlton's office was located. With our security watches in place from vehicles on university parking lots, Jay and I walked holding hands into the dimly-lit courtyard. Once behind the bushes, I turned towards the window as Jay kept watch. With a screwdriver, I was able to pry away the trim holding the glass window in place. Once the trim was removed, the old window caulking was so loose that I easily removed the two-foot-long piece of glass and set it on the ground. When Jay saw that I had removed the window rather quickly, she gave me a thumbs up and I began crawling into the darkened office. No alarms sounded, but I still wanted to keep my entry time minimal. Without rifling through records, I simply began making a pile of flammable materials under Knowlton's office desk. Once I had placed the incendiary device and set the timer for one hour, I knew the clock was now ticking, literally, on how much time we had to raid the Predator Research Facility.

The moment I had entered Knowlton's office, Jay radioed our two friends sitting in their car at the Millville Canyon trailhead. That was their signal to begin walking the half-mile towards the Predator Research Facility and start cutting the fence. After Jay and I returned to our own vehicle, I stripped off my student attire and put on black cargo pants with pockets and an equally dark, thin jacket. We then drove the eight miles, being very careful to stay under the speed limit. If we were pulled over for even the smallest reason, there would be a record of our presence close to where a fire would soon start. When we reached the trailhead, Jay took up watch from a vantage point over the road leading to the PRF, and I began jogging towards the distant outline of the watchtower that stood over the maze of coyote pens.

This felt like another action that would catch our enemies completely by surprise, not another attack on a predictably-defended fur farm target. With the WSU raid, we had targeted sarcocystis research being conducted on coyotes on behalf of the livestock industry, and by doing so had revealed that our strategy was expanding to other lethal wildlife research. But the numerous USDA/APHIS research stations spread across the country had drawn little critical attention—but enough to warrant strict security measures on the Wasatch Front of Utah where I now stood.

On radio now, I warned the other two warriors of my approach; I could see them up ahead, both cutting chain-link fence with bolt cutters. As I approached, I saw them both fighting back tears. Leif grabbed me by the shoulders and said, "They know, the coyotes know... They know what we are doing. As we were just cutting the fence, one was standing on the other side, digging at the fence! They know we're trying to set them free!"

It was not what I expected to hear, but I wasn't in the least bit surprised. After my experience on the plains with my coyote and hawk relatives, I knew a veil had been lifted between our species and we were rekindling an ancient kinship between our wild animal relations. This was no longer a political movement; it was part of a centuries-old spiritually-based resistance. The adrenalin told my own body that right now was not the time for tears; it was a time for flaming arrows.

I moved more slowly as I left my friends and approached the one-story research facility. Keeping the lab between me and the watch-person's house directly behind it, I crouched below the same bathroom window that I had earlier seen ajar. Unfortunately, there was a metal screen firmly in place that I'd have to wrench away. I knew in doing so, I might make enough noise to be heard. We hadn't come this far to turn back now, so I decided I just had to go for it, and get the screen off as quickly as possible. At that exact moment, as if on cue, coyotes began singing from the mountains behind me. Maybe they were those that were being freed, I'll never know; but when their singing had faded, a cacophony of coyote song erupted from the 100 prisoners being held in the main kennel building. I knew this was not a coincidence. I stood up and forced my large screwdriver beneath the screen and pried it off noisily, but any sound was surely drowned out by the coyotes' cries.

I climbed into the building and surveyed the scene before me. There wasn't much to be seen that was sinister; most of the research took place in the coyote pens. But amongst the sterile surroundings were stacks of small plywood signs with wire that read, "DO NOT FEED." These were the signs researchers placed on coyote cages when they wanted the animals to be forced to eat only the experimental tainted diet they had been given as part of a research project.

I took little more time exploring the lab. It was clearly empty of life. Utilizing the open window as an oxygen source for my planned fire, I took the plywood signs and piled them against a row of wooden cabinets. Taking the two plastic quart bottles of fuel from my pack, I placed these in the center of the pile and then took out my toilet-paper-cushioned incendiary device from its Tupperware container and gingerly set it up next to the fuel bottles. I then popped the cap off a Sterno can and placed the filament portion of the incendiary device in the flammable gel. The last thing I did was twist the one-hour timer—this time, for only 30 minutes—and connected the 9-volt battery power source. Thirty minutes was the time left on the other device, and we wanted them to trigger simultaneously. Should only one ignite, it could trigger a quick security search of related facilities, revealing my break-in at the lab.

When I had dropped from the bathroom window, I took out a can of red spray-paint and went to work painting a large spiral with four hawk feathers dangling beneath it, each representing our raids on Oregon State University, Washington State University, Michigan State University, and now Utah State University and the USDA's Predator Research Facility.

With quick coyote figures seen darting through the night towards the nearby mountains, we three warriors were now putting the lab and pens behind us and jogging back to our waiting vehicles at the trailhead. Our departure was uneventful, with Lief and the other warrior heading back west towards California, and Jay and I fleeing south towards New Mexico and the Gila Wilderness where she owned property. Around a campfire, we later burned computer disks and the few other valuable records we had taken during the raid.

It was weeks before we ever learned anything about the impact of our action. When Jay and I finally met up again with our Washington friend who was to carry out the action at the Pocatello Supply Depot, we discovered why we hadn't heard anything about the attack. Apparently, there was an alarm in the building. And when the sole warrior entered the building, the alarm sounded. He fled and hid as he watched a police cruiser circle the building with its spotlight searching. When the patrol car left, our friend assembled his incendiary device and returned for a second attempt. This time he set his device against the exterior of the building. Any subsequent fire probably didn't do enough damage to mention, even though the supply depot would now be on guard for future attacks.

Meanwhile back on the Wasatch Front, according to PRF officials, only 18 coyotes had been released. Perhaps that was simply the number of coyotes they were able to recapture and researchers wanted to say that all prisoners were accounted for. Even in media reports, there was mention that some coyotes had not been recovered. What wasn't argued was the coordinated fires that broke out in the two buildings connected with predator research. The campus fire burned briefly before it was extinguished, but not before irreplaceable research had been damaged or completely lost. At the Predator Research Facility, the fire was much stronger, causing so much structural damage to the entire building that it was deemed a total loss and had to be demolished. It would be weeks before we officially claimed responsible for the action, which would be the last for the Western Wildlife Unit of the ALF.

The Predator Research Facility continues to operate today. In the place where the lab was destroyed, another research facility has arisen, and though coyotes still live and die there, most of the experiments are focused on finding nonlethal ways to coexist with the coyotes. I'd like to think that our raid had something to do with that.

Terms of Surrender

With an ever-increasing focus on my past associations and whereabouts by federal authorities, I knew my arrest could possibly be imminent. And with the list of my friends who were being called before federal grand juries growing, the continued circulation of my composite sketch and threat of violence from fur farmers or federal agents, I decided that I would try to use my capture as leverage on behalf of some of the victims of Washington State University's wildlife research. I knew there was no way the Feds were going to negotiate with me, but I saw the offer as an opportunity to continue to shed light on the wildlife research I was discovering. I authored a "terms of surrender" agreement and sent it to a few journalists:

> Animal Liberation Front (ALF) spokesperson Rod Coronado, who has been in hiding due to threats against his life from the FBI and fur industry is willing to surrender to federal authorities under the following conditions:

That all grizzly bears being held hostage as experimental subjects by Washington State University be released to a wildlife rehabilitation center approved by People for the Ethical Treatment of Animals and Earth First! with the intent of returning the bears to their native homeland from which they were removed.

That Washington State University issue a public statement promising to never capture or acquire more endangered species as research subjects or for any other purpose.

That all taxpayer supported research being conducted on mink, coyote and otter by Washington State University, Oregon State University, Michigan State University and Utah State University be suspended.

Although the Coalition Against Fur Farms and the ALF do not approve of the incarceration of any native wildlife, Rod Coronado believes that the hostage exchange of one species for another is a reasonable alternative. If these three conditions are agreed to, met, and negotiated through PETA and EF!, I, Rod Coronado, will turn myself in to federal authorities in Montana at the tribal headquarters of the Blackfeet Nation. As part of the agreement, I, Rod Coronado, swear to cooperate fully with grand jury inquisitions into ALF activity that I am suspected of participating in relating to the defense of native wildlife and the environment. I swear to testify and answer all questions relating to my role as a spokesperson on behalf of the ALF and as the coordinator of the Coalition Against Fur Farms.

I, Rod Coronado, believe that my nonviolent actions in defense of the earth are innocent acts to protect the ecological integrity of this country's natural heritage. This statement of conditions of surrender is in no way an admission of guilt to charges laid by the United States government or any other agency. It is my belief that with a fair trial, the citizens of this country will recognize that the real acts of terrorism committed on university campuses in the last eighteen months are those carried out by Oregon State researcher Ron Scott, Washington State researcher John Gorham, Michigan State researcher Richard Aulerich, and Utah State researcher Frederick Knowlton.

Recent attempts by the FBI to portray me as a fugitive evading arrest are standard practices by the US government to convince the public that I am guilty and a violent criminal —the first steps in justifying the assassination of Native American activists who choose to maintain their cultural and religious beliefs.

Through the example of US history, it is my understanding that if I was to continue my defense of Native American wildlife and lands, that I would be murdered by the FBI or people within the fur industry. The FBI, while questioning David Howitt in June 1992, acknowledged a threat against my life. In May 1992, when the FBI and the Bureau of Alcohol, Tobacco and Firearms raided my mountain home in southern Oregon; the presence of automatic weaponry in my attempted arrest is a testament of the US government's willingness to use deadly force to squash my representation of Native American wildlife and those who defend them.

In over ten years of nonviolent resistance to the destruction of native wildlife and lands, I have never caused an injury or loss of life to any living being. Through my obligation as a citizen of earth, I have only ever targeted the implements of life's destruction i.e.; whaling ships in Iceland. I have never, nor will I ever carry or use a firearm or explosives in my defense of my Earth Mother. My religious beliefs recognize the sanctity of all life and would never allow me to justify a violent act that would result in the loss of life. It is only because of the FBI's record of violence against Native Americans such as Anne Mae Aquash, Leonard Peltier, Tina Trudell, Pedro Bisonette, and other American Indian Movement activists that I avoid contact with the US government by living a life in hiding.

In the Spirit of Crazy Horse,
Rod Coronado

My offer was not accepted, but it did receive some media attention by Northwest media outlets following the hunt for the ALF. What did receive national media attention was the December 12, 1992 airing of the *60 Minutes* news segment on fur farms that featured the footage Maureen and I had captured of Bruce Campbell breaking the necks of mink. Although I was in hiding and unaware of the airing at the time, having our footage be shown by the network to homes across the country was vindication for sacrifices I had made. Since that first Montana fur farming investigation, friends and I had rescued, rehabilitated, and released 65 fur farm prisoners, crippled fur farm animal research, cost the industry millions and exposed the treatment of animals on fur farms to the world.

While I was now focused on my own survival, it was still extremely comforting to know that our actions were still having an impact on the fur farm industry. Just before the 1992 Winter Solstice, my friend Griz and I drove to the Zuni Reservation in New Mexico where I would spend part of the winter in hiding. I would be again staying in a remote cabin on Indian land. It wasn't safe to return to Standing Rock and most of my friends were nervous to assist in my fugitive status for fear of the repercussions, like the raid on my cabin in the Little Applegate.

In addition to fears of police repression generated by our latest ALF raid in Utah, the recent August raid by the FBI and US Marshals in Ruby Ridge, Washington that resulted in the killing of Randy Weaver's wife, son, and dog was another example of federal law enforcement using excessive deadly force to serve a warrant. I began to fear that the federal "rules of engagement" that allowed federal agents to target and kill other political activists might be used in the many ongoing ALF investigations, especially after having demonstrated that our group was still capable of carrying out a coordinated attack.

Winter is a vulnerable time for a fugitive. I couldn't just escape into the wilderness like I could in other seasons. I needed a safe place to lay low for the next few months. On one of my first nights on the reservation, I joined my hosts in attending the annual Shalako dance ceremonies that take place annually on the winter solstice. The Zuni were very protective of their culture and did not allow non-native people to attend the ceremonies unless by special invitation. Even I who was Yaqui, but not Zuni, felt like an outsider. This was one of the first traditional indigenous ceremonies that I had witnessed, and all through the night my admiration grew for the strength of these ceremonies and their ability to tie a people together through all the challenges of the past five centuries. We visited homes where taxidermized deer heads were heavily draped with turquoise jewelry in an obvious display of great reverence for the wild animals the Zuni shared their homes with. In each home, prayers were sung in the participants' native language, which was the voices these mountains had been hearing from these people for centuries. Food was shared and the smell of juniper wood burning in traditional outdoor clay ovens wafted through the crowds of people going from house to house.

After stocking up with supplies in nearby Grants, I drove to my new hideout outside of Ramah. I was staying in an old jewelry-maker's cabin that had no electricity or running water, just like my cabins on Standing

Rock and the Little Applegate. I had no human neighbors, only the coyotes to keep me company. One day as the snow fell, I looked up from my desk where I had been writing, and standing about 15 feet away was a beautiful coyote with his full winter coat, standing broadside and staring right at me. I thought about all the coyotes I had known recently, especially the one on Standing Rock that came and spoke to me. The coyote was gone within a few seconds, but left inside of me was the unmistakable recognition of the chosen connection to these animals I was now feeling, especially after the events of the last year.

I then realized that Coyotes and other nations of animals were their own people, struggling to survive in the face of human eradication policies just like their human indigenous counterparts. This sacred relationship that some humans still share with animals was what I was beginning to witness more and more, not only as I fought to defend these animals, but more importantly as I began to witness and participate in the still-living ceremonies that indigenous people conduct to honor that connection between humans, animals, the Earth, and our creator.

Except for the cold and the constant necessity to keep a wood fire burning, I was again loving my life on the run. By avoiding cities and communities under surveillance, I was able to draw closer to the animals and people I was developing a loving kinship with. This was the beneficial relationship that I most wanted to share with my friends. Instead, many were seeing the state-sanctioned "consequences" of resisting the colonial and imperial forces that now govern our lands. Activists aligned with Central American, African American, and Native American causes were being killed by the US government in the 1960s and 1970s. That was what our opponents wanted us to connect with: the fear of losing our own lives for resisting, not the power awaiting us from connecting to the thousand-year-old relationship some humans still have with the natural world.

Into 1993: A Short Trip to Hawaii

A break in winter came when Jay showed up at my cabin with news that I was being invited to visit and hide out with some trusted acquaintances on the big island of Hawaii. These were the last days of being able to fly without a government-issued ID (the Unabomber would soon make the life of fugitives like me much harder), so we decided to take the risk and drive to Washington state where we would fly to Hawaii. When we arrived, we took a taxi to the town closest to where our friends lived and walked the rest of the way.

Hawaii was an idyllic setting, fresh fruits and vegetables were readily available, the weather was warm—unlike the windswept Dakota or New Mexico landscapes I was hiding in. But we were only there for a short visit. I wasn't ready to commit to living in Hawaii, but I had also come with the motive of getting a driver's license under a different name. Before leaving the mainland, Jay and I visited a cousin of mine I had grown up with. He was willing to let me use his birth certificate and social security number to get a license in another state—these being the days before any national database on government-issued ID's. With little effort, I passed my driver's exam and was issued a legitimate license with my photo yet under a false name. This would be the only alias that the Feds would never discover and the name that I used to travel across the country before my eventual capture in 1994.

I've never been a huge fan of beach life or tropical living. I missed the smell of skunks and the songs of coyotes. I thought I could never live on an island away from those things; they meant just as much to me as living. Not so much the skunks but definitely my growing relationship with the wild nations of animals from my own homelands.

One of the last things we did on the island was to visit the active volcano, Mauna Loa. We hopped over the portable guard rails set up to protect the public and inched as close as we could to the river of molten lava that led from the volcano's lip all the way down the mountain to the sea where we stood. We watched as the lava reached the sea and was cooled by the sea water, forming into rock and eventually more land. I remembered the Lakota origin story that the McLaughlin family had told me. How *Ina*, or rock, was the first being in the known world. This now made sense to me as I literally watched the living magma of the earth become solid ground. I missed living amongst people that believed in such things. I knew I felt safest among other indigenous folks who could relate to my own struggles.

When we returned to Washington state, Jay departed, leaving me in the college town of Olympia where my old friend, David Howitt, had moored his sailboat. Despite having recently been dragged before a federal grand jury, David was one of those friends who was always willing to help me. I slept on the couch of one of David's friends, daily checking the notice boards at the local food co-op, until I found a room to rent west of town on Summit Lake, ironically just ten miles from the mink farm we had tried to burn down. After the isolation, I enjoyed living in a college town where I met folks who were not connected to the animal rights or environmental movements, but very politically progressive.

One of the friends I made was Anne White Hat, a Sicangu Lakota woman attending Evergreen College. Anne was a bartender at a local watering hole where we could always get a break on drinks when she was working. In spring of 1993, Anne planned to drive home to South Dakota for a short visit and invited David and I to accompany her on the long drive. When we arrived at her family home, we met the rest of her immediate family, including her father, Albert White Hat. Anne's family was deeply rooted in the Lakota struggle for survival and her father was an indigenous scholar who taught the Lakota language for over 25 years. Like my elder friend, Pat McLaughlin, Albert had also been sent away to a boarding school where he was punished for speaking his language. His grandfather was Hollow Horn Bear, a leader who had fought at the Battle of the Greasy Grass, Little Bighorn.

When David and I weren't out smashing rocks in Albert's driveway, he spoke to us around his kitchen table about his efforts to reclaim his language and culture and to return to a traditional spiritual life that had been illegal in his lifetime. Albert told me that many Lakota he knew were using their traditional culture as a form of recovery from alcoholism. He told me that when he wanted to bring the Sun Dance back to his people, his family only knew a few of the songs required for the ceremony. He said an elder told him to pray for guidance and that the songs would come to him. Sure enough, in time, people came forward telling him they remembered parts of a song their elders had taught them from the Sun Dance. Other songs came in dreams, he said.

I remember talking to Albert about the wolves and other now-extinct native animals that once roamed the Plains. He told me a story from when he first moved back to the land where we were visiting. He said an elder was walking with him one day when the two men saw a group of hawks roosting in a nearby tree. The elder asked Albert what he saw, and when he replied that he saw the hawks, the elder instructed him to look even closer. When he did, Albert said he could tell that each hawk was different, that they were not the same species. The elder then told him that they were witness to a gathering of the Hawk Nation and that other animals would gather like this still across the Plains.

Albert said that every plant and animal has something to teach us if we are willing to be quiet and listen. To the Lakota and other indigenous peoples, animals and plants are sacred teachers and protectors. He said that when we are ready to again coexist and see animals as our relations, that animals that we thought were once extinct would return again. Albert said the animals and the knowledge and power they shared were waiting for us humans to again see all beings as our own relations.

David and I were invited to participate in one of Albert's weekly sweat lodge ceremonies, which he said was like an AA meeting for many Indians. David and I were the youngest participants and only non-Lakota at the ceremony, which was on the banks of a river. Inside the sweat lodge, red hot stones were brought in, each being blessed with offerings of tobacco. When the lodge door was closed, it was pitch black except for the glowing stones which, after prayers, were occasionally covered with water from a ladle in a bucket. The heat was intense, but what I most remembered were the voices of the Lakota men who were praying, singing, and talking in their own language. When they did speak in English, I knew it was for our own benefit so that we would understand what it was we were praying for. It was the first time I had ever participated in a traditional ceremony that honored a centuries-old connection to the Earth, humans, and animals.

I again found a deep connection with the Lakota and my own indigenous identity and culture which was largely unknown to me at the time. I knew I was Yaqui, but what little I knew of my own culture I had read in books written by white men. In my own flight and life as a hunted fugitive, I was discovering protection, but not the kind I originally had thought I would need for my survival. I discovered that the kind of world I innately desired and fought for was indeed real and still very much alive. I began to tap into a living history of spiritual power that had guided indigenous resistors and survivors since the Europeans first arrived on this continent.

When we got back to Washington State, I again was visited by Jay. This time she was traveling with David Barbarash, a friend and an ALF fugitive himself who was being sought by Canadian authorities for rescuing 29 cats from a research lab at the University of Alberta in Edmonton in 1992. I had met David in 1988 and we quickly became friends. He was a press officer for the North American ALF Supporters Group up in Canada and had also been arrested for smashing fast food outlets, as well as fur and butcher shops. Now the two were traveling down to California where they hoped to arrange a rendezvous with our common friend, Jonathan Paul. I advised against going so deep into the cities where the police had the ability to corner you, but they were determined to follow their own path.

Summer in South Dakota

With summer approaching, I decided it was time to move back to South Dakota. I had made friends with Lakota who were involved with the return of the buffalo and learned that an organization was starting in Rapid City to coordinate their efforts on behalf of many tribes: the Inter-Tribal Bison Cooperative. Not wanting to bring FBI repression back onto the Rez, I decided not to return to my cabin on Standing Rock, but to rent a small house on the outskirts of Rapid City.

I volunteered for the organization, attended a tribal bison round-up and traveled to Iowa to attend an international bison conference. At the conference it was clear the division between tribal bison operators and non-native bison producers who simply wanted to raise bison as they had beef cattle. Lakota friends spoke against such abuse and testified to the sacredness of the buffalo and how they deserved to be treated like relatives. It was another clear example of how indigenous views on animals were more aligned with my own thinking on the treatment of animals. To the Lakota, all buffalo were related, and represented tribal autonomy and the ability to survive without white assistance. To the Lakota, every part of the buffalo played a part in their existence. There was no waste. During this time, I also drove to the Arapahoe Nation's Wind River Reservation to witness the traditional butchering of a buffalo with stone tools by elders of the nation, who told stories to the local indigenous attendees who were packed inside a basketball court where the bison was being distributed to awaiting tribal members.

I didn't find the butchering disturbing; it was very different from the dark violence I felt when visiting slaughterhouses. This animal, while being killed for human consumption, was treated very differently from any cow slaughtered for a supermarket. All of us in attendance were told of the responsibility we had to protect and honor those animals whose lives were taken to feed the people. It was a sacred relation filled with human humility that was unknown in the dominant white culture that dictates how we treat animals.

At a gathering of tribal co-operative members, I listened as various elders spoke of the role of buffalo in their history and culture. One tribal elder from Montana spoke of his tribe's small buffalo herd that was being used as part of a restorative justice project for tribal members who had broken laws. He told us the story of a woman who was sentenced to the tribe's "Bison Watch" program, which required offenders to physically camp out near the growing bison herd and simply observe the animals. The elder related how the woman was angry to be spending time out with the herd. But later she would share the story of how she eventually began to watch the herd as it grazed and interacted with other members of the herd. She spoke of beginning to notice the relationship between the bison mothers and their calves. Within a few days, she had an overwhelming emotional breakdown as she came to the realization that she was not being the good mother that the bison and Creator wanted her to be. She had learned from the buffalo what she needed to do to not only be a good mother, but a good human being. The restorative justice wasn't only benefiting tribal members, it was helping to rekindle tribal members' interest in the life-saving values of indigenous culture and traditions.

As I also learned to see the world through indigenous eyes, I was finding the solace I was seeking in my own pursuits of animal liberation, which at the time was less a worldview and more a philosophy. Here was a way of seeing nature and animals that had existed on this continent since the first humans walked on these lands, not as conquerors but as cooperative members of a living community that included all living things.

My work with the Inter-Tribal Bison Cooperative came to an end when I began to be the subject of suspicion by some of the tribal members. Many of the indigenous members remembered the years of FBI repression that had resulted in the deaths of dozens of indigenous activists. Unbeknownst to me, my arrival on the scene had aroused suspicion because no one had any history with me, knew of my family, or had any idea where I was getting the money I needed to survive. Finally, a good friend of mine from the Cheyenne River Sioux Tribe confronted me with his own suspicions, telling me straight up that he and some of his friends suspected that I might be an FBI agent. When he told me in all seriousness, I couldn't help but laugh as I responded that I was the furthest thing from being an FBI infiltrator. I went to the local library and found a microfilm copy of a newspaper article from the 1986 Iceland raid that included my picture. I took a copy of the article and my real passport to my friend and revealed to him exactly who I was. The explanation made sense to him, but in revealing my true identity, I knew I must again leave my current home.

The Sun Dance

By this time, it was summer 1993 and Sun Dance season. Across the plains, nations of indigenous Lakota, Cheyenne, and Arapahoe were gathering to participate in the annual ceremony. I had been invited by Albert White Hat to attend his tribe's Hollow Horn Bear Sun Dance on the Rosebud Reservation, so I left my rented home and traveled back to the White Hat family land which was filling up with sun dancers and their supporters.

At the ceremony, I helped gather the stones needed for the daily sweat lodge ceremonies, wood for the fires, and assisted with preparing the arbor that the dancers would fill for four straight days. In the center of the arbor stood a lone cottonwood tree that was the focal point for the dancers' prayers. When the tree was first cut for the ceremony, I stood on a hillside as I heard dozens of Lakota singing as they carried the tree into the arbor by hand. Cedar smoke filled the air as a blessing and as a purifier. I spent the four days helping tend the fire used to heat rocks for the daily sweat lodge ceremonies. I also helped prepare the sweat lodges for family members who simply wanted to participate in their own purification ceremonies.

I had never so felt a part of a culture that truly honored and respected animals and nature as much as Albert White Hat's people did that summer on the Rosebud, and it was beautiful to know that this was a world very much alive for traditional indigenous peoples. Albert told me a story about how, when the dancers needed strength, they would sometimes walk up to the tree in the center of the arbor and place their hands on it to pray. Albert told me one time when he was extremely exhausted and thought he could dance no longer, how he approached the tree in his fatigue and placed his hands on the trunk. He said that when he did, he could not feel the bark of the tree at all, but only the warm flesh of another human being.

No one at the sun dance knew I was a fugitive from justice. On July 16, 1993, a federal arrest warrant was issued for me out of the Western District of Michigan. It stated that I was charged with "maliciously damaging/destroying property by fire or explosive materials." At that point, I was technically a federal fugitive from justice, and all parts of the federal judicial system were now formally empowered to track me down and arrest me.

But none of this affected the Sun Dance. Nor did anyone there know about the inner struggles I had as I fought for my own survival, both physically and spiritually. Yet, through the invitations I had received from fellow indigenous warriors, I found what I needed to not only survive, but to truly live. After the Hollow Horn Bear Sun Dance, I visited the Cheyenne River Sioux Reservation to attend a much smaller sun dance where only indigenous people were allowed to attend. The very private ceremony was held far away from any town. When elders arrived, they were introduced to the entire crowd of attendees and walked past everyone so that we could greet them with the honor they deserved.

At that point in time, I was less concerned with my being captured by the Feds than I was with my own feelings of spiritual absence. Here I was witnessing the living culture of a people still very much connected to the Earth, as I desired to be connected. Yet, I was not Lakota, I was Yaqui; but I knew nothing of my own culture. It became abundantly clear that I needed to learn about my own people as I had about the Lakota and other allied tribes. In my searchings, I quickly came to the realization that I needed to find out more about my own people and traditions, and that would mean another move, only this time it would be to the homeland of my own people in southern Arizona outside of the city of Tucson, where Yaqui communities still resided.

Return to Tucson

In the fall of 1993, I arrived back in Tucson and reconnected with friends I had made through Earth First! The radical environmental community was in the midst of building support with Apache resistors who were opposed to the construction of an observatory by the University of Arizona on the nearby Dzil Nchaa Si An, known to whites as Mt. Graham.

The entire Pinaleno Mountain range was a sky island wilderness that jutted out of the Sonoran Desert to an altitude of 10,000 feet, making it an ecologically unique habitat for endangered species like the Mt. Graham red squirrel. The mountain was sacred to not just the Apache but my own Yaqui people, as I would later learn.

The struggle to protect Mt. Graham brought indigenous and white activists together, and it was the first time I was part of such a coalition of resistors. One of the main organizers within Earth First! and on the University of Arizona campus was Guy Lopez, a Lakota activist whose wife, Cati, was Yaqui. I became friends with both Guy and Cati, and it was Cati who introduced me to the spiritual leader of the Yaqui Nation, Anselmo Valencia Tori.

I found a basement apartment on the same South Tucson street where Guy and Cati lived and soon got involved with other Native Americans who gathered weekly outside of the downtown Tucson Indian Center. In the parking lot, we sat around a large drum and learned different Pow Wow songs from a Dine (Navajo) singer named Alex. I quickly became friends with some of the other singers and together we formed a drum group called Catalina Mountain Singers; we traveled to various Arizona Pow Wows to compete with other groups for prize money, but mostly for the fun of spending time with other indigenous folks.

It was through the local Pow Wow circuit that I also met Raul Cancio, a traditional Yaqui who sang at Pow Wows but who also was the leader of the traditional warrior society. It was at one event in Tucson that he invited me to a Yaqui ceremony in one of the local villages. I drove through downtown Tucson to the south side of the city, which was still pretty low income and semi-rural. Amongst the neighborhoods and immediately below an interstate highway that ran past, Barrio Libre was a tiny enclave of mostly Yaqui families that lived around a small church. Opposite the church was a plywood structure that served as the traditional ramada for the non-Christian Yaqui ceremonies that took place in the shadow of the church. I parked my car next to the plaza and walked towards the lights of the church.

I heard music, but it wasn't coming from the church; it came from the plywood structure. As I came around the back of the ramada and into view, the music hit me like electricity. I had never heard it before but it was at the same time immediately familiar. Three men sat on the earth playing rasps and a water drum; they sang a song as another man with gourd rattles and a deer head covering his own face danced in front of them. As this dance took place, another was beginning in the same earthen ground by another man with a wooden mask and cocoon rattles who danced before a Yaqui playing a flute and hand drum at the same time. It was the first time I had ever seen or heard the sacred music and dances of my own ancestors, and it immediately resonated with something deep inside of me that I could not explain.

Let me say, straight out, that there are things that happened in my time with my own people that I will not write about. Some are too sacred to share with non-Yaquis, and other things are part of our culture which I have no intention of publishing. Anyone can still find such works available on the internet about Yaqui culture, but I was taught to be fiercely private with the lessons about the ways of my ancestors that were shared with me. Suffice to say, when I began living on the Yaqui reservation outside of Tucson and participating in cultural activities, it was a powerful and magical time spent rediscovering the lessons that would save my life.

Once I had visited my first Yaqui ceremony, I made the decision to prioritize my own culture over the Pow Wow circuit, which was more of an intertribal and public ceremonial activity. I still love going to Pow Wows, but I knew when I met Raul, Anselmo, and other Yaqui elders, that it was my responsibility to learn what I could while I was still able.

My immersion in Yaqui culture was supported by my Earth First! friends in Tucson, but my underground acquaintance Jay felt I was drifting away from the warrior society I had been creating with her and others. We had a falling out, and I never saw her again. Still, Jay was one of my first white allies who shared my belief in the spiritual power of the earth and animals—something that was available not just to indigenous people but anyone brave enough to still believe in those ancient sacred ways of resistance.

It was at another Yaqui ceremony where Cati introduced me to Anselmo. He seemed minimally interested when I told him that I was Yaqui but didn't know anything about my culture, though I was hoping to learn what I could...hopefully from him. He told me I was welcome to help him do repairs on the cultural kitchen. So I spent days cleaning and scrubbing walls at the kitchen, with Anselmo directing me to my chores in the morning, and returning with a sack lunch for me at noon. While I ate, he would point with his lips to a distant figure crossing the open plaza and say something about who they were related to, and how that person had been a soldier during the Yaqui war years—which he said went until 1927. Sometimes his stories would cause me to lose my appetite and start crying, usually because they involved the telling of a horrific event in our people's history that I had never heard about before. This was not the history I had been taught in school, but was the story of my very own family and how they had survived countless efforts, by first the Spanish and then the Mexican government, to exterminate them.

Soon, Anselmo and I began weekly youth meetings where we would cook traditional foods for reservation youth while Anselmo or other elders shared stories. Anselmo was also an activist and warrior for his people, having led the fight towards gaining federal recognition for our tribe from the US government. Anselmo had been chairman of the tribe numerous times, but when I met him, he was still vice-chairman but more focused on the cultural preservation of our nation. His dream was to create a Yaqui Museum.

When New Years Day arrived in 1994, the world woke up to an indigenous armed uprising in the Mexican state of Chiapas by the Zapatista Liberation Army (EZLN). News of the uprising was greeted with amazement and pride by indigenous people across Arizona, and Anselmo and I quickly began organizing relief caravans and hosting events to raise public awareness. I attended regular protests outside the Mexican Consulate and otherwise was living the life of the Yaqui "Martin Rubio," not that of Rodney Coronado, the fugitive from justice.

Although I had spent time in Tucson surveilling the University of Arizona and housing animals, I never made any attempt to reconnect with my indigenous and southern Arizona roots. Yet, my own father was born in Tucson and my grandfather was even the pastor of a local church after his return from World War II.

One evening when I was visiting Deborah, a Tohono O'odham woman I had worked with on Zapatista support, we smoked hand-rolled cigarettes and burned creosote, which her tribe uses for healing. On that warm summer night, as I recounted to her my father's history in Tucson, I was completely honest and not lying to support my alias. After a pause in the story, she asked, "Martin, what was your grandfather's name?" I told her the truth, that his name was Reyes Coronado. When she exhaled her drag of American Spirit tobacco, which I had picked up smoking on the Rez, she said, "I know your grandfather. And I know your father and your auntie too!" If it was one thing I had learned about Indian World, it was that everyone knows (or knew) everybody in the small worlds where indigenous people lived and died amongst themselves, most having never left the state of Arizona, except maybe to serve in the Armed Forces, as Anselmo did during World War II. But that's another story.

The next day, Deborah showed me an old black-and-white photograph of a group of children standing with two men in front of a church. One of the men was my grandfather, Reyes Coronado, and the other was Deborah's father. I recognized my grandfather's wide toothy smile and the children resembled those I had seen in my own family photo album. Deborah was one of the children, accompanied by my father's elder sister.

Not long after, when I needed to travel to California to ask for financial support to maintain my only slightly underground existence, Deborah accompanied me to Los Angeles. Not wanting to use the phone, I simply arrived unannounced at the home of one of the founding members of EF! Los Angeles, Peter Bralver, who lived alone with his father. Peter had helped me search for California condor traps in 1987, when the state was capturing the world's last wild birds for a captive breeding colony. He had also served alongside me on the Sea Shepherd's Divine Wind drift net campaign to the North Pacific the same year.

Deborah and I simply laid out our sleeping bags on Peter's front lawn, which was bordered with a high hedge, and waited for either of the men to awake. At dawn, Peter's father (who also was called Peter) walked out the door on his way to get fresh bagels. When he saw us, he laughed and invited us inside to wait for his return with breakfast. Peter had escaped the repression that was falling on every radical environmental activist within my path from California up to Washington, across to Montana and Michigan. But I doubt his welcoming would have been any different. Peter and his father were artists and intellectuals who saw the world their own way, with scientific evidence to support it. The younger Peter was a self-identified interdisciplinary theoretical mathematician.

While Peter slept, his father listened to my stories of the events that brought me back to Los Angeles, where we first met in 1987. When I told his father of my time with the Lakota, he led me to his library of leatherbound books. With his pipe dangling from his mouth, he searched until he found a book about American Indians written in the late 1800s. It had not yet recorded the Battle of the Greasy Grass (Little Bighorn). Peter Sr. presented me with the book, with the same gravity I've seen other elders use when presenting an indigenous warrior with an eagle feather. We spent the morning sitting and visiting in the family's backyard, where their garden of fruit trees served as a natural barrier from the city that surrounded the neighborhood. It would be the last time I ever saw either Peter.

When I collected the few thousand dollars I could raise from previous ALF supporters, Deborah and I drove north out of Los Angeles and headed to my grandparent's home in Fresno. I wanted to get a message to my family that I was safe and protected, and thought I could surprise my grandparents who had only late in their life expressed support for the path that I had chosen. Back in 1986, when the national news covered our raid on Iceland's illegal whalers, my grandparents chastised my parents for my behavior. My parents confronted the elder couple and recounted how, ever since my father had left the family church to marry my mother, they were critical of my own family's weak adherence to the apostolic values that my grandfather preached. After the confrontation, my grandparents began asking me more about what I was doing without me having understood what had transpired earlier between them and my parents.

When we arrived in Fresno, Deborah dropped me off in a park while she drove to my grandparent's neighborhood. She parked around a corner and walked up to the address I gave her. After knocking, my grandfather answered the door and exclaimed, "Don't tell me...Deborah Sotelo?" With the coast clear, Deborah collected me and we returned to have a meal of rice, beans, and tortillas that my grandmother prepared, just as she had my entire life. We talked about my family's life in Tucson and my grandmother told me about the Yaqui side of my family, her own grandmother having fled our homelands in northern Mexico during some of the worst repression in the early 1900s. Anselmo had instructed me to interview my Yaqui grandmother before she passed about everything she could remember about her own mother and grandmother. It was the only way to keep the history of our people alive, to carry the stories from our own elders for future generations.

My grandparents agreed to deliver a message to my parents—only they didn't wait to call them on the telephone to do it. Speaking in Spanish, my grandmother had told my father I had just visited them. My father immediately left work and began the two-hour drive, but I fled before he could arrive, suspecting that the message had surely been intercepted by the authorities. Deborah and I again drove north. I wanted to get away from the metropolitan areas of California, so we headed east across the Sierra Nevada Mountains, then north to Reno, Nevada, where we felt we could sleep safely across the state line.

The Last Match

Remembering that we weren't far from the beautiful open wildlands where wild horses still roam, I decided to take Deborah to Litchfield and camp in the same area where, in 1987, we hid out while surveilling the wild horse corrals for our Memorial Day liberation. From the same precipices where I had spied before, we again watched as wild horses continued to be shuttled from the wild through this holding facility. That night, we drove across the highway from the facility and walked a half mile to the first line of fencing. After determining that, despite our earlier horse liberation, there were no onsite personnel, Deborah and I walked onto the grounds and I began checking windows on the few buildings spread across the complex.

I gained entry through an open bathroom window. This was a spontaneous action that we had agreed to with little discussion. Once we knew I could get into the building, we left; taking tools from the barn, I headed to one of the wild horse pens that bordered the open desert. With only two of us, we were barely able to clear one thirty-foot length of wire, but it was enough for the extremely human-shy wild horses which we easily corralled out of the pen by walking from the far end towards the open side facing the desert. It would be the second time that I would witness wild horses running to freedom under the moonlight.

Next, while Deborah went out for the rental car, I climbed back into the Bureau of Land Management trailer that served as the facility's main office, with a gas can in hand. I began dumping the fuel all around the trailer, which contained a small kitchen space with cook range. Just as I was dripping gas across the counter of the stove, I wondered whether it had a pilot light...and suddenly flames burst from under the stove and ignited the trail of gasoline I had just poured. I ran for the door. As soon as I swung it open, and oxygen was able to fuel the fire, flames exploded behind me—just like a thousand action movies, but on a smaller scale. I fled with only singed hair, but as we drove away from the facility across the flat open desert, we could see the orange glow of the fire, along with flashing red and blue lights speeding from the nearby town of Litchfield. This unplanned, unannounced, and unclaimed action would be the second time the wild horse facility was targeted by the ALF, but it wouldn't be the last. It would, however, be the last time I personally lit a match for animal liberation.

Resistance on Mt. Graham

When we got back to Tucson, things were heating up in the Apache-led coalition of resistance to the construction of the Vatican's Mt. Graham Observatory atop a sacred mountain and home to the endangered red squirrel. The telescope was officially dedicated on September 12, 1993, with a delegation from the Vatican traveling to Arizona to participate.

Weeks before, Arizona Earth First!ers and I had traveled to the San Carlos Apache Reservation to essentially ask indigenous leaders for permission to engage in civil disobedience on the day of the dedication. Before I arrived back in Tucson, activists began building a relationship with Apache resisting the Mt. Graham telescopes. Now, though, the legal opposition to the construction had failed, and the facility was planning on further development in the heart of the mountain. Wensler Nosie and Ernest Victor were full-blooded Apache who looked like the faces staring from the famous C. S. Fly photographs of Geronimo's 19th century warriors. Together these men, their families and communities, would lead the opposition to the University of Arizona's desecration of Dzil Nchaa Sian.

With the approval of the Apache coalition, a handful of us traveled to the mountain a few days before the planned dedication to prepare for a series of road blockades on the single narrow road that snaked steeply up the mountain. At the base of the mountain was a federal prison, whose lights could be seen at night from across the desert. This was the only nearby law enforcement presence we would have to avoid. Our first blockade would be past the prison where a metal cattle guard crossed the road. Here, one protestor would use a U-shaped bike lock to secure themselves by the neck to the cattle guard.

On top of the mountain, a group of us would be waiting to throw up a tipi-shaped tripod of twenty-foot pine poles into the road with our Apache friend Dee atop the primitive device. We camped away from any roads or trails, with only small fires at night, and during the day we gathered logs and boulders that we could later roll into the road. Many of the Tucson Earth First!ers were Arizona history buffs, and at night we shared stories around the campfire that we had read—about Geronimo, Juh, Cochise, and other Apache warriors who used to roll boulders against unsuspecting stagecoaches not far from these very same mountains.

On the night before the dedication, we dry-camped in an area that was officially closed for the dedication and also part of an exclusion area that University officials claimed was necessary for the protection of the endangered squirrels—yet they had no problem logging acres of critical habitat to build the infrastructure for the observatory. Even tribal members had been arrested while praying and foraging in the area as their ancestors had done before them for centuries.

Three of us were spread out not far from one of the summits of the mountain, awaking before dawn to plan our attack. A caravan of activists from Tucson would be arriving in the morning, hopefully before police could set up any roadblocks in anticipation of the action they were highly suspecting. Here I was, back in the homeland of my own ancestors, working with non-native allies, indigenous leaders, and communities to oppose the continued destruction and desecration of our always-sacred lands. This was the resistance I felt that I was born for, a resistance against speciesism and colonization born from centuries of indigenous nations struggles— only now a resistance that included not just indigenous, but all peoples.

As I slept, I had a dream that I will never forget. It was less visual and more what I was hearing and feeling. In my half sleep, I heard the most beautiful music I could ever remember hearing. The sound was like many sounds from nature, like the cacophony of birds, monkeys, and insects in a jungle, but with the structure of a song. Accompanying the music was a human voice, also in song, whose words I could not understand through hearing, but instead in a feeling. The song was both a message and invitation: "This is the world that is waiting for you. This is the world that has been alive for centuries and that you will enter when you die." The feeling I experienced was so overwhelming in my half sleep that, when I was awoken a few moments later by a friend's voice, I started crying because what I had been experiencing was simply so beautiful and enticing that I regretted waking up. I wanted to enter that world right then.

Days later, when I recounted the experience to Anselmo, he listened across the dining room table, which was where so much of his wisdom was dispensed; and when I finished the story, he told me that, for centuries, not only the Apache had considered this mountain sacred, but our own Yoeme people as well. It was a place where tribal warfare was forbidden and a truce was observed by our warring people. Anselmo also said that somewhere on the mountain was one of those places that served as a portal between two worlds. These portals across our holy lands that currently stretched from northern Mexico to southern Colorado were entries into one of the enchanted worlds that our people still believed in. Anselmo told me that if a Yaqui of "good heart" were ever near one of these portals, he might hear the songs and voices of our ancestors.

Perhaps it was for this reason that Anselmo also supported the actions we were taking to defend Mt. Graham.

The morning of the dedication, we watched from the edges of the forest as state police patrols cruised the lone road, looking for us protesters. When we knew the buses were coming filled with University and Vatican guests, we sprang into action and threw up the tripod, with Dee perched high in it. A group of us young warriors then took to the trees where we had stacked logs and boulders, and began rolling them into the road, littering the road with debris that would have to be cleared before reaching Dee in the tripod.

We wore masks to cover our faces as we wrestled with a big boulder, trying to get a pry bar underneath it, when two older Indian men with long braids came walking down the road. They walked past us like it was nothing—like every day that you see young Indians rolling boulders into the road. They casually said, "The state police are unloading a bulldozer and heading this way..." Moments later, a bulldozer came tearing down the road, clearing everything in its path. We remained hidden just beyond the edge of the trees, as state police began yelling, "We know who you are, come out with your hands up." I fought a strong urge to roll a boulder towards their parked cruiser in response, but instead we remained hidden and silent. The police were in their regular uniforms and in no condition to run after us uphill into the forest. We knew this mountain was our place of power, not theirs.

The police first cut loose the protester locked to the cattle guard and arrested her. When they encountered Dee's tripod, they cut the legs in sections, lowering her slowly to the ground before also arresting her. The rest of us that fought in the forest, blended in with the later-arriving protestors and made it off the mountain without any arrests.

The following month, on Columbus Day (October 11, 1993), Earth First!ers and other environmentalists gathered on the Pascua Yaqui Reservation where Anselmo was to give a blessing to honor over five centuries of indigenous resistance and survival. We gathered in the plaza where ceremonies were held and where the tribe's warrior society was in attendance to participate in the blessing. It was no small coincidence to me that, as a fugitive from justice for crimes in defense of nature, that I had found myself back in the community of my own ancestors on a day of celebration of our continuing resistance. This was the world that had been calling to me, just as it literally had been calling to me on the mountain and in the plains. This was the world that was waiting for me.

After the blessing, we set up a tipi on the campus mall of the University of Arizona while a protester occupied the campus clock tower. We sang pow wow songs into the night at this latest action protesting the desecration of Mt. Graham. Our drum group, Catalina Mountain Singers would even be invited to perform at the opening of a Pearl Jam concert in Phoenix that was a fundraiser for the campaign. As much as I wanted to go, I made an excuse because I knew the event was being filmed and I would be risking being identified.

All this time, federal law enforcement was busy following leads in their relentless hunt for me and others in the ALF. By the end of the year, they were ready to issue an all-points bulletin: "Wanted by the FBI: Rodney Adam Coronado." Despite all evidence to the contrary, "Coronado should be considered armed and dangerous."

I didn't know it at the time, of course, but I would have about nine months of freedom left.

Into the Year 1994

It was spring 1994 and I continued to attend traditional ceremonies as a volunteer with the warrior society that Raul Cancio had reformed. Of all the indigenous nations I had spent time within recent years, I never felt more comfortable than I did with my own people. I couldn't help but think of how much I was yearning for a feeling of belonging and connection with others who shared my beliefs about the animal and natural world.

That longing had led me to the radical animal rights and environmental movements that fed my passions, but it did not provide the history, worldview, and stories that my own indigenous heritage could. Throughout my time on the Yaqui Reservation, I met the living descendants of warriors who had fought and survived a literal campaign of eradication and genocide. The Mexican government were every bit as brutal as their American colonial counterparts and Anselmo kept alive the stories of Yaqui babies having their heads smashed against trees and dozens of women who chose to jump to their deaths with babies in their arms rather than be captured and shipped to slavery on plantations across the Americas. These were the stories of my own people and, as disturbing as they were, they provided a certain level of comfort and understanding about my own commitment against cruelty and injustice.

Throughout 1994, as I immersed myself in the protection of my own people and became more involved with the struggles that our tribe was facing today, I felt like I had found a place where I belonged. As welcomed as I had been in the Dakotas, this was my homeland and these were my people, even though I hardly knew them. As I served as a volunteer and student of our culture, I was welcomed in a way that provided me with more spiritual than physical protection.

Finally, after a particularly beautiful all-night ceremony in the desert, Anselmo and I were driving one of the musicians from Rio Yaqui to the home he was staying at when I told him I needed to talk. After the harpist walked into the adobe house, Anselmo drove to the edge of the village and parked facing the wild open desert. He asked me what was on my chest. I began by telling him that I was Yaqui, but I wasn't who I said I was, that I had been using a fake identity to hide from the police who were looking for me. I started crying when I told him that I needed to learn more about my own people and that was why, despite the risk, I had come back seeking his assistance.

We sat staring forward into the forest of ocotillo that was swaying in the early morning winds and, after a pause, Anselmo said, "You must be

Rodney Coronado then. I'm glad you decided to tell me. I knew who you were the first time I saw you. I've just been waiting for you to be ready to tell me. Now, I know it may be hard to believe because I'm just an old man, but you see those plants and those rocks? They still give me some help when I ask them, so I'm going to do some prayers and we'll see what we can do... Try not to worry about it."

After I had revealed who I really was, Anselmo invited me to live in a building next to his home on the reservation. He felt that Tucson was not a safe place to be, as opposed to the Rez which was surrounded by the desert. I started hanging out less with my Pow Wow friends and hardly participated in our drum group, as the practices conflicted with my traditional participation in Yaqui cultural activities. Anselmo was recognized as the spiritual leader of all the Yaqui communities, including the eight sacred pueblos (villages) in the northern Mexican state of Sonora, which was the heart of our homelands. In 1994, as in other years, conflicts flared between traditional and government Yaquis in Mexico, so Anselmo was called in to help mediate the situation that had turned violent. A traditional leader had been shot and the pro-government gunman was in the custody of the victim's supporters.

It was decided that I should chauffer Anselmo to Rio Yaqui, Mexico, which was a 4-hour drive from Tucson. I had left the country once before, to visit a Sea Shepherd friend in Vancouver, but I hadn't gone south into Mexico. I still had my cousin's identity on a driver's license, but no passport, which was not required then to cross into Canada or Mexico. I wasn't too nervous about the crossing, Anselmo was then Vice-Chairman for the tribe and on official business. We left early in the morning and crossed into Mexico without incident, arriving at a small hotel off the international highway. When we drove into Torim, we were one of the few vehicles to be seen. This was still a place where most people traveled by walking, horseback, or boat. Anselmo showed me the bullet holes still in adobe walls where rebel Yaquis had been lined up and shot by Mexican soldiers. We spent the hours talking to factions on both sides and negotiating a resolution that would not involve the military being brought in to occupy the villages, as had been happening since the 1500s in Yaqui communities in our homelands of Sonora, Mexico.

On the first evening, we were present where the armed assailant was being held. He sat on the ground with his arms tied behind his back with bailing wire. Next to him were women from the traditional community who were officiating a wake for the still-living shooter with candles burning as they sang the appropriate songs. During breaks in the hours-long conversations, we were guests at the homes of Anselmo's relatives who fed us tortillas and beans cooked in front of us over a fire. And all outside under a ramada with hard dirt as a floor.

Life here was starkly different than that lived by most Yaquis a few hundred miles north in the United States. In Mexico, our people are still intimately connected to the lands they fought and died to hold onto for five centuries. From most Yaqui villages, the Bacatete Mountains can be seen in the distance, towering out of the desert. The steep mountains served as a refuge for Yaquis during armed uprisings, first against the Spanish and later the Mexican governments. We visited the Yaqui River, whose waters had been contested since the first Spaniards arrived. This was the river that was central to our sense of place, the heart of 'Hiakim,' which was what we call our homeland. Anselmo and I walked along the slow-moving water under the canopy of ancient cottonwood trees. I could almost hear the power of this sacred place, much as I had when fighting for Mt. Graham which lay on the northern edge of Hiakim. I mentioned to Anselmo that I could still feel the power and almost hear it, and he responded that when he was a young man, that voice was a roar. Anselmo believed all Yaquis were still capable of having strong relationships with the spirit and natural world, but most of us were too distracted to listen to the ancient voices of our ancestors, which speak to us still if we are willing to listen.

One hot afternoon, Anselmo was having a spirited conversation with another elder of his age. I couldn't understand our native language, but I was beginning to catch an occasional word that was repeated. After the elder departed, I said to Anselmo, "I heard you both saying the word, 'Geronimo'—what was that about?" He casually responded, "Oh, he was just saying that he had been raised with the story that Geronimo was a Yaqui kidnapped by the Apache and raised as one of their own. I told him that that was the same story I had been told…" The story illustrated how wrong most anthropologists were about indigenous peoples and our worldviews. Tribal identity wasn't determined by blood quantum, it was based on who you were raised with and whose stories you were told. When he spoke about the Yaqui connection to Mt. Graham, Anselmo spoke of the traditional warfare that existed between our tribe and the mostly northern Apache who also maintained strongholds in the Sierra Madre Mountains of northern Mexico. Our attacks were rarely aimed at causing loss of life. Instead it was horses, cattle, or other provisions we were forced to fight over after the Invader's arrival. Occasionally though, if a warrior from either tribe was killed in a foray, Anselmo said it was customary for the side with the loss to kidnap a child from the offending nation and raise them as your own to compensate for the loss. This was the case with the one they called Geronimo, as I was taught by my Yaqui elders. A story that would be sure to cause some lively discussion with my Apache friends!

"The Jig is Up"

While I was immersed in my culture, federal grand juries were still sub-poenaing witnesses for questioning about the ALF, and in particular, my role in Operation Bite Back. I had cut off all ties with anyone who might lead the Feds back to me and was living amongst others who looked like me. Of course, my last writings published in the *EF! Journal* were filled with connections to indigenous struggles and worldviews, and I thought that would eventually lead the Feds to the Yaqui Reservation where I was living in hiding. My mother had received a lot of harassment from both ATF and FBI agents searching for me, especially once the warrant for my arrest was issued in July 1993. Now my mom was being called before the federal grand jury in Oregon and questioned by the same ATF agent, John Comery, who had led the investigation since the first fur farm arsons in 1991. His only question to my mother was, "Is Rodney living on an Indian reservation?"

I always kept a "go bag" not far from where I slept each night in An-selmo's open desert yard. We didn't have a guard dog, but we did have guard geese and a domesticated deer that roamed the yard, ready to alert us to any visitors. The backpack against the wall of my shed living-quarters held dried food, water, a wool blanket, rain gear, and topographical maps that provided directions from my home on the Pascua Yaqui Reservation to our homelands in Sonora, Hiakim. My escape plan in case of emergency would be to use the same routes my ancestors had used to escape persecu-tion in Mexico and smuggle arms back for the fight for our lands. While in Mexico, I had made connections with Yaquis who I believed could help ensure I was never discovered. Maybe I would even journey further south to Chiapas and join up with the indigenous army of Zapatista rebels still holding onto many villages.

On September 28, 1994, I was washing dishes in the kitchen of An-selmo's home when there was a ring of the bell that was perched on our outside wrought-iron fence. When I poked my head out the door, I saw a white tribal cop I had seen around the village many times. She shouted that there was an injured hawk that had been brought into the fire department. Knowing we cared for animals, she asked if I could take a look at the in-jured bird. There was little that concerned me about the request; I had gotten close to tribal officials, and tribal police officers had seen me often around the village. I told the officer to hang on while I grabbed some gloves.

I climbed into her cruiser and she drove the half mile to the fire department which always had its front roll-up doors open. She must have noticed the change of appearance because she quickly said, "They shut the doors so the hawk wouldn't get out..." It was bright and hot when I stepped out of the car and walked towards the side entrance of the fire station. I could feel the tribal cop right behind me. I pulled open the windowless door and as I entered the building, several men in suits ran towards me, yelling my real name. Within a fraction of a second—but it seemed longer—I was overpowered by brute force, thrown to the ground, and handcuffed behind my back. John Comery was the lead agent in the raid and he immediately identified himself and relayed that he was in touch with my mother, who was on hand in case the situation escalated to some form of confrontation or occupation. She was informed of my nonviolent arrest.

Once the full gravity of the situation had dawned on me, I thought that this was probably the last chance I would have to attempt escape. I couldn't live with myself for years in prison knowing I hadn't tried to get away. I was led outside where I was placed sitting at a picnic table while calls were being made and my transportation arranged. I sprung from my seat and bolted towards the open desert. I was instantly subdued and again tackled, only this time leg shackles were added, while Comery yelled at me, saying he had chosen to do this "the nonviolent way" and my actions were causing him to rethink his position. "They wanted to bring in helicopters and a SWAT team to get you... How do you think Anselmo would have handled that?" It wasn't an idle threat; he knew Anselmo's heart was ailing and the shock of a full-blown FBI raid on his beloved community could have ended in tragedy.

I was led into a black cruiser and said goodbye to my simple life as Martin Rubio, as we drove off the reservation towards the skyline of downtown Tucson, where I was taken to the holding area for the federal court building. I was still wearing my own clothes when the agents deposited me in federal custody; and even though I'd been searched, they did not find my Hawaii driver's license in my cousin's name. I took the license and shoved it into a crack at the base of a wall, hoping my secret identity remained unknown.

Within a few hours, I was again shackled and placed with a group of mostly Mexican nationals, and transported in a van to the nearby federal prison outside of Tucson, where I was processed and placed in the Special Housing Unit, or "Hole," as it was known to prisoners. Here, I spent my first nights in federal custody, sharing a tiny barely-lit cell with another criminal defendant awaiting their fate. This was it. The jig was up, and I now truly did not know what my fate would be, except that it would involve years in a prison like the one I was now in. I was facing my deepest fear, worse than any of dying. For me, imprisonment was the worst fate.

CHAPTER 10

PRISON YEARS

Inside my small cell, I spent those first days wondering how many years I would be behind bars, now that the Feds had two years to build a case for my conviction. Before they could do that, I would first be extradited to Michigan where I was indicted. As I awaited the extradition hearing, I was kept locked in my cell 23 hours a day; anytime I left my cell, I was in handcuffs. An orderly went along the row of cells in the Special Housing Unit (SHU) and inserted an empty potato chip bag through the metal slot food-door of the cell. The small door was normally locked, but the orderly could get hot water to us through the potato chip bag, with the bottom corner cut off to serve as a flat funnel. Hot water meant instant coffee or soup.

Meanwhile, friends and supporters were holding rallies outside the federal building, and a collective of friends from my indigenous and activist circles of friends formed a "Rodney Coronado Support Committee" to help with my legal defense. My family flew to Arizona and my father took the lead on securing an attorney for my extradition hearing. Whenever I was brought to the federal building, my supporters caused security concerns when they burned sage in the secure building and otherwise drew attention to a criminal process that usually goes unnoticed. Although I was frightened with years of imprisonment, I was also filled with a huge sense of relief; I was no longer on the run and in hiding, and I could finally see my family.

When my extradition hearing was held, I was denied my petition to remain in Arizona; instead, I got shipped out on the US Marshals' air service commonly called ConAir. On a dark morning before dawn, I was again shackled and loaded onto a bus that would drive dozens of prisoners to the federal prison north of Phoenix to await a flight the following day. After another early morning departure, I was offloaded in El Reno, Oklahoma, where the Bureau of Prisons operated a hub that shipped federal prisoners across the country from an old brick prison.

This was a prison like in the movies, with rolling steel bar doors that slammed shut at night and tiers of cells six stories high. There were no windows and only minimal natural light. The highlight of the day was being led out to the chow hall.

When I finally arrived in Michigan, I was transported to a small jail operated by White Cloud County and again placed in solitary housing.

Only this time, I had the two-cell unit to myself, with my own cable TV that played country music videos most the day. It was also the first place I could begin to receive mail from family, friends, and supporters. The letters were overwhelming and helped lighten my stress around the upcoming criminal process. Now that I was back in Michigan, my father decided that he wanted to find a lawyer to represent me. People for the Ethical Treatment of Animals (PETA) notified my family that they would be paying for my legal defense.

We retained a local law firm that was excited to represent the controversial case, knowing it would be the first-ever federal trial of a member of the ALF against one of the state's most hallowed institutions, Michigan State University. But before any trial proceedings, I would receive a bond hearing to determine whether I could be released on bond to await my trial. The Feds were convinced that the federal judge would deem me a flight risk and deny bond, but my lawyers were prepared to argue that I was only on the run because of death threats made against me by fur farmers, and because of the history of murders targeting indigenous members of the American Indian Movement in the 1970s.

When it was time for my bond hearing, I was moved to Kalamazoo County Jail where I shared a cell with four black men. On the day of my hearing, I was in a US Marshals holding cell when a marshal came over and told me he was a member of PETA. It was a very humanizing and friendly moment. Here was a federal agent with sympathy for what everyone was calling a "terrorist attack" on MSU's research facilities. I think many law enforcement people in the federal justice system saw really violent criminals and were somewhat pleasantly surprised to be dealing with "organized criminals" who were against animal torture.

The hearing was expected to be brief, but when a break was called midway, my attorneys confessed that it was a very good sign that the judge was actually considering the merits of my argument for bond and this was freaking out the prosecutors, who were not prepared to argue strongly against my being granted bail. It was mid-December 1994 and with Christmas approaching, I couldn't help hoping that I might actually get out of prison; even if it was only to await my trial, it would still be a major victory for my family and supporters.

My father was called to the stand to testify on the second day of the hearing. He had come up with a $1.5 million bond using our family's home and business as collateral. The judge then called me onto the stand and asked if I would run out on my family; he made it clear that if I did, I would be forfeiting everything my father had spent his life working for.

My father and I had not always got along, but during this frightful stage of my criminal prosecution, he was my greatest defender.

On December 18th, I was granted bail—though I'd have to wait for my family to raise the $650,000 cash portion of the bond before I could be released. On December 23, I was pulled from my cell and told I was being transported back to the US Marshals holding cell in the Federal Court Building. I had time to call my lawyer and he was concerned that the amount of my bond was being raised since he had heard nothing about any new hearing. When I arrived at the US Marshals holding unit, a nice woman came up to the door of the cell and explained that they were aware that my father was getting together my bond, but that the office would close for Christmas the next day. In order to expedite my release before Christmas, they had transferred me early, knowing I'd be making bond by the end of the day.

In a few hours, I signed some documents and was led out of the building by my attorney. I only had random street clothes given to me by the jail, but I didn't care; I wore them proudly when my attorney took me out for a hot meal at the local vegetarian Gaia Cafe. I spent the night in a warm bed without other prisoners and the next day boarded a flight back to Tucson, Arizona. I had a huge criminal trial to prepare for, but at least I'd be doing it from the sanctuary of my new home with Anselmo and the Yaqui Nation. My parents would also be coming to Arizona for Christmas, which made it one of the best of my life. I wasn't out of the fire, but I had survived a two-year ordeal on the run as a "dangerous fugitive."

In the following days, my attorneys would explain that despite the media's claim that I was facing up to 65 years in prison, in reality the sentencing guidelines for my crimes were more like 12 years. Add to that the fact that they would be trying to negotiate a plea bargain for a much lesser sentence, and I began to think that I might stand a chance at a new lease on life after a few years, not decades in prison.

When I returned to Tucson, it was the first time I was not hiding my identity or my past from anyone. It felt like a rebirth to be in the Yaqui village and see my own parents talking to elders in my community. The radical environmentalist community of Tucson that I had befriended while fighting for Mt. Graham were happy to see me back, whatever name I was using. Anselmo wanted me in the village but he never asked me to do anything to get a shorter sentence. We all knew that the Feds would be asking for my cooperation if I expected a shorter sentence.

Meanwhile a debate was brewing in the animal liberation community that served as the support network for ALF prisoners. While ALF members had served prison sentences for years in the UK, here in the US, no federal prosecution of ALF members had ever happened. And everyone thought my criminal trial would also put the fur farm industry on trial. But when my lawyers and I began to explore plea options, there was dissent, and some of my oldest friends questioned my taking any kind of plea bargain. I argued that if I did not have to testify against any other ALF members or supporters, then a plea bargain was my safest bet. Only I knew exactly how many crimes I had committed and how truly guilty I was for the string of attacks and attempted raids I had carried out over the last five years.

I have to say that it bothered me that privileged animal rights activists who had never risked their lives for animals were so quick to judge me for my decisions on how to resist a possible lengthy prison sentence. I didn't want to be like Nelson Mandela or Leonard Peltier, spending decades in prison as a beacon of strength for an entire struggle; I wanted to do my prison time and get out and return to the fight.

The prosecution added five more charges to my indictment, covering both the theft of the cavalryman's journal and other Operation Bite Back targets. I was now being charged with arson, theft, transporting stolen goods across state lines, and conspiracy to commit arson. The government knew that any plea bargain would result in some charges being dropped and they didn't want to see my crimes in Michigan compromised for the sake of a conviction.

Most of the evidence against me was related to my handling of re-search documents stolen from MSU. Also submitted as evidence were my phone records and eyewitness reports that placed me near every Operation Bite Back action. The Feds could prove that I had handled the documents, stayed in a nearby hotel and visited friends near targets, but they could not pin the actual arsons and break-ins on me. There was still of course the typewriter ribbon found in my Oregon storage locker that recorded the letter I wrote, asking for funds to carry out more actions, and my finger-prints all over the plexiglass case that held the cavalryman's journal.

More smoking evidence in my case was the cigarette butt found at the Fur Breeders Co-op in Utah with my DNA. Adding to this was the fact that the Feds had submitted as evidence the video I shot of myself rescuing mink from the experimental farm at MSU. Though I wore a mask, the prosecution argued that a forensic anthropologist could determine it was me. A US attorney prosecuting the case said, "No known member of the ALF has ever been convicted of a felony." I would be the first. These and other facts that I felt could easily convince a jury of my total guilt led me to seek a plea bargain, but one that would not require my testimony about anyone's actions but my own.

In March 1995, I signed a plea bargain stating that I would admit my guilt for my role in the MSU arson and cavalryman's journal theft but no other crimes. I would not be required to testify against anyone or about anyone else. The plea bargain would be for a sentencing range between 33 and 41 months in federal prison. My lawyers hoped they could argue for a downward departure from 33 months to a period of just over two years. I was optimistic, even though I admitted responsibility for actions that had caused at least $2.5 million in damages.

Prosecutors were quick to capitalize on their secured plea agreement:

> Since the defendant's indictment and arrest, the fire-bombings and massive property damage that were a hall-mark of 'Operation Bite Back' have ceased. However, the intimidation and fear that these crimes were designed to inflict continues to this day. Nowhere is this continued intimidation more evident than in the events that have transpired since the defendant's guilty plea. In several instances, the defendant has appeared in the media to exhort others to take his place as a 'hero to the animal and environmental movement.' In contrast, the victims of the defendant's crimes remain so afraid of the defendant and others like him that they would not speak to the Court's own pre-sentence investigator unless he guaranteed their anonymity.

For my part, I wrote the following statement for my pre-sentencing investigation report, which offered recommendations to the judge on the length of prison sentence I should receive. Dozens of letters were written on my behalf by friends I had known before (and after) going underground. Also submitted to the court were dozens more letters from supporters of animal experimentation and the fur trade, asking for the harshest sentence possible. Here is my text:

> What I have been taught, and what I believe, is that all life is sacred. Everything on this Earth is a creation of god and should be cherished and appreciated. My earlier beliefs addressed the specific sacredness of animal life, but what I attempt to live is a life where the circle of respect and reverence is extended to all of god's creation. I may use the term

"god" but I also say Creator, and in my prayers and native language, the term is *Achai Ta'aa*, which means Father Sun. I believe in Jesus Christ yet I believe and practice pre-Christian and Catholic ways. I feel that my beliefs have become clearer ever since I moved back to a Yaqui community. My beliefs as a traditional Yaqui may have only come to surface in the last three years, but it has been such a revelation as to permanently change every way that I live; much to my relief, most everything I believe in has been reaffirmed as I learn more and more of my traditions and culture.

The belief that rocks, air, water, and animals are all sacred does not mean that I do not believe in their use or consumption. Appreciation is a strong belief of mine, and I believe in acknowledging appreciation for all the blessings we are given each day. I pray every day and give thanks for the Sun to have shone and for air, water, food, and family. Since my return to my heritage and homeland, I have also made a vow, or what might be called a religious promise, in return for my blessings and good fortune in my homecoming. Many Yaquis make vows or commitments to traditional religious societies in our culture.

My promise is to the *Wiko Yau Uura*, which means Bow Leaders. They were and are the oldest of our ceremonial societies and their foundation was at the instruction of prophecies spoken through a Talking Tree. It is our responsibility to protect the homelands, the people, and the culture. Our society was originally a warrior society formed to fight the Spanish conquistadors in the 1500s. I am one of very few members who is taught my responsibilities by our nation's spiritual leader, Anselmo Valencia Tori. Most members associate their involvement with the dancing and the ceremonial rituals. Though I share their appreciation, I consider the greater responsibility to be our civil obligation to the people.

I believe I had to go on a long journey to discover who I am, and now that I have, I must make amends for my behavior in the past that may have broken the law or hurt others. I believe the best way to do this is to live here amongst my people; I feel obligated to resolve all my legal matters so I may return to their service as soon as possible.

I cannot say that I was dragged into the wrong crowd or a criminal element. I was fully aware of what the consequences of my actions might be. But my community has given me the strength to pay the price for my criminal behavior. Though ideological differences still exist between the indigenous perspective and what might be called the dominant worldview, I still acknowledge that I stepped over the line of acceptable behavior in a free society. I do now honestly feel that I have discovered a much more effective way of influencing positive change in our society, and it is within legal bounds.

A Few More Precious Days of Freedom

After signing the plea agreement in March, I had a few months for the presentence investigation to be conducted before I would be sentenced in late summer 1995. I took the opportunity to visit my family in California and vacationed with them in the Sierra Nevada Mountains where we used to camp when I was a child. One morning in the mountains, I awoke before dawn and went for a hike before the others were awake. I stopped in a forest grove and lay down on the ground, listening as the animal world awoke around me. There was a cacophony of bird song that began quietly but grew into a symphony of song that was angelic and beautiful and quickly reminded me of the spiritual experiences I had found up on Mt. Graham and when I first heard traditional Yaqui music. This was the enchanted world of my ancestors and it was singing to me, giving me a reminder of the strength and resilience of the animal nations that were still suffering under the hands of men.

Suddenly, a loud manmade sound echoed from far away, and the singing stopped. The animal and spirit world knew that the Invaders and Destroyers were also awake for another day…

My time left with Anselmo was also extremely important to me. We spent every moment we could at ceremonies, but I knew the day was coming when I would need to say goodbye. Anselmo was already in his seventies and suffered failing health. No one said as much, but we all knew the chances were slim that he would still be alive whenever I was released from prison. My father had spent time visiting with Anselmo, and he later recounted the story he told my father. Anselmo had told my father that although he was indeed my father, that in a past life, Anselmo and I were father and son; only we met our fates before our work on Earth was complete. Anselmo said that I had found my way back to him so that we might continue the work we had started over a century ago.

When the date was scheduled for my sentencing, I rented a van and drove from Arizona to Michigan with five other Yaquis from my community as support. On the day of my sentencing, the courtroom was packed with supporters—and enemies wanting to see me sent to prison for a very long time.

The hearing was focused on whether the judge would approve the plea agreement between the prosecution and my attorneys, which he did before moving on to sentencing. Any hope for leniency was quickly squashed as the judge recounted the seriousness of my crimes and their impact on their victims. The judge questioned my acceptance of responsibility, especially because I had not come out flatly denouncing the actions of the ALF. My heart dropped with every point that was added to my sentencing category. It was clear that the judge intended to send a message to other potential ALF vandals. The judge agreed to the high end of my sentencing range, which went from 33 to 51 months. Then due to the severity of my crimes, he gave me an extra six months as an upward departure. I would be sentenced to a total of 57 months in federal prison, being required to complete 85% of my sentence before being eligible for early release.

I left the courtroom deflated, but accepting of the inevitable prison sentence I always knew was in my future. Only now it was no longer a question of how long.

When I got back to Arizona, I spent most of my time in the Yaqui village that had become my home. Not long after I arrived back, my lawyers contacted me with an offer that the prosecution was making. They would ask the judge for a re-sentencing downwards to as little as 18 months if I was willing to reveal the source of my ALF funding. I didn't hesitate to tell my lawyers that I was uninterested in the offer.

I was given just over two months to get my affairs in order before I was ordered to self-surrender at the Federal Correctional Institution in Safford, Arizona. I would be locked up within sight of Mt. Graham, the sacred peak I had been fighting for. As the days passed and the date approached, I spent less time sleeping and more time visiting friends and hiking in the desert. I tried to start a relationship with a woman I had been dating from the Yaqui community, but it simply was too much to ask, to begin a relationship with someone who was leaving for four years.

On the day I was to surrender, I awoke to the sound of birdsong out my window and knew it would be a very long time before I would experience such a serene morning again. My parents flew in to drive me to the prison. We spent the 90-minute drive mostly in silence; all of us were coping with the impending moment when I would no longer be free. My father drove us to a campsite in the national forest above the prison where we burned sage and prayed for my safety. It was a very sad moment for my family, but I was proud to have them by my side, especially my father, who did so much to secure my release on bond. Being out on bail had allowed me to reconnect with so many of my friends and family that I thought I might never see again; it gave me the strength I would need in the coming months and years.

The Moment Arrives

When we arrived at the prison, I walked into the lobby with my family and said my goodbyes as if I was boarding a plane for a flight. I was not allowed to bring anything inside. After being searched, I was buzzed through a set of doors that led into the main compound. Once inside, I was processed, given a quick medical inspection, and given my first set of prison clothes. I was led with a few other new prisoners to our unit, which was an open dormitory shared by about 85 men. There were no walls, only five-foot cinder block partitions separating each set of three bunk beds.

I quickly learned to seek out other indigenous prisoners, and I was introduced to the prisoners who ran the prison sweat lodge. Being imprisoned in Arizona meant being locked up with other Arizona Indians from the neighboring tribes. In those first months, it was members of the San Carlos Apache Tribe who befriended me and helped me learn the ins and outs of prison life.

When I first entered prison, I clung to my familiar life of friends, always looking forward to my next visit to keep me going. What I didn't realize was the toll it put on my friends and family, to make the two-hour drive to visit me. My girlfriend, Rosa, came to see me one day, and though my spirits were high, I could tell she was emotionally challenged being in the prison environment. After the visit, I went outside near the fence where I could see her drive away, and that's when I noticed her crying as she left. I knew it was too much to ask for her to wait for me for the next four years. After that sad day, I dug into my prison existence and depended less on visits to keep me connected to the real world.

After just two months into my sentence, there was a lockdown on the yard and I was hauled into the Captain's office to be questioned about a supposed fire that someone tried to set under the library trailer. I was aghast that I was suspected, but then again, I was a newly-convicted arsonist and this would not be the only time that my past would affect my future. Once cleared of any wrongdoing, I was informed that I was being transferred to a higher security prison—Safford being a minimum-security facility that I was happy with. I protested, but my pleas fell on deaf ears and the next morning I was woken at dawn and transferred to FCI Tucson, the medium-security facility where I had first been imprisoned after my arrest. I was stressed and depressed about the move, but as soon as I was taken to my new holding unit, I knew the change would be for the better.

Unlike the minimum-security prison, FCI Tucson had three main housing units for prisoners, each named for desert plants: Mesquite, Yucca, and Cholla Units. After being processed, I was again delivered to the Special Housing Unit, the Hole.

After two days, I was brought before the Captain and asked about the alleged arson at Safford. He did not appear to believe that I was involved, and when he asked whether I would cause trouble on the prison yard, I told him that my intention was to keep my head down and simply do my time. It was the most common prison survival strategy for those of us only serving a handful of years. When I was released from the Hole, I was assigned to a two-man cell with an older Navajo man. We indigenous prisoners would try to share cells whenever possible, and my new cellmate was a quiet man who spent most of his time working or out of the cell.

Rather than be stressed that I was living in a higher security prison, I was actually relieved. I was no longer in a large dorm unit where every prisoner could be heard snoring and farting each night; now I shared a quiet cell on the top tier with one man that I got along with. Also, the prison was just ten miles from Tucson, making visits much easier for my large support group of friends. I also was receiving letters of support from literally all over the world. Supporters in the UK were the most prolific, with the Vegan Prisoners Support Group being an established network to provide support to imprisoned activists like myself.

Inside of prison, every weekday after the 4pm "stand up" count, there would be mail call. Prisoners would come out of their cells and line the handrails of the upper tier, listening and hoping for one letter from a family or friend. I felt fortunate and selfish at the same time as the guard called out my name repeatedly, often handing me a stack of letters and magazines, when others received nothing. The attention at mail call led to curious prisoners asking why I received so much mail. I explained to them the nature of my crimes and the support for them amongst the free-living public. What most impressed other prisoners was that I was not a snitch and had chosen a longer prison sentence rather than selling out my friends.

Testimony from a co-defendant in exchange for a lighter sentence was the number one reason most other prisoners were convicted of their crimes.

Other prisoners became friends because I was someone who could provide interesting reading material. One particular prisoner was a shaved-headed white man with a huge swastika tattooed on his stomach. He would come visit me each evening before we were locked down for the night and ask for something to read. He liked the exposure to things happening in the world that were part of a bigger struggle. I shared with him radical environmental journals, vegan magazines, and books about the Irish Republican Army. One night as the guard was locking our cells, I ran downstairs to fill my jug with ice. As I walked past my skin-headed friend's cell, I peered into the narrow glass window in the door and saw him lying on his bunk reading an ALF supporters newsletter from the UK.

Other prisoners gained respect for my struggle because of how I acted in prison towards them. I used my good fortune to help others whenever I could. Whenever a new indigenous prisoner arrived, everyone who could chipped in some money so the new prisoner could buy soap, shampoo, soups, and other necessary items the prison did not supply, except for the poorest quality products.

In addition to the large volume of support mail that I received, I also had regular visits from my friends living just ten miles away. Anne Carl was a Tucson resident who always brought a new joke with her. Other friends came from afar to visit me, including some who would later be convicted of their own crimes for defending Earth and animals. I met my little nephew for the first time in the prison visiting room. And I also went there during non-visiting hours for interviews with different media outlets reporting on my crimes and the ALF. A journalist I had met in 1992 in Los Angeles, Dean Kuipers, wrote a feature story for *Rolling Stone* titled "The Tracks of the Coyote"; it required a professional photographer to come into the prison and set up lighting for a photo shoot. After interviews, the guards strip-searching me often expressed curiosity, and sometimes veiled support, for my actions.

One of the good things to come out of my plea bargain was the ability to publicly accept responsibility for my most publicized actions. I did not like it when I was first captured and many supporters were claiming that I was innocent of my "crimes." I believe now as I did then, that my crimes were nothing to be ashamed of and that I had an obligation to explain to the world why people like me were willing to risk their own freedom to save the life of animals. Even in prison, the guards knew I was neither a threat nor the "terrorist" that my file said I was. They dealt with people who had committed very violent crimes against innocent victims and they knew the difference, in their own way, between good and evil.

After the **THE** Animal Liberation Front firebombed a university research lab, federal **TRACKS** authorities accused a young American Indian of ecoterrorism Rodney Coronado **OF** lived under ground for more than two years. Now he awaits sentencing for **THE** a crime that he may not have committed — but refuses to condemn **COYOTE**

IN THE COLD PRE-DAWN HOURS OF FEB. 28, 1992, THE MEMBERS OF THE Great Lakes unit of a radical network called the Animal Liberation Front let themselves into the office of Dr. Richard Aulerich, a mink researcher at Michigan State University, in East Lansing. There were already a couple of students in the offices, labs and classrooms of Anthony Hall at that hour – research goes on there around the clock. The A.L.Fers, however, were not doing research. « No one knows if the Great Lakes unit was one person or 20. Whoever they were, they tore the office to pieces, looking for evidence of cruelty in Aulerich's mink data, dumping out files and destroying

B Y   D E A N   K U I P E R S

52 · ROLLING STONE, JUNE 1, 1995

Rolling Stone (1 June 1995)

Time Passes

I didn't count the days; I counted the months. I created little milestones for achievement, like finishing my first year in prison. The holidays were always a time when meals would be slightly better and the movies brought cheer and relief as we watched them under a patio outdoors in the recreation area. We microwaved bags of popcorn and drank ice cold soda as we watched current blockbusters like *Titanic* and *Men in Black*. I was no longer in the activist or Yaqui communities that I loved, but in this prison, there was something similar that I found with my fellow indigenous prisoners.

PHOTOGRAPHS BY MAX AGUILERA-HELLWEG
Rolling Stone (1 June 1995)

By this time, I learned that whenever I was transferred in the federal prison system, I needed to contact the prison chaplain and let them know I wanted to exercise my right to participate in any sweat lodge ceremonies. Thanks to the efforts of early American Indian rights activists, indigenous prisoners' religious freedom meant the availability of sweat lodges for prayers and cleansing. Within this federal construct of prisons, there are sweat lodges inside the walls and fences that allow us to connect with our Creator in ways that were prohibited in the recent past. I've never seen this right abused and it's a right that we as indigenous prisoners are allowed control over, even in prison.

So, every Saturday morning that I was in prison, except on a few rare occasions during lockdowns, I would be called out of my cell and let into the recreation yard where, in the far corner behind a hedgerow, there was our sweat lodge and outdoor shower. Opposite the sweat lodge was a fire pit used to heat rocks that were brought into the dome-shaped lodge, where they were ceremonially placed in the center, the first four in each of the sacred directions. Once the remaining hot stones were brought into the lodge, the canvas door was closed and we sat in pitch darkness except for the glowing orange of the hot rocks. Tobacco and other sacred herbs were placed on the rocks, before water was later poured to create steam. We always did four prayer rounds, each lasting about 15 to 30 minutes, depending on the length of prayers.

During the entire length of my imprisonment, I was able to participate in these ancient ways of honoring earth and ancestors that had first been introduced to me on that cold snowy day in South Dakota by Albert White Hat. Having this connection to the source of my own power and belief gave me the strength to not only endure prison, but to use the experience to continue to advocate for the wild, as well as support my indigenous brothers.

I also helped organize weekly meetings in the chapel for indigenous prisoners. An indigenous prison staff member was our sponsor, and every week I gave her a four-page newsletter I had put together from articles on indigenous struggles that I received in the mail. She made 20 to 30 copies and I distributed them to the indigenous prisoners interested, always with the advice to not share the newsletter with other prisoners who might complain of favorable treatment for native prisoners.

I also created a 'zine called *Strong Hearts* where I wrote about my alleged crimes, along with indigenous and animal issues. I read articles and books on a subject of interest and then typed out an article in the law library. I then used a copy machine to reduce the size of the text, which I then cut out with mustache scissors and overlayed on images that I cut from other publications and news articles.

When I had an entire issue of the 'zine completed, I was ready to send it out to the world. But the prison would not allow such a thing, so I had to get clever about it. Once in a while, I prepared a box of books to be sent to a supporter—but not without lining the bottom of the box with my latest issue. He then made copies and sent them out to a mailing list of other supporters. My 'zine was quite a hit; you can imagine my surprise when, decades later while living in Vermont, I walked into a record store and saw a poster made from the first issue of *Strong Hearts*.

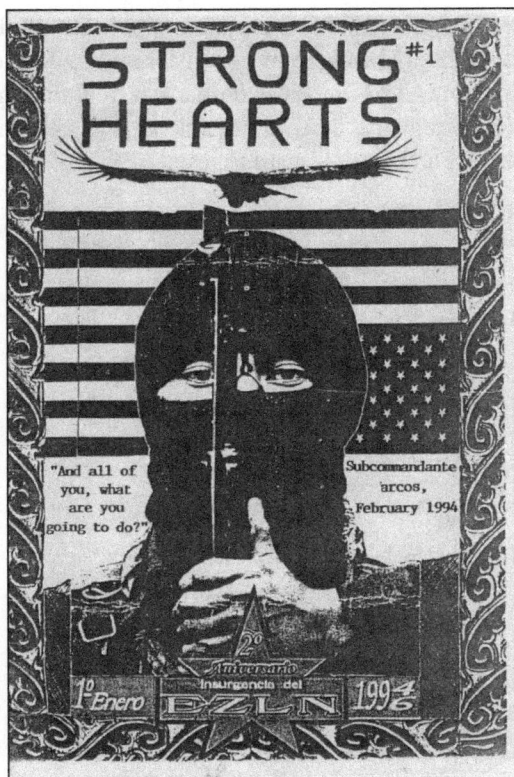

STRONG HEARTS #1

"And all of you, what are you going to do?"

Subcommandante Marcos, February 1994

1º Enero EZLN 1994

2º Aniversario Insurgencia del EZLN

I used my time in prison just as I had read that prisoners of war used their time: to further their own education on forbidden topics, as well as to plan escapes—granted, my only planned escapes were through lucid dreaming where I experienced adventures with friends that never lasted longer than one night.

Getting good sleep, three solid meals, and not drinking or smoking made my time in prison some of the healthiest years of my life. I worked out daily, walked the track, and read at least two books at once. If I had to be in prison, I was going to use the time to make myself a better person for it. Living for years with poor people from all races bought a level of awareness I could not have found anywhere else. I became friends with white separatists, Mexican Mafia, and other gang members as well as African American members of the Nation of Islam, whose meetings I was regularly invited to. Together we all realized the injustice of a colonial system that favored those already with wealth and power. The rest of us ended up here in prison because we struggled for a way out from our poverty—only for most poor people, that road is a criminal one. Many of the indigenous people I was locked up with were in prison for smuggling marijuana into the United States from Mexico, whose border ran right through the Tohono O'odham Nation. For many, making a quick $5,000 for simply driving a car across the reservation was too hard to resist.

One day while I was standing in the chow hall line reading a paperback book, I heard someone behind me call out, "Hey Martin!" No one in prison called me by that name except other Yaquis. When I turned, I saw a friend of mine from the village who had been busted for human smuggling. He wasn't the only Yaqui I knew in prison. When I first arrived in my designated unit, I was introduced to Triste, a Yaqui man a little older than me. Triste was one of those young indigenous men who was always in and out of prison. He helped me learn the ways of prison life and had a lot of respect from the other races because he was one of those prisoners that could get you what you wanted. Triste didn't go to the sweat lodge but he was familiar with Yaqui culture, and I often saw his family at ceremonies. Sadly, he was transferred early in my sentence and so I struck up close friendships with mostly Tohono and Akimel O'odham (Desert and River People.)

Zapatistas, the IRA, and Other Rebels

In December 1996, my Akimel O'odham friend Wade and I were glued to the Spanish-speaking TV station watched by Mexican nationals in our unit. The Peruvian Marxist revolutionary group, Tupac Amaru Revolutionary Movement (MARTA), had occupied the Japanese Ambassador's Mansion in Lima during a party for many representatives of multinational corporations exploiting the land and the (mostly indigenous) people of Peru. MARTA was a revolutionary group with many members serving life sentences for their actions. The demands of the occupiers included the release of the wife of one of the occupiers. Seventy-two hostages were taken without any loss of life, until four months later, when Alberto Fujimori, then President ordered a raid on the complex.

Wade and I would sit in the chow hall talking about what we had seen and heard from our Spanish-speaking friends. During the long occupation, the Red Cross allowed the police to hide cameras in food boxes delivered to the hostage takers. I remember one photo in particular that was published in the *New York Times*; in it, five members of MARTA were sitting without their masks or guns, laughing and playing a guitar. They looked like friends of mine; I admired that they were willing to risk their lives to save their imprisoned friends. When the truth came out after the raid that left all the hostage takers dead, it was revealed that as many as eight of the MARTA revolutionaries who had surrendered were immediately executed by Fujimori's soldiers.

I took great interest in the revolutionary movements of not only the Zapatistas and MARTA rebels, but I also read over a dozen Irish history books on the Irish Republican Army (IRA). Most of my activist friends considered the IRA real terrorists because they killed people, but I see the Irish history of armed struggle as no different from the armed struggles of indigenous Americans and of South Africa's anti-apartheid movement. Armed struggle is the only reason I am alive today and I still believe in the rights of anyone to take up arms against their violent oppressors. Personally, I've always drawn the line at physical violence, instead preferring to target only property. But I will never condemn the legitimate armed struggles against imperialism and genocide that continue today.

What I most admired about the IRA's struggle was the power of their prison campaigns in the 1970s and 1980s, in particular the hunger strikes and "dirty protests" that took place as a means to fight for the recognition of IRA fighters as legitimate prisoners of war. IRA prisoners demanded that their struggle not end in prison, and they taught each other their native language and Irish history. They also conducted some amazing escapes from Britian's infamous Maze Prison which held hundreds of IRA prisoners. Over a dozen IRA men made the ultimate sacrifice when they died after weeks on hunger strike. Their struggle was proof for me that a legitimate armed struggle could exist in a developed country and be a force to be reckoned with.

But all prisoners need supporters on the outside. My old PETA friend, Ingrid Newkirk, helped me during my prison years in many ways. One was to pay for my subscription to the Sinn Fein newspaper that was the voice of the IRA and its political party. Each week, I'd receive a little cardboard tube from Belfast with the weekly newspaper which I'd read from cover to cover. Like us Indians over in the Americas, the Irish Republican struggle really honored the sacrifices of their predecessors and ancestors, and I was envious of their memorial marches on important battle days and illegal armed salutes given to fallen IRA warriors.

Another regular newspaper I received was from the Vegan Prisoners Supporters Group, which listed all animal liberation prisoners in the world. I couldn't write to any kind of other US prisoner, but there was no restriction on my writing to animal liberation prisoners from other countries, namely the UK, where there were many like me. I corresponded with Barry Horne before he himself died on hunger strike, the first animal liberation prisoner to take that historic path of resistance. We prisoners were our own network and I really appreciated being able to communicate with others just like me who were serving time for protecting animal life.

I became fast friends with a British woman who was also serving time for arson attacks. Melanie Arnold was a longtime animal liberationist who was caught after torching a fleet of trucks belonging to a slaughterhouse. We both had over three years left in our sentence when we started writing each other, so we committed to support each other for the full stint of our sentences. And although I wrote hundreds of letters, trying to respond to every one I received, I never struck up a romantic relationship through the mail; that to me did not seem like a way to make the time go faster, only slower. It took five days for my letters to reach Mel in "Her Majesty's Prison" in the UK (actual name!). She responded the day she received the letter, and it would take another five days to reach me. In this fashion, for those three years, Mel and I wrote hundreds of letters to each other, receiving one from the other every week to ten days.

Although we were separated by an ocean and behind walls and razor wire, I'd have to say that I felt like Mel was one of my best friends in prison and was one of a very few I grew very close to while in prison. We did eventually fall in love with each other, which was a source of great joy! I was learning how strong platonic love could be and how much of a jerk I was for not spending the same kind of time I did with Mel just getting to know the women I had become lovers with. I still had much to learn before becoming capable of a truly loving relationship. But that's another story.

Rod and friends in prison

Springtime, 1998

Within the walls of my prison home, I became very adept at not only surviving but thriving. The lessons from the Northern Ireland prison struggles left me obligated to use the time to better not only myself, but my abilities as an animal- and Earth-defender. I wrote my own prison 'zine, the indigenous prisoners' newsletter, and articles for the *Earth First! Journal* and other international activist publications. My time was punctuated by the occasional in-person media interview as well as many visits from my friends.

At about this time, spring 1998, I began to get excited that I had begun my final year in prison. Being a longer serving prisoner meant I had earned a privileged position working in the prison commissary, which was the on-site grocery store where prisoners could purchase food and drink. Prisoners would line up, often for over an hour, to purchase commissary items. When they finally got to the head of the line, they would push their shopping list through a small slot where a prisoner on the other side (me) would take the shopping list and fill it in a basket, which was then put in another line to be delivered. One of the hustles I developed was to collect shopping lists from select customers ahead of time, fill them when I first started working, and then wait for my guys to come by the window and give me a nod. I'd move their baskets to the head of the line so they wouldn't have to wait; in exchange, I'd earn a six-pack of sodas.

Working in the commissary was the only place I ever got close to a physical altercation. A new white prisoner began working with us on the commissary crew and he wasn't stocking supplies like he was supposed to, which was backing up our busy shopping day. When I spoke up that he wasn't doing his job, the older white male—who was very aggressive to his fellow white prisoners—called me to the back of the building where we bumped chests while he chastised me for publicly telling him off. I was terrified by the much larger man, but I knew I couldn't back down, otherwise I'd lose the respect of not just "Tramp" as he was called, but other prisoners as well. When he finished his attempt at intimidation, I retorted that my problem with him was that he wasn't doing his job, which was slowing the rest of us down. The only prison staff onsite was our boss, who was in no position to intervene; and if he had, we all knew it would result in a prison-wide lockdown with both Tramp and I being thrown into the Hole. I was certain he could feel my heart beating as our chests bumped against each other, but instead of escalating, I was able to defuse the situation and he backed off. Only then did our boss come and ask if there was a problem, to which we both replied, "no." I'd seen Tramp belittling other white inmates who cowered under the intimidation. In this way, he would reaffirm his lack of respect for others, saying that they were "weak."

The funny thing that happened following our slight altercation was that Tramp and I began talking more, and in time, we became friends, despite his loud, sometimes racist and always offensive behavior. Tramp was someone who had spent more time in prison than out. He was a product of institutionalization and I couldn't fault him for the person he had become, living under the control of others. He used to be a biker tattoo artist, and in prison he continued the hustle. I had already paid an O'odham friend of mine to tattoo me, but the young artist was not good. I decided to ask Tramp to complete the tattoo, which he did. I chose to honor my crimes by creating a Native American shield with a coyote's paw in the center. From the shield, five hawk feathers hang, marking our ALF raids on Oregon State, Northwest Furbreeders, Washington State, Utah State, and Michigan State university laboratories. I also had Tramp tattoo me with a Celtic design of a mink. I wanted a sacred design from my indigenous relations overseas to honor the sacrifices my white friends had made defending Earth and animals.

Also early in 1998, I received word that my elder, Anselmo Valencia, wanted to visit me. I was deflated. Anselmo had clearly expressed that he did not want to see me in prison; we would reunite after my release. Knowing he had changed his mind, I could only think of one reason for the change, that he now knew that he would die before my release. His wife and I knew this but did not speak of it during our visit. When Anselmo came into the visiting room, he was energetic, and we instantly began conversing about Yaqui history and culture as usual. He told me stories that I had heard before, but I said nothing. When our visit ended, I thanked him in our language and shook his hand; Anselmo had taught me that Yaquis do not hug.

When I got back to the privacy of my cell, I broke down and cried—one of the few times that I did in prison. It was indeed the last time that I ever saw Anselmo in person. He passed into the spirit world on May 2, 1998. It was my greatest loss while in prison.

My grief was slightly overshadowed, fortunately, by my impending release. With less than one year remaining, I no longer counted the time in months but began breaking it up into weeks. I was fortunate to have created a busy prison life and spent much of my last year helping to organize a Pow Wow that would take place in the prison. Outside visitors would be allowed, which was an exciting prospect for those indigenous prisoners who rarely received visits. For the event, all of us traditional indigenous prisoners organized not only the Pow Wow, but an indigenous feast for the entire prison population. We spent the day working together in the kitchen, cooking fry bread and other native foods. I chose to make *calabacitas*, a squash dish that Yaquis always ate at ceremonies.

When summer 1998 arrived, my prison pen pal, Melanie Arnold, was released from prison. She not only continued writing me but got her passport and flew to Arizona to visit me in prison. When I walked into the visiting room and saw her for the first time, it was very unusual to be so excited to meet someone you already knew so much about. Mel visited me every day that she could for a month, and met with an immigration lawyer to discuss our prospects of being in a relationship. The lawyer brought our heads out of the clouds, telling Mel that part of the conditions of my release would include a prohibition on associating with other known felons. We could be together, but it would be at the risk of my being re-imprisoned and Mel deported from the US. Maybe we both knew the greatest strength of our relationship was that it had served us well in prison, providing joy in a dark place. With much sadness, we enjoyed our last times together, knowing that although we could not stay together, I too would soon be released from prison.

My release plan was to serve five months of halfway-house time in Eugene, Oregon, where I had been told I had a job waiting for me at the *Earth First! Journal* as a member of the editorial collective—a job being one of the requirements of halfway house release. I wanted to hit the ground running and help continue to promote the direct-action defense of Earth and animals by not just the ALF, but the emerging Earth Liberation Front, another UK offshoot that had taken roots in America, targeting genetically modified research farms and sport-utility vehicle dealers. On October 18, 1998, televisions across the country and in my prison featured helicopter footage of the massive Vail ski resort smoldering after an ELF group ignited a massive fire at the complex, causing over $12 million in damages and making it the costliest act of eco-terror yet in the country. Again I was interviewed about the action; I could easily see that while it might not be possible to continue engaging in ALF or ELF actions, I could however serve an important role as a media spokesperson for such actions, which were on the rise.

The fur farm industry had not escaped the growing movement for Earth defense and animal liberation. Within a year of my own imprisonment, others would take up the ALF name in defense of fur animals and continue attacks on fur farms across the country. No longer were fur farms operating in secrecy; many were the targets of massive mink releases that, while devastating for the local environment, were a severe economic loss for the fur farmers, leading many to close their doors forever. There would be consequences. Fur animal defenders in Utah who targeted the same Furbreeders Co-op with pipe bombs that caused extensive damage, faced terrorism charges that led one ALF member, Alex Slack, to commit suicide. While attacks on fur farms and ELF raids increased, there were also arrests, and some people testified against their former comrades—something I was fortunate to have never experienced.

Like all prisoners nearing release, I hid my excitement from friends, especially those with years left in their sentences. The weeks became days as my excitement was replaced with pure nervousness. I was finally finishing a long sentence that had forced me to adapt to a harsh but regimented environment. But that was coming to an end. No longer would I be able to predict where or what I was doing every moment of the day, as I had for the past nearly four years. I became totally accustomed to sleeping in a room locked from the outside and being in the company of hundreds of mostly poor men from many cultures. I had routines that provided predictability, not uncertainty. That was all about to change.

Parting with my indigenous support network would be my greatest loss. The men inside of those walls had reminded me of the endurance of our people and our ability to remain true to our beliefs, even in the depths of the enemy's prisons. At my last sweat lodge ceremony in the prison, I was invited to lead the ceremony, which I did with little confidence and less ability to hide how I was truly feeling. Inside this sweat lodge, I was able to pray weekly and keep my connections with my Earth-centered ways strong and resilient; these brothers were there to support me, much as my Lakota friends had when I first found myself as a fugitive.

On one of my last weeks in prison, I was walking the track, as I daily did. As I rounded the portion that bordered the desert, thirty feet away across two fences of razor wire, I saw a lone coyote standing beside a creosote brush, unafraid and staring at me. I froze in my tracks and removed the headset of my Walkman radio. The coyote and I locked eyes, and I said hello in Yaqui. I felt what I believed to be the thoughts of that animal. He was just checking on me, while reminding me that what I most wanted to believe was indeed true. Animals were just other people like us, with their own nations, tribes, and languages, all struggling to survive in a war that pitted all of us wild ones against the dark forces that invaded these sacred places centuries earlier in a war that rages on, each and every day.

Freedom Regained

On the day of my release, I awoke excited but more nervous. I hauled my duffel bag of belongings to the same receiving room I had entered a few years earlier. For one last time, I was placed in a holding cell to wait—staring at the walls, knowing this time that within moments I would be walking out of this place. My parents, brother, and old friend (now girlfriend), Turtle, would be waiting to drive me to the airport, where I'd fly to Eugene to self-surrender at the halfway house run by the county sheriff's department. As I signed for the money that remained in my prison account, I saw my own hands shaking as I scratched my name on the paper without reading a word. One of my former bosses with the landscape crew was just arriving to work, and with a smile on his face said, "What's the matter

Rod, a little nervous?" I laughed nervously but also took the moment to thank him for treating me like a human.

When the electronic buzz indicated that the doors to the prison were opening, I stood alone in the chamber as the metal door rolled open. Across the room I could see my family and friends sitting in nervous excitement, all with huge smiles on their faces. They sat forward in their chairs, unsure when it was safe to approach and embrace me.

My smile was so huge it hurt my face. I felt like I was taking in fresh air for the first time in years. The new clothes my family had sent me to wear felt uncomfortable—so unlike my usual prison outfit. I was most appreciative that my parents were there for the big moment, especially my mom, who had suffered so much because of harassment from federal agents looking for me while I was a fugitive.

Rod and his mother at the airport

We only had a short time before my flight to Oregon, so friends from Tucson gathered at the airport and we all shared some apple cider before I boarded my plane. As it lifted off, it banked and flew directly over the prison, a small quadrant in a huge wild desert that grew smaller and smaller out my window before disappearing completely in the clouds. Though I still would be in custody for another five months, I would be free to work and travel, once I became settled at the halfway house. This would be the first time I returned to Oregon since going underground, and I was returning just as the radical environmental movement in Eugene was on the verge of exploding. I was ready for the next chapter in my life as a warrior. I followed the IRA model: once captured as an insurgent and imprisoned, upon release, you return to the struggle, albeit in a different capacity. I had survived and grown stronger; now it was the time to show others that prison does not have to defeat you. Rather, it is the test that all true struggles must endure before victory can be seen on the horizon.

A New Life in Oregon

When I walked off the airplane and entered the small airport in Eugene, Oregon, I was met by a group of friends who each were carrying a letter in the words, "Forever Wild." They weren't sure whether I was going to be in the custody of marshals on my way to the halfway house, so they opted for the sign. When they realized I was accompanied by my brother, not a cop, we all embraced and they asked if I had time to visit the Willamette River that ran through the small mountain town.

I still had five months of custody to complete in the halfway house, so I wasn't really free from prison, just released under my own supervision until I arrived in Eugene, where I would self-surrender to the Lane County Sheriff's Department, which operated the halfway house. I had been planning the move to Oregon for over a year. I was required to have a job at the halfway house, so I had arranged for financial support from People for the Ethical Treatment of Animals, which offered to provide my salary for the low-paying job of being an editor on the *Earth First! Journal*, which was operating out of Eugene at the time.

After a couple days of orientation at the halfway house, I was allowed to go into town and search for employment. When I came back on the first day with the news that I had found a job, the deputy supervising my case complimented me. I didn't say I was working at the "Earth First! Journal" but at Daily Planet Publishing, which was the radical newspaper's official business name. There were strict conditions that allowed me to travel only to work, the gym, church, and an occasional social pass which required a sponsor to be with me at all times.

Sponsors would come to the halfway house, sign me out, and then we were allowed to travel to a pre-approved list of destinations, usually starting at a restaurant and then moving to a movie theater. At any location, I was required to provide a phone number so the police could check up on me. Security was low; there was little reason yet to be concerned with my going abouts in the small college town hosting the *Earth First! Journal*, yet it was a simmering hotbed for radical politics, of which Earth First! was at the center.

When I arrived in Eugene, the occupation of a proposed timber sale at Warner Creek had recently disbanded after more than a year of blockading a forestry road that led into sensitive spotted owl habitat. Not long after the occupation ended, the US Forest Service's Ranger Station at Oak Ridge responsible for the timber sale was burned to the ground—one of the first actions in Oregon that would be credited to the Earth Liberation Front (ELF). Not long after, in December 1998, a fire destroyed the offices of US Forest Industries in Medford, Oregon, with the ELF again claiming responsibility.

Warner Creek was just one occupation organized by the Cascadia Forest Defenders, which took up occupations and tree-sitting as their primary tactics for opposing old growth logging operations in the Pacific Northwest. It was now summer 1999, and perhaps the most famous tree-sit occupation was taking place in northern California, where an activist by the name of Julia Butterfly Hill was living in an old growth redwood tree named Luna. Butterfly did not identify as an Earth First! activist; she chose to operate independently with her own support team which coordinated both material support and media interview requests that were arriving from all over the world.

Each morning, I was always the first one to arrive at the Earth First! house. I had no desire to be in the halfway house for one minute longer than necessary, so each morning I left at 7 a.m. to go to work and make my breakfast there before other members of the editorial collective had arrived. Being the first one in the office meant that I answered the phones, and Julia would often call to provide an update on her tree-sitting occupation. Through these conversations, we struck up an unlikely friendship, her being a devout pacifist, but me being a supporter of illegal direct action and guerilla warfare.

The radical environmental movement was in transition. Recent violent actions—that had really begun as far back as 1990, when Darryl Cherney and Judi Bari were the targets of a car-bomb attack in California—caused many in the movement to reevaluate their stance on committing crimes in defense of Earth and animals. Possibly the biggest impact on the previously nonviolent environmental movement was the 1998 death of David Chain, a California forest defender, who, while opposing old growth logging in an active timber sale, was killed when a tree was deliberately cut near the group of protesters. No charges were ever filed against the logger, but it did become public knowledge that the timber company, Pacific Lumber, was in violation of numerous logging regulations when the death of Chain occurred.

I spoke to Chain's mother on the phone numerous times during my time at the newspaper, and in my position as editor, I was able to reconnect with many of the environmental struggles taking place in California and Oregon. On June 18, 1999, as I was working out at the local gym in Eugene, I watched the news on the gym television which was showing crowds of protestors confronting police in the streets outside. By the time I got back to the halfway house, the facility was in lockdown due to the "Carnival Against Capital" protest that had turned into a full-blown riot in downtown Eugene. One protestor went to prison for seven years for hitting a police officer with a rock.

At about this same time, my ruse with my employment had also been discovered, and the deputy in charge of my case became irate with my deception, yet he was unwilling to void my early release agreement and send me back to prison, thankfully.

I met many people during this time who would later become the focus of other federal investigations into ALF and ELF activity. One of these people was Josephine Sunshine Overaker, one of the young activists I spoke with as I biked to work at the *Journal*. On one of our early morning bike rides, Josephine confessed to me that she was one of the people that had read of the rehabilitation of fur farm animals we had done in 1990 and taken action, travelling to the Fraser Fur Farm in Ronan Montana, where they had hoped to carry out some form of direct action that never occurred. I then began to realize the impact my actions had had on the larger movement, something that had only grown while I was in prison.

This was also the time of the Unabomber. Ted Kaczynski was arrested while I was finishing my prison sentence, and now the *Earth First! Journal* was one of the only media outlets that he was willing to talk to. Ted's use of explosives and his causing of physical injuries cost him much support from us radical eco-activists, despite the fact that his targets were aligned with our philosophy on technology and its significance to the destruction of wild nature. His willingness to be interviewed threw the *Earth First! Journal* into an internal quandary. Some editorial collective mem-

bers were adamantly opposed to printing an interview with the Unabomber, but others like myself saw it as an excellent opportunity to explore the
reasons behind his controversial actions which had garnered international
attention. How could we as journalists ignore such a scoop? We agreed to
do it, but by the time the interview was actually published, much of the
attention had been lost by the fickle public.

Not long after the Eugene riots, it was time for my last stage of incarceration: home confinement, which would last a month in southern Oregon. I had been invited to live with friends outside of the small mountain
town of Williams, not far from the Little Applegate River Valley that I had
fled in 1992. I drove my father's truck to southern Oregon, following a
Lane County Sheriff's Deputy cruiser with an officer who would set up the
device to monitor my physical movements via an ankle bracelet. I would
have to wear the device for the last month of my prison sentence.

After the officer left, I was alone on a mountainside without another
visible human being as a neighbor. My trailer had no outside lights, so
when the sun had disappeared, I experienced my first night of natural star-
light in nearly four years. I laid out a sleeping bag in the bed of my truck,
with my leg close to my bedroom window where the receiver for my ankle
bracelet could register that I had not left the location. I lay awake, staring
at the same sea of stars I had seen while living in my cabin at Standing
Rock or on the Little Applegate. When a falling star shot across the sky, I
was reminded of the night of the Washington State University raid eight
years ago, when stars could be seen falling from the skies.

In the next days, I was reunited with my old friend, Jonathan Paul,
and others I had known in my Little Applegate days, but the vibe had
changed since the early 1990s, with increasingly radical actions in defense
of Earth and animals regularly showing up in the headlines of Oregon
newspapers. Jonathan and I were able to attend a sweat lodge ceremony
that month in southern Oregon, and I felt blessed to have the opportunity to
be in another sweat lodge, only this time outside of prison. It was seven
years since Jonathan and I said our quick goodbyes on the shoulder of a
South Dakota highway, with the FBI in hot pursuit.

Back to Arizona

In addition to my prison sentence, I also had a three-year term of supervised
release or probation that I would be under while going about my post-prison
life. As much as I felt at home and with community and friends in Oregon,
my homeland in Arizona was calling, so I decided to return to Tucson in

the fall of 1999. Not only would I be returning to my own Yaqui people, but friends I had met while underground and organizing with the Student Environmental Action Committee were opening up a high school for indigenous youth, and they wanted me to join the staff of the new school.

As excited as I was for my new beginnings and with the state of the radical environmental and animal movements, I did not come out of prison with the tools to sustain a healthy personal relationship. I was fortunate to fall in love, but maintaining those relationships was something it would eventually take many years of therapy to unpack and understand. I had begun a relationship with a close friend in Tucson before I left prison and was now planning to live with the same woman upon my return there. Yet, on the last days of my stay in Oregon, I spent the night with a woman I met during my time in Williams.

This is not the story of my own hoped-for recovery from violating the trust of my partners; that is a story still being written, and one that is as important as any other value I hold for life and Earth. I simply want to confess that I have a history of infidelity with women and it is a part of my own history that I am dedicated to breaking and changing, in order to be truly happy.

My Tucson homecoming in August 1999 was punctuated by the heat I had become familiar with since returning to my newly discovered home state. The first week of my employment with Ha:san Preparatory and Leadership Academy had me camping out with all of our students and staff in the Baboquivari Mountains, that were the homelands of the Tohono O'odham Nation, whose members comprised the vast majority of our students and staff. In time, I recruited Yaqui youth who became the second most populous tribal members at the new high school. The school's focus was not only on basic education but cultural preservation as well, with the state's foreign language requirement being met with our teaching of the Tohono O'odham language. Traditional basketmaking and the sustainable growing of traditional foods were also curriculum at the school.

I was the receptionist for the school, answering the phones and calling parents when a student was absent or showed up late. During breaks, students gathered around my desk and asked questions about the food I was eating or the flyers I was making for local events, some of which were being hosted by the school. During my tenure, I helped bring in guest speakers from Pastors for Peace, Buffalo Field Campaign, the indigenous artists, Blackfire, and other social change agents who shared their stories with our students.

It was about this same time that the family of my former elder, Anselmo Valencia, asked if I wanted to move back into the family home that I shared with Anselmo before my imprisonment. At the time, I was living in the South Tucson Yaqui community of Barrio Libre, where I was regularly volunteering with the local traditional religious societies.

Moving back to the Pascua Yaqui Reservation was bittersweet. I returned to my former role as a volunteer with the warrior society, but there was a noticeable absence since Anselmo's passing. Yet, the traditions of our people continued and I was happy to spend New Year's Eve 1999 in the plaza of one of our villages with other traditional Yaquis, who had gathered in ceremony on the eve of what was thought to be a chaotic entry into the 21st century. When the church bells rang at midnight, the world remained the same.

Rod with some Yaqui kids on Mt. Graham

The VA Dog Raid

Not long afterward, I read an article in the newspaper about dogs being used for research by the nearby Tucson Veterans Administration Hospital. Apparently, the researcher was under scrutiny and had his experiments halted, but the dogs were remaining at the VA Complex in South Tucson. I had first heard of vivisection on greyhounds at the VA when four dogs were rescued in 1989. Now, all these years later, the experiments appeared to be continuing. I remembered reading about VA security staff chasing away the earlier bandits, who they said ran off "into the desert." This made me think that there was undeveloped desert surrounding the facility where the dogs were held.

My friend, Turtle, and I decided to investigate, so we rode our bikes south of downtown along the path that ran behind the VA complex. We soon identified one building separate from the others with kennels attached to it. In the ensuing evenings, we carried out surveillance, climbing underneath the chain-link perimeter fence to sit and watch the dog kennel. One night, a lone security guard drove ten yards away from where we lay in the dark, watching the building. After an hour, we crept backwards and disappeared back under the fence without notice. It had only been a few days since I first read about the experiments and we knew that time was of the essence.

Unlike the Pacific Northwest in 2000, there was no dark cloud of federal investigation hanging over the activist community in southern Arizona. That was still to come. Despite my history with such surveillance in the past, I felt that I could carry out this one particular action with a few local unknown friends who had never been arrested, but could certainly be trusted. I felt like these were the people I could most trust, especially after all the support they gave me through their friendship and prison visits. These were also people I saw demonstrating good security culture in regards to other protests that involved confrontations with the police.

When the weekend came, we rented a room in a hotel with a window looking out over the VA complex. This would be our security patrol. None of us were too concerned about triggering federal investigations; it had been ten years since the ALF last visited the University of Arizona in one of my most favorite nights of action. Perhaps my being a primary suspect in any dog rescue might have warranted more vigilance, but this seemed like a unique opportunity to save lives within a bike ride from my house.

It was now the year 2000, and this would be my first criminal animal liberation since those actions I carried out while a fugitive in 1993 and 1994. It appeared that the only time I was not acting in defense of Earth and animals was when I was literally locked up and kept under constant surveillance. Even then, I'd like to believe that my letters to supporters, my 'zine, and my writing for outside publications were all methods in furtherance of Earth defense and animal liberation.

For this raid, I planned to climb onto the kennel's roof to evade an infrared sensor, similar to that I encountered at Fred Gilbert's laboratory at Washington State University in 1991. From there, I would cut a hole into the kennel fencing, drop into the kennel, and retrieve any dogs through the kennel dog door separating the outside kennel from the inside of the building.

The two of us cut through the outside chain-link fence, rather than crawl underneath as we had done during surveillance. We didn't care about leaving a trace at this point and we needed a quick exit with any dogs. At the fence line, there were two others to receive dogs while we returned to the kennel, taking more dogs until it was empty.

When I reached the kennel, I took a ladder that lay against another building and leaned it against the top of the kennel fencing, being careful not to break the infrared beam below the ladder. As soon as I was on the roof, I fumbled for my wire cutters and quickly cut enough fencing to fit my body into the kennel. When I dropped onto the floor, I crouched and looked for my partner, who gave me a thumbs up that everything was still ok on the security front. But when I lifted the door separating the outside kennel, I saw and heard no dogs. The lit interior of the kennel was empty. On the inside of the door I came through, I saw only muddy paw prints but no other signs of life. The dogs were gone.

We retreated without detection, but we left signs of entry at both the perimeter fence and kennel itself. With the history of the 1989 raid, VA security must have linked this attempted break-in to the ALF, although to this day, I have never seen any mention or evidence of our failed rescue of VA dogs. But if nothing else, it signaled that I was indeed not done being a member of the Animal Liberation Front.

Meanwhile, my role with the *Earth First! Journal* had come under scrutiny and, despite the newspaper moving its location to Tucson, I was not allowed to work for the paper while under supervised release. The move to Arizona was an idea first floated amongst local Earth First! activists while I was still in prison, and I even authored a proposal to move the paper back to Arizona where it began in 1982.

The Ongoing Defense of Mount Graham

The struggle to defend Dzil Nchaa Zian, or Mount Graham, was also continuing. With the observatory now complete, the University of Arizona and Vatican owners of the complex were constructing a powerline that would exclusively serve the observatory. The powerline was opposed by the San Carlos Apache Tribe because it desecrated graves along the route of the line. While I was forbidden from overtly working on the *Earth First! Journal*, I was not under such surveillance that prevented my contemplating an attack on the powerline under construction. I was still under federal supervision and such a crime would certainly mean my return to prison. Yet, despite having been out of prison for less than two years, I knew I had to act to defend the sacred homelands of my ancestors.

When we drove along the remote state highway that threaded the southern edge of the Pinaleno Mountains on a scouting mission, we easily found the huge excavator being used to dig the trench where the powerline would be buried. The machine was sinister looking, with a toothed blade on one end that stood over six feet across. Strung out behind the excavator were numerous line-laying vehicles, machinery, and large spools of wire.

I worked with someone I knew to be an active member of the Earth Liberation Front. At the Winter Earth First! Organizer's Conference in the Mojave Desert in 2000 that I was able to attend, I was invited to join a private meeting of what would become the Praxis Book Club. The Club was the name given to members of both the ELF, ALF, and other radicals currently engaging in various acts of economic sabotage. Under the ELF name (and without my knowledge), Book Club members had successfully carried out numerous arson attacks and other raids between 1996 and the early 2000s, causing federal law enforcement agencies to label both the ELF and ALF as the most active domestic terrorist organizations in the United States.

One of the first gatherings of the Praxis Book Club was in Tucson in 2000. Using a supporter's vacated home (which one of us was entrusted to house-sit), about ten of us who had gathered at the winter event now were together to skill-share in Tucson. In preparation for the weekend event, I had scoped out the University of Arizona's genetically-modified crop research on corn that was being conducted on and off campus. We weren't looking for a target, but we wanted a live example to practice some of our techniques. Inside the house, we discussed the needs for greater security protocols following the new round of federal investigations that were now hunting the ELF and ALF. We also practiced lock-picking and manufacturing incendiary devices, much like those I perfected in the 1990s. At night, we carried out surveillance and hopped fences to access greenhouses where GMO crops were being raised, practicing entry techniques we had discussed during the day.

One evening as we explored GMO crops at an off-campus location, I noticed a few trailers on the University property that were associated with invertebrate research. In this case, it was shrimp that were a focus of aquaculture research intended to aid the farmed shrimp business. Security was non-existent, so I approached one of the trailers and found a side-office window open. Inside the building were tanks filled with shrimp, but in another room was a cage with two seagulls inside. Next to the cage was a binder detailing the experiments the gulls would soon be subjected to; while not inherently lethal, the experiments would end in the gulls' deaths so that their organs could be examined.

After I found the birds, I went back to the Praxis Book Club and proposed that we rescue them. No one was against the action, but none of these friends, who were currently being hunted, wanted to be in Tucson when such a raid went down. It was agreed that I would (if I could) carry out the action only after the Club had disbanded.

The binder accompanying the seagulls listed the date of the planned death of the animals, so I went to work recruiting a few local friends for the job. I easily found three Earth First!ers willing to do the job—one of whom was a woman who had helped with our attempted raid at the VA hospital. I took one of the women onto the grounds and showed her how to enter the building and where a driver could park in a nearby river-wash to await the birds. As much as I wanted to simply take the birds on the night I had discovered them, I knew that doing so might begin a string of events I was hardly prepared for. Instead, I planned to be out of state, visiting my family, when the liberation occurred.

The gulls were rescued without a hitch, and released, although not back in Utah where they had come from. These two birds were freed at Kennedy Park in Tucson, a green oasis with ponds where the birds could decide if they wanted to continue receiving human handouts or wing it out of the area. When I returned from my trip, I thanked my three friends with hawk (not gull) feathers, which are a symbol of respect and victory in my own culture.

Back in one of our Tucson homes, three of us wiped tools and packed go-bags for our raid on the powerline under construction. We would be dropped off by our driver who would return hours later at a set time. If we were not at the meeting point, they were instructed to return to Tucson and we would walk overland the 70 miles back home.

In the desert, we agreed to come together to share skills related to breaking into buildings, constructing incendiary devices, and remaining undetected as we traveled into areas with active law enforcement investigations. When I discovered the powerline under construction, I decided to ask for help from someone I had only met since leaving prison, but his resumé was indeed impressive. Together with others, they were responsible for multiple raids on facilities experimenting with genetically modified plants, where experimental plots were often destroyed and the plants pulled.

Except for the brief urban attempt at the VA Hospital in Tucson, this was the first time since the 1993 arson at the BLM Wild Horse Facility that I was again in the field, operating at night, in defense of sacred indigenous lands and endangered species habitat. This was obviously my calling; prison had not dampened my desire to act when others would not. Federal investigators had yet to target southern Arizona in their active hunt for ELF and ALF members, but our planned action would surely change that.

Along with my friend, who I will call Sage, we walked alone on the dark highway towards our target in the far-off distance as bursts of lightning illuminated the clouds covering the mountains. Thunder could be heard rumbling with the lightning strikes and bursts of light looking like mortar blasts and bombs exploding on a battlefield. As we walked, we both spoke of other humans who had walked these same hills with the same intent of sabotaging the works of the colonizers invading these sacred lands. I remembered the sacredness I felt when defending Mount Graham and the dream I had the night before our action in 1993.

When we reached the excavator, there was no security in sight, so we went to work cutting hydraulic lines and smashing equipment with sledge-hammers and pry bars we found when we broke into a tool storage trailer. I climbed into the trench dug by the excavator and, using a huge pair of wire cutters found onsite, began cutting the line every hundred feet that was still exposed. After over 90 minutes of grueling work that reminded me of our raid on Iceland's whaling station, we began the long walk back to our pre-designated pick-up spot where we were thankfully met and driven back to Tucson, thoroughly exhausted.

The action went unclaimed; we did not want to provide any information to law enforcement investigating the crime. But less than two weeks later, Sage and I returned to the scene of the crime, and this time we saw trucks regularly patrolling the excavation equipment left out along the highway. While they were focused on the equipment, Sage and I hiked back to the powerline already laid in the ground. This time we brought drill and nails to penetrate the insulated powerline, using the nails to conduct between wires, causing an electrical short that would have to be located and later repaired at great costs. We again escaped detection on this second phase of the raid.

Luxury Homes Torched

The University of Arizona and its Vatican partners eventually completed the powerline up Mount Graham at a much greater cost than originally anticipated. This wasn't a surprise; we just wanted them to know there would always be continued resistance to their continued desecration of the mountain and their destruction of endangered red squirrel habitat.

Elsewhere in Arizona, another presumed "eco-terrorist" was capturing headlines in early 2000 for his burning down of luxury homes built near the Phoenix Mountains Preserve, on the edge of the sprawling city. In April 2000, the arsonist first struck, leaving behind the note, U BUILD - WE BURN AGIN! "C.S.P." at the remains of a luxury home under construction that was totally destroyed. The arsonist used the name "Coalition to Save the Preserve," and when the first target was rebuilt, he followed through and burned it down again. In total, eight luxury homes under construction would be destroyed; everyone was convinced that the culprit was environmentally motivated because of the proximity of the homes to the desert preserve.

Anti-sprawl campaigns were certainly much of the focus of the environmental community in Arizona, as homes were pushing further and further into the Sonoran Desert to meet the needs, not of the poor, but the very wealthy. Stringent rules were put into place by county officials hoping to minimize the impact of human sprawl on the sensitive desert ecosystem, but growth was nibbling away constantly at the home of many plants and animals living in the desert long before the first Europeans set foot in this dry landscape.

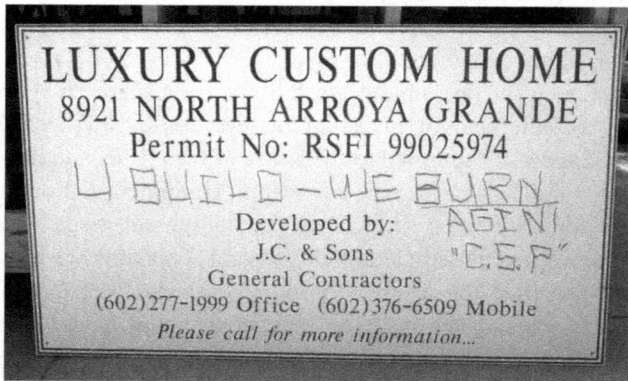

Our local Earth First! chapter engaged in protests and street theater targeting urban sprawl at home expos, and we even disrupted Tucson's Earth Day Parade which was sponsored by luxury home developers and Raytheon, the local weapons manufacturer. Now, the presence of a serial arsonist (like myself) targeting luxury homes pushed the envelope and became a reality in the current fight against sprawl encroaching on the desert. I was still very much under federal supervision as part of my three-year probationary period, so while I reported monthly to my probation officer, who also made unannounced visits, I wasn't questioned about the Phoenix arsons or even viewed as a suspect.

In June 2001, I met a friend from the Praxis Book Club late one hot evening at an all-night cafe. He proposed the idea of targeting luxury homes under construction in a high-end development project called Pima Canyon Estates; it was controlled by Don Diamond, a local developer responsible for not only building luxury homes in the desert, but also for grazing domestic goats in the desert, which had spread an infectious disease to endangered desert bighorn sheep, causing them to go blind and eventually stumble to their deaths. We decided to check out a series of houses under construction; these were some of the first in the new wealthy neighborhood inserted into an otherwise untouched desert oasis that was Pima Canyon.

We rode our bikes through the warm night air up Ina Road which rolls east from downtown right up against the Catalina Mountains, which form a crescent around Tucson. This wasn't just where I lived, it was and is my homeland. Although the eight traditional pueblos of the Yaqui Nation are in what is currently called Sonora, Mexico, the Yoeme had established villages throughout southern Arizona. This wasn't by choice, but for survival. As our people continued armed resistance long past the turn of the 20th century with our Mexican aggressors, we were forced to take shelter over the international border in Arizona, where our injured warriors could recover; other Yoeme worked in mines to gain the funds necessary to purchase more guns and ammunition for the struggle in Jiakim, the Yaqui homeland.

My elder, Anselmo Valencia Tori, told me stories from his childhood of waking up in a house in South Tucson with injured and battered Yaqui warriors laying everywhere in their tiny home. His mother was a known medic and healer, so their home was a safe house for soldiers fleeing the battlefield 300 miles south of Tucson. Anselmo also told me that our people ranged all the way north to southern Colorado, and I always remembered what he had told me about our tribe's own history with Mount Graham and other such sacred places outside of our traditional homelands in today's Mexico.

One day, Anselmo told me that, not far from Pima Canyon, he and some others were hunting javelina when they stopped to rest. His companion was tossing small stones when they both heard the distinct "clink" sound of a stone hitting metal. When they investigated, they unearthed a four-hundred-year-old Spanish conquistador's helmet.

The longer I spent in Tucson and the greater Sonoran Desert, the more I truly felt at home. And it wasn't just because I was living in my homeland, but I was living with my own people and participating in our still-thriving culture. Since my return from prison, I had returned to volunteering with our nation's warrior society, which meant attending the occasional all-night ceremony. This was a parallel world that existed amidst the colonized land and mindset called Tucson, Arizona, with its military bases and arms manufacturers that had established themselves here, originally, partly to vanquish the then-Apache threat.

The fight for indigenous autonomy and against colonization continued, only for me the focus was on protecting our non-human relations and the habitat they needed for their own autonomy and survival. This was what I saw as my role in our centuries-old fight for survival from conquest.

When we reached the foot of the canyon, we ditched our bikes in the desert and began walking up the newly-paved road that wound like a black snake up the canyon. The road was the first phase of development, but we also walked past one-acre plots where luxury homes would soon be built overlooking the Tucson desert. There was virtually no security present other than a few "no trespassing" signs at the actual construction sites.

We had no intention of setting any fires; we simply were investigating whether such an action was possible ... and it appeared that it most definitely was. Our simple plan was to use the cover of the Phoenix-area arsonist, more than 100 miles away, to carry out similar actions targeting a luxury home developer with a bad reputation on our side of the Sonoran Desert.

When we returned to the city, my friend said that it would be best if I had a solid alibi for any local arsons, so I shared with him my plans to visit my family in California the following week. That was the last I heard of any plan until late June, when I was visiting my parents. My girlfriend from Arizona had driven to California and brought with her a few local newspapers that reported that, shortly after midnight on June 12, 2001, four luxury homes under construction in Pima Canyon Estates were destroyed by fire in what was an obviously coordinated action. At one home, the letters, "C.S.P." were found spray-painted on a wall. Damages were reportedly in excess of $2 million, and investigators said it was thought that the arsonists were onsite, setting the third and fourth fires, while firefighters were still battling the first and second.

Two days after the Tucson fires, Phoenix police arrested Mark Warren Sands, who they said was responsible for the string of luxury home arsons in 2000 and 2001. He eventually served 15 years in prison for those fires. Meanwhile, the luxury home arsons in Tucson remained an unsolved crime—as they are to this day.

White Sands Research Center

It was now summer 2001. I visited a friend in New Mexico who told me about the campaign against the notorious Coulston Foundation, a chimpanzee research facility that housed the famous "Space Chimps" that were part of early NASA research into space flight. The lab was also home to hundreds of other apes and experimental animal subjects. My friend described the financial pressure felt by the besieged lab, which was failing to even make payroll for its employees. Anti-vivisection organizations had been lobbying the owners of the lab for years in an attempt to have former research chimps given better homes where they could naturally socialize with others of their own kind. But the calls fell on deaf ears. My friend, knowing my connections in the ALF and ELF, asked whether something could be done to help push the vivisector closer towards bankruptcy. He suggested smashing windows of the offices, but I had other ideas.

When I arrived back in Tucson, I went back to my life as a receptionist at Ha:san Prep and as a practicing traditional Yaqui, but I also wasted no time in finding some Praxis Book Club members with whom I could discuss any possible Coulston Foundation action. This time I met with a woman who I had first met while interning with the *Earth First! Journal* in Eugene when I first got out of prison. When I initially met her, she looked like any other young college student at the University of Oregon, but now she was a committed member of the Earth Liberation Front.

With a third person to act as a lookout and driver, we drove the five hours to the outskirts of Alamogordo, New Mexico, where Coulston's White Sands Center was located in a largely agricultural area. We found a vantage point high above the facility, where we used the day's remaining light to monitor activity through our spotting scope and binoculars.

From our vantage point, we saw only one person occasionally walking amongst the buildings before returning to sit in a car. The facility did not have a perimeter fence, nor any signs identifying the business as an animal research laboratory, yet many buildings did not have windows. In the hot New Mexico sun, the scattering of brick-and-mortar buildings with air-conditioning equipment atop told us little of where any chimpanzees might actually be housed.

From the beginning, the intent of any raid was to cause infrastructure damage that would make continuing business as a primate research facility economically impossible. We already knew the lab was in dire straits. Now we were seeing just one security guard for the entire multi-acre compound, which was consistent with what we had heard about a reduction in staff. We didn't know what we would find when we scoped out the compound, but what we saw gave us confidence to take a closer look, once night had fallen.

We were dropped off half-a-mile from the facility on an unlit paved road and walked past the main offices that sat closest to the road. There were no lights on or any signs of human activity, so we continued past the administrative building to where the security guard had been parked. The car was gone. We walked past the entire grounds and circled behind it, where we crouched in the shadows and watched the same buildings we had earlier surveilled from above. After about 30 minutes, without any further signs of physical security, my partner and I donned black ski-masks and walked upright towards the first building.

We didn't see any infrared security or motion-detecting lights, so we quietly walked along the first row of buildings which each emitted a cedar-like scent from their extracting ventilation fans. From university labs, I knew that this was usually an indicator of a vivarium where animals were housed before or after experimentation. The actual laboratories themselves were usually under much greater security.

I looked at the doors and roofs of each building and saw multiple ways we might gain entry with limited force or noise, even though I knew this was not the objective of this mission. Still, we couldn't help but imagine how many trucks we would need to rescue the hundreds if not thousands of non-primates Coulston was using for research. With so little security, I wanted to do as much as possible to shut down this lab once and for all, just as we had done with the Oregon State Universities Experimental Fur Farm in 1991—except this wasn't the past, but a new era where both the ALF and ELF were quickly becoming the most active "domestic terrorist group" in the United States and a growing concern, especially now that arson had become a primary tactic, because of its ability to inflict maximum damage to animal abusers who were the real eco-terrorists destroying our natural world for profit.

I also had to deal with the reality that I was a known and convicted eco-terrorist who, while publicly no longer associated with the ALF, became a regular spokesperson for both the ALF and ELF as their actions raged on in the early 2000s. Already I had attempted a break-in and rescue at the VA Hospital, followed by our successful attacks on the Mount Graham powerline under construction, not to mention the still-unsolved luxury home arsons in Tucson. Another arson on an animal research facility in the Southwest would surely lead to me as a top suspect.

As in Pima Canyon, Alamogordo on that hot September night was just a recon mission to determine whether others might be able to carry out an attack on a worthy target. We continued our onsite surveillance, quickly confirming that most of the buildings we had seen earlier housed laboratory animals. We then shifted our attention to other buildings, where I saw a large corrugated metal barn with large extractor fans on each end and sides. The ground-floor doors were all locked, so I climbed onto a low roof and found an entry door that allowed access to a catwalk over the interior of the barn.

As soon as I opened the door, the smell told me that animals were housed inside, and the size of the wire mesh in the cages below told me it was most likely chimpanzees. As I crouch-walked along the catwalk with my headlamp as the only light, I heard movements and grunts as apes awoke to my presence. I shined my light into each cage until I saw movement, usually as a chimp crossed the beam of my light. As I came to one cage, I could make out three small, young chimps on the ground. They grasped each other and peered into my light, unable to see who was there. Finally, one chimp climbed the wire to inspect. I reached into my pack, looking for the Ziploc bag of raisins I had carried as a snack and just in case I found any apes. When I pressed my fingers through the cage with a few raisins offered, a small wrinkled warm hand reached out and touched mine as it took the offering. I sat there feeding raisins to this chimp for about a minute before retreating back the way I came; for reasons of animal safety, this was another building off limits to any possible attack.

I had never before literally held hands with one of the animals I was trying to rescue, and the experience left me feeling obligated to act in the same way that I felt after witnessing the brutal neck-breaking of mink on a Montana fur farm eleven years earlier. I knew it was now my obligation to act; in bearing witness to yet another atrocity against life, I felt morally obliged to fight it.

My partner and I regrouped and compared our individual discoveries. She had located a maintenance building that did not have animals housed in it, but was full of the equipment necessary to operate the research facility. The large building also housed records that were stored above the offices inside. Fortunately, the building lay far away from the chimps and other buildings housing animals.

When we got back to Tucson, we were shocked to hear of another arson in Tucson, only this time the target was a McDonalds restaurant which was gutted by the fire ... which was claimed by the ALF and ELF. We knew nothing about the action, thinking it resembled a non-strategic approach, perhaps indicating that it wasn't an experienced ALF or ELF member, but possibly an inspired citizen who knew it was within their right to claim such an action under the banner of both the ALF and ELF because of the notorious reputation the McDonalds Corporation has globally, both regarding environmental destruction and animal abuse.

While we supported the action, we knew it would only draw attention to possible suspects in my own hometown. I was asked about the arson by my probation officer, but he knew it wasn't my style to act against such a target, especially while I was getting closer every day to finishing my three-year sentence of "supervised release." I was also expecting my first child to be born in October, back in Michigan. I was certainly someone capable of such things, but so were so many others, as was evidenced by the increasing amount of arsons and property destruction claimed by both the ALF and ELF in 2000 and 2001.

By this time, I was a school bus driver for Ha:san Prep. I had spent a week over the summer in Phoenix receiving the state-required training to be a bus driver, and while there, got the opportunity to see the British punk band, Conflict, famous for their animal liberation lyrics and songs like, "This is the ALF," which lyrically details how one can take direct action against animal abusers. The band had its heyday when I did, in the 1980s, but like me, they were still alive and strong, just a little more grey and a bit heavier around the middle.

At the concert, I ran into Stan Islas, as I knew him, another Praxis Book Club member who I presumed was also in the more-organized cell of the ELF that was launching raids across the West in the early 2000s. Stan and I met at a Denny's restaurant after the concert and I shared with him what we had discovered in Alamogordo. He said he was willing to help if needed. I said I'd be in touch. It would be the last time I ever saw or spoke to him before we both would be later arrested by the FBI.

The September 11 Attacks

On the morning of September 11, 2001, I began my day at 6 a.m., inspecting my school bus before my early morning route to South Tucson and the Tohono O'odham and Yaqui Reservations to pick up students. After starting the bus, I turned on the radio and heard early reports of an airplane that had crashed into the World Trade Center in New York City. Like everyone, I was dumbstruck. I couldn't believe something like that had happened, but when the skies went silent and no planes could be seen in Tucson's normally busy skies, I knew the country was in the midst of a cataclysmic event.

Later that day at school, as students watched live television reports in their classrooms, concern appeared in some students for their own safety. One young man approached me at my desk and asked me if I thought we had anything to be worried about. I clearly remember telling him that, to the best of my knowledge, neither the Yaqui or O'odham people had wronged the people being blamed for the attack and that those of us living on Indian Reservations should have nothing to fear. Later I heard the noted indigenous writer, Simon Ortiz, describe how, when he saw video footage of the villages in Afghanistan that were supposedly harboring Osama Bin Laden, he was reminded of how similar the homes were to our own traditional homes.

When I saw my Praxis friend later that week, he totally dismissed any idea of further participation in a raid on the White Sands Research Center, because of the heightened security everywhere. I reluctantly had to report how I had seen a vehicle following my bus as I went on my usual route, believing it to be a federal agent from some agency checking up on the government's own list of domestic terrorists. My friend then made me an offer I couldn't refuse. They said if I promised to stay in my routine and remain visible at home in Tucson, they would make sure the action happened.

I didn't have to wait long. On September 20, the Animal Liberation Front accepted responsibility for the destruction of the maintenance building and storage facility at White Sands Research Center. Damage was estimated at $1 million and Coulston soon announced it was going bankrupt after first losing its government research contracts and then being saddled with heavy fines for violating the lenient Animal Welfare Act. The ALF raid was the last straw for Coulston; not long after its bankruptcy announcement, the entire chimpanzee population was acquired by Save the Chimps, which would eventually relocate the animals to its sanctuary in Florida where they are currently living out their lives in peace.

Arson damage at White Sands
(courtesy We Animals Media)

Arson damage at White Sands
(courtesy We Animals Media)

Another University of Arizona Protest

My son's due date was October 12, 2001—Columbus Day. The same day we planned a "Counter-Columbus Day" poetry event, followed with a protest the next day at an unannounced target. It would be the University of Arizona's underground mirror research laboratory, where the lenses were being made for the still-uncompleted telescopes on Mount Graham. The poetry event included indigenous students reading their own poetry and we were blessed with readings from the noteworthy author and poet Leslie Marmon Silko, whose book, *Almanac of the Dead* (1991), was a kind of subculture revolutionary bible for my desert friends, with its foretelling of an indigenous rebellion that starts in the south of Mexico, like the Zapatista Liberation Army did in 1994, moving north to our homelands. The event was inspiring and empowering for our indigenous students who, the next day, marched the few blocks to the University of Arizona's campus, led by myself and other teachers from Ha:san who also were members of the radical environmental community.

Earlier that morning, we gathered first at Pascua Yaqui Pueblo, in the ceremonial grounds where Raul Cancio and the Bow Leaders Society gave a blessing for our actions in defense of Dzil Nchaa Siann, Mount Graham.

It was heartening to be back here where I first met Raul some six years earlier and where my exploration of my own culture had begun. I hoped I was keeping the tradition of indigenous resistance alive in southern Arizona while also strengthening the coalition between environmentalists, animal liberationists, and indigenous peoples. We were joined by the family members who comprised the indigenous punk band, Black Fire. The band had performed at Ha:san the night before and were happy to join us in our protest.

After the blessing, we returned to Ha:san where we gathered and began marching silently to the University. When we got onto campus and under the cavernous stadium built over the mirror lab which was accessible only by elevator, we began beating hand drums and singing the A.I.M. song—the anthem of the American Indian Movement that was sung by Lakota warriors as they rode into battle with General Custer on the Greasy Grass aka Little Bighorn River.

The protest caught University staff totally off guard. As we approached the doorway entrance of the Mirror Lab, a university employee attempted to block our entry with his own body. It was a good tactic. We wrestled with him as nonviolently as possible while others in the office called for police back up. We knew we weren't going to get inside the lab like we had hoped. When the University Police cars began pulling up, we turned towards the main campus plaza and continued marching with drums beating and an upside-down American flag waving. There were about 30 of us, students and adults, and the police were obviously trying to corral us. When they had completely surrounded us, I realized any arrest would constitute a violation of my conditions of supervised release. I also knew that any arrest might mean I'd miss my scheduled flight to Michigan to be present for the birth of my son.

Reluctantly, I decided to make a run for it while the police were still getting organized. The campus was busy with students walking everywhere, which made it easy to ignore the calls from the police and run from our rowdy assemblance and disappear into the nearby library. I went up a few floors and, while walking between aisles of books, bumped into another Yaqui friend who had also fled the protest.

I walked back to the school and waited as people began to slowly make it back to Ha:san Prep with news of what had happened. In total, 17 people were arrested, including two Ha:san students and one teacher. I spent the night at the county jail, awaiting each of our friend's release as bail was made from local supporters. Before I made my flight, I had to call the parents of one of the students arrested and inform them of what had happened. I expected to be yelled at for allowing such a thing to happen, but instead the O'odham parents scoffed and said it was a valuable lesson for their child to be learning about standing up for their rights as indigenous people.

Meanwhile the mother of the two brother members of Black Fire, Clee and Clayson Benally, who were also arrested, was angry at me for the way the protest had ended—with her sons under arrest. I responded that the two were warriors who knew what they were getting involved with. From the protest, I will always remember Clee and Clayson singing the loudest as they perched on cop cars waving the upside-down American flag. I hope they felt it was worth it, because I sure did. Again, it wasn't necessarily about winning any concessions; it was more about making a stand and a statement about the colonizers' continued disrespect for indigenous rights and the rights of all beings which whom we shared our desert homes. Our voices will never be silenced and our actions shall always be remembered!

CHAPTER 11
RESISTANCE IN A POST-9/11 WORLD

It was now into the year 2002. After almost getting arrested at our Counter-Columbus Day protests in Tucson and almost missing the birth of my son, I slowed down and spent the summer visiting with new family members in Michigan. Ironically, my son's mother was from West Michigan, so I found myself finishing my three-year sentence of supervised release in the same federal district I had been charged for the Michigan State University mink farm raid. I was fortunate to not be staying there long enough to require in-person reporting to a probation officer, but that would unfortunately change a few years later.

As soon as my probation was over in August 2002, I accepted an invitation to lecture over in England in a speaking tour organized by two British Earth First!ers, Jen and Giles, who I had met earlier in the year when they were both visiting Arizona. I said goodbye to my young family and promised to be back in time for my son's first birthday in October.

Fortunately, I had no problems getting into the United Kingdom. After news of my arrival had spread amongst the animal liberation community, I was invited to speak at additional venues in London, Manchester, and Leeds. While in Brighton, where I was staying with Jen and Giles, I went shopping and bought a pair of boots from the famous Vegetarian Shoe shop there. Not wanting to wear or carry them, I asked if I could pick them up later. After lunch, I returned to the store and, while waiting to pick up the boots, I noticed that two other people there were openly staring at me. Before I could even process it, the woman said, "You're gonna come all the way to Brighton and not even say hello?" It was Melanie Arnold!—my prison crush and pen pal who I had first met, and last seen, while I was still in prison.

Mel and I talked alone for the first time in our then-seven-year relationship, which began via correspondence while we were both in prison for animal related arsons. We sat on cliffs overlooking the Atlantic Ocean and talked about many things, but largely we spoke about our continuing desire to rescue animals destined for miserable lives on fur farms and in laboratories. We cared about all animals, but we knew there was still a need for attacks on vulnerable links in the chain of animal abuse industries. We knew we could never again get away with underground attacks in our home countries. We never did raid any labs together, but we did get to visit a carnival in Brighton, where Mel told me she loved the rides. We both laughed and enjoyed something we could only ever dream about in prison: spending time together alone.

While I was in the UK, I decided to take advantage of the close proximity to other European countries, so I accepted more offers to speak in Holland and Finland. I gave lectures at anarchist squats in Amsterdam and another Dutch town before flying to Sweden, where I decided to take a ferry the rest of the way to Finland—a journey of 16 hours that would be on the Autumn Equinox. I traveled alone, and while the rest of the ship was indoors at the casino or nightclub, I sat on the rear deck watching the sunset. I hadn't been on a ship in years and it felt great to be sailing off to another country I had never visited. When I arrived, I connected with animal liberation activists in Helsinki who I had corresponded with while in prison, including a young woman who was convicted of releasing mink from a fur farm. Finland was in a new domestic battle with illegal direct action on behalf of animals, corresponding to increased action in the US and Canada.

My Finnish lectures focused on my own path to becoming an animal liberationists and eco-defender, and my realization that when letters and protests failed, history showed that many pro-justice movements were forced to break unjust laws to defend life and liberty. I spoke of my awakening to my own indigenous heritage and the lessons in coexistence I had learned from elders like Albert White Hat, Anselmo Valencia Tori, and Paul Watson. I spoke from my own experiences of what I had witnessed with my own eyes: that, to whales, mink, and other animals, humans are the real terrorists. We have waged genocidal wars that have led to the eradication of entire nations of species, all for the sake of money. And I supported nonviolent illegal direct action in defense of Earth, animals, and indigenous sovereignty—not as our chosen first tactic, but only as a measure of last resort. Animals in laboratories and fur farms, apex predators and others dependent on wild lands, and the indigenous survivors of this continent have waited centuries for justice. Now was the time for action.

At my Finnish lectures, it was no problem speaking in English because most people there were bilingual. Local media had also came to listen and interview me about recent raids on fur farms in Finland, which I supported.

After the lectures in Helsinki, I joined up with another activist to drive north to the town of Tampere, about two hours away. On the drive, I asked him about an experimental fur farm I had heard about that was not far from where we were going. He offered to detour to the area to investigate. There was no discussion of action; we just were both curious, especially about any security the facility might have, in light of the recent fur farm raids. We drove by other smaller mink farms on small dirt roads before we arrived at a much larger fur farm, surrounded by eight-foot fences.

We parked past the facility and walked back, surrounded in beautiful forests. We didn't see any cars present, which was why we risked stopping, and now that we had walked the perimeter, we concluded that no one was on the premises. I returned to a spot where a tree made it easier for me to cross the fence, and climbed into the grounds of the farm which appeared to focus on foxes. I remembered my conversations with Mel about how raids in our own countries seemed no longer possible. Suddenly, I was beginning to think that, once again, I might be able to continue carrying out attacks on a part of the centuries-old fur trade I most despised: the research and development tentacle that was keeping the larger monster alive in the face of depressed fur prices.

I had been off probation for less than two months. Not even counting the crimes I had already abetted while still on probation, I knew that if I wasn't careful, it might not be long before I became a criminal and fugitive in another country. In this case, I decided to not act; as they say, sometimes discretion is the better part of valor.

We left the fur farm and arrived in Tampere, which was not far from where recent fur farm raids had occurred. I gave my usual lecture, and afterward, we agreed to gather at an activist house for a meal and sauna. I drove. On my way to the festivities, I noticed that a car had pulled out behind us and appeared to be following—police. At a stoplight, when the light turned green, I waited...until the light turned yellow, and then I punched it across the intersection. The police in the car behind us couldn't make it through before the light turned red, and, not wanting to expose themselves, they remained behind at the intersection. We quickly detoured and decided not to meet up as planned, where the police were surely already planning to greet us. Instead, we drove two hours back to Helsinki. The next day, I said my goodbyes and took the ferry back to Sweden, where I caught a flight back to London. I would never return to Finland ... at least, not yet!

I returned to Brighton, where an activist collective was organizing an action for Indigenous Peoples' Day, otherwise known as Columbus Day. The target of the radical protest would be the New Tribes Mission, a Christian non-profit that sent missionaries into rainforests and other remote areas to preach the 'virtues' of Christianity to the last remaining nations of indigenous peoples—people desperately struggling to preserve their own traditional worldviews in the face of ever-encroaching civilization. We had not publicized the protest nor the target, which was located outside a tiny village in the countryside of northeast England and consisted of multiple buildings, with one main administrative building.

Our main target was the admin building. Our plan was to arrive unannounced and catch the staff off-guard; this would give us a small window of time to act before "the bobbies" arrived. In that rural area, we had about eight or ten minutes, by our reckoning. We drove to the quiet small coastal village outside of Grimsby and found the target, dead-quiet. As soon as we arrived, about 16 of us masked up and started walking towards the main buildings. I did not wear a mask. I was the only indigenous person there and I wanted the missionaries to know it. And this is not to mention that I had brought my Yaqui war drum and was now beating it loudly.

When we entered the main offices that were our target, the few staff were stunned and didn't know how to respond. There were simply too many of us, and while most of us distracted the staff, others slipped into a bathroom where they hoped to possibly flood the building. Others removed hard drives from computers.

Once we accomplished what we set out to do, we began exiting the building—which the staff were more than happy to facilitate. Now outside, other staff congregated, thinking of ways to detain us long enough until the police could arrive. But it was time to leave. I was with one group that had traveled together and suddenly, as we crowded back into our van, one of our members was being physically restrained by missionary staff. We weren't going to leave anyone behind. I called for help from others; a few of us then approached the men holding our friend and we started physically prying their hands off him, saying, "We are trying to be nonviolent, please let go." With our reclaimed friend now in our van, we made our escape through a maze of countryside roads, flinging out hard drives onto sheep pastures for fear we might be intercepted by the police. We got away and, for the second time in a year, I again narrowly escaped an arrest situation and made it home for my son's first birthday. I was still trying to be a warrior, but at the expense of my own new family. I would need to rethink my path if I hoped to remain out of prison and off probation.

Back in the USA

After returning from my speaking tour in Europe, I lived for a short time in Humboldt County in northern California, where my parents owned a small home. I tried to focus on being a father, but the easiest way for me to support my new family was to accept the honorariums being offered by universities wanting me to lecture. More accurately, student groups wanted me to speak to my recent imprisonment and past activism with Sea Shepherd, Earth First! and the ALF. I had convinced myself that I couldn't possibly get arrested for simply speaking about earth and animal defense, but with the growing wave of both ALF and ELF actions on the rise, I was beginning to be seen as a leader of these otherwise faceless movements. I accepted any consequence that might come from my lectures, even though I knew I was poking the bear—especially by including demonstrations of how to build a crude incendiary device with a plastic one-gallon jug, a sponge, and an incense stick.

In January 2003, I was invited to a conference at American University in Washington DC, where the topic was nonviolent civil disobedience and direct action in the United States. I made a flyer for my lecture that featured the silhouettes of both Apache and white eco-defenders from Dave Foreman's infamous book, *Eco-Defense: A Field Guide to Monkeywrenching*. In bold black letters, I added the words of a 19th century Lakota warrior, "It is Time Once Again to Burn their Forts to the Ground."

The lecture was of course recorded, and would later be used by federal officials to demonstrate the growing threat eco-warriors were beginning to pose to United States commerce. It wasn't just fur farms anymore; experimental genetically-engineered crops were targeted by the ELF, costing researchers millions of dollars and the loss of vital research. On the animal rights front, a new organization, Stop Huntington Life Science (SHAC), was targeting not just the New Jersey based vivisection company, Huntington Life Sciences, but its subsidiaries and affiliated businesses. Their tactics included demonstrations at the homes of animal researchers and others associated with the abusive company, whose cruel experiments on beagles and other animals were well-documented by both the ALF and other undercover investigators.

I later learned that a long-time pen pal of mine from prison, Bonnie Rasmussen (not her real name, but the one she used on envelopes and letters), was herself undercover at Huntington Life Sciences for six months. During the entire time we corresponded, not once did she ever reveal anything that would lead me to believe she was so active for animals in labs. We didn't write about the struggle; we spoke of our love for camping, the outdoors, and good food. When we finally met, she revealed that I was one of the few people she maintained contact with during her undercover investigation, which provided the evidence of animal abuse that SHAC used in its effective and strategic protests.

Back in December 2002, I had been invited by SHAC to speak at an event organized for the 50th "birthday" of their target, Huntington Life Sciences, in New Jersey. Other guest speakers were Bobby Seale, founding member of the Black Panther Party, and Robin Webb, the UK Press Officer for the ALF. There would be multiple protests in New York City and at the site of the lab. This was probably the first place I had used a plastic jug to demonstrate how to make a firebomb—and it wouldn't be the last!

I traveled with the SHAC activists to the many protests, and while I was at the New Jersey site of the infamous lab, I left the protest and walked through a park to what might be the backside of the labs' property. Before I was out of sight of the protest, a dark SUV came driving across the grass, following just feet behind me, until I returned to the main protest, where only 50 people were being allowed at a time to actually protest at the entrance of the laboratory. It was about that time when Webb, an elderly man, albeit the ALF press spokesperson, also chose to leave the main protest. He was arrested and spent time in jail before being required to not leave the country until his case was heard. Robin became a fixture of the SHAC movement during his forced stay in America. It reminded me of the precarious risks associated with aboveground protests, something I was never fond of. These were historically the sites of violence, but always directed towards those *protesting the violence*, not the actual targets of the protests.

Taking On Pacific Lumber and Maxxam

Back in California, I became aware of the continued logging of old-growth forests by the Maxxam Corporation, which had bought out the locally-owned Pacific Lumber Company (PL) in 1985. Throughout the early 1980s, PL had become a notorious logger of endangered spotted owl habitat, often as part of agreements with government officials to protect spotted owl nesting sites in other areas. To protect some, the timber industry learned they could leverage the lives of the owls to continue logging in both the endangered owl and marbled murrelet's shrinking home territory.

Over the summer of 2003, I helped other forest defenders set tree-climbing lines in old-growth trees painted with a blue line, indicating their being targeted for cutting. In the Mattole Forests, I saw a spotted owl perched on a branch of a tree slated for cutting. We were setting lines for climbers who would later come to build tree-sits, where forest defenders could occupy the trees to delay their cutting.

I was now one of the older activists in the scene, and having experienced the effectiveness of SHAC's protests, I advocated for protests at the home and business of the tree-climber hired by PL to evict tree-sitters. We were responding to numerous incidents where peaceful protesters were being cut out of trees and handcuffed, to then be dangerously lowered to the ground and hauled off to the Humboldt County Jail. It took only one protest to get the company's attention.

After more arrests of tree sitters in the Freshwater Forest outside of Arcata, I hiked into active logging areas to observe loggers when I noticed one stashing his saw at the end of the day in the hollow stump of a recently-cut tree. After he left, I climbed down from my hidden observation point and grabbed the expensive saw, hauling it back to where I could pick it up later. Later that week, as I was parked on the shoulder of the road overlooking the active logging area with my friend Steve, a PL truck pulled up and parked next to us. The logger asked us if we knew anything about a missing chainsaw. We laughed—as if we were going to help him find a saw used to cut the forest we were there to defend.

Later, there was another incident, this time in Freshwater Forest, where I chose to cross the line and engage in illegal activity. After a group of tree-sitters was violently evicted from a thousand-year-old redwood tree which was then cut, I decided to exact a little vengeance on a diesel road grader used at the logging site. Another friend and I returned to the site just past midnight. While a public meeting was being held by protestors on next steps, we climbed onto the grader and proceeded to remove the engine valve covers, and then injected a grinding compound to cause damage when the engines were next started. We left no sign of our sabotage, but later saw a full-page ad in the local newspaper offering a reward for the saboteurs responsible for the $10,000 in reported damages.

Maxxam Corporation was a Houston-based company, where I had many friends in both Earth First! and SHAC circles. It was decided that we would launch a "Dirty South Earth First!" group, whose inaugural campaign would be organizing demonstrations at the homes of Maxxam's corporate officers. The protests were extremely effective at shocking those targeted, but in the end were not sustainable. The group created a tree-sit in a local park that generated attention, but I was being called back the lecture circuit and other SHAC protests.

Freed from federal supervision, I returned to my natural role as a spokesperson for direct actions on behalf of animals and the Earth, and my presence in the old-growth forests of California had again triggered the FBI's investigations into my activities. One day, while staying in Boulder,

Colorado, I went out to my truck to install a towing hitch. When I crawled under my vehicle to install it, I was stunned to discover an odd-looking electronic device wired to the truck. My housemates and I immediately suspected that the device was for tracking our movements, so we inspected the two other vehicles we owned, finding similar tracking devices in those vehicles.

My housemate, a local animal rights activists, took one of the devices to the local newspaper, which in turn took the device to a GPS specialist who confirmed that they were indeed custom-made tracking devices, costing about $2,000 apiece, with obliterated serial numbers. The devices could be turned on remotely, long enough to send a location, before being turned off remotely to save battery life. The FBI would neither confirm nor deny that the devices belonged to their agency, probably because they knew that they were overstepping their authority to track activists not charged with a crime. Years later, a Supreme Court ruling would indeed determine that the agency did not have the authority to place tracking devices on a suspect's vehicle without a warrant. The last word on the GPS tracking devices came from my old Earth First! musician friend Darryl Cherney, who wrote a song about it called, "Sell It On Ebay"—because that's what I said I was going to do!

Summer 2003, In the Southwest

In August 2003, I was back in Tucson, living at the home office of the *Earth First! Journal* where I was again a co-editor, pushing for more representation for the continuing raids by both the ELF and ALF. I was frustrated that the other editors were not investigating the targets of the groups to better understand why they were being attacked. This was the time, for example, when gas-guzzling Sport Utility Vehicles were beginning to be targeted for attacks because of their heavy carbon footprint.

A SHAC supporter I knew since my release from prison invited me to give a lecture in San Diego at the Hillcrest Community Center. It was a short and cheap flight from Tucson and only a couple hours from Los Angeles, where I was also scheduled to attend the Animal Rights National Conference which was organized by Alex Hershaft's Farm Animal Reform Movement.

When I arrived in San Diego on the early morning flight, my host, David Agranoff, picked me up and took me to his home for a quick rest. When I rejoined the activists organizing my evening event, they shared breaking news from that early morning. At about 3:00 AM, a large fire was reported in University City at a controversial apartment complex under construction in the undeveloped Rose Canyon. The fire had quickly spread through the mostly-wooden structure, shooting flames a hundred feet into the air and melting a nearby crane. There were no injuries reported, as firefighters did not risk their lives on an uninhabited building. When the dust settled, a crude handwritten banner could be seen by passing news helicopters, stating, "IF YOU BUILD IT, WE WILL BURN IT. THE ELF IS MAD!"

I was of course shocked but pleasantly surprised by the brazen arson, which I couldn't help but think was done by someone who knew I was coming to San Diego, to condone and explain such attacks. And that is what I did, calling media to offer my explanation for the arson. Though I did a few interviews, I was never questioned by police.

That night, at the planned lecture, I gave my standard talk covering my history as an ALF activist and an indigenous warrior to the crowd of roughly 50 people. I knew it was highly probable that there were undercover police in the audience, but why should I care? I wasn't involved in the San Diego arson, nor did I know who was. All I could do was speak to why folks such as myself might take such action.

When I finished my lecture and began to take questions from the audience, one question came from David Agranoff, who asked how I had carried out my arsons on fur-farm research targets. It was too complicated to explain how to make the actual one-hour timed incendiary devices that were my signature fire-making tool, so I instead decided to explain how to build a much simpler device with a one-gallon jug of fuel accelerant. I walked over to the snack table and picked up a jug of apple juice to use as a prop. I had given the same demonstrations in New Jersey and Washington DC, but I knew giving a demo on the same day as the apartment complex arson might raise some police eyebrows.

After the lecture, another SHAC activist and I boarded a Greyhound Bus for Los Angeles, where the Animal Rights 2003 Conference was being held. The next morning, newspaper headlines announced the ELF's latest arson, claiming that damages were in excess of $50 million—making it the costliest act of environmental sabotage by the ELF. I was a keynote speaker at the conference and was voted by attendees to be inducted into the conference's Animal Rights Hall of Fame. I was awarded a plaque recognizing my contributions to the greater struggle, and used the opportunity to remind the activists in attendance to always support our movement's warriors and imprisoned comrades. I was proud that the conference had chosen to highlight my contributions rather than condemn them.

Unfortunately, because of the rising tide of ELF and ALF direct actions in the United States, the Humane Society of the United States, led by

Wayne Pacelle, decided to pull its funding for animal rights conferences that supported the ALF. I confronted Pacelle about the decision and told him that his and my own mentor, Cleveland Amory (who died in 1998), would be appalled by such an action. Cleveland had funded Paul Watson's purchase of the first Sea Shepherd ship, and as long as I knew him, he was a supporter of direct action on behalf of animals. Yet, under Pacelle's leadership, Cleveland's Fund for Animals was dissolved and merged into the larger HSUS that Pacelle controlled. By the following year, the Animal Rights National Conference actually began to *condemn* illegal activity to rescue animals. (The conferences ceased completely after 2016.)

Back in Tucson, I continued as press spokesperson for the ALF and ELF, which made others in the *Earth First! Journal* office a bit nervous because of the recent media attention to direct actions. I argued that it was our job as movement journalists to give voice to actions that the perpetrators themselves could not risk explaining. This was also the time when a greater left-wing "social justice" presence came into Earth First!, with more and more people interested in building community gardens than firebombs. I grew more and more frustrated, and decided that my time was better served in the field.

Sabino Canyon—Sab the Hunt!

The year 2003 was quickly ending and the FBI had made no arrests in any major ALF or ELF crimes, yet the actions were continuing. In a report by the FBI's Office of Inspector General, the agency recommended allowing the *criminal* division of the FBI to investigate eco-terrorism, rather than the agency's *counterterrorism* division. I continued traveling the country, giving lectures in defense of both the ALF and ELF's actions, but I also still worked as an editor of the *Earth First! Journal*. I lived in the Dunbar Springs neighborhood of Tucson, near the University of Arizona that I had raided over ten years ago.

One morning as I was drinking coffee outside of my favorite cafe, one of the new, young editors working with the *Earth First! Journal* came to talk to me about recently reported mountain lion sightings in the popular hiking area known as the Sabino Canyon Recreation Area, which lay just a few miles northeast of Tucson and is surrounded by the Coronado National Forest. Urban sprawl was on the march, with more and more luxury homes encroaching into suitable mountain lion habitat. Adding to the problem was the fact that residents often liked to feed the local wild peccaries called javelinas, a favorite food for mountain lions. To make it worse, lions had been seen drinking from swimming pools, which to them was a source of water in the desert.

In early March 2004, cafeteria workers at a local elementary school saw a lion just behind the school near Sabino Canyon, prompting the Arizona Game and Fish Department to launch a hunt for the animals; at the same time, the US Forest Service decided to close the popular recreation area which normally saw hundreds of visitors each day. I followed the story closely and had hopes that with such a popular recreation area and with the focus on a species like mountain lions, that local environmental groups would succeed in obtaining a temporary injunction stopping the now-controversial hunt.

Zach was a young eco-radical from Colorado, and he wanted to know whether I had any plans to get involved with stopping the hunt. I told him what Paul Watson had taught me: to exploit instances where the public was outraged at the failure of the government to stop a particular injustice. In this case, 'the public' was the many Tucson residents who loved hiking in Sabino Canyon because it was an area normally closed to activities like hunting and trapping, not to mention that many people loved mountain lions and felt partially responsible for the hunt, which was arguably being held in the interest of public safety.

Not long beforehand, the Arizona Game and Fish Department was sued by the victim of a black bear attack, which held the agency responsible for her injuries. The case left the department afraid of more litigation from people experiencing conflicts with wildlife, so they decided that the best course of action would be to hunt and kill the approximately five mountain lions believed to be living in or near Sabino Canyon.

On March 10, a federal closure order was put in place at Sabino Canyon. I told other activists in the Tucson community that such closure orders were commonly overturned when challenged by forest defenders opposing timber sales on national forest lands—my point being that the order should not preclude us from considering action to stop the hunt. By this time, I was in daily contact with a friend working at the Center for Biological Diversity, which was attempting to stop the hunt with a request for a temporary injunction. In the end, I was told that no injunction would be coming from either the Center or the Defenders of Wildlife. It was time for action.

Zach and I recruited other local Earth First!ers who were willing to hike into the closed canyon at night to investigate the lion hunting operation. We drove to an adjacent canyon that was not in the closure area and hiked into Sabino and past the posted "closed" signs. Our initial visit to the canyon was very mild: we brought along a box of sidewalk chalk and, at different intervals along the paved canyon road, we wrote messages to the lion hunters in three-foot-high letters. Unfortunately, these were quickly washed away by a spring rainstorm.

Back at work the next day, I was frustrated by the lack of support for ALF and ELF actions within the editorial collective of the *EF! Journal*. Despite the growing attempts by federal agents to catch eco-saboteurs, such actions were continuing, and I felt we as radical journalists owed it to those taking the real risks to cover the reasons behind their actions. I was told by other editors that the communiques and press releases provided by the ALF and ELF were not very informative on the issues and left little to report on. I responded that it was our responsibility to explain why illegal actions were necessary to save lives and protect wild places, and that we can't expect members of those groups to risk exposure and capture simply to "better explain their actions." But the other editors were not interested; they wanted to cover the community garden movement and other social justice issues.

I decided it was time for me to return to my roots as a radical organizer. I then started my own Earth First! chapter, calling our new hunt sabotage group, Chuk'shon Earth First!—taking the name from the Tohono O'Odham word for "Black Mountain" which the name "Tucson" was derived from by Spanish settlers ("Chuk'shon" became "Tuk-son" became "Tucson"). I also wanted to set myself apart from being continually labeled as an 'animal rights activist' by reminding others about the history of indigenous resistance to colonization. This was actually part of the original impetus for the formation of Earth First!, which began with a crude monument created by early Earth First!ers for the Mimbres Apache warrior, Victorio, who chased miners from his homelands in the (now) Gila Wilderness Area. The monument was later dynamited by white Arizona miners.

Within just a few days, the media was reporting that more than a thousand letters, faxes, and emails had flooded the mailboxes of Game & Fish, legislators, and the governor's office—all opposed to the hunt for Sabino Canyon lions. With the hunt receiving top story coverage by local media, it was a good time for Chuk'shon Earth First! to go public with our hunt sabotage campaign.

While the Center for Biological Diversity and Defenders of Wildlife fought the hunt within legal confines, CEF! mobilized for direct action. By midnight on the first day of the hunt, an eight-person patrol was in Sabino Canyon carrying out reconnaissance and "hunting for the hunters." An AGFD spokesman told reporters that 95 percent of the calls flooding his office were in opposition to the hunt, but that it would not sway the agency's decision to kill the lions.

Zach and I gathered camo clothing and a video camera for our planned debut. We snuck into Sabino Canyon at dusk and took up a position overlooking the entrance to the park. From our high vantage point, we could monitor all activity coming and going into the closed park. Next, we filmed ourselves masked up with binoculars and spotting scopes, patrolling the area for hunters. The next day, after making multiple VHS copies of our actions, I contacted local media stations and offered them copies of the tape, which they immediately aired on their stations. It was the top story on all three networks; suddenly the one-sided war against the mountain lions of Sabino became a Robin Hood-esque battle between CEF! and the federal and state agencies. The Tanque Verde Homeowners Association even voted unanimously to support Earth First!'s presence in Sabino Canyon, and local residents offered us refuge in their luxury homes.

Stopping this hunt was a community responsibility that warranted an open and honest call for some public-friendly illegal direct action. If we acted like criminals, the media would portray us as criminals. If we presented ourselves as monitors and nonviolent defenders of the lions, we might actually win public support; where there's general public support for lawbreaking, real change becomes possible.

On March 13, in a television interview, I stated our intention to stop the hunt by placing our bodies between any lions and their hunters. Next, we began holding nightly organizing meetings where we created a schedule with the goal of always having two saboteurs in the canyon during the hunt. We coordinated daily rides into the canyon and I began receiving requests for media interviews. The AGFD was furious at the coverage we were receiving. The narrative was just as we had hoped. The state and federal lion hunters were the bad guys and we were being hailed as heroes for attempting to stop a hunt that the courts had refused to halt. State wildlife officials tried to paint us as criminals for violating the closure order and for our willingness to interfere with the hunt. But this wasn't a justifiable burglary or arson to save animals that we were defending; we were using our own bodies as shields and we never threatened violence or even destruction of property. We knew that, in order to maintain the moral high ground, we could not engage in any activities the public would not support.

CEF!'s campaign strategy was to be in the canyon every day and night, searching for lion hunting and trapping activity, with the intent to disrupt the process by, among other things, using masking scents and actual lion hound training scent to lead the dogs down false trails. I ordered a bottle of mountain lion urine from a trapping supply business to plant false trails and hopefully throw the lion hunters off the real scent of any lion in the area. With stopping the hunt as our end goal, we knew that growing opposition to the hunt might increase if we could document AZGF's activities and provide such evidence to the media to expose the secretive operation. On March 13, AGFD held a public comment hearing, but the room couldn't hold the crowd that showed up to oppose the hunt. CEF! went public and announced that we were actively interfering with the hunt despite the federal closure and the penalty of up to six months in prison for violating it.

CEF! became a legitimate liability to AGFD's plans to kill lions in Sabino, and we showed no mercy to the good ol' boy agency that mismanaged wildlife in relative secrecy and was unanswerable to the public and even to the governor's office. AZDGF was not accustomed to the attention and scrutiny of their policies, and they defended them foolishly. After only five days pursuing the shoot-to-kill policy, AGFD imposed a three-day moratorium on the hunt. Vocal opposition from the public was only one PR nightmare. Governor Janet Napolitano openly criticized AZDGF's decision to kill the Sabino lions and 27 state legislative members signed a statement condemning the hunt.

A Change in Strategy

On the day before the hunt was to resume, AGFD announced that they would no longer kill the lions, but imprison them instead at a private wildlife rehabilitation facility for the rest of their lives. But on March 15, AGFD restated their authority and intention to use deadly force, should the hunt encounter a lion it deemed to be "a threat to public safety."

Meanwhile, a local resident opposed to the hunt asked the question, "I have kids. I can watch kids, make sure my kids are safe, and keep them in the house. There are other animals in the desert: bobcats, wolves, and coyotes. What are we going to do? Shoot every animal out there?" School children began joining the protest as well, holding signs outside the park, imploring officials to stop the hunt. Next, Governor Janet Napolitano joined Defenders of Wildlife and the Center for Biological Diversity in questioning the logic behind the hunt, arguing that it was not unusual for young dispersing lions to seek new territory and thus they should not be categorized as threatening to humans. The scientific mountain lion community was split. Three lion biologists claimed that the recent lion activity

did constitute a threat and justification for lethal removal, while three others (with award-winning research credentials) were opposed to the hunt.

I delivered another videotape to television stations depicting us
spreading false trails with mountain lion urine. The growing opposition
forced AGFD officials to re-evaluate their tactics, and by March 20, a
three-day halt in the hunt was ordered while officials devised an alternative
approach. No longer would hired hunters be used to hunt and kill the lions
in question; despite the announcement that any lions would be captured
and taken to a wildlife sanctuary to live out their lives in captivity, we were
still very much opposed to the plan.

Bringing in the Choppers

During the pause in the hunt, I was on patrol in the canyon when we heard
the loud thumping of an approaching helicopter. As the sound intensified,
from over a mountain top came a military Blackhawk helicopter flying into
Sabino Canyon. When the media questioned the presence of the military in
an already-overblown wild goose chase, AGFD officials claimed the chopper was scouting landing sites to receive any captured lions. Under yet
more pressure, the state agency decided to charter an expensive private
helicopter for their continued hunting operation.

As it happened, at that same time, my personal life was in turmoil. I
had just broken up with my son's mother—a crisis of my own doing,
thanks to my infidelity. At the time, the dissolution of my new young family
left me heartbroken, and so I threw myself into my work as I had always
done, ignoring any self-evaluation that could help me end the cycle of my
unhealthy behavior. Instead, I remember crying as I was being driven to
the drop-off location in nearby Bear Canyon, wiping away my tears as I
climbed out of the vehicle and disappeared into the desert landscape. For
the time being, I was still able to spend time with my son, but he no longer
lived exclusively with me. I now only had him for a portion of the week.
On some days during the hunt, I would drop off my son at daycare before
heading out to the canyon to look for lion hunters; I told him I was "protecting the kitties."

Soon thereafter I was contacted by a reporter with *Esquire* magazine,
John Richardson, who wanted to do a story about my activist career. When
I told him what I was involved with at the moment, he agreed to immediately fly out and shadow me during the lion hunt. John was also a war
journalist and believed he could only get his story by immersing himself in
the lives of the subjects of his stories. I thought it would be a great advantage

to have a reporter embedded with us in the canyon, to help dispel any myth that we were eco-terrorists willing to harm humans to save animals.

On March 23, as the hunt was beginning again, I was again quoted in media reports stating that no lion would be captured in Sabino Canyon without a fight. By now, our actions—and mine in particular—drew the attention of the FBI. No longer were state and federal authorities only hunting mountain lions; now they were hunting for us as well. Unbeknownst to us, state and federal trappers were now using motion detecting devices near their traps that would immediately alert them to the presence of any two-legged foot traffic. That night, under the gaze of Orion, we jogged the trails near the hunter's camp, dragging the lion scent-soaked training bag, creating a trail that would lead the hounds away from any real lion scent further in the canyon.

The next day, a group of about ten activists gathered at one of our houses where we made plans for the following day. I burned sage and blessed those who would be entering the canyon the next day. In the morning, after dropping off my son at his daycare center, I drove towards the canyon with John Richardson and another Earth First! friend, Matt. After being dropped off, we climbed a precipice that gave us an overview of the canyon. From deep inside the canyon, along the paved road, came a pack of hunting hounds followed by a solitary man on horseback. We filmed the hunter and delivered the videotape to our friends awaiting us at the drop-off point. As I handed over the tape, I felt an eerie foreboding, as if I was saying goodbye forever to my friends receiving the tape.

By this point, we knew that the hunting campaign could not last much longer. The park was losing between $5,000 and $10,000 a day in visitor fees, and AGFD admitted that they were paying $6,000 a day for the helicopter and for the hunters. If CEF! could delay the hunt for just a few more days, the cost would likely become too prohibitive to continue. And all the while, we feared that a lion might just wander into Sabino and thus into the middle of one of the biggest lion hunts in Arizona history.

Busted!

It was March 24, 2004; and once again, the hunt resumed for the (estimated) five lions that were deemed a "public threat." John, Matt, and I retreated back into the canyon in our continuing search for traps. From a high vantage point, we watched the landing site for the chartered helicopter that was on hand to transport any captured lions. We spoke of the possibility of locking ourselves to the chopper, but feared such an action might warrant a more serious crime. But we would never have the opportunity. John and I both wore desert camouflage, but Matt was dressed in black, which, ironically, made him highly visible. I loaned Matt a camo hoodie to wear.

But as I returned to viewing the chopper landing site with my spotting scope, I suddenly noticed three uniformed men glaring back at us with their own binoculars. We had been spotted. We descended back into the canyon just as the helicopter started up its engines.

The helicopter swept into the canyon and circled over us before hovering just above the cottonwoods of Sabino Creek. I could see two AGFD officers through the open helicopter doors, videotaping us. When we realized that we had now become the prey, we ran down the creek trail until a brush barrier blocked our path. Along the edge of a narrow passage in the barrier was a steel cable connected to a snare set by a USDA trapper and intended for a mountain lion.

This was not unexpected. The day before, my biologist friend had told us that, in addition to the horseback hunters with hounds, a federal trapper would be setting snares along the creek to capture the lions, which would then be incarcerated for life, never again to roam these native canyons that comprised their home. Since the hunt began, we had been in the canyon looking for traps or snares, and now, with a helicopter bearing down on us, we finally found one.

I didn't care anymore about getting caught. I had already publicly accepted responsibility for interfering with this hunt and now we were being filmed doing just that. But I wasn't going to sleep in a jail cell that night knowing we had left a trap awaiting an unsuspecting victim. I dove onto the trap, the spring-loaded arm tightening the snare as I ripped it from the ground. I unthreaded its cable from the mesquite tree that anchored it, before flinging the snare into the nearby creek.

I didn't see which way Matt ran, but John and I ran toward some nearby undergrowth, trying to hide there as the helicopter crept lower and lower towards us. Finally, it was only feet above me, whipping leaves and dirt into a dust storm all around. It felt like the chopper was going to land on top of me. We knew that, as soon as the helicopter had spotted us, that law enforcement officers with the US Forest Service (USFS) and AGFD would be coming in hot pursuit, searching the canyon on foot for us. The helicopter pinned me down until the pursuing officers could arrive. Not wanting to simply lie there in plain sight waiting to be captured, I decided to run down the creek towards the mouth of the canyon that offered the only remote chance of escape.

Pretending that the helicopter wasn't only feet above me, I stood up, tightened the straps of my pack, and began jogging down the creek, hopping from boulder to boulder with the helicopter following about 30 feet overhead. When I reached a trail, I heard a voice scream, "Show me your hands!" I turned to see a trembling AGFD officer in a crouch position pointing his Glock semi-automatic handgun at my chest. No sooner had he ordered me to the ground and handcuffed me, than an FBI agent arrived, greeted me by name, and took over from the arresting state officer. I was led out of the canyon, handcuffed and shackled, and loaded into the bed of an FBI pick-up truck. John was apprehended not long after.

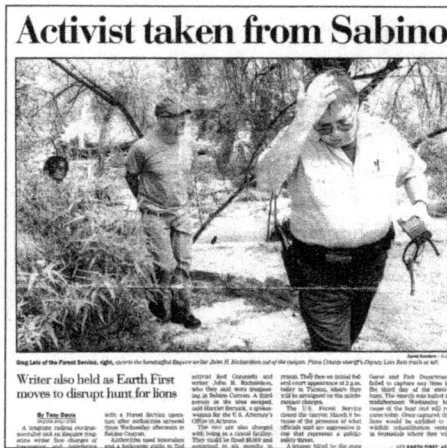

John Richardson (center) being arrested

Meanwhile, the third hunt saboteur in our group, Matt, lay further up the canyon in the creek-side brush where AGFD, USFS, and FBI agents were combing the area. For seven hours, the agents searched the canyon, sometimes standing only a few feet from the cloaked warrior, whose only camouflage was the hoodie I had lent him. We joked later that it must have been an Invisibility Cloak like the one used by Harry Potter! When darkness finally descended in the canyon, Matt fled and reached a convenience store where he called his girlfriend for a ride.

My capture and arrest lent credibility to our promise to disrupt the hunt, and every news station ran it as the top story. The FBI, USFS, and AGFD mistakenly thought my arrest would decapitate CEF!'s campaign; instead, my arrest and that of a prominent New York journalist in Sabino Canyon demonstrated to the AGFD, the USFS, the governor's office, and the media that the situation was truly spinning out of control. Despite my arrest, we were winning. If we could keep up the presence in Sabino Canyon, AGFD would be forced to recognize that they could not economically support the law enforcement presence necessary to now *police* the lion hunt, in addition to the cost of the hunt itself.

Rod and a mountain lion, both shackled

As the intensified hunt entered its fourth day, the AGFD regional supervisor said they were "approaching the limit of our budget endurance." On March 26, the same spokesperson said, "No agency can withstand expending all of its resources on any one project." That night a CEF! patrol entered the canyon and located and disabled another snare they had discovered.

On March 27, a Wildlife Services lion hunter and AGFD officer trailed their hounds on horseback into Sabino Canyon. The only lion scent they found was that left by CEF!. On March 28, after five straight days of intensive hunting and our hunt sabbing, AGFD ended the morning hunt for lions in Sabino Canyon with the announcement that they were suspending the hunt indefinitely, having not seen a single lion during the entire length of the hunt.

Unbeknownst to us, on April 7, a USFS employee found a partially-eaten deer killed by a lion in nearby Esperero Canyon. Despite any evidence proving this particular lion posed a threat to humans, the USFS, AGFD, and the USDA's lion hunter set three snares using the deer as bait. The snares were checked the next day, and the following morning, an 80-pound female lion was captured with a fractured tooth caused by the trap.

On Good Friday, newspapers ran a front-page photo released by AGFD showing the 4-year-old lioness draped on the tailgate of a AGFD pick-up truck with police handcuffs on her front and rear paws, just like when I was captured. It was a deliberate "Fuck You" to Chuk'shon Earth First! and to everyone who questioned AGFD's authority by opposing their hunt. The media believed AGFD had lied, or at least deliberately misled the public to believe the hunt had been called off. Now a lion who did nothing more than hunt its natural prey was beginning the first days of a lifetime prison sentence.

We could have stopped her capture. Had we recognized AGFD's history of lying before the hunt was called off, we might have kept hunt sabs in the field to ensure they kept their word. From our regular vantage points, we could have easily seen AGFD activity in the Esperero Canyon area; it was already an area where we had seen lion hunters before. Ultimately, we didn't have enough experienced people to continue patrolling the area after my arrest. I was knocked out of the game, and any other hunt sabbers with the skill to evade police had to return to their normal life's responsibilities.

In the immediate need for action, security culture was not practiced at the level it should have been. Not having reliable or "clean" radios, we used our personal cell phones to rally patrols and even coordinate drop-offs and pick-ups, most of us using our real names. But this shouldn't have been a big problem; hunt sabbing isn't firebombing, after all (though it has the potential to be every bit as effective). It is low-level psychological warfare with a sprinkling of guerilla tactics, effective enough, while committing nothing more than a misdemeanor...or so we thought. Still, I believed hunt sabotage was an effective training ground for activists unfamiliar with the rigors of serious eco-warfare.

What we failed to anticipate was that CEF!'s effectiveness was enough of an excuse to drive them to operating covertly, out of the public eye. It was an important lesson, for not just the public, but even me, to remember that no corporation or government agency that sanctions physical violence is above lying about it. We should never believe their words, only their actions.

As a previously convicted felon, my arrest had effectively returned me to partial custody of the US Government. Like every arrest our resistance faced, resources now needed to be redirected towards legal defense while my ability to organize was only slightly curtailed. This was a very local and public campaign, and one I knew I must use to further the goal of that campaign rather than focus solely on receiving a favorable sentence. I had no problem with sitting in prison for a few months if it meant being able to make these lion hunters squirm in the witness box. The lions we were protecting deserved nothing less.

Back in Custody Once Again

After being arrested, John and I were taken to an office within the park complex, where we were separated and given water. I wasn't just hand-cuffed; I was shackled with a chain around my waist that was connected to my handcuffs. I sat outside under the midday sun, feeling very much like how I imagined Geronimo felt when he was arrested in the same desert: each time led to a period of imprisonment, followed by his release, which would then be followed by another break-out from the disease-filled reservation where he was forced to watch his people slowly die.

The FBI was now involved, and we waited for transportation to their downtown Tucson headquarters where we would be interviewed. We had been warned that anyone entering the canyon would be arrested, but we also knew that this was likely what it was going to take to end this lion hunt. As long as no lions were captured or killed, we were happy with the exchange of prisoners. Or at least I was. I knew our crimes weren't serious and I was willing to return to court, especially for actions that were being widely supported by the public. These weren't arsons or break-ins; we had simply sprung a trap set for lions that everyone wanted free.

Still, my involvement ramped up the state's response. I wasn't just some protestor; I was also still a spokesperson for organizations (ALF and ELF) that were now deemed 'domestic terrorist groups.' The Tucson public didn't care about my association with radical groups; they were extremely supportive. And in my own Yaqui community, others thanked me for defending our lions. But in a post 9-11 world, the FBI was going to take full advantage of the fact that I had chosen to engage in illegal activity on federal lands.

Back at FBI headquarters, we were chained to chairs and waited to be processed. When the FBI came to talk to me, I told them I'd only talk to the media. John, who sat next to me, was stressed out; he chastised me for falling asleep between questioning. We had been up since 4:00 AM and now, in a comfy, air-conditioned room, I couldn't keep my eyes open. John had also complained, several days ago when, while on patrol and awaiting the sunrise, I took a quick nap on the rock we were perched on. He couldn't believe I could sleep in such a stressful situation. For me, living a life at war, where you sleep very little and are always on alert for a surprise ambush, I learned to use quiet moments to grab some much-needed rest. I also loved sleeping outside in the warm desert where huge boulders remained warm for hours from the daylight sun, offering comfort to tired warriors like myself.

Finally at about 7:00 p.m., after the courts had closed and no judge was available to offer bail or bond, we were fingerprinted, processed, and again shackled for our next journey. We would be spending the night at my old home, the Federal Correctional Institution in Tucson, where I had served most of my four-year prison sentence. I found myself more than content to return to my familiar prison, although I was held in a pre-trial unit away from the many prisoners serving sentences who I still knew. John was nowhere to be found; I later learned he had chosen to be detained in the solitary housing unit, being afraid to "mix" in the general population.

An Old Friend

In the morning, we were transferred back to the federal courthouse for a bail hearing, where we were placed in a holding cell together. I told John that, next, we would be seeing a pre-trial officer who would determine our eligibility for release on bond. This officer would be the one determining whether we would be released or not. If we were deemed a flight risk or a danger to the community, the judge could order us detained until we went to trial—which could be months.

When the door in the interview room opened, and the pre-trial officer entered our cubicle, I was greeted with a smiling familiar face: Al Carranza, the Latino pre-trial officer assigned to my earlier ALF case in 1994, when I was arrested by the FBI on our tribe's reservation. "Hey Rodney!" Al said, as he pulled up a seat. We chatted like old friends, as he jotted down notes. He told me the FBI claimed that I was homeless, in an effort to sway the judge to deny me bail. I told him I lived less than a mile from where we sat. Mr. Carranza then asked how much I could afford to put up for bail. I told him $1,000. This was the amount he recommended in his report to the judge; and it worked.

Within the hour, I was holding my sleeping son against my chest as I answered questions from the media outside the courthouse. Would I be pleading guilty? Were we ready to go to jail to save these lions lives? How were they treating us? In my heart, I was relieved that, in less than 24 hours since my much-publicized arrest by FBI agents, that I was being allowed to return home. But we knew this campaign was different. Despite the much-hyped coverage of ELF and ALF actions that were being carried out during this same time period, we had engaged simply in nonviolent civil disobedience, using our own bodies as weapons to put between the hunter and the hunted. And despite the FBI clasping their hands in glee because they had me back in their grasp, I was ready and willing to accept the consequences of this latest action.

Al Carranza was assigned as my pre-trial supervision officer. Every week, I called him or stopped into the federal building to provide a urine sample, and we talked casually about what I was doing in my life. Al told me the FBI were calling him constantly to report on my every political activity, including attending anti-war protests. He told me the agents had said that I carried a United States flag upside down at one protest (which of course was true). His response was to ask if that was illegal, which of course it was not. Finally, in frustration, he told the FBI, "Hey, look, either you bring me a photo of Rodney doing something wrong, or you stop calling, because unless he's doing something illegal, I'm not concerned."

One day, we were organizing a protest at the local Arizona Game & Fish Department office, which happened to be the same day that Al visited my house. As we spoke in front of the house, other activists were busy shuttling signs we had painted outside to our vehicles, walking between us as we spoke. Al chuckled and said, "Well, I guess I should ask what you are doing?" I laughed nervously, and truthfully told him we were protesting the imprisonment of Sabino, the lion that had been captured in April, after the hunt was supposedly ended. I gave him a copy of our Chuk'shon Earth First! press release, and he was satisfied.

While the Animal Liberation Front, Earth Liberation Front, and even a new group calling itself Revolutionary Cells carried out illegal actions on behalf of animals and the Earth, I had found an avenue that I felt could be sustainable, one where we used covert civil disobedience to interfere with controversial and unethical hunting practices, yet not risking potentially years in prison. I was still of the belief that "hunt sabotage" as a tactic could result in, at most, a misdemeanor charge, not a federal charge of eco-terrorism.

Chuk'shon Earth First! was an idea shared mostly by activists in Tucson and Phoenix. It had started with a young crowd of radicals who loved the idea of spending days in the desert, following hunters, in the hopes of keeping them from their prey. After my early years in the Mojave Desert, together we began traveling to the Kofa National Wildlife Refuge every December to hopefully prevent desert bighorn sheep hunters from bagging a ram. The trophy hunts were offered only through a lottery, allowing hunters a once-in-a-lifetime opportunity to kill a desert bighorn. We combed the desert mountain range looking for hunters—except that, unlike our earlier days in California, we weren't using compressed air horns, but again our own bodies to scare away the hunter's prey. In those remote hunting areas, anyone seen or smelled could scare away a timid bighorn.

So, despite my pending court case for the Sabino Canyon lion hunt, friends from Phoenix and Tucson joined me in targeting other hunting practices in Arizona that were within our reach. We sabotaged desert big-horn sheep hunts, the lion hunt in Sabino Canyon, and now we were targeting other unethical hunting practices. We learned of hunts, for example, for Gunnison's prairie dogs in northern Arizona, where hunters would set up shooting stands and blast prairie dogs with high-powered rifles with no intent to use the animal; simply killing was the objective. We traveled to the northern Arizona plains where hunters were shooting prairie dogs and approached them in the field with our cameras. It wasn't long before we were told that we were no longer allowed on the property where the hunt was taking place. Still, we had learned that most hunters do not want their activities seen by the outside world, especially when done for pleasure.

Protecting the Sandhill Cranes

Not long afterward, we decided to target Arizona's sandhill crane hunt, which saw a few hundred permits sold each year to kill the large migratory birds. We began driving 90 miles south to Whitewater Draw, a wildlife area for sandhill cranes. It was a haven for bird watchers, but also one for water-fowl hunters. On one of my first scouting trips to the area, I saw duck hunters trudging into areas closed to hunters, simply to scare the flocks into fields where they could be shot—hardly ethical hunting.

When the sandhill crane hunt began in November 2004, I was one of the permitted hunters. I had applied for and received a permit, both as a tactic to deny a permit to another hunter, but also as a legal way to arguably be in the field "hunting." My thinking was that, with hunter harassment laws in most states by the early 2000s, the best way to sabotage hunts was as a licensed, albeit "bad," hunter—one who scares away more wildlife than they get close enough to kill. We got busted in Sabino because the police knew everything that we were doing and when; our tactics were open and public. But what if we sabotaged a hunt and the hunters didn't even know that they had been sabotaged? That was our new tactic.

On the very first crane hunt sabotage, a vegan activist from LA named Sasha drove out to help. I told her I had located the blind where the hunters would be shooting from on opening day; it was amidst corn fields where the cranes would come to feed on waste corn left behind after the initial harvest. When the cranes approached the fields, hunters would ambush them as they descended. We, on the other hand, had arrived earlier than the hunters—at about 3:30 a.m.—taking up a stand in the open field about 100 yards ahead of the hunters. We were nestled in a depression of the land that offered invisibility, but only if we continued laying on our bellies. From this position, we would be the first to see the approaching cranes, who were very skittish and would veer away at the sight of trouble. If the birds saw even a glint of a reflection off a hunter's gun, the flock would yield and turn away.

We used empty potato chip bags turned inside out, CDs, and our arms and legs to wave away approaching birds as we lay prone in the ground, all out of the sight of the hunters, who we heard swearing as yet another flock of cranes steered away from them. Our reward was to not have heard a shot from this particular group of hunters the whole morning. Only when they left in frustration did we finally stand up from our hiding spot and stretch our cold and tired bones.

But we didn't always succeed. Sometimes there was nothing we could do, as sandhill cranes descended onto a corn field to feed, only to be shot out of the sky. I will never forget the morning I saw a crane injured and unable to fly away as the hunter approached to finish the kill. As some cranes flew away in fear, others tried to help the wounded bird into the air with their own wings, only abandoning their kin when the hunter was just feet away. When he reached the bird, he took it by the legs and flung it hard against some nearby farm equipment, finally killing the poor animal.

Our Latest Trial

On the legal front, Matt Crozier, the third hunt saboteur who escaped capture in Sabino Canyon on that ill-begotten day, had been arrested after the FBI learned of his identity through his mention of an acting class while being recorded by John Richardson for his story for *Esquire*. John's tape recorder was seized by the FBI, and they used the tape to hunt down other supporters. Now Matt and I were issued state charges for our actions in Sabino Canyon, and the federal government was also preparing to indict us on more serious charges of "intent to harm, interfere, or harass a federal officer"—meaning, the tracker/hunter/hounder brought in by the feds to kill lions.

With these more-serious charges looming, I began to see the flaws in my strategy. I had thought that, by avoiding serious crimes, I could avoid serious charges. But that was before the United States revised its anti-terrorism law book that allowed them to go after animal and environmental activists as if they were members of the Taliban. I guess some would say that I couldn't have it both ways: to be a spokesperson for *illegal* direct action, yet only be a practitioner of *legal* direct action. To the state, I was one and the same, and they weren't far off their target. Now I again was under federal indictment, not for arson, but still for a charge that could put me back in prison for more than just one night to see old friends.

In December 2005, Matt and I finally stood trial for sabotaging the lion hunt nearly two years earlier, in March 2004. One of the first court tasks was jury selection. Over two dozen random registered voters from Pima County, Arizona, were chosen to be potential jurors, and as they sat quietly listening, the judge read the federal indictment detailing our actions to stop the Sabino Canyon hunt the year before. Finally, he asked, "Are any of you familiar with the events I mention?" At which point, every juror raised their hand—eliciting subdued laughter. One juror excused herself because, as a wildlife advocate, she could not promise that her judgment was impartial. She didn't care that she might be able to aid in my acquittal.

With a jury finally seated, our trial began. It was quickly revealed that, despite the state's public announcement of the lion hunt ending in Sabino Canyon, it indeed did continue, with the use of private bowhunters; they used hounds to tree and kill four more lions in the area. Our charge of violating the federal closure was dropped, as predicted; the US Forest Service had not followed proper procedures, so any conviction for violating the closure was not possible. But Matt and I were both found guilty of interfering with a federal officer, which carried a possible two-year sentence.

On the morning of the verdict being read, I remember telling another Earth First!er that we were about to either see the ranks of Chuk'Shon Earth First! grow (with a verdict of "not guilty") or dwindle (with a guilty verdict). It was indeed the latter, and I again was facing years imprisonment for a crime for which, in the 1980s, I would only have received a citation and/or a fine.

The prosecutor in the case was quoted after the verdict, saying, "He is a danger to the community. I know he wasn't tried here for being a violent anarchist. This trial wasn't about Rod Coronado being a terrorist...but he is one." Although the consequences of the lion hunt sabotage had grown beyond my expectations, I still did not regret using nonviolent direct action to protect the mountain lions I shared my homelands with.

CHAPTER 12

THE SAN DIEGO TRIAL

The worst was yet to come. While my trial was being held in Tucson, the FBI had finally made a break in their ELF investigations, having turned one member, Jacob Ferguson, into a snitch. Once Jake began testifying against other ELF members, those members also provided testimony to the state; most named Bill Rogers, known to friends as 'Avalon,' as the ringleader of the ELF. One by one, new friends I had made upon my release from prison were now being rounded up to face years in prison.

I ran into Avalon when I traveled up to Prescott University to give a lecture on my activism; I was happy to find that he and his partner had started an Info Shop in the small college town. On the Winter Solstice, knowing other friends had begun cooperating with federal prosecutors, Avalon chose to take his own life while awaiting transfer in the local county jail, rather than face the years of imprisonment that would surely come his way. Left behind in his cell was this note:

> Certain human cultures have been waging war against the earth for millennia. I chose to fight on the side of bears, mountain lions, skunks, bats, saguaros, cliff rose and all things wild. I am just the most recent casualty in that war. But tonight, I have made a jail break. I am returning home to the earth to the place of my origins.
>
> —Avalon

I began to stress out more about the possibility of being roped into the larger group, mostly because of my participation in the "Praxis Book Club" meetings where the very same ELF members and I shared information on how to break into and burn buildings. I had only been involved with the group in the one action in 2001 against Coulston's chimp laboratory, but I knew my role was enough to constitute a federal charge of conspiracy.

One day after having been found guilty in the Sabino case and while I was awaiting sentencing, my family and I were participating in a community art project, when out of the blue came Lacey Phillabaum, one of my former fellow *Earth First! Journal* editors and one of those named in the ELF indictments. Lacey was from Oregon, but she wanted to talk to me about the recent arrests. Before I could meet with her, my then-girlfriend responded with shock when I told her about this. She told me the timing was too suspicious and, more than likely, Lacey was wearing a wire and looking to gain some leniency by providing intelligence on a much bigger fish, namely, me. Months later, our suspicions would be confirmed when it became public that Lacey was indeed turning state's evidence in the hopes of escaping a long prison sentence.

With my upcoming sentencing for the mountain lion hunt sabotage scheduled for spring 2006, I tried to go about my life as normal and without fearing the consequences of the FBI's most recent string of arrests. I worked for a fossil dealer, where I received and shipped various dinosaur bones and teeth to customers all over the world from a warehouse where I was the only employee.

One February morning, I decided to take my three-year-old daughter to work with me, something I loved to do. We ate breakfast before going to the warehouse. A friend of mine also planned to stop by there. When he arrived, I came to the front of the building to greet him, when all of a sudden four black SUVs came screeching into the parking lot with federal agents spilling out, all focused and shouting at me to raise my hands. My friend was forced onto the ground while I was pushed against one of the vehicles and handcuffed. I knew I was being arrested for the lecture I gave in San Diego back in August of 2003, on the morning of the ELF's largest arson attack to date.

My attorney for the mountain lion case was aware of the grand jury in San Diego and wrote a letter to the court, advising them of my willingness to turn myself in if indicted. But the FBI wasn't going to miss the opportunity to arrest me for a third time in the same state.

As I sat in the FBI's vehicle, I could see my daughter standing alone back in my work area. I begged the arresting agents to call her mother and told them I'd cooperate as long as my daughter was safe. Thankfully, these FBI agents weren't monsters and soon returned her to her mother with the news that I was being taken back into federal custody.

I was held in solitary confinement in a prison in Florence, Arizona, where I paced the small barren concrete cell. I had already been found guilty of another federal offense and was awaiting sentencing. Now I had been indicted a third time, only here, the central charge—Conspiracy to Distribute Information Related to the Assembly of Explosives and Weapons of Mass Destruction—meant that I was now facing almost 20 years in prison if found guilty.

I remember thinking, "How in the hell am I going to get out of this…" With multiple other friends languishing in prison as they also awaited their fate, I felt at that moment that the odds were pretty good that I would not be seeing my young children for a very long time, and only then, maybe in a prison visiting room.

I was transported yet again to the same federal building in downtown Tucson, where I was brought before a judge who would determine whether I should be released on bond or not. Again, my old friend in the federal justice system, Al Carranza, recommended that I be granted release on bail. When my attorney explained to the judge that I was well aware of the pending charges in San Diego and had offered to turn myself in, he responded with surprise and asked the prosecutors if this was true. Upon confirmation, the judge granted me bail on only a $1,000 bond.

When I walked out of the federal building, I broke down crying as I approached my girlfriend and daughter. I now truly felt like my number was up and I would again be facing years and years in prison. The only solace came in the form of an amazing team of *pro bono* lawyers that were assembling to defend me. It was clear that I was being targeted and that the FBI were frustrated that despite my continuing activism, I was at the time only facing less than a year in prison for the lion hunt sabotage.

Back at my home in the Dunbar Springs neighborhood where many local Earth First!ers lived, the FBI combed through my belongings, confiscating materials that were still in the boxes the FBI had placed them in after my first arrest. In addition to my upcoming sentencing for the lion case, I was still facing state charges for the same event, as well as the new federal charges for my lecture in San Diego. Now the feds were filing additional charges, having seized from me some eagle feathers I had been given, as well as my Yaqui regalia used in our warrior society's ceremonies. They were alleging that I was in violation of the Migratory Bird Treaty, despite being a "sincere practitioner of a Native American religion," which is the clause in the law that allows such indigenous people like me to practice our religious beliefs without fear of persecution or federal prosecution. It was clear that the feds were looking for any charge they might be able to pile on me.

As one might easily imagine, I felt like the deck was stacked against me. Having been unable to rope me into the larger FBI's "Operation Back Fire" (which was an homage to my earlier "Operation Bite Back"), the feds now charged me with everything that they could think of, knowing even if I beat one or two charges, others might get me further legally entangled.

I owe so much to my then-fiancée, who not only stood by my side with her own one-year-old daughter that I was now raising, but who also began coordinating my legal defense in the San Diego case where I easily faced the most years in prison. She had already supported me during the Sabino Canyon trial, knowing I was destined for prison, albeit for a hopefully short sentence. We were together for less than a year, trying to raise two young children, when my life began to legally unravel. I was fearful that this young mother would see the dangers in a life with me, and take her child and run as far away as possible; but instead, we grew closer.

Despite facing certain uncertainty, on one beautiful spring day atop Dzil Nchaa Si Aan, the mountain we had fought for, she proposed to me, and I of course accepted her offer of marriage. She knew I wanted to marry her, but how tragic it would look for someone facing the dangers I faced to propose a lifelong marriage to a woman with a young child, who needed not just a partner, but a present partner. Her proposal humbled me and I was glad our children were there to see me crying my tears of happiness. Those are the moments that, as an indigenous warrior, give you the strength to continue fighting, even against insurmountable odds.

Sentence Coming Down

A few months later in March, Matt and I stood before the judge, awaiting our sentences. Matt was a young white man who had gone into a recovery program to address his drinking while awaiting sentencing. He was desperate to increase his chance for a lenient sentence after having been arrested again for stealing an idling Hummer at a gas station. The judge looked kindly upon him; here was a man trying to alter his path away from illegality. Matt was sentenced to nothing more than probation.

But when it came time to hand down my sentence, US District Judge David Bury said he wanted to send a message: if you use "force and violence in civil disobedience, you are going to be punished for it; it's anarchy." He chastised me for continuing on my path of illegality as a means of defending wildlife. I knew any sentence could be as long as a year; instead, the judge sentenced me to eight months in federal prison for my crime of destroying a lion snare and interfering with the killing of Sabino lions. I was not even allowed to say goodbye to my two young children; instead, I was handcuffed and led away. Once again shackled and transported with a busload of other prisoners to a privately-run prison in Chandler, Arizona, I began the first few weeks of my sentence.

While awaiting transfer to my old home at the Federal Correctional Institution in Tucson, I can recall how, on the anniversary of our arrest in Sabino Canyon, a large storm tore through southern Arizona. The storm was so powerful it knocked out the power briefly in my prison cell, but back in Sabino Canyon, the entire paved road used to ferry tourists was destroyed, closing the canyon yet again—but this time, nature, not the federal government was in control.

When I arrived back at FCI Tucson, I was saddened to see some of my old indigenous friends still serving their sentences. I was one of the lucky ones. I had a support network, a team of lawyers, and many friends, while many of my comrades in prison had no one. Many had been convicted of crimes that would make returning to their old homes difficult or impossible, but as indigenous people today, most had nowhere else to go.

One day as I was walking to lunch, a correctional officer (they hate being called 'prison guards') stopped me and immediately offered me his hand and started talking about the Sabino Canyon lion hunt. He wanted to thank me for trying to save the lions. He said his entire family was rooting for us. It meant a lot to me to know that my captors were not blind to the fact that they saw me as more an activist than a criminal deserving to be in prison.

My lawyers told me not to worry about the San Diego case while I was serving my sentence for Sabino. The judge was well aware that I had other cases pending and motions had been filed delaying proceedings to spare the hardship of transferring me back and forth from Arizona to California. Instead, I tried to focus on preserving my own sanity and any hopes for raising children in a normal fashion. Already, my daughter was becoming familiar with visiting me in prison, while my son's mother did not want him seeing me in prison, which I understood. I returned to my regiment of reading, writing letters, and of course, attending sweat lodge ceremonies held each Saturday.

Serving a prison sentence is the easiest part of being imprisoned. The worst is when there is no determined date for your release. For example, when I was picked up as a fugitive from justice, the media reported that I faced decades in prison for my crimes. Once I was picked up, and after having consulted with lawyers, I knew that my time might instead be only two to six years. Once I was sentenced and imprisoned for the Sabino Canyon case on an 8-month sentence, I didn't have the peace of mind of knowing that I'd be returning to a semi-normal life upon completing that sentence because I still had the San Diego case and the federal "feather case" hanging over me.

I remember a conversation I had with Antonio Felix, who had become my lawyer for my "Arizona" cases. I asked him for advice on sorting through the million and one possible outcomes in my situation, when he said, "Usually, I council my clients to not focus on the outcome of their case until they've made it through the preliminary motions, trial, etc. ... You, my friend, have three cases to survive through..."

While I had lived my life believing that having children would only take me away from my struggles for Earth- and animal-liberation, I began to learn the lesson that all indigenous warriors have known for millennia: that your family does not take you away from struggle, it give you the reasons to continue fighting and to survive. Not only to continue to exist as a conquered person, but to live life as a free indigenous human being, honoring the sacrifices made by one's ancestors so that the cycle of natural life could continue and other families such as your own could survive. Now I had two young children and a soon-to-be strong wife that I desperately wanted to spend my life with...outside of a prison visiting room.

Finally, the day arrived when I was released from prison...again. I returned home to Tucson and my semi-normal life, only this time my full-time job was defending myself in what was to be an upcoming trial in San Diego sometime in 2007. And my fiancée and I began to plan our marriage for the fall, although at this point in our lives we didn't know whether I'd be spending future anniversaries free or behind bars. I went back to my job at the fossil dealer, as well as working as a barista at a Tucson coffee shop. My fiancée and I were now living together and raising our daughter, but I only saw my son part of the week. His mother had decided to move back to Michigan, where she was from, taking my son with her. I was heartbroken. All I wanted was for my new family to survive this ordeal and remain together, yet I was already losing my son, in a way. But I had no leverage; in hindsight, I can appreciate that my son's mother was acting in our child's best interest.

Meanwhile, I dove deep into the legal defense with my team of attorneys. Gerry Singleton was the local San Diego attorney leading the case, but the team included Tony Serra, Omar Figueroa, and Ben Rosenfeld, with legal assistance from Steve Christiansen. Tony Serra had defended many controversial clients in the past, including Huey Newton of the Black Panthers, members of the White Panthers, Hell's Angels, and even the Symbionese Liberation Army. Tony had also won acquittals for many convicted innocent people who were ultimately freed. He lives a simple life, having taken a vow of poverty and refusing to pay taxes because of the 2003 Iraq War. He himself was federally convicted for violation of tax laws and served a ten-month sentence at Lompoc Prison in California. As soon as he was released from prison and custody in March 2007, he began working on my case.

To say the least, my legal team was unconventional, but we were fighting an unconventional war against a superior state power. Tony and Ben were the attorneys responsible for winning a $4 million settlement from the FBI for Judi Bari's family for having been wrongly accused of carrying the bomb that crippled her and injured my friend, Darryl Cherney, way back in 1990, when they were on the way to my house.

None of my lawyers asked for a dime. Tony told me, "I represent people who pay me with stacks of hundred-dollar bills... That allows me to represent people like you for free." Omar was a younger version of Tony, who had met his legal mentor when he came to lecture at his Stanford Law School. I was also fortunate to be out on bail and able to attend pretrial hearings as a free man, not shackled in an orange jump suit.

So, I drove the 6 hours to San Diego where my lawyers and I met in a federal courtroom. I had drawn a federal judge that was known for his staunch defense of constitutional rights, Jeffrey Miller. I gained respect for him when he invited us into his chambers to discuss matters. I had never participated in my own defense to such a degree in my earlier cases and now, with a team of amazing lawyers, I started to believe that with these legal angels I stood the best chance possible of beating the power of the Department of Justice which was bearing down hard on the ALF and ELF, whom they considered the most active domestic terrorist threat in America.

Sometimes my fiancée and I stayed with Gerry and his family while in San Diego for a hearing. Gerry's daughter was the same age as our daughter, so the two could play while we adults talked legal strategy; other times, we relaxed and watched *The Sound of Music* with the kids.

The trial date was still unknown, but we expected it to be in the fall of 2007, the same time that I was scheduled to be married. Chrysta and I had to juggle our wedding plans with my trial preparation. We chose September 8, a Saturday, for our ceremony, which would be held at the Tucson Botanical Gardens. We asked my old Earth First! friend, Peg Millet, to conduct the ceremony, which was a legal problem because, as a convicted felon herself, I was not supposed to be associating with her—as per my federal conditions of supervised release (probation) in the Sabino Canyon case.

Chrysta and I asked for a meeting with my probation officer to discuss the matter. When we arrived, he was there with his supervisor and we explained our dilemma. The supervisor was immediately amiable, saying, "We aren't monsters! Why don't we just get the judge to sign an order allowing you an exemption for the day…" We couldn't believe our luck—a great omen for our preparation of a life together and for my literal freedom.

The New Trial Begins

My federal trial on charges of distribution of information related to explosives and weapons of mass destruction was planned to begin on September 11, 2007. We knew we could expect the prosecutor's opening statement to mention the September 11, 2001 attacks, so my lawyers would speak to it first, acknowledging only that this was not a case about a terrorist attack, it was a trial about constitutional rights and free speech.

For our wedding, we had a Lakota friend conduct a pipe ceremony, followed by Peg Millet's bonding ceremony. We had written our own vows, inspired by the wedding ceremony from JK Rowling's *Deathly Hallows*, the final book in the Harry Potter series. When I was in prison the previous year for sabotaging the lion hunt, I read the first six Harry Potter books, which both of my kids were deeply into. I wanted to have something to connect with my son about through letters, but I also loved the world created by Rowling with its deep connections to earthly powers, plants, and animals.

At our wedding, we also had my old Earth First! friend, Dana Lyons, perform Johnny Cash's "Ring of Fire" with a Yaqui mariachi band I knew from the reservation; and my Navajo friend Chucki Begay also sang her own songs. Afterwards, I stayed up late into the night around a campfire with my hunt saboteur friends from Phoenix, drinking home-brewed beer while my new wife Chrysta and daughter slept in a tent nearby.

On the first day of the trial, I stood outside the Edward J. Schwartz United States Courthouse in San Diego with my wife and lawyers in a circle. We passed a bundle of sage between us, smudging ourselves and saying prayers for the battle for my freedom that would soon begin inside the courtroom. Passersby watched us, but more noticeably, so did two FBI agents who had been investigating my case for the last four years.

The first process was jury selection. A pool of about thirty registered voters from across the southern district of California answered questions put to them by the judge. That night, my lawyers researched the names of the jurors, rooting out those who had penned right-wing commentaries in local papers and determining who we wanted on the jury.

Once the jury was chosen, opening arguments began from Gerry and Tony. We had clear instructions from the judge that the jury must find not only that I did indeed show an audience how to make an incendiary device, but that it was with the intent that someone in the audience would go out and commit an imminent crime. No one could argue that I wasn't telling people how to make an incendiary device; it had become part of my stump speech. I even used the same jugs as donation containers, passing them around the audience where people stuffed in cash at the end of my fiery lectures. But were these demonstrations with the intent that folks would then rush out and commit arsons? No…and yes. On the one hand, I encouraged my audiences in the early 2000s to carry out further attacks in defense of Earth and animals, but in the 2003 San Diego talk, I was responding to a direct question about how I had made the incendiary device used in my attack on Michigan State University's mink research program. That device wasn't a jug and fuel-soaked sponge; it was the one-hour kitchen timer device we had developed in California in the 1990s, only I found it more practical to demonstrate the easier-to-build jug than a device requiring an understanding of electrical circuits. In my efforts to encourage action, I wanted to demonstrate something not only easy, but a device you could make from supplies found at any supermarket.

But the judge's ruling on jury instructions made the definition of 'imminence' the primary focus of both the prosecution and my defense. The prosecution wouldn't say it, but they knew that my encouragement of arson during a lecture was protected free speech; what they needed to prove was that I intended my audience to *take imminent action*. Federal prosecutors argued that I was making a call for action, except that the fire they wanted to use as evidence occurred hours before, not after, my San Diego talk.

After opening arguments, we entered our second day of the trial with the prosecution's introduction of evidence. The lights were dimmed in the courtroom and a screen was unfurled. The government had seized a videotape of my lecture in San Diego, but it did not include the question-and-answer portion of my talk where I demonstrated the incendiary device.

Nonetheless, the filmed portion of my lecture was now being presented as evidence. Until now, the jury wasn't clear whether I was a bomber captured in some dark basement or simply a common criminal. They had no idea that I was a seasoned political activist, long targeted by the government and charged for simply talking about a crime I had already served one prison sentence for. We couldn't introduce evidence of my past or an explanation of my beliefs (to defend sacred lands, people, animals, and waters), but now the government was making that very case by allowing the jury to witness my entire 90-minute lecture in which I recounted my Yaqui heritage and history, my exposure to the commercial slaughter of wildlife, what I saw during my investigation of fur farms—my whole story was being told without having to take the stand and exposing myself to cross-examination.

After the jury became aware of the political nature of my trial, they took greater interest and also weren't afraid of making eye contact, often seeing my wife and I eating lunch in the same cafeteria. We knew we had a few jurors already on our side, but there was no confidence it was enough for an acquittal. After the trial began, my lawyers held a brief press conference during a lunch break, where Omar used the presence of the FBI to make a point about their attempts to criminalize free speech. When he pointed to the two FBI agents hovering amongst the press, they immediately scattered in different directions. When we returned to the courtroom, the judge heard about the antics and admonished my team to tread carefully when discussing the case with the media. Tony begged the judge punish him, not me, for any misconduct.

Without a factual record from the question-and-answer period of my lecture, where I discussed the incendiary device, it was now up to both the government and my lawyers to explain and interpret to the jury exactly what I actually said. The prosecutors brought forth a witness who had attended the lecture undercover, San Diego Police Detective Joe Lehr. In his testimony, he stated that I was asked "how to make a bomb for an action." It was only then that my legal team submitted evidence we had received of an actual audio recording of that portion of my lecture, where I was clearly asked about how I carried out the action at Michigan State University, not how to do it in the immediate future. Tony's questioning of the detective led to his retracting of his earlier statement, leaving our recording as the final evidence received by the jury.

Tony made a closing argument that lasted over three hours. The focus of his argument was to illustrate to the jury several historic examples where inflammatory speech was indeed protected by the First Amendment.

He spoke of the Longshoreman protests, the early gay liberation movement, and even the Boston Tea Party. With each example, he explained the fiery speech used by early activists and how it was protected by the Constitution. He argued that the beauty of living in our free society was the hallmark of our ability to exercise free speech without fear of government repression. When it came time for the government to make their closing case, prosecutors drifted away from my San Diego speech, using instead an interview I gave to Ed Bradley of "60 Minutes" about the ELF and the use of arson. In the interview, I clearly advocated for arson as a tool for animal and Earth defense, but again I was not calling for any *specific* and *immediate* action, and this was the key point.

If found guilty, I was probably facing 8 to 12 years in prison—not a lifetime but long enough for me to miss most of my children's youth. My wife and I sat on a bench outside the courtroom, her cradling my head on her lap as I fretted about the jury that was deliberating. From my horizontal position on the bench, I saw a pair of legs walking by, and when I looked up at their face, I recognized one of my jurors. Their mouth formed into a small smile as our eyes connected. When we were called back into the courtroom after a full day of jury deliberations, my wife held open the swinging courtroom gate for the jurors as the re-entered the court. As they passed, the majority thanked her for the courtesy. The prosecution was pissed. They accused my wife of attempting to sway the jury with kindness. The judge reluctantly agreed and, although appreciating the gesture, instructed her not to interact with the jury.

I was asked to stand by the judge as the jury read their verdict. Within minutes, I would know whether my future would be filled with raising my young children or nearly a decade behind bars. "We the jury are hopelessly deadlocked and unable to agree on a verdict." The judge declared a mistrial. I was confused. I asked Tony, "What does that mean?" His response was, "You were not found guilty. I consider that a victory." Later we learned that it was either 9-3 or 10-2 in favor of acquittal.

We drove back to Tucson after a celebratory dinner with my legal team to await the next word from the federal government. Within days, federal prosecutors informed my team that I would next be indicted for the lecture I gave in Washington DC in 2003 at American University, where there was indeed a much clearer call for action. Prosecutors said they would continue to seek indictments for other lectures I had given as well.

Meanwhile, my real fear was based not in my fiery speeches but on the actual conspiring I had committed with my friends in the ELF through the Praxis Book Club, where we met and shared break-in and fire-making skills. Now some of them had turned into snitches and were informing on former friends. I feared that I would be one of them. The last thing I wanted was to fight more cases about free speech, only to ultimately be convicted of more than speech. When I came clean with my lawyers, they advised that I consider a plea deal with immunity for any crimes I might have committed since leaving prison in 1999.

My legal team was willing to continue fighting future indictments for free speech, but the real question was whether I wanted to put my family through more trials that could end with me spending much more time in prison. The feds wanted a conviction; if I was willing to plead guilty to the charge I had just beat, it gave me some bargaining power. Gerry told me if I wanted to be done with activism and focus on my young family, no one would blame me, but if I was planning on continuing my radical career, he advised I continue fighting.

I talked it over with Chrysta. We eventually agreed that if I was granted immunity for my associations with ELF members, the Praxis Book Club, my role in the Coulston chimp lab arson and for sabotaging the Mount Graham telescope power line twice, *and* spend only one year in prison, then that would be a deal I would take. On their side, the feds were offering a deal with a prison sentence of 21 to 24 months. I called my lawyers and came to the agreement with them that I would accept a federal prison sentence of one year and one day—in the US federal system, any sentence longer than one year is eligible for a 15% reduction for good behavior, meaning a fair chance that I would spend just over ten months in prison. My lawyers also bargained to drop the state charges in the Sabino Canyon case and the federal feather case.

It was a unique opportunity to wipe my slate clean without having to testify against anyone else. The feds had cracked their largest eco-terrorism case ever with the arrest of my new post-prison friends and other ELF members, and they knew that my involvement was peripheral at best. From my perspective as a member and student of a revolutionary movement, I saw my plea deal as a kind of conditional surrender with favorable terms. I was agreeing to no longer engage in revolutionary actions against industry and state in exchange for my freedom. So, I entered my guilty plea in December 2007 and my sentencing was scheduled for March 2008. I then wrote the following letter to my supporters, explaining my actions:

Dear friends and supporters--

On December 14th, before Judge Jeffery Miller in Federal Court in San Diego, I entered a guilty plea to one count of distribution of information related to "the assembly of explosives and weapons of mass destruction." This was the one count I have fought for almost two years now and for which I faced approximately five to ten years in prison if found guilty. In September of 2007, a jury instead voted 8-4 for acquittal, and in the ensuing weeks, prosecutors in the case informed us that they would seek an additional indictment in Washington DC, for a speech I delivered at American University in January, 2003.

In exchange for a guilty plea in the San Diego case, the US government has agreed to ask only for a one-year prison sentence, drop pending charges in Tucson for my possession of raptor feathers, and not to indict me in DC. I am not required to testify against anyone else in any other investigations, and hopefully this plea agreement will once and for all grant me closure in a well-known campaign of repression against me for my past involvement: association and support for covert campaigns against environmental destroyers and animal abusers.

It has long been my desire to put my past behind me and instead build a sustainable existence for myself, my wife, Chrysta, and two children, Anheles and Maya. This decision to take a plea bargain comes only after much careful consideration and a sincere desire to do what is best for my family. Such unconstitutional assaults on my free speech beg for a continued legal battle and defense, but I am instead choosing to reach a settlement that will allow me to move on with my life rather than face years of litigation that might lead to many years in prison. My children need me. I am a father first and foremost, and have given 20-plus years to the battle against corporate and government policies which destroy our Earth. Now it is time to give of myself to the purpose of raising a family in these troubling times.

For the Earth, and all of her Children,
Rod Coronado

I prepared a list of crimes I had committed since my release from prison in 1999, in addition to requesting immunity for any involvement with the skill-sharing I did with members of the ELF in 2002. I listed scouting missions I did at the USDA's wildlife research campus at Fort Collins, sabotaging logging equipment in Northern California, Mount Graham power-line sabotage, breaking into the kennels at the VA Hospital in Tucson, and of course my role in carrying out recon at Coulston Labs in New Mexico. When we went to the meeting with prosecutors and the FBI, they plopped an old-school tape recorder on the middle of the table and pushed the record button. We had already provided my list and were simply there to answer any questions. I found it interesting that I was never asked whether I knew anything about the San Diego arson the morning of my lecture. In the end, the feds knew all along that I wasn't connected to it; they were simply exploiting the opportunity they had been provided with my pre-planned lecture, which gave them a target—not the best target, but a target nonetheless.

Omar Figueroa, Rod, Chrysta, Tony Serra, Gerry Singleton

As I awaited my sentencing, I was torn over where to request that I be interned in the federal prison system. Chrysta wanted me to return to my familiar prison in Tucson, but I also wanted to be close to my son, who now lived in Michigan. On the positive side, I would only be away from him for less than a year.

Awaiting Sentencing

The week before my sentencing, I flew with my wife and daughter to Oregon to visit my parents. While we were there, we drove to a friend's house in Olympia, Washington—but to do so, I had to inform my probation officer from the Sabino Canyon case because it was a deviation from my scheduled travel. My wife's best friend had invited us up for a visit and a stay at a cabin on the rugged coast where our kids could play on the beach.

After the trip, upon our return to Arizona, we learned from my lawyers about an arson attack that occurred on March 3rd, while I was visiting the Pacific Northwest. I was only days away from my sentencing in San Diego when the ELF claimed responsibility for torching three more luxury homes under construction in what was called "Seattle Street of Dreams"— a luxury home contest in Canada and the US, whose theme was "green building." At the site of the fires, someone painted: "Built Green? Nope black! McMansions r not green. ELF." Even the prosecutors in my San Diego case were not suspicious that I might have been involved, but the FBI had some questions, which I fielded to my lawyers with the instructions to only inform them of my actual movements during my stay in Washington. My parents were also visited one last time by the FBI in Portland, asking about my stay with them. The issue was dropped, and we remained focused on my strategy, which was to begin my new life again after completing any sentence for the San Diego case.

When it came time for my sentencing, there were no arguments for a longer sentence; the prosecution was pleased with the conviction. When I told the judge I would no longer be associating with members of the radical environmental and animal movements and instead working on raising a family and building community, he instead expressed hope I would still be involved, if only to share my story of personal development toward more legal forms of advocacy. The judge was in no rush to send me to prison, instead giving me a date on which I was to self-surrender to the designated prison: the medium-security federal prison in El Reno, Oklahoma— unfortunately not close to either my wife or children.

I bought a one-way ticket to Oklahoma City. The night before I left, my wife, daughter, and I had dinner in Phoenix before checking into a hotel so I could catch an early morning flight. It felt awful. The next day, after painful goodbyes, I boarded my plane, arriving some hours later in Oklahoma City. I called a cab and asked him to drive me to the prison in El Reno. The driver assumed I was on my way to visit someone, until I told him I wouldn't need a return ride until the end of the year.

When I got to the prison, I pressed the call box located near the parking lot and informed them that I was there to self-surrender. They instructed me to walk a few hundred yards along the perimeter fence to a gate where I waited outside the prison, alone on the prairie, for 15 minutes, before the gate buzzed and I was instructed to enter. It was another state, but the same routine: I was strip-searched, given prison clothes, and led to my new home in the dorm-like setting of the prison complex.

I dove right back into my familiar routines of hanging out with the intellectually-interesting prisoners in the library, connecting with the indigenous population, and attending weekly sweat lodge ceremonies. Most of the other native prisoners were from the Oklahoma area, but that didn't matter in prison. I was grateful for the familiar support network and was eventually assigned to work for the Chaplain as the sweat lodge caretaker.

I didn't like the prison layout. We didn't have normal cells with toilets; instead, we were divided by cinder-block cubicles only five feet high. The only way I could sleep at night was with earplugs and with my eyes covered, but I was counting months, not years, on my sentence.

My wife and daughter visited me on their way to Michigan. They had agreed to move so I could be closer to my son, who was living in West Michigan with his mother. The only thing worse than being in prison is being in prison when you have young children. The four years I had earlier spent in prison were much less stressful than the time spent locked up after I had kids. Still, I was grateful to be one of the few short-term inmates.

One evening, while sitting in the TV room watching the Discovery Channel, a commercial came on—and I nearly fell out of my chair. It was for a new show called "Whale Wars," starring my old friend Paul Watson. There on television was Paul and his black pirate ship, going to sea against the Japanese whaling fleet in the southern oceans of Antarctica. I was so happy to see that Sea Shepherd was becoming more of a mainstream organization, now making its debut in the era of reality TV. Of course, no one else wanted to watch Whale Wars, so it would be many months before I got to watch my first episode.

Ten months passed. The day I was released from prison, I was issued a pair of blue jeans and a shirt, and driven to the bus station in Oklahoma City. There, I met a supporter who gave me a box containing my own clothes and a cell phone to keep in touch with my wife as I journeyed from Oklahoma to Michigan via bus. I was no longer a federal prisoner, although I would still be required to be on supervised release for another three years.

"Facebook Friend"

Upon arrival in Grand Rapids, Michigan, I was driven to the halfway house where I'd finish the remaining two months of my sentence. It was the thick of winter and snow covered the ground, but I still hit the streets every morning looking for a job. On every job application that I filled out, I was required by law to check the box that identified me as a convicted felon, which made it ten times harder to find a job. Meanwhile, I was only allowed to leave the halfway house to go to work or church, so I started attending a progressive Unitarian Universalist Church, where I could spend time with Chrysta and my two children. Finally, I got a job at a chain restaurant where the manager was sympathetic and supportive of my efforts to reintegrate into a semi-normal life.

One day while on lunch break, I was walking to a neighboring grocery store with my two kids when I was approached by a man identifying himself as an FBI agent. He had questions about the arson that was committed in Washington state the same time I was visiting my family in Oregon. In all my years of being investigated by the FBI, rarely have I ever spoken to a single agent who was arresting or questioning me, except to respond to irrelevant questions like, "Are those handcuffs too tight?" It has always been the number one rule of the American revolutionary to not co-operate with the FBI. I listened to the agent's question and then said, "You know I have a rule about not talking to the FBI, but I'll give you one answer because I'm here with my kids and on my lunch break... I didn't even know about the fires in Seattle until your agents asked my lawyers about it. I was visiting friends on the coast with my wife when the fires occurred."

It wasn't long before I saw him again. On February 4, 2009, I was called into the offices of my halfway house and told that, based on FBI advice, I wouldn't be allowed to leave the building the following day. The next day was the scheduled sentencing of my old friend, Marie Mason, who had visited me 16 years earlier in White Cloud County Jail in Michigan while I was awaiting my bail hearing, after having been picked up as a fugitive on the Yaqui Reservation in 1993. Marie was convicted for an arson on Michigan State University's Agricultural Hall that caused over a million dollars in damage to genetic engineered crop research on New Year's Eve 1999—the very night that I was with my nation's warrior society at a ceremony in Tucson, having myself finally completed my own sentence for arson at the very same university. I was learning that Michigan was not welcome territory for radical environmentalist or animal activists, after both ALF and ELF arsons had cost Michigan State millions of dollars and years of irreplaceable research intended to genetically modify food and aid fur farmers.

Mason got arrested, only thanks to the turncoat actions of her ex-husband, Frank Ambrose. It began in 2007 when Ambrose's house was raided following the discovery of evidence he had dumped in a Detroit-area dumpster. Someone rooting through the trash called the police after discovering personal records, writings, and a gas mask belonging to Ambrose. Jacob Ferguson was the snitch that helped bring down the Western ELF, and now Ambrose was being used to break the Midwest contingent that he and Mason began back in 1999 when they jointly torched MSU and, later, some logging equipment at another location in Michigan. Prosecutors admit that, as an informer, Ambrose traveled outside the state a total of seven times gathering intelligence and recording conversations with former friends. In the end, Marie—now 'Marius,' due to a 2016 transition to male—was sentenced to 21 years in prison.

Meanwhile, life on the home front was becoming a challenge for me. I wasn't allowed to associate with anyone I had known previously if they had an activist history—and that was pretty much everyone I had known in my entire life. My wife Chrysta also hated living in the Midwest and had developed a relationship with a male co-worker that was threatening the survival of our young family. I was afraid that if we broke up, I would lose not just my wife but my daughter as well. I never told my probation officer of the struggles I was facing at home, for fear that it would somehow be used against me. Instead, I did everything I could to try and keep my family together.

As part of my conditions of supervised release, I was subjected to computer monitoring, where I had to pay for a service that recorded literally every keystroke I made on my monitored computer. With winter set in and having been socially isolated from friends, I took to Facebook for support, reaching out to others I thought might be supportive. Unfortunately, I did not ask my probation officer whether it was permissible to be Facebook friends with someone with an activist path; as I now realize, she would have said 'no.' Instead, in late August 2010, my probation officer called me into the federal building where she gave me a summons to appear in court for violating my conditions of probation. The offense was "using an unauthorized computer" and "becoming Facebook friends" with my old Earth First! buddy, Mike Roselle, who himself had become a convicted felon after being charged with hanging a banner decrying acid rain on Mount Rushmore.

In the early 2000s when I was on probation for ALF actions, my western probation officer would speak with me first about any concerns she might have with my behavior before taking action. Here in Michigan, the feds were much tougher; they used any excuse to continue their vendetta against me. My lawyers in San Diego were the first to warn me, after filing a motion requesting that my sentencing district in California remain as my formal supervisory district. But the federal attorney in West Michigan said "this isn't California and that's not how we supervise felons." Instead, with little warning, I was taken before the same judge that had sentenced Marie Mason and asked by the judge, in a very hostile tone, what I didn't understand about supervised release. He said any further violation of conditions would result in extended prison time. For now, his punishment was to return me to the federal prison in Milan, Michigan for four months. At least the prison sentences were getting shorter!

This would be my fourth federal prison sentence. I again self-surrendered, stripping off my street clothes and folding them carefully before placing them in the paper bag where they would remain for four months. Before being placed into the general prison population, correctional staff pulled me aside and asked if there were going to be any problems. They saw that I was convicted of injuring or interfering with a federal officer, and they took that to mean that I had assaulted prison staff. I explained what happened and told them that I wanted to do my time and return to my family as soon as possible. They would have no problems from me.

I again found other indigenous prisoners and got on the call-out sheet for the weekly sweat lodge ceremonies. The hardest part was being in an institution where so many other prisoners were years into their sentences, far removed from their families and all outside connections. I tried not to talk too much with other prisoners about my sentence. I had no right to complain; I was just going to be there "a prison minute."

Becoming familiar with prison life, however, doesn't mean you ever get used to it. Again, I was in dorm housing and found it impossible to get a good night's sleep, with all the snoring and other disturbances each night. Most people fear getting beat up in prison; I hated not getting a good night's sleep.

In the 1990s, when I served four years, I built a regiment around my writing, exercise, religious and political activities, and visits. Now I was a father and a husband taken away from his children and wife, with all my thoughts on returning to them as soon as possible. Such feelings made even a week in prison feel like a year. The day I was released, I was again called into an office and asked if I understood how strictly I would continue to be supervised and whether I understood that any deviation would lead me right back into prison. I guess I learned my lesson; I haven't been back since.

I returned home, but not to a happy life. My wife, not wanting to live under the same restrictions as I did, chose to travel overseas where she again fell for another man. She broke the news to me on the day I got out of prison. I still loved her and the life we tried to have, but she was miserable living in Michigan and our marriage paid the price. We separated, I moved out, and we began divorce proceedings. Somehow, I felt responsible, that I deserved what was happening. Over the years, I had cheated on several girlfriends and hardly ever been held accountable. I didn't realize it at the time, but I lived in a subculture that, like its mainstream counterpart, enabled men to treat women with disrespect. Having children and, later, getting into therapy encouraged me to change my patterns of behavior towards women, so that my son would not grow up like I did. But at the time, I felt like it was karma; all I could do was allow my wife her freedom to love whoever she wanted.

My remaining time on supervised release was spent entirely in the state of Michigan. I was not allowed to fly out West to visit my family, although I was allowed to travel to the Upper Peninsula of Michigan and Lake Superior, which was a form of natural escape for me. I continued working as a waiter at a brewery in Grand Rapids, biked everywhere, and got into yoga. I moved into a cooperative housing situation for artists and activists, and began taking community college classes. When I was offered a scholarship to attend college full-time, my probation officer made me refuse it; she wanted me to work, not go to school. She believed education was a privilege that I did not deserve.

In the waning months of my supervised release, I was instructed to report for a polygraph examination to determine if I was indeed following the conditions of my release. When I reported for testing, I was interviewed by the examiner before the test. He asked about my family and children and where they went to school. He then excused himself to make a call, and when he returned, he informed me that there was a conflict of interest because, during my interview, he realized that both our children were in the same class. I told him it didn't bother me, so he proceeded with the test—asking if I had used an unauthorized computer, traveled outside the district without permission, or accepted financial aid from any old contacts in the movement. I passed the test. Sure enough, some weeks later at one of my son's school events, I ran into the polygraph expert and we shook hands. I was happy to see that he did not view me as a terrorist, like my probation officer did.

CHAPTER 13

WOLF PATROL

Life continued, a mixture of normality and unpleasant experiences. I remember asking for permission to visit my parents for Christmas, and my
probation officer responded, "Oh, you celebrate Christmas, but you also do
yoga?"—as if it was some kind of hypocritical contradiction. Another horrible consequence of probation was drug testing. I have never been charged
with a drug crime, yet while on probation in Michigan, I was required to
call a testing center *every day*. If it was my 'color' or 'code' that day, I had
to report for a urine test before the end of the day. If I was camping, I'd
still have to ensure that I was close enough to drive to the testing center
before 7 pm. Finally, on an August evening in 2013, on the last day of my
federal period of supervised release (probation), I picked up my phone and
called Dwight, my old Earth First! comrade from Tucson who had helped
shelter me while I was a fugitive from the FBI. He laughed when he picked
up the phone, saying, "Well, how does it feel to finally be free?" I told him
I'd be sure to let him know, if I ever truly felt free.

While staying in West Michigan to be close to my son, my attention
fell to the recent decision in the Midwest to again hunt wolves recreational-
ly. Having been almost totally wiped out by the early 1900s, only a few
wolves remained in the far reaches of the Upper Peninsula of Michigan.
These wolves would eventually breed with wolves from Minnesota who
also survived extirpation, and from these animals would come the current
wolf population of Minnesota, Wisconsin, and Michigan. Having only recently been removed from the federal list of endangered species, wolves,
for the first time in almost a century, were going to be hunted again.

Every indigenous nation in the Great Lakes region is opposed to recreational wolf hunting. For many, especially the Anishinabeg, the wolf is
considered a sacred brother, having been sent by the Creator to keep the
first human company. Those nations believe what befalls the wolf, will
befall them, and for that reason there was overwhelming opposition from
indigenous people.

I wanted to take some form of action—not a straight-up act of hunt
sabotage like in Sabino Canyon, but some form of monitoring that might
elicit outrage that could be channeled into action against the wolf hunt.
With the loss of federal protections for wolves across the Rockies and the

Great Lakes, I wanted to use the model Paul Watson had taught me: to go into the field and find wolf hunters, document their hunting practices, and use the evidence to raise public awareness and advocacy in favor of wolf protection.

In Michigan, the hunt would be in three small zones with up to 1,200 permits being issued for only 43 wolves, in total. We knew we couldn't risk following hunters into the field without their knowledge, so we decided to set up surveillance of the big game check-in station where the first wolf killed in Michigan's first hunt might be brought in. If we could film that first wolf killed, surely the media would want to hear our side of the story behind the photo.

My best friend at the time was Kevin, the father of my children's schoolmates who also kayaked and bicycled with me. He was an anarchist and college professor, someone who didn't show up on my probation officer's radar. Now, he was willing to drive with me to a hotel overlooking the check station that we would be staking out.

We spent hours during the first day of the hunt, watching the station. Twice we saw hunters pull up, only to report deer not wolves. While I was in town getting batteries, Kevin called to say that a wolf had been brought in. He was able to take a few photos without arousing any suspicions, but unknown to us, earlier that day another wolf had been killed and it was that animal that was featured in news stories about the hunt.

Nonetheless, an idea was born. With a return to recreational wolf hunting in the Lower 48 states, it was time to use some form of nonviolent and legal direct action to oppose the renewed hunting of wolves. I drew on my knowledge from past campaigns against trophy hunting which had begun with that first desert bighorn sheep hunt in the Mojave Desert of California in 1987. I had to learn from my mistakes and evolve if I was going to survive, just like the wild animals I fought for. I needed to find a way to oppose wolf hunting in the field without committing an act of hunter harassment or other crime.

With this objective in mind, I set out on a small speaking tour with a self-identified hunt saboteur from Oregon named Airrick. I had never heard of him but he claimed to be a representative from the British group, Hunt Saboteurs Association, and he was willing to coordinate a series of lectures, so together we set out on the road, visiting activist cafes and college campuses where I gave lectures on the renewed threats to wolves in the Rockies and Great Lake states. It was the first time in years that I had returned to the lecture circuit, only now my talks focused on what could be done legally to prevent the continued slaughter of wolves.

It was liberating to be speaking as an activist again, and to be speaking to other activists about the latest assault on the natural world. I was invited to speak at an animal liberation conference in Portland in the summer of 2014; as it turned out, this was not far from where the Earth First! movement's annual summer rendezvous was taking place in Northern California, so I drove out to attend both events and promote my latest wolf campaign. It was quite an eye-opener for me: the movement had certainly changed in the years I was absent. The younger generation was moving beyond environmental and animal defense, to include social justice and human welfare issues. On the one hand, this was good because it expanded the concern about human oppression; but on the other, it took the focus away from animals and nature.

Unfortunately, as soon as I left Oregon, I was contacted by one of the new editors of the *Earth First! Journal* and informed that some people at the rendezvous were "uncomfortable" with my presence and behavior at the event. I asked for details and names, and was only told that some folks didn't appreciate seeing me sharing my camp with one of the women I had met at the conference in Portland. The woman, in her thirties, had chosen to meet me at the rendezvous and stay with me, which apparently troubled some folks. It was only the beginning of my understanding that I would no longer be welcome in the movement that I helped build.

The new, inner politics of the radical environmental community were impossible to navigate unless you devoted much of your time to adhering to an unwritten code of behavior—one that excluded many older activists. Activists who were unfamiliar with the negative implications of mainstream phrases like "you guys" or "ladies" were condemned for not being more conscious of their language. So be it; who was I to judge? This was a new generation's movement now and I was hopeful that, in its own way, it would make the world better for the Earth and animals. Unfortunately, I soon learned that those were not the chief concerns of this new movement.

The Summer of 2014

Over the summer, I recruited a crew to go into Montana's backcountry to document the hunting of wolves just outside the boundary of Yellowstone National Park. This was where wolves from Canada were first reintroduced back into the park, heralding an era of ecological changes that humans were finally beginning to understand. Again, it was the ranching interests of Montana that were opposed to the return of wolves, with many taking the law into their own hands and illegally killing wolves they suspected or blamed for killing livestock. The truth was, indeed some wolves were killing livestock, but the state response to eradicate entire packs once a depredation occurred was extreme to say the least. Instead, the state of Montana authorized recreational hunting of wolves around Yellowstone and the entire state, with the season overlapping big game deer and elk seasons. This meant that, for a few extra bucks, a deer or elk hunter could purchase a wolf tag and shoot an animal if they happened to encounter a wolf during a hunt for a different species.

Photos started circulating of illegal wolf hunters posing with dead wolves, their faces covered with white sacks not unlike those worn by Ku Klux Klan members. Another early image was of a USDA wolf-trapper posing with a live wolf attached to a bloody foothold trap laying behind him. These visual messages were sent by many opposed to wolf reintroduction in the Rocky Mountain region. They did not welcome the return of the wolf like I did; they believed that they were eradicated for a reason, and that reason still existed. I spoke of this kind of hatred for an indigenous species and how it resembled the campaigns of eradication directed towards indigenous humans. That was why these renewed wolf hunts were being opposed by many indigenous nations—because they still reflected an imperialist and colonial belief that has been infecting this continent for centuries since the arrival of European explorers.

For me, it was about reversing the damage we now know we did when we targeted apex predators like the wolf, mountain lion, and other large carnivores. The large predators of North America were especially hated because they killed the domestic livestock so important to early settlers. By the early 20th century, the gray wolf had been all but eradicated from the Lower 48 states, although remnant populations survived in the Boundary Waters Area of Minnesota and a few in Northern Michigan. I, like many others, was raised with the lesson that wiping out an entire species to serve human needs was no longer acceptable, and that the ecological value of such species far outweighed any real threat posed by any animals continued existence in its native habitat. Yet, for many still raising cattle and sheep, or others hunting deer and elk, wolves were competitors for the same wild and domestic animals that humans wanted. A generation of men had already been raised on a landscape devoid of wolves, and many ranchers, farmers, and hunters preferred the absence of a predator that could threaten their sport or livelihood.

I was ready to dive into the controversy with an addition of quasi-hunt sabotage-like actions that I believed might thread the needle between illegal and legal actions. We would not be on the ground to interfere with any wolf hunting, but we would be there to document it from a legal and safe distance, so that we might show the world what the return to wolf hunting looked like—all with the hope that it would lead to greater public awareness and advocacy for the returning wolves across America. From Michigan, I raised funds and prepared for our September journey to the Yellowstone area. I would be driving out with a caravan of other activists I had met earlier that year in Oregon and Michigan. Most knew each other from other Earth First!-supported campaigns, but I had only known them a few months, at most.

We hiked into the backcountry from a remote trail head with the objective of locating the camp of licensed guides, who were leading clients into the national forests along Yellowstone's boundaries to catch trophy bull elk migrating from the park. Wolves following the elk were now being offered at an additional cost. We targeted one of the outfitters whose base was just outside of Gardiner, Montana. From there, they led hunters deep into the wilderness on horseback. When we reached our destination, we set up a base camp and began scouting for the guided hunters.

It felt great being back in the field in a remote wilderness area with others ready and willing to defend the wolves. I had been befriended by a Blackfeet medicine man, Jimmy St. Goddard, who gifted me with tobacco and instructed me in how to offer it as a protection for the wolves. This was just the first of what I hoped would be many campaigns in a new era of wildlife defense—one that would not end with us, or namely me, sitting in prison. The goal was not just to protect wolves, but to do so without the loss of our own freedom. Or at least, that was what I was selling to this ragtag group of mostly young activists that had followed me into the field.

In my lectures and around the campfire, I explained to people that in our fight to protect wildlife, we could accomplish much by utilizing the hunt sabotage tactics we had refined in Arizona. Only now, more could be accomplished through documenting controversial hunting and trapping practices rather than sabotaging, which ultimately lead to court cases and possible jail time. Instead, by acting as citizens monitoring these practices on public lands, we could ultimately contribute towards policy changes that would save more lives than we ever could in the field. Using the power of the camera was something Paul Watson had taught me, and it remained the best way to draw attention to the atrocities we were hoping to end.

Back in the wilderness, we were having a leisurely exploratory hike when I saw a single person on horseback approaching from down the trail. We ditched into the surrounding woods until the rider passed. This was surely someone headed to the guide's remote campsite. We waited, and after an hour, picked up the rider's tracks and followed them until they led to a campsite tucked away in the trees. We had located the hunters; now we just had to catch them on a hunt.

In the following days, we did encounter the hunters, but always as they were coming or going from a hunt. They did not suspect of us anything, and we gave them little reason to. In the end, we would only see the hunters take a bull elk, not any wolves, so we hiked out of the wilderness and met with a reporter who followed us on a patrol of the northern boundaries of the park. The article appeared on the cover of the Missoula paper, and was some proof to my crew that we could be effective without getting caught for anything illegal.

We ended our weeklong campaign on the high note of having successfully introduced a new kind of activism onto the scene: citizen monitoring of controversial hunting and trapping practices on public lands.

Our new crew met in the park and formulated our next plan, to document the Wisconsin wolf hunt which would begin on October 15, 2014. At this same time, I was interviewed for a job with the Center for Biological Diversity (CBD), to be part of their wolf education and awareness efforts. It was interesting and ironic timing. Here I was on the brink of launching a very new, grassroots, legal direct-action campaign, while at the same time being considered for a position with a national non-profit where I'd just be another employee, starting at the lowest level but with a regular paycheck. It was the organization that many of my former Earth First! friends had successfully settled into, litigating for wildlife with much more effect than we ever could as Earth First!ers. Still, for many of those I'd known in activist circles, paying jobs awaited in the many nonprofits dedicated to protecting wildlife, some with more effect than others and some with much more money.

In the end, the decisive issue wasn't bringing national attention to the wolf issue that CBD saw me accomplishing with the campaign to protect Yellowstone wolves; rather, it was the media's mentioning of my past conviction for ALF crimes that bothered them. They were concerned that associating themselves with such a controversial figure as myself might negatively impact their fundraising and public image. I'll never forget being told by CBD's endangered species director that their organization raised more funds for wolves than any other species. It appeared that, once again, what mattered most wasn't effecting real change as much as maximum fundraising; I was not very surprised.

So, instead, I continued preparing for our first field campaign in Wisconsin. We had settled on the names: Yellowstone Wolf Patrol and Great

Lakes Wolf Patrol; but in the end, the name that would be cursed by wolf-haters across the Midwest would be simply, Wolf Patrol.

In October, I again led a caravan of activists from Michigan north across the Upper Peninsula into northern Wisconsin. This time, Airrick from the Hunt Saboteurs would be joining me for the first time in the field, along with a handful of those activists that had been in Montana. We all met up at a campsite and broke up into groups to patrol the network of dirt roads that threaded county and state public lands. On this trip, I was accompanied by Joe Brown, a documentary filmmaker who was also a professor of videography at the nearby Marquette University. Joe wanted to make a documentary about Wisconsin's wolf hunt, and I believed that the more cameras we had, the better. I saw such a professional presence as part of our effort to achieve legitimacy as citizen monitors attempting to draw attention to an important issue, not to mention the protection that cameras offer against unkind attacks from those opposed to our witnessing of their behavior in the woods.

On the very first day of the wolf hunt, I returned to camp after having luckily discovered the location of a wolf trap. I found the other group of activists sitting in Airrick's rented vehicle, drinking beer and being grumpy about the direction the campaign was taking. We all gathered and held a meeting where Airrick and a few others expressed dissatisfaction with Joe's presence and our intention to making social media posts and YouTube videos. They wanted to do more than just take pictures. I explained that if they wanted to sabotage traps or interfere with the hunt, that it would be me, not them, that would be blamed for it and that this was a campaign to legitimize our right to expose the abuse of wildlife on public lands. We were operating with the knowledge that any illegal acts, however minor, would be used to again criminalize our efforts. I wanted my crew to know that they could save more wolves with video evidence of their suffering in traps than they could by sabotaging the traps themselves—an action which would inevitably lead to someone being charged with the crime and the state again knowing that our intent was criminal. This would unleash an unknown level of federal anti-terrorism attention towards our efforts to protect wildlife, thereby neutralizing any action whatsoever.

As frustrated as I was at the misunderstanding of the intent with Wolf Patrol, I still saw these folks as my friends. When they asked me if I was opposed to illegal action to sabotage the wolf hunt, I said absolutely not, as long as it wasn't anywhere near me! At that point, Airrick and most of the others hopped in the vehicle and left. The next day, we discovered a fabricated press release online that Airick with the hunt saboteurs claimed he had received. The statement alleged that hunt saboteurs had rescued a wolf from a trap in Wisconsin, and after taking it to a veterinarian(!), had released the animal. I was livid. I called Airick and told him his fake claim of actions were putting our crew in the field at risk. It was only us, not those who abandoned the campaign, who would be suspected of any such crime. He agreed to remove the press release; but his actions left me wary of anyone in this new animal rights movement.

But we were still a group of five after the split, so the remaining crew and I began setting up a trail camera that would film the wolf trap that two of our crew had seen a trapper setting. We had noticed the trapper taking his ATV down a forested trail and decided it would be best to send the two women in our crew along his path on foot with cameras, posing as birdwatchers. The women didn't walk far before coming on the trapper setting his trap. The two women listened as the trapper explained that he was setting a trap for a wolf without any suspicion that these two women were there exactly for that reason. Once we knew the trap location, we could set a camera with the goal of documenting any wolf getting captured.

One morning, as we patrolled county forest lands looking for other traps, we were parked on the shoulder of a dirt road when we heard an eerie sound that I had never heard before, yet I knew what it was—the howl of wolves. It wasn't the dark of night, in the shadow of a full moon, but mid-morning as we scanned tracks near a bog. In the distance, just out of visual sight came the low, long, drawn-out howls of a wolf, followed by other low howls nearby. Actually, this was the first time in my life I had ever heard wild wolves. Once in Vancouver, Canada, while on the Sea Shepherd's Divine Wind, we went into Stanley Park at night with a local who howled to the wolves imprisoned in the zoo there. But this was something different. There were no walls or bars separating us; these wolves lived in this place, and we were only visiting.

Wisconsin's 2014 wolf hunt only lasted a week, the quota being filled far more quickly than the state's Department of Natural Resources (WDNR) ever imagined. When the hunt came to a close, we monitored the wolf trap closely to ensure that the trapper removed it, as required by law. When he didn't, we reported it to the warden. The report led to an investigation, where our actions of monitoring the trap were not questioned, but only the actions of the trapper which we alone had documented. The trapper was given a verbal warning and I was invited to a meeting with WDNR officials to discuss our presence in the upcoming hound-hunt for wolves, which was set to begin December 1st.

Before our meeting with DNR, myself and our three remaining crew met at a cafe where everyone was given the opportunity to air their grievances. Matt and Stef were the two crew members who had shown a deep commitment to our campaign objectives and I valued their opinion on any developing problem amongst our crew. They now expressed concerns with some of Julie's behavior during the Yellowstone campaign. After our meeting, I was left with the decision to either ask Matt and Stef, or Julie, to step away from our new group and campaign. With just days before the hunt, I asked all three if they would participate in an accountability process to remedy their grievances with the other crew. Matt and Stef agreed, but Julie did not. I later learned that Julie had secretly recorded conversations she had with Matt and Stef in Yellowstone and that she was using these recordings to cast Wolf Patrol crew in a negative light to other activists. I never suspected Julie or any other crew member of being a cop, but I absolutely did not support anyone secretly recording conversations we were having in the field. The only recording we supported was that done to document the wolf hunting tactics we were opposing, so we could educate and advocate for an end to the hound hunt for wolves.

Meeting with the DNR

On November 20, 2014, we met with Wisconsin DNR officials at their headquarters in Madison, Wisconsin. The meeting was called by Dave Zebro, a supervisory warden I had spoken to after reporting the wolf trap violation back in October. DNR law enforcement officers expressed a willingness to outline the legality of wolf trapping and hound hunting of wolves, as well as answer any questions so that Wolf Patrol's citizen monitoring activities could have a greater law enforcement, as well as fact-finding value. We were also informed by DNR wardens patrolling the wolf hunt in October, that there were no complaints related to our monitoring activities. We were told that wardens had been patrolling us in October undercover. DNR wardens also welcomed our illegal hunting and trapping reports to their anti-poaching hotline. During the meeting, we informed DNR officials that in addition to patrolling for illegal wolf hunting, that our objective during the December hunt was the video documentation of the legal hound hunting of wolves as well. We always knew that if we could capture video images of hunting hounds fighting with a cornered or bayed wolf, that could help end such a cruel hunt.

Since we were new to opposing these controversial hunting practices, Wolf Patrol's intention in northern Wisconsin was to establish a working knowledge of what hound hunting for wolves actually was and what it looked like, so that we, as citizens, might better understand it as a wildlife management tool. We also wanted to understand the logistical complexities involved in enforcing hound hunting regulations and policing such a hunt involving dogs, multiple hunters, and vehicles. It was hoped that our monitoring would simply present the evidence that citizens could then use to educate themselves accurately. All our evidence we obtained would be free to use by any individual, group, or media outlet. We believed that *the truth* was all that we needed to present, and if the public saw dogs fighting with wild wolves, our objective would have been met.

During our meeting with DNR officials, specific concern was expressed for the stage of hound hunting when a wolf became exhausted from pursuit. Hound hunting of bears, mountain lions, or raccoons often ends with the pursued prey taking shelter in a tree. We questioned DNR wardens about this stage for wolves, and were told that in such instances, the wolf could effectively protect itself while causing injury to themselves and the dogs. We referenced the many fatal conflicts between hounds and wolves that occurred each summer and fall, but nothing was provided to assure us that hound hunters could control their hounds when far from their reach and in pursuit of, or cornering, a wolf. From our experience, the hounds were frequently out of the hunter's control and oftentimes, as is quite common, could not be easily located. Much was unknown about the hound hunting of wolves. Hence, the focus of our December monitoring of the hound hunt for wolves, was to determine whether hounds were indeed biting, attacking, or killing wolves while free-roaming in public lands in Zone 3 of the wolf hunt area.

In the previous year, 35 wolves were killed with the aid of dogs, all in Zone 3. That would be our first patrol area during the hunt. The Wisconsin wolf hunt quota in 2014 was 150 animals. By the time the hound hunt for wolves began on December 1, 146 wolves had already been killed by hunters and trappers. This meant that it was highly probable that the hunt would go over its quota with the new addition of hound hunters.

Wolf Patrol monitored hound hunts on three separate occasions during the five-day wolf hounding season, on December 2 and 3, when we encountered two separate hound hunting parties in Polk and Burnett counties. The monitored hunters were informed that they were being monitored by us, and there were no further interactions during the short encounter when no wolves were pursued with hounds.

During the monitoring, fresh wolf tracks and scat had been observed at locations where the hound hunters were stopping, so it was believed that wolves were or had been in the immediate area in the last 12 hours. Monitoring in the Polk County forest area was uneventful, with two patrol vehicles maintaining a buffer zone of 50 yards from the hound hunters when operating in the field.

It was no secret that Wolf Patrol was out in the woods monitoring wolf hunters—and they did not like it one bit. But we knew the difference between having an intent to interfere with a hunt and simply wanting to document controversial practices occurring on public lands against a recently recovered endangered species, and we knew we had a constitutional right to do it. Once Wisconsin's wardens knew our intent was not to break the law, they accepted our presence on the landscape and Dave Zebro would call me personally if there ever was a concern.

After following wolf hunters in the early days of the December hunt, the hounders decided to call the local sheriff. As I drove back into town after the patrol, I saw the sheriff's cruiser, so I decided to pull over and wait for them to turn around. The Deputy approached my truck and asked what I was doing in the area, and I explained exactly what we had told DNR officials in Madison about monitoring the hunt. I told the deputy who I was, gave him my card, and invited him to call me if he or the sheriff had any concerns. The deputy sent me on my way; moments later, I saw him questioning the hound hunters we had been following. They didn't look happy being questioned and having their licenses and dog registrations checked by the cops. I learned that the more time that hunters spent worrying about us following them, the less time they had to kill wolves.

While we were unable to document any physical encounters between hounds and wolves that year, we did observe on three separate occasions, the hound hunting of wolves, yet hunting hound and wolf interactions are at their worst in the *bear hound* training season which runs from July 1 to September 30, the day before bear hunting season begins. In 2014, 18 hounds were killed by wolves while bear hunters trained their dogs in known wolf rendezvous areas. It was less likely for wolves to attack bear hounds in winter, when bear hunters are not baiting bears, which also attracts wolves.

We had been following another wolf hunter we had hoped was thwarted from making a kill, only to find a photo on Facebook later that day of the same hunter holding a dead wolf by the hind legs as he stood on his truck. The hounder's kill brought the total take up to 149 wolves, just one shy of the total quota. We knew that the warmer weather and upcoming weekend would mean an increased number of hound hunters hunting, with a high probability of exceeding the statewide quota of 150 wolves. In the interest of keeping it at the limit, Matt, Stef, and I decided to try and pressure DNR to close Zone 3 to hunting before the weekend.

I called warden Dave Zebro and asked if, with the statewide quota at 149, whether the process had begun to close Zone 3 to wolf hunting. He informed me that the season would remain open despite the statewide quota. So, we immediately started contacting supporters and initiated a phone campaign, to respectfully request that DNR biologists begin the process to close Zone 3 to wolf hunting within the next 24 hours, due to the likelihood of exceeding the statewide quota of 150 wolves. Later that morning, Zebro called me back and said that the process had begun to close Zone 3 to wolf hunting at noon that day, before the weekend. A small victory! Zone 3 would be the only one in Wisconsin to close under quota, with only 30 of the allotted 40 wolves killed.

A proud hunter with his "kill"

Bottom line: Our first year in the field and we had not only avoided arrest, but we also managed to save the lives of ten wolves that would have surely been killed by hound hunters had the hunt remained open in our patrol area.

While we observed no illegality or cruelty in the hound hunt, what we did document was a recreational hunt for wolves that involved an excessive degree of technology that demonstrates unethical hunting and unfair chase. Primary to successful hound hunting is the use of vehicles in the pursuit of wolves. Hound hunters routinely hunt from their vehicles, something illegal in other big game hunting, and use cell phones to coordinate their activities.

This is not the only time satellite technology is used in wolf hunting with hounds. A common component in hound hunting today is the use of GPS-equipped dog collars that allow hound hunters to follow their dogs remotely from miles away. While this is convenient for the hunters, what it also does is reduce the amount of time a hound hunter is physically monitoring his/her animals. Every hound we ever observed in Wisconsin wore GPS collars.

What we also discovered in northern Wisconsin, was the blatant encouragement of illegal wolf hunting on social media sites, where frequent comments were posted during the wolf hunt encouraging Wisconsin residents to kill wolves out of season and "Shoot, shovel (bury), and shut-up." or "SSS," which is a frequently-spoken acronym on anti-wolf social media sites. Many of these kinds of statements originated from residents in northern Wisconsin who were actively engaged in big game hunting, not merely keyboard warriors from far away. We would soon learn that social media would be as good as any physical trail to find illegal and unethical hunting and trapping practices in Wisconsin.

After the wolf hunt was over, I got a call from the WDNR's wolf biologist, to whom we had directed our calls requesting an early closure. He wanted to let me know that, in all his years fielding calls from angry citizens about wolves, that our supporters were the politest callers he had ever encountered.

The only better thing that could have happened for wolves in Wisconsin in 2014, *did* happen in late December, when a federal judge returned the Great Lakes population of gray wolves to "protected status," thereby ending any future wolf hunts...for the time being. I was with my then 13-year-old son when I heard the news in Michigan, and practically cried with happiness. Wolf Patrol had nothing to do with the federal decision to re-list wolves, of course, but we had carved a place for ourselves on a landscape wrought with unethical hunting practices. Although wolves would be returned to federal protection, they would never be protected from the *illegal* threats that they continued to face every day. We had only scratched the surface of what we would soon discover was a haven for hunters and trappers—and a hell for the wolves and other native wildlife struggling to survive in the 21st century.

With only the funding from Wolf Patrol's GoFundMe page, we continued throughout the winter of 2014-15 to investigate wolf hunting and trapping as well as other organized predator hunts, especially coyote hunting with hounds. Our travels took us back to Montana where a known trapper by the name of Jason Maxwell was organizing what was being billed as the Great American Wolf Hunt. Dozens of hunters and trappers would be gathering to compare their kills, so we infiltrated the event with the hope of obtaining some graphic videos. In the end, only one wolf was brought into the contest, but we gained yet more confidence in our unconventional approach to opposing the renewed killing campaigns against wolves in the United States.

We weren't the only ones in Montana documenting controversial hunting practices. My old Earth First! friend, Mike Mease, had founded Buffalo Field Campaign (BFC) once the renewed campaign of extermination of wild bison from Montana began in the 1990s. Now there was a base camp in West Yellowstone where activists could be based during the bison hunting season. We worked with the BFC crew to infiltrate the wolf killing contest, and later that winter, a few crew members and I drove back to Montana to aid in the patrols of the bison killing areas immediately outside of Yellowstone Park—in the exact same area where we operated against the wolf hunt the previous fall.

Things had definitely changed in Earth First! The new people I met when I finished probation in 2013 were a different breed than those in the 1980s. I remembered a trivia contest an older friend of mine had done at the last Earth First! gathering I attended in 2013. He asked the mostly younger crowd in attendance who was Edward Abbey and other early movement icons. The crowd responded with yells, "He was a racist!," "A misogynist!," and so on. They repeatedly denounced folks I had met in the 1980s who inspired me to start my own ALF cell and fight back against the corporate destruction of the Earth that we all loved. I didn't want anything to do with people who had no respect for the elders who created our movement. I would continue without their support—but not without their attacks.

Beyond Matt and Stef, most of the dozens of crew members who served on Wolf Patrol campaigns weren't Earth First! or animal rights activists, they were simple citizens of rural areas sick and tired of the abuse of wildlife that they were witnessing in Wisconsin and other states.

We returned to Wisconsin and decided to begin investigating the hunting of coyotes with hounds which took place every winter with no season or bag limits. We had first heard of the practice after hounds being used to chase coyotes were killed themselves by the recolonized wolves of Wisconsin. Without wolves on the landscape, a generation of hound hunters had been raised hunting the Northwoods without fear of a predator larger than a coyote. Now with wolves returning to the landscape, more and more free-roaming hunting hounds were becoming wolf meals, and hounders got more and more angry, demanding a continuation of wolf hunting and killing, even illegally if necessary.

Hounds bay an exhausted wolf

We went back to the area of Luck, Wisconsin, where we patrolled during the wolf hunt and encountered some of the same hound hunters. They never called the sheriff, but they did swear and accuse us of running past stop signs—while they themselves sped throughout the countryside in multiple trucks, following unpredictable packs of hounds as they chased a coyote. Often, hounders would have to trudge through the snow to reach the place where their hounds had finally bayed an exhausted coyote. Sometimes the dogs did the killing; other times, hounders would wound the tired animal just to allow their dogs to safely attack it. This was but one of the annual practices taking place in Wisconsin that contributed to growing conflicts with recently re-listed gray wolves in the Great Lakes population.

The deadliest time of year for hunting hounds in Wisconsin is during the summer bear hound training season, which begins July 1st. Bear hound training is the term used to cover the practice of both running hounds on bear and baiting for bear as a method of obtaining a track for your hounds to follow. Every year beginning in May, about the same time black bears are emerging from hibernation, hound hunters in Wisconsin begin baiting for bears with an assortment of human food waste and food oil by-products that would give anyone a heart attack. Donuts, cookies, cereal, chocolate, candy, syrup, any past-due-date bakery item in Wisconsin often becomes bear bait. And it's completely legal to feed bears up to ten gallons of this crap every day, in as many bear baits as you can manage to refill. It's esti-mated that an average of about 4 million gallons of human food waste is fed to black bears in Wisconsin by bear hunters every year, with a study conducted by Wisconsin's Department of Natural Resources (WDNR) finding that as much as 40% of a wild black bear's diet in the Chequamegon-Nicolet National Forest of northern Wisconsin consists of such bear bait. The high calorie intake increases fertility in bears, leading to more four-cub litters, not to mention an artificial dependency on bait placed by hunters.

And the baiting isn't only attracting bears; deer and other wildlife come to feed from these man-made feeding stations, themselves attracting predators like wolves. We've documented wolf parents taking pups to bait sites to feed, and in such areas when bear hounds are released in July to chase the bears that have become accustomed to feeding from bear baits, wolves in the area will defend the area as both a feeding area and because of their protection of young pups, who have only just left their dens in July.

The ensuing literally thousands of hounds released to crisscross our national forests in Wisconsin annually result in about two dozen being killed and often eaten by wolves every year. The state provides compensa-tion for the hound hunters losses, to the tune of $2,500 per depredated hound. Often we would see the same bear hound hunter continuing to re-lease their dogs in areas where hounds have already been killed, surely knowing if it happened again, they would be compensated as usual, from the state Endangered Species Fund—whose funds are mostly generated from the sale of vanity license plates with pictures of wolves.

With a new (to us) Toyota Tacoma 4x4 truck purchased with grant funding from LUSH Cosmetics, Stef, a new crew member named Ben, and myself headed back to Polk County, Wisconsin, for opening week of bear hound training season. It didn't take long for us to find our first bear baits and the hound hunters using them, nor did it take long for them to find us. After just one encounter, they called the county sheriff. I remember driving down one of many dirt roads in the county forest, only to see two police cruisers coming from the other direction with their lights blazing.

I pulled over, knowing they were looking for us. They promptly exited their vehicles and came to my window, asking what I was doing in the area. I explained that we were monitoring bear baiting and hound training practices without any intent to interfere, and I told them about our agreement with WDNR's law enforcement division. The superior officer told me that their county prosecutor was informed of our activities and that, in this county, it was considered hunter harassment. I politely disagreed but told the officer he could issue me a citation if he thought I had violated any law. The two cops went back to their cruisers and minutes later came back to tell us that there was a "technical difficulty" and they couldn't issue us citations then, but they would the next day.

The next morning, we drove to the Sheriff's Department and asked the clerk on duty whether they had our tickets ready. The clerk said it was the first time someone had ever asked *them* for a ticket, but sadly, they did not have any for us. When we tried to call the officer, he was unavailable. It was clear that the sheriff was hoping we would be intimidated with the threat of a ticket, but knowing our rights, we were undeterred and continued patrolling. We had faced wolf hunters in Wisconsin, but not bear hound hunters, who were a unique breed. They operated often in large parties, sometimes with the entire family in tow, especially during the Fourth of July weekend.

We decided to head north to the Chequamegon-Nicolet National Forest (CNNF) where the bear-baiting study had taken place and also where a majority of bear hounds had been killed so far that year. When we got there, within the first hour we located 14 bear-baiting stations consisting of hollowed out logs filled with bait and covered with a "cookie" or lid cut from the round of a tree; often these were anchored with a rock which a large bear could easily roll off.

It was easy to find the many unlimited bear baits in the national forest; all we had to do was look at the "Wolf Caution Areas" on the WDNR's website, which were established once a hound had been killed by a wolf. They were an invisible 4-mile radius around the depredation site, and whenever we investigated such sites, we found the areas almost always had bear baits, which of course were also attracting wolves.

In addition to our in the field patrols, we also started attending Bear and Wolf Advisory Committee meetings. The committees were all hunters and trappers, and the clear goal of the committees was to increase hunting opportunities. Despite the obvious bias in favor of mostly bear hunters, we wanted them to know we would also be asking for greater restrictions on bear baiting. Behind the bear hunters was the Wisconsin Bear Hunters Association (WBHA), a member-based organization with a powerful political lobby. The WBHA worked closely with WDNR and they were very much aware of Wolf Patrol's arrival in Wisconsin. As soon as we began targeting bear hunters, the organization began lobbying for a stricter hunter harassment law that would make our citizen monitoring efforts illegal.

On opening day of Wisconsin's hound hunt for bear, we were in the Chequamegon-Nicolet National Forest monitoring the army of hound trucks following loose hounds. One hunter tried to intimidate us by blocking our truck with his own. I got out of my truck with a camera and thanked him for demonstrating intimidating behavior, which we could use for our YouTube channel—at which point he slowly backed away. Bear hunters began calling the local sheriff whenever they encountered us filming them, only to be told that we were not doing anything illegal. Instead, we used our knowledge of the minimal bear baiting regulations to investigate whether baits were in compliance with the regulations.

We also began collecting data on the number of bear baits within Wolf Caution Areas and the contents of the bait. Chocolate, which is toxic to bears and canids, was often an ingredient in bear bait, yet neighboring states like Michigan had already banned the toxin from being used as bear bait. We knew most states had already outlawed feeding bears, but of the 17 states that still allowed the practice, Wisconsin appeared to be the worst—and the only state where wolves were killing so many bear hounds.

Meanwhile on the political front, Wisconsin's bear hunters got their wish when Representative Adam Jarchow introduced "The Right to Hunt Act" in the Legislature, which went quickly through committee with just one opportunity for the public to provide testimony. We knew the law was written specifically for us, so I was obligated to speak in defense of my new group and our campaign tactics. We drove to the state capitol directly from our monitoring activities. Two busloads of bear hunters had been bussed in by the WBHA and we all were crowding into the capitol legislative floor to testify. One by one, the hunters testified about being stalked and harassed by Wolf Patrol, and Jarchow spoke of the group being led by "a convicted terrorist." When it came time for me to speak, I recounted that had any of the allegations against Wolf Patrol been true, we would have surely been cited for violating any law we broke. But we had never been cited for anything. The only purpose of this law was to stop us from exposing the preventable conflicts with wolves that were steadily increasing because of bear baiting and hounding.

Wolf Patrol at the Capitol

That winter, we began investigating the many wildlife killing contests taking place in Wisconsin—especially those in the Northwoods where coyote killing contests could easily become illegal *wolf* killing expeditions. Another crew member and I arrived early, and we went to a bar in Argonne, Wisconsin, where the contest was going to be held the following day. We were having a beer when a senior citizen asked me if I was there for the contest. I said I was. We spoke for a short time before he departed; but when he returned, he was pissed off and wanted to fight me. Apparently, he had realized that we were Wolf Patrol and not just some casual attendees.

The next day, while investigating human-made trails in the snow in the Chequamegon-Nicolet National Forest, we discovered five treble fishing hooks hidden inside some chunks of raw meat. Each baited hook was dangling from fishing line that had been tied a couple feet off the ground, and located on trails where wild canids like wolves and coyotes could find them. We had heard of such cruel methods. Among the many anti-wolf social media sites on Facebook were some in Wisconsin that told of ways to illegally kill wolves, and this was one of them. We reported the illegal and deadly baits, and then stayed until an investigating warden removed them. Later I tried calling the FBI—me, the "terrorist"!—to report the illegal attempt to kill endangered gray wolves, but I never received a return call. I guess they didn't care about my activism unless they could come after me for it.

Summer Comes Around

In the summer of 2016, a greater number of hounds than normal were killed by wolves while being released from bear-bait sites to chase bears during the hound training season. We returned to the Wolf Caution Areas on the Bayfield Peninsula to investigate—only this time, we had to contend with the new "Right to Hunt Act" which had been signed into law on April 1st by then-Governor Scott Walker while he attended the Wisconsin Bear Hunters Association annual conference. Now the WBHA was sending out postcards to all of its members, alerting them to the new law and misinforming hunters that it was now illegal to follow and film them.

One day, we were following an out-of-state hunter on a dirt forest road as his dozen loose hounds followed behind his truck. When the hounder realized we were behind him, he jumped out of his truck and started yelling that we better not be filming him. When he saw the camera in my hand, he began demanding my film. I climbed onto the top of my truck and continued filming him as he attempted to climb up towards me. There was no way I was giving him the SD cards recording the event. I would never turn over my camera; they'd have to beat me up if they wanted it. When I reached for the shovel I kept in my truck, he retreated.

Immediately after the incident, I contacted David Zebro with the WDNR Warden Service. I told him that WBHA had been misinforming its members that our citizen monitoring was now illegal, and with the season now in full swing, more bear hunters would be accosting us, misbelieving that what we were doing was illegal. There was clear language in the new bill language that clarified that someone violating the Right to Hunt Act had to have an intent to interfere with hunting, which our monitoring was never intended to do. Hence, despite the new law stating that filming hunters was questionable, we knew our constitutional rights guaranteed us protection for filming on public lands where there was no reasonable expectation of privacy. Zebro agreed that the situation could easily escalate to violence and suggested a meeting between WDNR, US Forest Service law enforcement, and the local county sheriff's department. Zebro told us that the Chief Warden would personally be meeting with WBHA officials who were refusing to meet with Wolf Patrol.

We drove to the county sheriff's office in Bayfield, where we met with about eight law enforcement representatives from federal, state, and local departments. I explained the nature of our monitoring and that our intent was to gather evidence to provide to US Forest Service officials on the impacts of the unlimited bear baiting occurring on our national forest lands.

Next, WDNR wardens explained that some of our monitoring was very close to the line on interference. The wardens lowered a projection screen and played one of our YouTube videos that I recently had posted. During this particular patrol, we had been monitoring radio communications between bear hunters like always, when we heard that they were in pursuit of a bear. We could identify the area they were in on our maps, so we drove to where we expected the bear would exit the woods. We parked exactly where the bear exited, followed by the hounds in pursuit. The hounder then showed up to try and retrieve his dogs, and found us in the spot he was headed towards. I asked the wardens what was a reasonable distance to maintain between us and the hounders we were monitoring. We agreed that 50 yards was reasonable, and they agreed to communicate this to WBHA officials. The seasoned older County Sheriff told us what he tells his officers: if you are in danger, get out of there, even if what you are witnessing is illegal. Safety was his biggest concern. He also told me I would make a good warden! It was the best compliment I had ever received since starting Wolf Patrol, and it came from a cop!

Friendly feds... (with Matt, Jeremy, and Rod)

The death toll at that point was 34 bear hounds killed by wolves so far in 2016, when the hound hunt for black bear began in September. We positioned ourselves in the heart of the overlapping Wolf Caution Areas that had been established following the bear hound depredations. On opening day, it wasn't only hound trucks plying the roads in the early morning

hours; in addition to our patrol vehicles, the US Forest Service had decided
to dispatch a cadre of law enforcement to also monitor bear hunters. We
couldn't have been happier. Without our monitoring efforts, bear hunters
were having free rein in our national forests. Now, with the attention we
generated about the conflicts created by bear hunters, forest officials were
taking action. Instead of criminalizing our actions, the WBHA's efforts
had galvanized law enforcement to *recognize* and *admit* that we had as
much right to be doing what we were doing in the forest as the bear hunters
did. In just two years, Wolf Patrol had become a force to be reckoned with,
and one that would not be easily swayed from our task of protecting the
recolonizing wolves of Wisconsin.

Pipeline Protest

With our citizen monitoring of the 2016 Wisconsin bear hunt in my rear-
view mirror, I next took some time away from Wolf Patrol to return to my
old home on the run, the Standing Rock Indian Reservation—home of Sitting Bull's Hunkpapa Lakota and the McLaughlin family who sheltered
me while I was a fugitive from the law in 1992. This time I'd be returning
to the largest protest and occupation I would ever see in my life: The No
Dakota Access Pipeline movement that had begun earlier that year.

The movement began when plans were released to route a pipeline
across the Missouri River and various sacred sites, including burial
grounds. One of the main protest camps was led by LaDonna BraveBull
and her husband Miles, two of the first indigenous resistors I had ever met
way back in 1992, when we sat together drinking coffee in their kitchen in
North Dakota and recounting our experiences with anti-indigenous racism.
Now the Standing Rock Reservation became an ocean of resistance as indigenous people and their supporters poured onto the traditional lands of
the Hunkpapa Lakota to occupy the pipeline construction site and resist
desecration of sacred lands.

I volunteered to drive with my girlfriend, who was a member of the
medic team assembled to serve the growing occupation. As we approached
the reservation, along the state highway that led to the protest, we encountered a full-scale US military blockade with concrete blocks in place to
force all traffic to slow to a halt. At the roadblock, soldiers asked where we
were headed before allowing us to pass. It was a harsh reality, revealing our
government's instinctual response to an uprising by any people, regardless of
the cause or justification. When the people rise, the state must crush them.

After passing through the roadblock, we next passed a portion of the pipeline construction site that was covered in anti-DAPL graffiti and slogans declaring this land as sacred. When we crested the rise of the hill before the main encampment, I saw something I thought I'd never see in my life: a camp with literally thousands of people from all over the world, mainly indigenous, who were gathered to defend our Earth Mother with their own bodies, if necessary. I'd be lying if I didn't reveal that the sight brought me to tears. Flags from every indigenous nation lined the main road leading into camp, which was filled with tipis and tents and the sound of drums and singing. I had never witnessed a gathering of so many indigenous people, let alone for an act of resistance.

After setting up camp, we walked through the occupation area and I found old friends from past resistances and new friends I had yet to meet. I thought of the indigenous elders I had known—people like Anselmo Valencia Tori, Albert White Hat, and Pat McLaughlin. I knew they were there with us, as were the spirits of so many other ancestors. My visit came before the worst attempts to crush the massive protest would begin, when our very presence wasn't just a protest, but a celebration of the centuries of resistance and survival that made our presence that day possible. Now it was our time to fight for what we believed in.

I didn't want to ever leave. I could have easily shifted my entire focus from wolves and the Northwoods of Wisconsin to joining this historic resistance, but I knew as I always have, that my most important constituents were those with four legs not two—those without the ability to rise against human oppression themselves. But here was the kind of movement I had always wanted. It was one where the collective wisdom and knowledge of indigenous peoples was seen not as a threat, but instead as a roadmap towards a more sustainable future. I drank it all in; and as night came, I drifted off to sleep in my tent to the sounds of drums, laughter, and singing. A few days later, when I reluctantly had to pack up to leave, a Lakota man yelled from the riverbank, "Remember! Tell your friends what it feels like to be free!" The experience changed me forever; it showed me that mass occupation and protest was still possible.

Return to Wisconsin

Upon my return to Wisconsin, I enrolled as a volunteer tracker for the state's Large Carnivore Survey whereby public trackers patrolled forest roads in winter to record wolf tracks. The information was then used to formulate a census of Wisconsin's growing wolf population. I would drive up to northern Wisconsin and spend my free weekends tracking wolves while also keeping an eye out for coyote hunters who were using dogs to hunt in the winter when tracking animals was easier. In January of 2017, a wolf was illegally killed and dumped just over the state line in Michigan, probably to confuse investigating wardens.

We decided to investigate this other portion of the Chequamegon-National Forest, where I suspected the wolf poachers had originated from. We were driving down the state highway where the wolf had been found when we saw a man dressed in winter camouflage standing on the yellow line in the middle of the road. When I slowed down to hear what he had to say, he began to accuse us of harassing him, even though *we* had to slow down to avoid hitting *him* as he stood in the highway. He demanded that we wait until law enforcement arrived and started yelling at one of our crew members, before he finally departed. We waited, but no cops ever arrived. We had found another portion of the national forest where both bear and coyote hounders operated, and they both hated the wolves that were killing their dogs. Following the wolf poaching, Wolf Patrol began a reward program, offering $1,000 for any information that led to a wolf poaching conviction; we began posting reward posters across northern Wisconsin.

In the summer of 2017, the Animal Legal Defense Fund filed a federal lawsuit challenging the Right to Hunt Act, and naming two of our crew as plaintiffs in the case. The lawsuit clearly argued that the new law's prohibitions on filming were restrictive to the constitutional rights of our crew and the journalists we carried into the field. In every state where hunter harassment statutes were challenged, they were often overturned because they gave favorable legal protections to hunters, but not others using public lands. It would be years before a final ruling, but it would come; and when the Right to Hunt Act was overturned, again our citizen monitoring efforts in Wisconsin would be vindicated.

One of the interesting developments with Wolf Patrol's new presence on the Wisconsin landscape was that most of our support came from rural residents in the areas we patrolled. I had thought I needed the support of the radical environmental community, but in the end, what made our tactics so effective were that they were supported by local residents. These weren't folks opposed to hunting itself, but they were opposed to hounds trespassing on their land and disturbing their peace. One such supporter was a bear hunter himself who had been targeted by hound hunters because he didn't allow them on his lands. This hunter told me that once he started pissing off hounders, the locks on his gate were glued and threats were made to burn down his summer cabin. We accepted the hunter's invitation and spent the weekend documenting bear hound trespass on private property. This would be another angle to attack hound hunting, one that resonated with the many rural residents experiencing bear-hound trespassing.

In January 2018, when winter rolled around, we returned to patrolling national forest lands for coyote and bobcat hound hunters. We were in the same area where we had earlier been accosted by the angry hound hunter when we encountered a large hound hunting party operating on the edge of national forest lands. When I tried to drive down the forest road to investigate, a hound hunter blocked my path with their truck. As more hounders arrived, they formed a barricade around our truck with their vehicles, demanding that we were interfering with their hunt. At one point, when I got out of the truck, a hound hunter began rolling his truck towards me until it was touching my body. I slammed my fist on his hood, creating a nice dent and the hounders went wild with anger. They began bumping chests with our cameraman and threatening to beat the shit out of us. When the police arrived, both groups were separated and their stories heard by the deputies. In the end, the deputies demanded that we turn over our film. While we argued with them, we subtly removed the SD cards from our main cameras and only turned over footage from our GoPro cameras. It would be months before the cameras were returned, but we did get them back and we again were not charged with any crime.

Needless to say, I became one of the most hated people by hound hunters in Wisconsin. While our efforts began with a focus on the wolf hunt, once wolves were returned to federal protections, we uncovered the source of most wolf conflicts—and it was hound hunters releasing their thousands of dogs every year into reclaimed wolf territory. Now we were exposing not only bear baiting, but the vicious practice of coyote hunting with hounds, illegal wolf killings, and wildlife killing contests taking place annually in Wisconsin.

Yet, while I was reviled by many, there were a few hound hunters that I befriended after conversations revealed a common love for being outdoors. I had no problem with these guys, so long as they obeyed all wildlife laws and didn't promote illegal killing of wolves. These hunters recognized that bad behavior by one hound hunter would eventually hurt every hound hunter. It was also these friendlier hound hunters who told me that it was commonly other hound hunters who were creating bigger problems for them than we were causing with our patrols. These hunters complained that while they had been hunting in the same area their entire lives, others were now coming in and trespassing, and sometimes even sabotaging other bear hunters' baits.

In February, five pro-hunting and anti-wolf legislators from Wisconsin penned a public letter to the DNR demanding that I be held accountable for my actions of harassing hunters and that I no longer be allowed to participate as a volunteer in the annual Large Carnivore Survey. Ironically, the same politicians were sponsoring legislation that would have cut funding for the survey and DNR law enforcement. Here is the content of that letter:

> *Today, several state legislators call on environmental terrorist and convicted felon Rod Coronado to be held responsible for his most recent aggressive confrontations with hunters.*
>
> *Rod Coronado has a past riddled with violent and inappropriate behavior. Most notably he admitted to firebombing a research building at Michigan State University in the 1990s, destroying more than three decades of research and causing millions of dollars in damage. He's been involved in sinking whaling ships, breaking into facilities to impair important research, and was charged with half a dozen Animal Liberation Front attacks. It seems his disruptive path continues.*
>
> *In 2013, Coronado turned his focus to denying the constitutional rights of hunters and outdoor enthusiasts. He has been wreaking havoc in the Midwest ever since. The group Coronado leads, Wolf Patrol, has spent their time harassing*

individuals across northern Wisconsin exercising their constitutional rights to hunt. ...

We, as a legislature, stood with sportsmen across Wisconsin in condemning these types of aggressions by passing the Right to Hunt Act. Despite that fact, the Wolf Patrol has continued to disrupt legal hunting and agitate hunters. In late January, near Laona, Coronado and his crew once again had an aggressive confrontation with hunters. ... We hope that Coronado and all involved in disrupting legal hunting are held responsible for their actions and prosecuted to the fullest extent of the law.

We are calling on the DNR to not allow Coronado to participate in the winter wolf tracking and summer wolf howling surveys as part of the wolf tracking program. We also call on members of the environmental community to follow the lead of Wolves of Douglas County in denouncing Coronado and his actions. Let the repudiation of Mr. Coronado bind us as a community that will no longer allow the systematic abuse of human life.

It didn't surprise me that these legislators, the same who had endorsed the Right to Hunt Act, were now launching a personal campaign against me. What bothered me was that my opponents in Wisconsin were capitalizing on the allegations made against me by Earth First! and attempting to use them to cut off support from the environmental community, which never really existed anyhow. "Wolves of Douglas County" was the only group to take the bait, but its founder and I had already distanced ourselves from each other over tactics. What really saddened me was that they were targeting something that I loved to do: track wolves and other animals in winter. Since my divorce, I had not been allowed to see my daughter, and losing my larger family pitched me into depression. Living in Michigan was something I only wanted to do because it is where I could have my own family. But once it was just my son and I, often I would be alone. I used my free time to reconnect with the wild nature of the Northwoods and began falling in love with the area we frequently patrolled in Wisconsin. Spending long days driving remote wilderness roads in winter wasn't only peaceful, it was healing. I worried that it would only be a matter of time before I was kicked out of the tracking group.

"Wanted"

Online Activism

I took my sadness and frustration and turned it into fuel for a new kind of citizen monitoring campaign; this time, we would begin investigating illegal hunting activities online, or at least the evidence of them. One of the women living in rural Wisconsin that I met in 2014 had created a fake Facebook profile for a Wisconsin hound hunter, and then began friending every other hound hunter she could find in the state. By 2018, the fake account became one of those entrenched in the hound hunting community, documenting all of the year's hunting activity of those who maintained Facebook pages. The online sleuth had already discovered numerous videos filmed by Wisconsin hound hunters, documenting cruelty and abuse of bobcats, coyotes, raccoons, and other wildlife.

So, the very next day after reading the letter against me from legislators, Wolf Patrol launched its "Wildlife Crimes Cyber Division" and began publishing videos of hound hunters abuses in Wisconsin. Every day, I would release another video detailing horrific abuse by hound hunters, mostly towards coyotes. The coyote hound-hunting season was in full swing and suddenly hound hunters were desperately trying to sanitize their personal Facebook pages once it became known that there was a mole in the community. I was also contacted again by WDNR's warden, David

Zebro, who condemned the treatment of wildlife I was highlighting and promised that there would be criminal investigations. With little effort, I took the legislators' attack on Wolf Patrol and used the attention to again demonstrate what it was we were exactly doing in Wisconsin: uncovering and exposing illegal behavior towards public trust wildlife.

By mid-March, just two weeks into the "Wisconsin's War on Wildlife" video campaign, authorities announced criminal charges were being filed against one of the Wisconsin hound hunters we were highlighting in our campaign. His videos depicted his hounds viciously attacking raccoons and other wildlife, something we knew many hound hunters were doing, but until now, hard to prove.

Once I had weaponized the fake Facebook account (yes, it still exists and the identity has yet to be compromised!), in addition to long days in the field, I now spent countless hours trolling Facebook for other wildlife violations. They weren't only in Wisconsin either. I began calling wildlife law enforcement in other states where I found evidence of violations on personal Facebook pages of hounders in Michigan, Idaho, Illinois, Pennsylvania, and even Florida. In March 2018, I reported bear hounder Bo Wood to Florida's Fish and Wildlife Commission. Bo's Facebook page was filled with videos of his running hounds on bear in Florida, where it was illegal. After reporting him, I was contacted by Florida authorities and told that there was a current investigation already underway. On December 19, 2018, Bo Woods and eight others were charged and arrested in Florida on counts of conspiracy to commit racketeering, animal cruelty, illegal baiting, and the taking of a black bear.

At that time in my life, it was not uncommon to have a law enforcement agent call me about a report I had made earlier. After all the years of evading law enforcement in my efforts to protect wildlife, now conservation officers and game wardens were my familiar allies. Again, with only a handful of committed warriors, I was able to find a safe and sustainable form of direct action that could be used to defend persecuted native wildlife. And we were doing it all with very little money and almost no support from any environmental or animal protection movements, most of whom were more focused on fundraising than protecting animals.

I never paid myself for all my work; and most of the funding for Wolf Patrol came from Wisconsin residents in donations ranging from $5 to $50. Most of our budget went for gas. My regular 10-hour drives to northern Wisconsin, not to mention patrolling hundreds of miles of forest roads, was our biggest carbon footprint. Joe Brown, our videographer and documentarian, taught me how to create short videos and even donated the $5,000 camera that was on loan from Marquette University, where he taught and managed the Video Department. Our opponents in Wisconsin created Facebook pages targeted at us, with names like "Anti-Wolf Patrol" and "The Wolf Pack." Sites like these demonstrated that we were having an impact on the culture of hound hunting in Wisconsin, and that we had successfully created a culture of fear, whereby hounders were beginning to even be suspicious of each other. Talk about turning the tables!

Back in Forest County, Wisconsin, which had become our stomping grounds, we continued to document bear baiting and the corresponding conflicts with wolves. It didn't bother us to know that many of the hound hunters that hated us the most also hunted this portion of the national forest, or that this was the only place our cameras had ever been seized. This was where wolves were returning, to a place they had been eradicated—and a place where many people wanted them eradicated again.

In addition to my most-trusted crew members, Matt and Stef, who lived in Wisconsin, I had found other highly skilled crew for our controversial patrols. From the Red Lake Band of Chippewa (Anishinabe) came Jack Baz, a member of the Bear Clan who, with his partner Sophie, joined me on patrols and, more importantly, rescued me when my patrol vehicle broke down.

There were other indigenous supporters who we built relationships with, like Mike Wiggins Jr, the then-chairman of the Bad River Band of Lake Superior Chippewa. We were patrolling national forest lands near his reservation one summer disguised as hound hunters, with a dog box in the bed of our truck and the high antenna from our CB scanner, both signature giveaways. We had stopped for lunch by a small pond when Mike came over and asked what we were doing. I knew he was most likely going to be an ally, so I told him the truth, that we were monitoring hound hunters and opposed to the bear baiting occurring throughout the area. Mike then said, "Well, in that case, let me shake your hand. I thought you were someone else!" Later Mike would put our crew up in the tribe's casino hotel for the opening weekend of the hound hunt for bear.

Another invaluable crew member and friend that I made in Wisconsin was Jeremy. Like most of my crew, Jeremy had no activist background, wasn't vegetarian or vegan; he simply cared deeply for wolves and all the other wildlife he saw growing up in Wisconsin. Jeremy was a deer hunter but he also rescued cats in Green Bay where he lived. Like me, he was hated online where he was very good at antagonizing Wisconsin's hound hunters. His online persona differed greatly from who he really was.

We first met Jeremy when we encountered him on remote forest roads, also patrolling for hounders during another coyote-killing contest. After that, he began showing up at our base camp, fully equipped and fully willing to follow us on our dangerous adventures. I felt like we were a wolf pack ourselves. We had found each other for the common purpose of not ours, but the wolves' survival. In order to protect them, we moved about secretly through the woods pursuing our prey. We hunted the hounders. Jeremy brought with him not only years of backwoods knowledge, but a familiarity with firearms and a willingness to always be armed and prepared, should any of our crew members become seriously threatened. Over the years, I would be getting a tongue lashing from some hounder, as Jeremy slowly surveyed the scene and silently positioned himself in a place to intervene, should a threat escalate. He never had to draw his gun, but seeing his hand casually resting inside of his camo jacket always gave me a sense of security.

One beautiful fall day on the last day of the hound hunt for bear in our patrol area, Jeremy and I were cooking some venison from a roadkill deer I had salvaged. I've always, whenever possible, pulled dead wildlife off roads so that other wildlife isn't attracted to the carcass and also killed. In some of these situations, I've also collected salvageable flesh for my own consumption, always believing as my elders taught me, that by sustaining ourselves with our animal relations, we maintain our sacred connection to them. In my Yaqui culture, deer are a sacred relation, and I've always taken great care to show them respect, especially when I'm pulling victims off the battlefield that our roads are to animals.

On this particular night, Jeremy and I had concluded another season of patrols with plenty of tense confrontations and we were now simply relaxing and enjoying the serenity of the wilderness that had become our second (if not first) home. As we sat back in our camp chairs watching the fire, a long low howl arose, very close by, from the surrounding forest. The one howl was followed by other low rolling howls as other members of what we lovingly called The Firekeeper Pack checked in with each other, and us. We had seen fleeting glimpses of wolves as they crossed roads in front of us and often saw them on our trail cameras. But hearing wolves is truly special—something I wish everyone could experience. It was as if there were people, just out of the sight of our fire's light, peering out from behind the trees, calling to us. I took the venison I was cooking and placed it on a plate and started walking towards the howls. When I reached the edge of the woods, tears were streaming down my face as I lay my offering gently onto the Earth. I wished it was the whole deer, not just this small portion, but I think they understood.

A New Hunt is Approved

By the end of the 2019 bear-hound training and hunting seasons in Wisconsin, 21 hounds were killed by wolves in 19 separate bloody fights. It was a predictable yet preventable outcome. Every year we reported on the bear hound and wolf conflict, and on the illegal killing of wolves it was causing, but little to nothing ever changed because of the political power of hunters and their control of the Natural Resources Board and every other committee setting wildlife policy in the state. In Wisconsin, there is a "Conservation Congress" whereby any citizen can put forward a resolution to change hunting, trapping, or fishing regulations. It's a good idea, but every resolution must first pass through committees of sportsmen adamantly opposed to any rules changes that negatively impact their constituents. As a result, every year Wolf Patrol supporters or other wildlife advocates successfully introduced resolutions limiting bear baiting or wildlife killing contests, they would be predictably denied.

In what we always knew was going to be a likely outcome, on October 29, 2020, federal officials announced the latest delisting of gray wolves from endangered and threatened wildlife protections, once again placing wolves under state, not federal management in Wisconsin, Michigan, and Minnesota. The announcement came after years of political pressure from state legislators sympathetic to the gun and trophy-hunting lobby in Wisconsin and other states. Wolves in the Great Lakes were placed under federal protection in December 2014, after having been returned to state management in 2012. In that short time, Wisconsin conducted three recreational wolf seasons in 2012-2014, "legally" killing over 500 wolves. The new delisting by US Fish & Wildlife meant that Wisconsin's wolves could once again be legally hunted. In recent years, a *mandatory* recreational wolf hunt was legislated by the state, stating that anytime wolves are under state management, the state's Department of Natural Resources must facilitate a public wolf hunt, including with the use of hounds.

Wisconsin's Department of Natural Resources (WDNR) was not in full agreement that there should be a hastily-organized wolf hunt, although some politicians were calling for one to begin immediately. Legal counsel for the state advised that a poorly-organized hunt could hurt relations with tribal authorities who were opposed to the hunt. Despite the loud calls of opposition from tribal officials and many residents who spoke out against a wolf hunt, the DNR Board rubberstamped the hunt and set the opening day as February 22, 2021.

I scrambled and put the call out for warriors. What had always upset me was the feeling of many wolf advocates that Wisconsin's wolves were only now being threatened. No one sounded the alarm when bear hunters were poisoning wolves in the years leading up to 2021. Yet many of those same groups regularly raised money to protect the wolves of Wisconsin. Now with wolves again in the crosshairs, the Humane Society of the United States (HSUS) and other groups were calling for legal action to stop the hunt. None came. No other organization would be witnessing the actual wolf hunt; Wolf Patrol was the only nonprofit actually on the ground. No one from Earth First!, no one from the Hunt Saboteurs or any other animal rights group responded to my calls for help. We were on our own.

Thankfully, Stef, Matt, and Jeremy did show up—the three people who had been by my side on dozens of dangerous patrols in hostile Wisconsin country. Now we gathered at a rented cabin near Eagle River on the eve of the hunt, recharging camera batteries, pouring over maps and talking strategy. This would be possibly the largest hound hunt for wolves in Wisconsin's history. Over 100 hound hunters had drawn permits and would be hitting the ground in areas where their own bear hounds had been killed. This wasn't a recreational hunt; it was a *revenge hunt*.

We couldn't be everywhere with just four people, so we chose to focus on protecting the areas and the wolf packs we knew best: the Firekeepers. Our patrol area in the Forest County portion of the Chequamegon-Nicolet National Forest was continuing to be a flashpoint for human/wolf conflicts and we knew they would be out in force.

It would be yet another against-all-odds battle in what had become a decades-long personal war against the abusers of indigenous North American wildlife. Again I would be facing unsurmountable odds, but I would not be alone. By my side would be warriors I could trust and who I knew were ready to put their own lives on the line to protect animals that by now had become our own relations. This wasn't an ALF action, but as we again prepared for battle with little more than cameras as our weapons, it sure did remind me of one.

With my son now in college and my daughter living with her mom in Arizona, there was nothing left for me in Michigan, so I moved to Vermont to begin a new chapter in my life. Now I made the 20-hour drive from Vermont to northern Wisconsin, where I rendezvoused with Stef, Matt, and Jeremy.

The Hunt Begins

With very little sleep, as soon as I arrived in the Chequamegon-Nicolet National Forest where we had been patrolling and protecting wolves for the last five years, we took to the snow-covered roads to scout for wolf hunters, trappers, and hounders. Like those trying to kill wolves, we also knew the hunt areas would focus on those regions where dozens of bear hounds were being killed by territorial wolves protecting their families. We quickly found a discarded deer carcass that would probably be used as bait in one of the areas where our trail cameras were monitoring a newly-formed pack of wolves.

Before dawn on the first day of the hunt, we drove to national forest lands where we had earlier seen tire tracks and footprints. We drove slowly until we noticed the location where a vehicle had stopped and someone had gotten out and walked into the woods. At the very first site we stopped to inspect, we detected a strong aroma in the air, like a scent lure used by a trapper. As we walked back to our truck to get flashlights, Jeremy stepped on a hidden foot-hold trap intended for a wolf—he wasn't hurt, thankfully. It wasn't our intention to interfere with any trappers or hounders; we were again there to monitor and document the hunt for the world to see and judge. We were there to bear witness to atrocities. Like the motto on my old Greenpeace membership card from 1977, we knew we couldn't stop the hunt, but maybe, through education, we could help prevent another from happening.

We now knew that a trapper was setting his traps along the forest road, hidden just feet from the tire tracks, where any animal or even person might step on them. In total, we located 14 separate traps set for wolves. We placed trail cameras near a few, and had one camera stolen and another tampered with. When I checked the camera, I could see and hear someone fumbling with the on/off switch, saying, "Fucking Paw Patrol."

With knowledge of trap locations now included on regularly scheduled patrols, we turned our focus to hound hunters. We easily found two separate groups, but they had found no wolves to pursue, which surprised us. We would learn that the hounders were looking for the tracks of solo wolves, not multiple wolves traveling in a pack. Sending their hounds after a pack of wolves in winter would surely end badly for the dogs. Once we realized this, whenever we encountered tracks of lone wolves on the snow-covered roads, we hopped out with brooms and swept away the tracks.

Within hours of the hunt beginning, there was a trickling of reported wolf kills. But at the same time, all over the social media pages of Wisconsin's hunters and trappers, a call was made to not report your kill so that the hunt would remain open. Many were saying, "Shoot or trap a wolf, then keep hunting." The blatant calls for illegal hunting did not surprise us. Nowhere have I seen a stronger culture of support for poaching than I have in northern Wisconsin. Later, I discovered that a convicted poacher who had had his own hunting privileges revoked, went on multiple wolf hunts during the 2021 hunt. I reported his violations to WDNR wardens, who took the case back to the prosecutor in the original case and came back with the excuse that Tyler Belott, the hounder in question, wasn't aware he couldn't continue hunting. I supplied multiple photos from Belott's Facebook page showing him engaged in hunts during his term of revocation, but prosecution never came.

In another criminal incident, we had discovered a cow calf carcass being used as bait at a trap site. We were told that it wasn't illegal to use a carcass for bait, as long as it was 25 feet away from the actual trap. But it was illegal to dump livestock carcasses without a permit, and the trapper's use of a livestock carcass would eventually be recognized as violation— but again, one that the warden chose not to prosecute. We had discovered some wolf traps set literally two or three feet off roads and clearly visible. We documented the trap sites immediately adjacent to public roads and began publishing our findings on YouTube, calling on the public to express their dissatisfaction with the hastily organized hunt. Our YouTube channel became known to local media outlets on the first day of the hunt, as they were looking for reports from on the ground during the hunt. Our videos began to appear on the news.

On the second day of the hunt, as we checked trap lines, we noticed that a few of the traps had been sprung. I thought it was unintentional, until we got to the location of the trap featured on the local news the previous night. At this trap site, there were multiple burning incense sticks placed in the snow around the trap. We surmised that someone wanted to sabotage the trap site without actually touching the trap. It was clever! But it was also illegal, and I knew we would again be suspected of any actual sabotage if it occurred during the hunt. We also heard media reports of traps being sabotaged in other parts of the state, which we of course had nothing to do with either.

We did, however, engage in one instance of hunt "sabotage" (more like, obstruction), which was to ask folks to apply for one of the 2,000 permits being offered, and then simply not use them. The tactic could have a broader impact on a hunt, with a smaller number of licenses being offered, but it still was a way for people to do something without having to leave their homes. What the tactic also did was really piss off the people who wanted to hunt wolves. Even though over a thousand permits were being issued to legitimate wolf hunters, the fact that Wolf Patrol supporters actually won nine licenses in the lottery really incensed those who had waited seven years to legally hunt a wolf. I took one of the permits we had won and, during a lull in the hunt, made a video of myself saying, "We got a wolf permit...and you know what we do with wolf permits...we burn them." I then burned the permit with hound trucks behind me and dogs in the field.

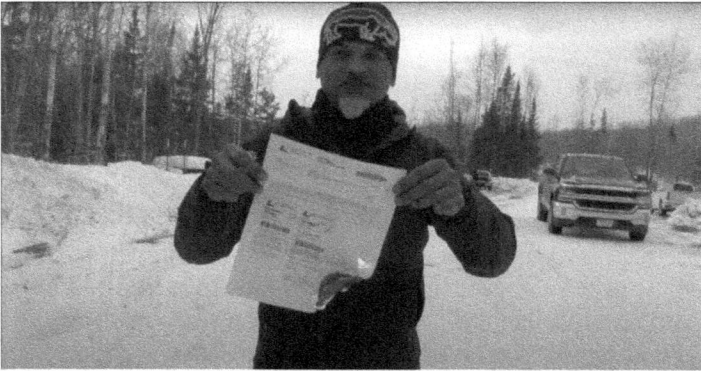

It was one of our only joys during the hunt. We sat in a parking area with six empty hound trucks with empty snowmobile trailers. Heavy snow had fallen, giving hound hunters perfect conditions to track and chase wolves. Now this party was in pursuit as we listened to their conversations over our scanner. They were in pursuit of a single wolf; the animal was cornered by dogs near some empty cabins and the hounder on the radio described a "vicious battle" between multiple hounds and the one wolf. It was exactly the scene that we needed to capture on film if we were ever going to end the hound hunt for wolves in Wisconsin. Unfortunately, because we didn't have a snowmobile, we couldn't access the fight area.

As darkness fell, the hunters began returning to the parking area where we sat surreptitiously filming them. On the back of one of their snowmobiles was their trophy—a young wolf. The men took turns lifting the still-limp body up, as their friends snapped photos with cellphone cameras. Luckily, this would be the only dead wolf we would actually see with our own eyes. In the end, however, more wolves were killed during the two-day hunt in Forest County than in any other county in the state.

The illegal call to not report wolves actually killed during the hunt made the news on the second day, and murmurs were being made that the hunt would soon close. With hound hunters becoming more difficult to locate, we decided to focus on the 14 traps we knew had yet to catch a wolf. Of those 14, about three had been sprung.

We wished we could be in more places at once. Old friends with the Bad River Chippewa Tribe requested our help to patrol their nation's reservation border to ensure that wolf hunters were not trespassing onto tribal lands where wolf hunting was forbidden.

On February 23rd, on only the second day of the hunt, with the reported kill at 82 wolves, the WDNR announced that the hunt would officially end at 10:00 the next morning. The quota for the entire hunt was set at 119 animals. I called the local warden, who by now knew me by name and reputation, and asked if he would be checking to ensure that traps had been pulled in areas where the hunt was closing the next morning, particularly in our patrol area. We now knew that we had only one night left to keep wolves out of the traps we were monitoring. Our frustration was at an all-time high as we continued monitoring calls for illegal wolf killings on social media. These weren't hollow threats being made by armchair warriors; these were calls being made by active hound hunters.

It was ironic to see the flagrant calls for poaching by numerous legitimate hunters being ignored by law enforcement, in light of the FBI's recent investigation into my one simple call for nonviolent civil disobedience against unregulated bear baiting a few summers ago. The FBI doesn't give a shit about killing wolves, but when I was willing to break the law to save them, my actions became a "credible terrorist threat," according to the FBI agent who spoke to my lawyers.

If the wardens weren't going to take action against illegal hunting, we would. We decided that any traps we located after the actual close of the hunt at 10 a.m. would be sprung. We didn't even have to break the law. At 10:00 sharp, as we sat in our patrol vehicle on the road laden with traps, we encountered the trapper in his truck. As he drove past us, he yelled, "I'll see you in court!" We drove along the trapper's route and discovered he had indeed removed all his traps, as required by law. Not far behind us was the warden, who had come to ensure the hunt would end peacefully in our district. He confirmed to me that there were multiple reports of people tampering with traps during the hunt and asked if I knew anything about the incidents; I honestly told him that, as promised, my crew adhered to all relevant laws.

By that time, the four of us had slept very few hours, and we were completely exhausted, emotionally and physically, as the hunt ground to a halt. As expected, once the hunt was officially over, there was an increase in the number of wolves reported killed, as hunters scrambled to report their kills they had made earlier. In the end, Wisconsin's February 2021 wolf hunt ended with a total reported killing of 218 wolves in less than 72 hours. Hound hunters were responsible for 188 kills, with the remaining wolves taken with the aid of foothold traps, snares, and electronic callers at night. A total of 160 wolves were killed on public lands. The hunt had gone grotesquely over the quota by 119 animals, almost double. The news was shattering; all over the nation, people began to hear, for the first time, about the abuses we had been reporting for years. National media attention on the hunt was somewhat vindicating, but what really mattered for our small band was the actual impact we had had on the ground during the hunt. While Forest County had the highest reported number of kills, we could say with certainty that none of the wolves in our small patrol area had been killed by trappers. Of the 14 active wolf traps we had monitored, not a single one captured a wolf.

The following winter, Stef, Matt, and I were again preparing to monitor the wolf hunt when word arrived that, due partially to the abuses in the previous year's hunt, a federal judge had returned the Great Lakes population of gray wolves to federal protection. There would be no 2022 Wisconsin wolf hunt.

Wisconsin hunters kill 216 wolves in less than 60 hours, sparking uproar

Kills quickly exceeded statewide limit, forcing the state to end the hunting season early

Gray wolves in the North American wilderness. Photograph: GatorDawg/Getty Images/iStockphoto

Hunters and trappers in Wisconsin killed 216 gray wolves last week during the state's 2021 wolf hunting season - more than 82% above the authorities' stated quota, sparking uproar among animal-lovers and conservationists, according to reports.

The kills all took place in less than 60 hours, quickly exceeding Wisconsin's statewide stated limit of 119 animals.

As a result, Wisconsin's department of natural resources ended the season, which was scheduled to span one week, four days early.

While department officials were reportedly surprised by the number of gray wolves killed, they described the population as "robust, resilient" and expressed confidence in managing the numbers "properly going forward".

The Guardian (UK), 3 Mar 2021

By now I was living in Vermont, having left Michigan once my son started attending college away from home. With the wolf hunt less than two months behind us, Stef, Matt, Jeremy, and I decided to regroup one last time. We wanted to infiltrate and film Wisconsin's largest coyote killing contest, "Moondog Madness," which took place annually in southern Wisconsin. The contest operated in secrecy despite being perfectly legal, because of concerns about possible protests. We registered for the hunt using my fake Facebook account and met up in a hotel to plan our operation. Stef and another crew member, Erik, would attend the weigh-in where piles of dead coyotes could be filmed. The hunters were mostly hunting at night, using infra-red and thermal imaging optics to locate and shoot coyotes that responded to their electronic calls.

Stef and Erik walked amongst the groups of hunters, filming with a smartphone hidden in their breast pocket. As expected, it was a grizzly scene, with hundreds of coyotes being weighed and inspected; many had their legs blown off by rifle fire. One hunter was surprised when he found only mice and rodents in the contents of the stomach of the animal he had killed. After all, this was a hunt that was being justified because of concerns about coyote predation on livestock.

We got the footage we wanted, shared it online, and returned home. In the course of just three months, we had witnessed this nation's largest-ever hound hunt for wolves and the state's biggest coyote-killing contest, both of which could now be viewed by anyone on our YouTube channel. In the weeks following the wolf hunt, I did many interviews with international journalists about my experiences, which were useful but emotionally difficult to recount.

After a lifetime of searching out and exposing animal abuse and environmental degradation, I felt like I had reached my limit. The wolves that had been killed in Wisconsin were not just numbers to us, they were individual family members that were struggling to survive. We saw their tracks, heard their howls, and on rare occasions, caught a glimpse of these indigenous survivors. In the end, it wasn't laws that protected these wolves; it was other 'wolves'—human ones. I didn't know if I could witness another wolf hunt, but I certainly wasn't going to miss the next slaughter.

I wasn't the only one deeply troubled by what we had witnessed during the wolf hunt, and later at the coyote killing contest. We all had reached a kind of breaking point. In the past, I would respond with aggressive direct action targeting the offenders, but we all knew the outcome of such an outburst ... my return to prison. I reluctantly left Wisconsin after our trusty patrol vehicle finally died, with over 400,000 miles on it. And in any case, living in Vermont made it expensive to travel to Wisconsin. But together, a handful of us have vowed to always return, as long as there is breath in our lungs, to protect and defend our gray wolf relations—not just the Firekeepers, but every single wolf following their heart and returning to their native homeland where they belong.

CHAPTER 14

LIFE IN VERMONT

I never really liked living in Michigan. The first time I ever went there was to scope out Michigan State University's experimental fur farm in 1992. After being sentenced to 57 months in federal prison in Kalamazoo three years later, I could be forgiven for never wanting to go there again. But having a family changes a man, and it certainly changes a warrior. Always in the hardest times, my Yaqui ancestors had to make difficult decisions and leave their beloved homelands. That's how I felt in 2008, when I moved from Tucson and my connections to my tribe to the racial disparities of the Midwest, in order to be closer to my son. I had moved there with my wife and daughter, but after my divorce in 2013, I lost them both. As with most difficult personal times in my life, when things got tough, I turned towards my work—in this case, my commitment to Earth and animals. Wolf Patrol gave me an outlet for my desire to continue fighting for change and it confirmed for me that there was still a way to use nonviolent direct action in defense of wildlife without risking years of freedom.

When my son went off to college, it was time for me to think about where I really wanted to live. By luck, at this same time, I had the opportunity to take a job as a caretaker at the 600-acre botanical sanctuary in Vermont where I now live. My ex-wife had wanted to move to Vermont, but I always said there weren't enough Indians there. I was right! But that's a different story.

I spent my first years getting accustomed to living a rural life again, and I loved it. I began cutting all the firewood we needed for the long Vermont winters, and essentially doing all the upkeep and repairs for the multiple buildings on our forested campus. I also began to get to know my neighbors—not the human ones, but the ones who have lived here the longest. In my time here, I've been able to become a caretaker for not just the land but for the indigenous nonhuman inhabitants as well. It's actually part of the job.

In my first years, I encountered a local bear hunter using hounds and I had the pleasure of telling him he was not welcome. There are thousands of nearby acres of public lands where he is legally allowed to harass bears from summer until fall, but in the (just over) one thousand acres that I protect, hound hunting is not allowed. I'm not against all hunting. In the years that I hunted myself or interacted with hunters as part of Wolf Patrol, I learned that many hunters share more of my beliefs than one might imagine. But I also strongly believe that some areas, like where I live, should be a safe haven for wildlife. They need it and they deserve it. A place where they can live without the fear of being harassed or molested, but allowed to live their lives in harmonious coexistence with us, their human neighbors.

Once, when a raccoon kit was injured and separated from their family, I took them food and water as they huddled in my neighbor's garage. I had contacted a local wildlife rehabilitator who told me it was best if the animal could stay close to where it lived. So I fed and watered them until they finally disappeared one day.

I also use a network of trail cameras to monitor wildlife and human crossings, and I had seen on multiple occasions a family of four raccoons: a mother and three kits. After the injured raccoon showed up, I noticed the family had dropped to three members. But then weeks later, after the injured raccoon had disappeared, I was reviewing the SD cards from my cameras when I again saw a family of four, not three raccoons. For me, the realization that I can make a difference in the life of even one animal gives me cause to never stop fighting and never give up hope that one person can make a difference.

In Vermont, everyone has multiple jobs; I'm no different. I am the local gravedigger—or as we call it here, a "cemetery commissioner." In addition to burying our dead, I also care for our town's six small cemeteries. One day, on my way home from one of them, I ran out of gas and had to walk the last mile home. As I walked along our forested state highway—the nearest residence is about a mile away—I crossed the road, and as I approached the ditch on the opposite side, I could see an emaciated cat hunkered near some human trash that had been thrown out a car window. I calmly started talking to the cat until it bolted into the forest. I took note of the location, and after filling my truck with gas, returned to the spot with a borrowed live-trap and cans of cat food. After only a couple hours, the cat was in the trap. We brought her home and kept her isolated from our other cats. She immediately began eating and would eventually put on 40% more weight. We found her when the trout lilies were just popping out in early spring, so we call her Lily Trout. She has slept on my lap as I wrote much of this book.

When we took her to the vet, we discovered she was spayed and probably abandoned. When I borrowed the live-trap from our town's animal control officer, she said that every spring, when tenants who haven't paid their rent are kicked out of their homes, they often abandon their pets.

Since then, we've rescued several chickens and another cat, Grey Cloud, who were all dumped like trash in our forests, left to an almost certain death. What kind of people can treat another living being like that? When I caught the license plate of one of the animal dumpers, the state police paid him a visit and asked why he dumped his chickens on our road (the police initially said they couldn't do anything about it, but then we cited the state's animal-cruelty laws, we got their attention). The dumper said he thought it was more humane than snapping their necks.

Whatever you might have heard about Vermont, don't for a moment think it is free of the kind of human beings who treat other living beings like garbage. Don't get me wrong, I love Vermont and I love rural life and the communities that make it possible. But I've learned over the last 40 years of fighting animal abuse that it exists everywhere there are animals.

A New Struggle Against Coyote Hunters

It didn't take me long to discover that the same kind of wildlife abuse that I had fought in Wisconsin was right here in the Green Mountain state. In 2022, the Vermont Legislature introduced a bill that would have banned the hunting of coyotes with hounds. I was asked by a local wildlife advocacy group to look into the practice here and see what I could find. I first turned to my fake Facebook account and easily friended a few local hound hunters. Once I had identified those who hunted coyotes with hounds, I pored over every single photo and video. This wasn't Wisconsin, obviously, but there were definitely some unsavory players here—which is never a surprise in a legal sport that allows dogs to chase and sometimes fight other dogs (namely, coyotes). I found videos of coyote hounders shooting animals as they tried to hide in their dens, photos from a Vermont hounder of his dog standing over a wounded and bloody coyote as the two animals fought. Most people don't know that it's a common practice for hounders to shoot to wound a coyote, so that it stands less of a chance of injuring the dogs that will then be allowed to maul and kill it.

Next, I called a rural resident who had some negative encounters with a group of hounders. He told me the exact area where the group operated and said they'd be there like clockwork every Saturday. When I took to the field the next day, I drove to the spot, and as I came over a ridge in the road, I saw a dog bound onto the road right in front of me. I slammed on my brakes. It was a coyote hound, unmistakable with the long, curved antenna of the GPS tracking collar around its neck. Moments later, I saw the dog's handler standing in the middle of the road with a .22 caliber rifle waiting for any coyote that might pop out of the woods. Shooting from roads is illegal here, as it is in most states. Since then, I've monitored coyote hunting with hounds in Vermont, but it's only done by a handful of people; most see it as a dying tradition...even though folks have only been doing it since coyotes filled the void after the wolf's extermination around 80 years ago.

Vermont is a small state, and it didn't take long for hunters and trappers to discover that I had relocated here. And it wasn't just because I began citizen monitoring of hound-hunting practices; I also started testifying to committees voting on bills affecting hounding and trapping. I was disappointed when I started watching televised Vermont Fish and Wildlife Board meetings and saw the familiar demographic of all-white, mostly male hunters and trappers filling nearly every seat. I say "nearly" because there was one member at the time, representing diverse opinions on wildlife. But overall, the scene wasn't that different from Wisconsin. Here again was a state wildlife agency being controlled by the agendas of the hunters, trappers, and anglers appointed to the board by the governor. Like most states, most of Vermont's fish and wildlife budget is spent on fur-bearers, game animals, and non-native fish.

Trappers Here, Too

Nothing brought home the continuing exploitation of wildlife for me here in Vermont more than when I discovered trapping on the lands we love and steward. On about the third week in October of 2022, which is also when recreational trapping season begins in the state, I saw a hound truck parked at the bottom of our road where the headwaters of our local river cross the state highway, entering a wetland that we also caretake. I couldn't see the human operating the truck, nor did I see any dogs in the dog boxes, but I did see a pile of rusty body-gripping traps, like those used to trap beaver.

A bit later, I came across two women accompanied by a state highway worker and asked them whether they had set traps in the area. One of the women said they had set about six. When I told them that we were the caretakers of the land for our neighbors living in Colorado, who strictly forbade trapping, the trapper responded that the Agency of Transportation owned the right of way along their highway where the river crossed and that she was a contracted trapper for the state.

We immediately notified the landowners and discussed the right to trap on these particular lands. Wanting to know whether other traps had been placed in our town, I drove to another beaver-created wetland that intersected the state highway and soon found two traps: one body-gripping trap set underwater near a culvert crossing the highway, and on the other side of the same culvert, a foot-hold trap submerged in just inches of water. I took pictures but did not touch them. I also placed trail cameras watching both trap sites. When I got home, there was a message from the landowner in Colorado; she had spoken to the local game warden, who informed her that the traps on their lands had been removed until the misunderstanding between us all was cleared up.

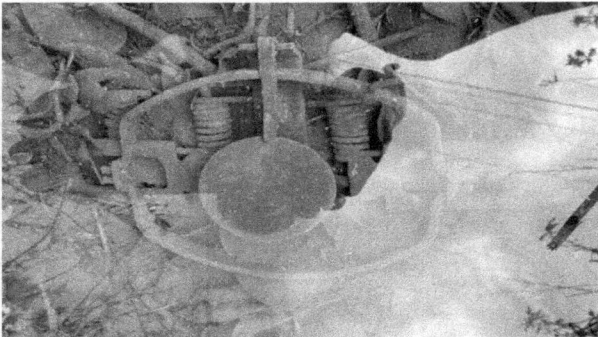

After the call, I returned to my trail cameras and sat about a hundred yards away, watching the area from my truck. Here were two traps that were intended for the local beavers who had recently returned from the last bout of trapping, which I later learned was every fall—ever since beavers had returned to Vermont after they were completely eradicated by trappers in the mid-19th century. I knew that if I did anything to tamper with the traps, I would be breaking the law in my own small town, where I am also an elected official. Still, somehow simply by knowing those traps were there, I felt responsible for any deaths that might occur. I didn't have to wait long. The next morning, when I returned to check on the traps, one was missing; and in the water, lay a young beaver kit, dead.

After I discovered the state-contracted beaver trapping in our own wetland, I made a public records request with the Agency of Transportation to determine how much the state was spending in our town to address "beaver conflicts"—specifically, blocked culverts. Multiple times a year, the state sends out a crew with an excavator to break up beaver dams and remove debris the beavers used to block culverts. In addition to paying trappers $150 for every beaver they kill, the state spent just over $22,000 on beaver-related work in our one town alone. Multiply that cost by the thousands of culverts and roads impacted by beavers across Vermont, and you'll come up with a sizable amount of public funds being used annually to kill beavers in our state alone.

But it doesn't have to be that way. Like all wildlife conflicts, there are non-lethal alternatives that should always be tried and exhausted before lethal measures are considered. That isn't just my position as a "radical environmentalist"; Vermont's own Best Management Practices for managing beaver conflicts says as much, recognizing the incredible ecological value that beavers bring to wetlands. In almost every conflict situation with beavers, a non-lethal "flow device" can be installed which allows water to pass through a culvert while also allowing beavers to continue creating flood-resilient wetlands. Vermont is home to the pioneering inventor of flow devices, Skip Lisle, who, with the Penobscot nation of Maine, invented the "Beaver Deceiver" and other non-lethal tools that have spared the lives of countless animals. The problem was and still is the institutional thinking that sees beavers only as a nuisance, and one that needs to be eradicated. Most cities and towns have been trapping beavers since they rebounded from near extinction, with all of our infrastructure having being built in their absence. Now as beavers are returning, they pose problems for roads and bridges built without taking into accounts the needs of extirpated native species who are now returning.

I also started investigating the underwater trapping practices used to kill beavers and many other animals—some intended, others not. It didn't take long for me to return to the published research of furbearer researchers like Fred Gilbert, whose trap research on behalf of the Fur Institute of

Canada I tried to sabotage back in 1991 at Washington State University. Now in Vermont, state lawmakers had passed a law directing the state wildlife agency, Vermont Fish and Wildlife, to establish Best Management Practices for trapping; but they followed those guidelines established through horrific experiments on literally every trap ever manufactured, to determine if they were capable of "humanely" trapping and killing their target animal. That state relied solely on the standards established by researchers like Gilbert, whose research subjects sometimes took up to 15 minutes to die in drowning-tank experiments.

I was further disgusted to learn that research on lethal body-gripping traps continues to this day at a lab in Alberta, sponsored by the Fur Institute of Canada. I also learned that the trapper hired by my state was cited for failing to check her traps and for trapping a fisher out of season, after a live fisher was found on a snowmobile trail with the same trapper's body-gripping trap crushing their head. (The animal was shot by a snowmobiler who couldn't bear to see the animal suffering any longer.) I learned that even the BMP experiments on some body-gripping traps had determined they were not capable of humanely killing a fisher. In addition to taking my complaints about BMP trap research to state lawmakers, where I testified that our state's new rules should not allow the use of certain body-gripping traps, I also began asking our town to explore non-lethal alternatives to beaver trapping, and I wrote commentaries about the practices.

As soon as I began to publicly speak out against trapping, and to testify in support of legislation that would restrict trapping and hound hunting, I was identified by opponents who were quick to expose my past and again accuse me of being a terrorist—as if that label alone should be cause for me not have some constitutional rights, like free speech. Before long, there were residents who wanted me to step down from my position as a cemetery commissioner because they believed I didn't have the same rights as they did. And when I asked that a flow device be considered for use at the wetland where I witnessed trapping, the town government responded with a failed attempt to open all town lands to trapping. Only when I presented legal evidence from Fish and Wildlife's wardens stating that state, not local, laws governed trapping, was their attempt derailed.

In 2023 I also began attending, in person, every monthly state Fish and Wildlife Board meeting, where our state's wildlife management policies are decided by a 14-member board following recommendations from Vermont Fish and Wildlife Department. Both the Department and the Board have it as their mission to protect not just game animals, but all species and the habitat necessary for their survival...for all the people of

Vermont, not just those who take pleasure in hunting, trapping, and fishing. Yet, as one might guess, even in Vermont, like most other states, it is hunters, trappers, and anglers who control our state's fish and wildlife agency. This, even though in recent years the income generated from license sales has continued to decline as a younger generation replaces one that spent much more time doing things like hunting and trapping. Some practices, like deer hunting, remain somewhat steady, but trapping continues to decline from what it once was, largely because of the collapse in fur prices.

To this day, I attend every Fish and Wildlife Board meeting, which allows members of the public two minutes to speak to board members, to the Commissioner of Fish and Wildlife, and to their staff in attendance. Every month, I use my two minutes to raise issues that I believe are important or are currently before the board. I speak to wolf and cougar recolonization, the inefficiency of some body-gripping traps, our need for better wildlife crossings, the legal practice of shooting bear sows with cubs, and a host of other issues threatening wildlife in the Green Mountain State.

Like most states in America, Vermont's Fish and Wildlife Department and board are focused on increasing hunting, trapping, and fishing opportunities for the license holders providing some of their budget. It used to be user fees like licenses that made up the majority of a state's wildlife budget, but nowadays much of the funding comes from general funds or from taxes. Gone are the days when wildlife agencies served only hunters, trappers, and anglers. In today's Vermont, hunting and trapping don't even make the top ten most popular outdoor activities; those places are held by folks who hike, bike, kayak, or simply enjoy walking in the woods without taking anything more than pictures.

Yet, in Vermont, the Fish and Wildlife Board continues to be dominated by members who are hunters and trappers looking to guard the gates from the threat posed by wildlife advocates. They call us "anti's" or "animal rights activists"—and some might be, but not me. I'm just looking out for my wild animal relations and our future generations. I do not like being labeled when so few of my opponents have ever taken the time to talk to me. When I started attending board meetings with another wildlife advocate, it was months before board members were willing to even acknowledge us. But eventually even the Commissioner of Fish and Wildlife took notice of our civil approach and began having conversations with us.

The Vermont Fish and Wildlife Board is composed of 14 members, each representing one of our state's counties. After a year of attending meetings, and speaking to the board as a resident of Orange County, I would have expected that my representative would have been on speaking terms with me; but such was not the case. In the beginning of 2024, law-makers introduced legislation that would have reformed the composition of the board, allowing greater diversity and representation of the many people of Vermont who care about wildlife. During the legislative session while I was supporting the bill, I used my time for public comment before the board to call out my county representative for not ever having attempted a conversation with me on wildlife issues. After the meeting, he finally introduced himself and agreed to talk.

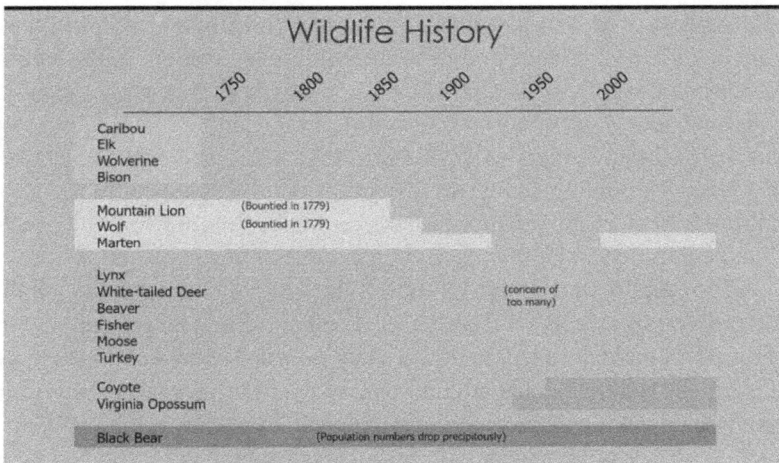

Wildlife History

1750 1800 1850 1900 1950 2000

Caribou
Elk
Wolverine
Bison

Mountain Lion   (Bountied in 1779)
Wolf   (Bountied in 1779)
Marten

Lynx
White-tailed Deer   (concern of too many)
Beaver
Fisher
Moose
Turkey

Coyote
Virginia Opossum

Black Bear   (Population numbers drop precipitously)

Vermont's history of extirpated wildlife

Attached to the same bill that would reform the Board was proposed legislation to end coyote hunting with hounds. The year previously, the same attempt to ban the practice turned into legislation that merely regulated the practice. The rules established "control of dogs" to mean the use of GPS collars, which advocates argued was hardly a form of control—something that I could testify in support of, after monitoring hound-hunting practices in Wisconsin for years now. I conducted my own investigation when the rules went into effect, and what I saw was that some hound hunters could control their dogs and others could not. The proposed legislation never made it to a vote, but at last count, we had less than a dozen permits issued to coyote hounders.

Sometimes simply regulating a previously unregulated bloodsport is enough to bring about its demise. Participating in the legislative process, as well as with the Fish and Wildlife Board on wildlife policy issues, was something I had only ever dabbled in over my long career as a wildlife advocate. Yet while living in Vermont, which is a relatively small state, I learned that even the voice of one person can be heard. We live in a state that prides itself on the accessibility of our elected leaders, with most just a phone call away. What I learned was that if you are willing to spend time at the state capitol, you can find your elected representatives there and alert them to your concerns and to the legislation you support.

Last year, I did just that. Previously, my elected House Representative drove up my driveway while I was working in my barn, wanting to talk to me about supporting his campaign, which I happily did. I told him we cared deeply about wildlife, and if I voted for him and he won, that I would be looking for his support for pro-wildlife legislation. In the following legislative session, I sought his support on a bill that would have reformed the state Fish and Wildlife board and ended coyote hunting with hounds. He disagreed but was willing to talk to me about his concerns. I enlightened him on issues he was not aware of, and as we sat in the Capitol's ornate but empty assembly room, he thanked me for my willingness to find compromise with other stakeholders like hunters and trappers.

When the legislation died, I took it upon myself to work on building better relationships with staff of the Fish and Wildlife Department and the Board, who continue to be extremely wary of wildlife advocates. Vermont is full of the polarization that comes from wildlife advocates, largely informed by social media and who vilify anyone who hunts or traps. There is no tolerance for some practices, which I totally understand, having come from a very abolitionist perspective on most forms of animal abuse. I came from a generation who believed we might end the fur trade or vivisection in our lifetimes, but now I realize that is as unlikely as our ability to end violence against women or death by police. Some forms of abuse are integral to the fabric of our capitalist society, which has always profited from the abuse of others.

I began to realize that the best hope I had of improving the lives of animals in the wild was through effective lobbying for stronger regulations and always for the reduction in any level of suffering. I might not say any longer that I'm "opposed to trapping," but I will always be opposed to the cruelty that is sometimes, if not often, associated with it. Wolf Patrol and my time in Wisconsin taught me this. There were ethical bear and hound hunters, just as much as there were bad actors. My efforts to reduce wolf conflicts with bear hunters could only ever be effective if bear hunters recognized and accepted their responsibility for contributing to the conflict.

I may no longer hunt myself, but I do support ethical and humane subsistence hunting, as long as it is done to feed one's own family. It's not sustainable for the world's population, but there are many places in America where one can still be connected to the land through sustenance from the life found there. In my own heart and mind, when I consume the flesh of my sacred relation, *sailo maaso* (brother deer) which I have taken from a road-killed animal, I still give thanks; I promise to take responsibility for the future generations of those animals who I could not live without. We owe that much to the plant- and animal-nations that sustain us. Even if we do not eat them, by simply living in our consumptive "First World" society, we still are responsible for animal death and environmental destruction. My reverence for nonhuman life also means that I could never justify the domestication of animals for food, medical use, or recreation, although I do support small family-run animal-producing farms that raise livestock humanely.

Lecturing at a college in Canada

Looking Ahead

One of my greatest hopes for change in wildlife policy in the United States is for the governing state agencies to become more representative of the diverse groups that enjoy and appreciate wild nature today. It has traditionally always been the users of wildlife, hunters, trappers, and anglers whose voices are heard, and who are continually favored by decision makers. But that needs to change. But the problem isn't only that others' views on wildlife are not being heard, it's that other voices for wildlife are simply not

380

Memories of Freedom

speaking at many of the public meetings where comments are heard and where opinions are solicited from state wildlife agencies.

In early 2025, I attended the annual spring Vermont Fish and Wildlife Department public comment meeting, which addresses proposed changes to moose, deer, and turkey hunting regulations. Like most states, hunting seasons in Vermont are set to achieve a "harvest objective," with the belief that recreational hunters are the most effective management tool for maintaining wildlife populations. And like most states in the US, many of the native predators of ungulates like moose and deer no longer exist in their Vermont home range. In their absence, coyotes and bobcats have become the dominant predator on much of our landscape, but gone are the wolves and mountain lions that once called N'Dakina (Vermont) home.

When I first moved to Vermont, I re-read Farley Mowat's *Sea of Slaughter*—the book Paul Watson introduced to me in the 1980s that chronicled the exploitation and eradication on many of the native species of the Northeastern North Atlantic Seaboard region that I now call home. I re-read stories of the commercial exploitation of "furbearers" and was reminded why Vermont and many other states no longer have wolves, mountain lions, wolverines, lynx, or even bison...they were all hunted to their extinction by European colonizers.

At the public meeting, as I expected, I was the only person in the room of about 80 attendees who wasn't a recreational hunter. Everyone else concerned enough about wildlife to attend the meeting was there for their own interests, though many would say those interests are for the deer, moose, or turkey in our state. As also expected, every biologist working for the VT Fish and Wildlife Dept on their deer, moose, and turkey policies are also hunters. This isn't something that I believe will ever change; but what I do hope will change is our state's belief that humans are the best wildlife management tool, rather than native apex predators.

Due to the impacts of a warming climate and other habitat factors, moose in the far northeastern corner of our state are suffering from a severe winter tick infestation that is killing off 50% of newborn moose calves every year. In an effort to control the ticks, the state says we must reduce the density of moose in some areas of persistent infestations. For many years, Vermont has conducted a lottery for a limited number of permits to kill moose, though almost half of those killed are bulls who are the most resilient to winter tick loads. Yet, bulls are killed because human hunters, unlike native apex predators, are after trophies, not a meal to feed their starving families.

My vision for wildlife has led me to speak for the restoration of those native predators that not only belong on our landscape, but who can provide better management than the ever-dwindling numbers of recreational hunters. In Vermont, I learned that, in 1980, there were 130,000 deer hunters. Now there are only 67,000. Our state's lead moose and deer biologist said, "we can make longer seasons, but hunters don't hunt more…" Yet, my voice has become the only one asking, "Why don't we restore native predators to address population imbalance in our deer and moose herd?" At this particular meeting, after having reviewed the state's proposal for the 2025 moose hunt, I asked also, "Why are we offering either-sex permits for a hunt whose objective is the taking of cow moose?"

Despite the goal of reducing cow moose, every year, three moose permits are also auctioned off to the highest bidder, with the hunters always choosing to take mature bulls. The auction hunt is justified because it generates revenue that the state uses to support a summer camp program promoting even more hunting, trapping, and fishing. I suggested that funds from those auction sales go into further non-invasive research currently in progress into the non-lethal use of fungal pathogens to control winter tick numbers.

I use my voice to represent wildlife, even when I know I might not be heard, because I am certain it won't be heard if I don't use it at all. I do believe change is possible, but only if we show up and remain an advocate for the greater good that wildlife brings to our world when we choose to coexist with our wild neighbors.

In the summer of 2024, I attended the Northeastern North America/ Turtle Island Landscape Connectivity Summit, which took place in Montreal; it brought together agency officials from both sides of the border to discuss large landscape conservation and habitat connectivity. The event featured conversations about habitat preservation, weaving indigenous knowledge with Western science, coordinating conservation efforts across borders, and helping preserve the ecological integrity of habitat necessary for the survival of indigenous peoples and the animals that we all share our homes with. It was an amazing event, where visions I had only heard people like Dave Foreman with Earth First! talk about were now being discussed by state and premier natural resource managers. In attendance at the meeting were also Vermont's Fish and Wildlife Commissioner and the Director of Wildlife, both of whom welcomed my own attendance. By the end of the event, I had identified long-term ecological visions that the state of Vermont is committed to and that I am now committed to supporting. This support transcends what have become divides between various wildlife stakeholders over more controversial issues.

A Task for Everyone

One of the things I love most about advocating for better wildlife crossings or habitat connectivity is that it's work that should be supported by literally everyone. There should be no stakeholders hoping for more developed land or roadkill wildlife; everyone should support protecting habitat necessary for all wildlife's survival, from animal rights activists to trappers. We may always be at odds over issues like trapping or hound hunting, but we should never be divided on the existential needs of wildlife, especially in light of the dangers facing wildlife due to climate change.

So, while many might be disgusted that this one-time Animal Liberation Front warrior is making friends with trappers and defending small farmers, I only ask that you have a little faith that my intentions are still the same as always: to do the most that one human can do for the benefit of our nonhuman relations.

I know what it's like to go to war for animals. I know what it's like to witness unspeakable cruelty towards animals. And I know what happens when we choose to follow our hearts rather than the law, when it comes to trying to stop that torture. Almost every day, I still struggle with what is the best thing I can do for animals. But I know that attacking and antagonizing can only get you so far. At some point, someone has to fight for change on the policy level and ensure that any progress made for animals is enshrined in law. That's where I am at right now. And although I think I've accomplished a lot by burning down some buildings and breaking into labs to rescue their prisoners, now, I believe I can do the most good for animals by again setting a strategic course for uncharted territory.

In many of the meetings I attend in Vermont, where I am the sole indigenous person and often only advocate for extirpated and hunted species, I speak up even when I am a lone voice. After nearly two years of attending such meetings, policy makers have recognized that I am not going away. I have been to meetings where Fish and Wildlife Board members come up to me afterward and thank me for my comments, even though they don't agree with me, I had a Republican state representative at the deer, moose, and turkey meeting say that he appreciated my comments and that they were based in lived experience and with accurate knowledge of these lands. All our state wildlife meetings are recorded, and I want my pro-wildlife testimonies to be a part of that public record.

I still believe that I am doing radical work. Only now, being radical means doing what others have yet to realize is the most important and necessary action to achieve change for animals. We need to make friends, not enemies, in our efforts to protect wildlife, even if it means building relationships with people whose practices and traditions are sometimes offensive.

Make no mistake, in my lifetime I have seen my share of animal abuse. But rarely have I ever met an "animal abuser" who was truly a monster. There are some pretty sick and depraved individuals in the hound hunting and trapping community who take joy in seeing an animal suffer, like some I know in Wisconsin, but there are many more trappers, hunters, and fur farmers that I have met who were simple, decent people.

What I have found to be effective is to not position myself as an opponent of an entire practice like trapping, because at the end of the day, there are some decent people engaged in the practice—not all, but some. I can say the same thing about other practices. But what I have found that resonates with groups of both anti-trappers and ethical law-abiding trappers is that there is no room for cruelty and illegality in the practice. Most people, if not all, when asked, support the ethical treatment of animals; so to people I know who trap and hunt, I always ask that they speak out against abuse and that they report violators of hunting and trapping regulations, because if they don't, then everyone would believe illegality and cruelty are inherent and acceptable.

I don't expect everyone to support my evolution. But I am not here to satisfy everyone, or even people at all. I am here to serve my constituents: my animal relations and the wild lands necessary for their survival, and those human communities that still see animals as their sacred relations. There will always be talk and action that might make us believe that our world is ending, but where man's world ends, nature's can begin. I believe in not only wild nature's rebirth through restoration and the return of extirpated species like the wolf and mountain lion, but I also believe in our own rebirth as well—into a world where we can once again coexist with our nonhuman neighbors. It is a future where the veil between our worlds becomes thin again, revealing our return to a deepened connection with not only nature but those human communities still embracing peaceful coexistence instead of commercial exploitation. That is the world I know still exists; that is the world I fight for.

As mentioned, I regularly attend public comment meetings held annually by the Vermont Fish and Wildlife Department to solicit opinions on proposed changes to hunting and fishing rules. I've been to similar meetings in many states but they are always the same—completely filled with hunters and anglers but zero non-consumptive users. Since the early 2000s when I started Chuk'shon Earth First! and began organizing legally to stop trophy hunting, I quickly discovered that every state wildlife agency supports wildlife management through hunting and trapping. Their budgets largely come from the sale of licenses, and they work closely with trophy hunting organizations like Safari Club International, believing that such partnerships are vital links between wildlife agencies and stakeholders like hunters and trappers. Like many states, Vermont is still in this pattern, and from my own personal experience, it sees non-consuming wildlife advocates more as a threat than as potential partners in conservation. The expectation I've learned to accept from most wildlife professionals in state agencies, is that they believe we are all against hunting, trapping, and fishing and will do anything we can to end it, which is simply not true.

I get it. I've spent a good part of my life trying to destroy the fur trade and I've sabotaged hunts since the 1980s. When my kids were little, I'd tell them, "If the Indians had won the war, people who abused animals would go to prison, not those like me who rescued them." My kids knew it didn't make sense to protect practices that we know in our hearts are wrong. What kind of a world would that be? I believed this myself as a child when I discovered humanity's inhumane stance towards the other beings we share this planet with. The cozy relationship between state wildlife agencies and hunters and trappers is why I started Hunt Saboteurs in America back in 1987, Chuk'shon Earth First! in 2004, and Wolf Patrol in 2014.

In the movement for reforming the Fish and Wildlife Board, one hears many wildlife advocates accurately cite that both the board and Fish and Wildlife Department's stated mission and purpose is "the conservation of fish, wildlife, and plants and their habitats for the people of Vermont." Missing, they say, are the voices of the many non-consumptive users of wildlife that enjoy nature and wildlife without leaving a trail of blood. What has always troubled me is our anthropocentric belief that wildlife and all nature belong to us. The idea of 'public trust wildlife' is a good thing; it dates back to the time when all wildlife was the property of the monarchy. But what it lacks is the understanding that nature serves a far greater purpose than simply the needs of one species, humans. I've always believed that nature, and animals in particular, have their own reasons for living. Yes, they serve a greater ecological role as part of a beautiful fabric of life that makes our world inhabitable; but beyond that, they have their own desires and capacities for freedom, love, and other things—none of which I need to understand in order to defend them. That is something lacking in the Western-based conservation community: an understanding of wild animal communities as their own nations of other beings, with whom we must share our world.

Reconnecting with an Old Friend

During the Covid epidemic, I learned that my old friend Paul Watson also had a connection to Vermont, living here for part of the year and maintaining a small office in nearby Woodstock. We got back in touch, and not long afterward, he and his son Tiger were over at my house for a reminiscing visit. In my living room, Paul awarded me "The Captain Paul Watson Medal for Courage in Defense of the Ocean" for shutting down Icelandic whaling operations by sinking half the fleet in 1986. It was one of my greatest honors to both receive the medal and rekindle my friendship and mentorship with my old friend and Captain.

Paul Watson and Rod, in Vermont (2022)

Paul was still the figurehead and leader of Sea Shepherd, but the group had grown into a global organization, complete with a fleet of its own ships and helicopters. His Woodstock office was filled with mementos and war trophies from the dozens of campaigns that the organization conducted annually. I was proud to see Paul's conservation success and his unwillingness to ever compromise his principles in defense of the seas.

Sadly, in the ensuing year, there was a hostile takeover at the group, ending as it had with Greenpeace: with Paul being ejected from the organization he created and loved. Everything was taken from him by the turncoats within his own group, including his fleet of ships, some of which were literally scrapped. I was disgusted. Here again, the growth of an environmental organization had led to its takeover by people who cared more about fundraising goals and "image" than saving lives. It was another story of the industrial non-profit complex that is eating up the environmental and animal movements, leaving in its place national organizations with no grassroots leadership or campaigns, no vision, no passion—just endless fundraising and well-paid executives.

Paul rose from the ashes and started another organization, The Captain Paul Watson Foundation. And while his former friends and crew continued their drift away from direct action, Paul obtained another ship, the John Paul Dejoria, which was soon joined by a second. Not long after the hostile takeover, Iceland announced its intention to resume commercial whaling despite the international ban that led to our first attack on the nation's whaling industry. For years, Iceland's only whaling company, Hvalur Limited, had indicated that they wanted to continue whaling. Now, neither Greenpeace nor the Sea Shepherd Conservation Society would respond to the threat, but Paul would.

In the summer of 2023, the John Paul Dejoria sailed into New York Harbor where I stood watching from a bridge overlook. The ship was on its way to Iceland, and I drove down to bring donations and visit the crew. It had been decades since I was onboard one of Paul's ships, even though it was only in harbor. I was so inspired once again, witnessing the tireless dedication of Paul's crew to both the mission and Paul. Like me, these were the kind of people Paul could count on not to betray him again.

When I reluctantly said my goodbyes and began driving back to Vermont, I broke down in tears. It had been so damn long since I felt that energy and dedication towards a mission to save animal lives, and I wanted to feel it again. As it happened, that summer no whales were killed by Iceland and a confrontation was averted. The following year, 2024, I was prepared to fly to London to join the ship, but this time, the government of Iceland did not issue a permit to the whalers; another confrontation was averted and I had no need to join.

Even at 74 years of age, Paul's tireless dedication to fighting for the world's whales remains a threat to this day. Without Iceland's threat that summer, Paul turned his attention back to the Japanese whaling industry which had just launched a brand-new factory ship for processing whales at sea. When the John Paul Dejoria pulled into Nuuk Greenland to refuel in July 2024, Danish authorities raided the ship, arresting Paul and detaining him on an Interpol warrant for interfering with Japanese whalers in Antarctica many years earlier. Paul spent five months in prison before being released, after Danish authorities refused to follow through on Japan's request for extradition. Meanwhile, Iceland has recently granted a five-year permit to Hvalur Limited to kill endangered fin whales again beginning in the summer of 2025. The battle never ends.

I believe in Paul more than ever. I admire his refusal to be defeated where others would surely quit. Where so many others I have known in the movement now hold down well-paying jobs in the organizations that many of them started, Paul has never wavered in his commitment to this planet, and for that reason, he will always be my friend and Captain. And if he asks me again, I will rejoin him on the John Paul Dejoria as it sails into harm's way to again save lives. I want to rejoin the ship, not only to again protect whales, but because I believe we must always support those like Paul who are willing to take action. The times desperately require our continued willingness to engage in nonviolent direct action to save lives. Many of us believe we would act when faced with unspeakable injustice, and now we are again at that time.

All my work and all my efforts would be negated if I failed to answer the call. In my daily life, I continue to work to change policy in Vermont for wildlife, but never will I ignore a call for help from a warrior friend, one who has always put the lives of others before his own. That is the definition of what it means to be an indigenous warrior, and I remain ready to serve my nonhuman constituents.

I end this book with this message: that now is again the time for action. Maybe not burning down buildings, but action that will speak for those that cannot speak for themselves. The cycle of abuse will not end until it is no longer tolerated. We can't simply wait for others to answer the call; we must take action ourselves. That action can be small, as in how you spend your dollars, or it can be large, involving your whole body and spirit. But we must always speak out against injustice or it will forever be a part of our world.

I am reminded of the words of John Lewis, about getting into "good trouble"—this is where we are at. Don't expect anyone else to do what you know in your heart must be done. Believe me, you will sleep better. You will laugh louder and you will find peace. Together we must continue to speak for our nonhuman relations and for the lands they need to survive as independent nations. Don't think about winning, just know that we must always fight and never give up. So many other lives depend on it.

Mink crossing a beaver dam

Rod with Stuart Mylow, Wolf Clan representative from the Mohawk Council (2024)

EPILOGUE

August 28, 2025
48° 16' 29.9" N, 69° 27' 40.6" W
St. Lawrence Seaway, Quebec

There's a very special place in the world that I've found, that I would like to share with you. It is where I go when I need to recharge my body and spirit for the battles I face in my daily life. Camping on the shore of the mighty St. Lawrence, where the waters can be over a hundred feet deep, it is not uncommon to be in your tent and hear the blow of a whale as they cruise closely by the shore.

During the day, folks sit on the rocks or in folding chairs and wait for the whales to arrive. Last year, we saw breaching humpbacks, minke, and beluga and even a blue whale, the largest animal that has ever lived on this Earth. When I saw their long body curling into the water as they made a dive, I was awestruck at the sheer size of this wondrous being. I come to see the whales, but I also come to be with people who are looking for a deeper connection with this wild world still before us.

Today, I heard the call, *"Baliene!"* ('whale' in French) and saw campers walking towards the cliffs from all directions. I clamored out onto a small island that can only be reached at low tide. All eyes were scanning the horizon, waiting for the submerged animal to surface. Suddenly, and just thirty feet from where I stood, a large humpback whale erupted from the silent waters with a loud exhale of warm air that I could see as well as hear. I heard joyous cries and when I turned around, there must have been a hundred people lining the rocks, reverently witnessing this visit between our worlds. I felt like a child again. I felt the way I have learned to allow myself to feel when the veil is removed between the worlds of humans and all other animals, when we are all connected.

I watched as the animal slowly swam past me, feeling a strong sense that this being knew it faced no danger from me or the others gathered here. This is how the world used to be and how it can be again. Seeing and being in a place where animals are revered with such deep respect is what I live and will die for.

I hope there is a place like this for everyone. But if you don't have one yet, come to Quebec in summertime and we can watch whales together with plenty of other two-leggeds! Thanks for taking this journey with me and allowing me to share my stories of resistance and memories of freedom. Now it's your turn!

FURTHER INFORMATION

The following sources are useful for further information:

YOUTUBE CHANNELS:
"Wolf Patrol"
"Vermont Wildlife Patrol"
"Vermont Fish & Wildlife Department Board Meetings"

WEBSITES:
Wolf Patrol: wolfpatrol.org
Vermont Wildlife Patrol: vtwildlife.org
The Captain Paul Watson Foundation: paulwatsonfoundation.org
Wildlands Network: wildlandsnetwork.org
Staying Connected Initiative: stayingconnectedinitiative.org

LINKS:
"Strong Hearts" zines: al-archive.nostate.net/strong-hearts/

BOOKS:
Operation Bite Back (2009) by Dean Kuipers
Sea of Slaughter (1984) by Farley Mowat
Earthforce: An Earth Warrior's Guide to Strategy (2012) by Paul Watson
Crossings: How Road Ecology is Shaping the Future of Our Planet (2023)
      by Ben Goldfarb
Wild New World: The Epic Story of Animals & People in America (2023)
      by Dan Flores
Once They Moved Like the Wind: Cochise, Geronimo, and the Apache Wars
      (1994) by David Roberts
In the Spirit of Crazy Horse (1991) by Peter Matthiessen
All About Love (1999) by Bell Hooks

www.ingramcontent.com/pod-product-compliance
Lightning Source LLC
Chambersburg PA
CBHW032047020426
42335CB00011B/226